THE IMPACT OF THE 1916 RISING

THE IMPACT OF THE 1916 RISING

Among the Nations

EDITOR

RUÁN O'DONNELL

University of Limerick

IRISH ACADEMIC PRESS
DUBLIN • PORTLAND, OR

First published in 2008 by Irish Academic Press

44 Northumberland Road,
Ballsbridge,
Dublin 4, Ireland

920 NE 58th Avenue, Suite 300
Portland, Oregon,
97213-3786 USA

www.iap.ie

This edition copyright © 2008 Irish Academic Press
Chapters © individual authors

British Library Cataloguing in Publication Data
An entry can be found on request

ISBN 978 0 7165 2964 4 (cloth)
ISBN 978 0 7165 2965 1 (paper)

Library of Congress Cataloging-in-Publication Data
An entry can be found on request

Printed by Biddles Ltd., King's Lynn, Norfolk

For Anthony Coughlan and Muriel Saidlear
and in memory of
C. Desmond Greaves.

Contents

Notes on Contributors

Peter Berresford Ellis is a well-known writer, novelist and historian. He holds an MA and Hon. D. Litt. and his many books include *Eyewitness to Irish History* (New Jersey, 2004).

Anthony Coughlan was the inaugural professor of Social Policy at Trinity College Dublin. Coughlan, a leading member of the Connolly Association and Wolfe Tone Society in the 1960s, has maintained an active interest in the defence of Irish sovereignty.

David Granville is the online editor of *Irish Democrat*, journal of the Connolly Association, and also edited the print edition between 1996 and 2002. He is researching the history of the British labour movement and the Irish question in the twentieth century.

Ann Matthews is a PhD graduate of NUI Maynooth. Her thesis focused on the participation of women in Irish republican politics from 1900 to 1941. She has also researched the history of Cumann na mBan and the Irish Citizen Army.

Ian McKeane received his PhD from the Institute of Irish Studies, University of Liverpool, where he now works. McKeane is an organizer of Liverpool's Irish Festival and has researched the history of Franco–Irish connections.

Priscilla Metscher taught Irish Studies at Oldenburg University, Germany, from 1974 to 1999. She has published many articles on the history of radical Irish politics and is the author of *James Connolly and the Reconquest of Ireland* (Minnesota, 2002).

Brian P. Murphy, OSB has written extensively on the subject of the Irish revolutionary period. He attended Oxford University and University College Dublin. Dr Murphy's publications include *The Origin and Organisation of British Propaganda in Ireland, 1920* (Cork, 2006).

Róisín Ní Ghairbhí is a lecturer in the Department of Irish, St Patrick's College, Drumcondra. Her research includes an assessment of Patrick Pearse from Irish language sources.

John O'Callaghan holds an MA from University of Limerick and a Higher Diploma in Education. He is completing postgraduate studies at the University of Limerick on the Irish revolutionary period and is the recipient of a scholarship from the Irish Research Council for the Humanities and Social Sciences. O'Callaghan is the former co-editor of student journal, *History Studies*.

Máirtín Seán Ó Catháin is a lecturer in history at the University of Central Lancashire. He is the author of *Irish Republicanism in Scotland, 1858–1916: Fenians in Exile* (Dublin, 2007). Ó Catháin received his PhD from the University of Ulster in 2001.

Ruán O'Donnell, a graduate of University College Dublin, holds a PhD from the Australian National University and is a Senior Lecturer in the History Department, University of Limerick. He is the author of several books on the history of Irish republicanism, including *From Vinegar Hill to Edentubber: The Wexford IRA and the Border Campaign* (Wexford, 2007).

Rory Sweetman teaches Irish history at the University of Otago, New Zealand. He has written on the history of the Irish in the southern hemisphere, including *Bishop in the Dock: The Sedition Trial of James Liston in New Zealand* (Dublin, 2007).

Matt Treacy is a writer, political activist and doctoral student at Trinity College Dublin. He is researching the history of the republican movement in the 1960s.

Bernadette Whelan received her PhD from University College Cork and is a Senior Lecturer in the History Department, University of Limerick. Recent publications include *United States Foreign Policy and Ireland: From Empire to Independence, 1913–29* (Dublin, 2007). She researchers and writes in the area of US–Irish diplomatic history.

Acknowledgements

I wish to acknowledge the help and encouragement of the following: Tony Coughlan, Frank Keohane, Finbar Cullen, Mary Cullen, Charlie Murphy, Muriel Saidlear, Owen Bennett, Helga and Cathal MacLiam, Roy Johnson, Ann Matthews, John O'Callaghan, Lisa Hyde, Aonghus Meaney, Joe and Mary Jamison and all the contributors.

Introduction:
Among the Nations

Ruán O'Donnell

Although confined to Dublin and just a few of Ireland's thirty-two counties, the week-long 1916 Rising was immediately regarded as a highly significant event. The fact that the insurrection occurred in one of the main cities of the British empire and at the height of a ferocious war against the Central Powers all but guaranteed international attention. Several factors set the Rising apart from other dramatic incidents of 1916.

The First World War was characterized on its western front by the subterranean world of field entrenchments and bunkers. Yet in 1916 British troops were deployed night and day in house-to-house fighting in Dublin streets where artillery and machine guns had a markedly different effect on the combat environs. Images of the devastation wrought by modern firepower in a built-up area were a striking harbinger of what many in Paris and Berlin hoped to visit on rival capitals in their quest for victory. From a British perspective, the Rising represented a challenge that was militarily manageable but politically problematic. It was not simply a matter of overwhelming rebel positions and the ritual exaction of retribution. The nascent Irish Republic had petitioned the same neutral American administration for recognition that Britain wished to manoeuvre into the conflict. Unsurprisingly, the initial response of London to the Irish crisis was confused and veered from an often ineptly conducted phase of counter-insurgency to a more pragmatic stance.

There were other troubling paradoxes. Irish soldiers had formed a substantial part of the imperial army in the Dardanelles in 1915, and in the early months of 1916 were poised to participate in the great Somme offensive. They numbered thousands who had first coalesced in the ranks of the Volunteers, a nationalist organization which, as recently as 1914, had weighed the prospect of fighting the same British army in which they served two years later. They and other supporters of home rule in 1916 were perplexed by what occurred in Ireland. Many grasped that the Rising altered the context in which they had embarked, at great cost in lives if not also compromised principles, to struggle for Irish freedom in France. At Easter 1916 a minority faction of the Volunteers under the influence of the Irish Republican Brotherhood (IRB) had unilaterally changed the fortunes of all who supported self-determination for Ireland.

Moreover, the separatists in Dublin fought alongside the small but potent Irish Citizen Army (ICA) which, under the command of James Connolly, comprised one of the first socialist militias to rise in arms in the twentieth century.

The nature and timing of the Rising ensured that it could not be ignored by the international community and a range of canards, myths and misconceptions were generated that have clouded discussion of the episode ever since. The longevity of many of the more questionable viewpoints stems, to a large degree, from an incomplete and vitiated historiography of 1916. The military history of the period remains in its infancy and several leading protagonists either lack authoritative biographies or have been subjected to assessments that are not supported by archival evidence. Comprehensive histories of the ICA, IRB, Volunteers and other political bodies are much needed. Interim discussions of the Rising are typically narrow in focus, as if it stood apart from the First World War and the trends of international socialism. This is patently not the case.

In 1803 Robert Emmet declared his wish to see Ireland take its place 'among the nations' and this objective was explicitly referenced in the 1916 Proclamation. The extent to which the Rising advanced this objective may be a matter of debate but contemporaries knew from the outset that its significance reached beyond the suburbs of Dublin. The essays in this collection address a number of key questions posed by the Rising, its revolutionary aftermath and contested legacy.

Social and political tensions within the Volunteer movement prior to and following the damaging 1914 split are explored by John O'Callaghan. His case study of the Limerick Volunteers reveals salient aspects of this transition and offers insights into the subsequent incidence of fighting in the provinces in 1916.

The Irish Citizen Army was at the heart of events in Dublin and arguably formed the 'vanguard of the revolution'. The ICA has been represented as if they were a heterogeneous presence during Easter week, rather than a coherent, clear-sighted and militant body of armed socialists. Ann Matthews contends that issues of class and social mores were much in evidence during interaction between the ICA, Cumann na mBan and the Irish Volunteers between 1913 and 1916.

Máirtín Seán Ó Catháin analyzes the contribution of Scottish-based activists to the Rising in Ireland. While the IRB was strongly embodied in the US and Britain and linked to adherents as far afield as Australasia, a Scottish presence was actually manifested in Dublin. Ó Cathain's essay highlights the fallacy of removing the Rising from the all islands political environment from which it emerged.

Similarly, the comparatively muted response of the British Left to the Rising is explored by David Granville. His account of the predicament faced by Britons who wished to voice sympathy for the rebels reminds that wartime censorship and forced solidarity did not reflect the diversity of informed opinion.

Rory Sweetman surveys the Rising from the outer reaches of the British empire where the Irish communities of New Zealand and Australia were caught off-guard and were, at first, ill-equipped to rationalize what had occurred. However, those who had advocated an extension to Ireland of the legislative rights enjoyed by the empire's 'white settler dominions' quickly recovered from the shocking news. Persons of more militant inclinations, not least Bishop James Liston of Auckland, subsequently faced imprisonment for their open identification with the revolutionaries.

The potentially decisive influence of President Woodrow Wilson on Irish nationhood is assessed by Bernadette Whelan. Nuances surrounding the issue of American diplomatic intervention are detailed by Whelan, not least decisions with a bearing on US neutrality, 'small nations' and the tentative alliance with London. The rejection of Irish delegations to the Paris peace talks in 1919 is more explicable in this broader context.

Paris also features in Ian McKeane's essay on reactions to the Rising in a country where the First World War was being waged. McKeane charts how the French view of Ireland's 'days of blood' was coloured by their military pact with the British and suspicions that their German enemy was deeply implicated.

Priscilla Metscher argues that Connolly's role in 1916 should be assessed in terms of the agenda of international socialism when under great strain from the war. Certainly, Connolly's writings and world view evince a strong sense of connection to the European Left and the policies, theories and tactics that promoted the advancement of the workers.

The other iconic and controversial figurehead of 1916, Patrick Pearse, is presented in a new light by Róisín Ní Ghairbhí. Pearse, it is argued, was far more cognizant of the ancient culture and revolutionary traditions of Ireland than hitherto entertained. Ní Ghairbhí contends that aspects of Pearse's early political formation have either been suppressed or ignored by commentators wishing to present him as a conflicted, estranged maverick.

Peter Berresford Ellis examines popular concepts of 1916 which he believes cannot be sustained by modern scholarship. He takes issue with the esoteric notion of 'blood sacrifice' as an alleged motivational force underpinning 1916 and rejects criticism of Connolly as military strategist.

Brian P. Murphy also finds fault with the research methodology employed by several historians of the revolutionary period. In a robust essay Murphy identifies examples of selective quotation of documents, curious silences and problematic assertions which undermine the integrity of the published works.

Matt Treacy rejects the theory that the republican movement exploited the fiftieth anniversary of 1916 to build towards an armed campaign. Treacy details the internal discussions within republican circles in the mid-1960s and his findings suggest that 1966 cannot be viewed as the catalyst for the violence which broke out in 1969.

1

The Limerick Volunteers and 1916

John O'Callaghan

The Irish Volunteers in Limerick were, on paper at least, one of the strongest units in the country. However, like the Volunteers in most counties, they had minimal impact on the events of Easter week 1916. This article assesses the development of the Limerick Volunteers in the national context and highlights certain problems that may have been unique to Limerick. The evolution of the Limerick Volunteers from their formation in 1913 until the Rising of 1916 is examined within the framework of Irish Republican Brotherhood (IRB) stratagem. There is an element of comparative analysis between conditions in Limerick and those in areas where the Volunteers did take action during the Rising.

Patrick Pearse's final manifesto of Easter week 1916 asserted that the military council of the IRB had planned a general mobilization and simultaneous rising of Irish Volunteer companies throughout the country. Yet the Volunteers of just four counties – Dublin, Wexford, Galway and Louth – rose in arms during Easter week. Only fragmentary documentary evidence exists of detailed plans for a nationwide rising; most of this relates to the landing and distribution of arms from Germany. Instructions were couched in vague, generalized terms about 'holding lines'. The report of the Royal Commission on the Rising commented admiringly on the military planning and implementation of the Dublin insurrection.[1]

Here again, however, the evidence is incomplete, much of it having gone to the grave with the executed rebels. It seems plausible that the Rising, as it occurred on Easter Monday, was a modified version of what had been planned for Sunday, that the rebel forces were smaller than envisaged and that this affected the pattern and nature of the military action. In any case, there is a strong impression that, as is the case for many historians, the provincial rebellion was something of an afterthought for the military council. The insistence in the original instructions to all provincial commandants that no action should be taken before 7 p.m. on Easter Sunday, when Dublin would already be in action, shows that not only was Dublin of primary concern to the leaders but that the initiative had been taken out of the hands of local officers. The Rising was planned and instigated by the IRB as distinct from the Volunteers. The plans of the military council were based on the assumption that the IRB would be able to commit the whole Volunteer organization to a rising, including the chief of staff, Eoin MacNeill.

MacNeill saw the role of the Volunteers as strictly defensive, unless the government attempted to enforce conscription or disarm the Volunteers. Tom Clarke and Seán MacDiarmada defeated the conservative elements within the IRB in 1910–11 and took control of the supreme council. The Royal Commission on the Rising found that Clarke and fellow Fenian veteran John Daly of Limerick were at the centre of the 'inner circle by which the plans for insurrection were no doubt matured'.[2] The triumvirate of Daly, Clarke and MacDiarmada were one of the main catalysts of the Rising, and the Daly household was the hub of significant seditious activity. Clarke and MacDiarmada believed that the betrayal of plans by spies and informers had contributed heavily to the failure of previous revolutionary efforts.[3] With this in mind, they set out to plan an insurrection, the details of which would be known to only a select few. In the Volunteers they had their instrument of rebellion; in the Great War they had their opportunity. All the members of the military council, with the exception of Clarke, who deliberately stayed in the background, were on the central executive of the Volunteers. Pearse, director of organization, Plunkett, director of military operations, and Ceannt (from August 1915), director of communications, were on the general council. However, the 2,000 IRB men around the country did not know that they were to follow only the instructions of this clique at the critical moment. In the end, the almost absolute secrecy maintained by an elite cabal who were relying on the unquestioning obedience of a nationwide revolutionary organization that they kept in ignorance undermined their objective of staging a nationwide rebellion everywhere except in Dublin, where they were in a position to directly control events. In fact, the military council encountered greater direct opposition to their plans from within the ranks of the Volunteers than they did from the British authorities.[4]

In 1911 the Limerick city IRB was reorganized under the guise of the Wolfe Tone Club debating society. As well as debating, the society purchased six .22 rifles and trained in their use.[5] On 14 November 1913, eleven days before the Irish Volunteers were publicly inaugurated, Fr John Fitzgerald, chairman of the West Limerick United Irish League (UIL) executive, had urged the creation of a volunteer force to resist Carson and the 'weak-kneed Liberals' and threatened bloodshed if home rule was not enacted. In December however, local MP Thomas Lundon told the east Limerick UIL executive that a volunteer army was unnecessary and urged restraint in committing to the movement until the party leaders gave direction.[6] His comments reflected the reservations of nationalists about the significance of the Volunteers and their potential to undermine Redmond and the Irish Parliamentary Party (IPP). Given the strength of opposition to the IPP in Limerick, these fears were well justified. In January 1914 the county inspector reported that John Daly 'and his followers are the principals in this movement as a large section of the Nationalists believe there is no necessity for it at the moment'.[7]

In December, just as Bulmer Hobson had engineered the national foundation of the Volunteers for the IRB the previous month, local members of the IRB made arrangements to establish a corps of Volunteers in Limerick city. Mayor Philip O'Donovan presided at a public meeting in the Athenaeum Hall, Cecil Street, on 25 January, and stated that should the movement 'be in any way hostile to the cause so ably advocated by Mr. Redmond and the Irish Parliamentary Party he would not officially support it'. However, the IRB, in the guise of the Wolfe Tone Club, and through acting as representatives of trade unions, were able to dominate the original provisional committee of the city Volunteers. As well as mirroring the IRB infiltration of the national Volunteer executive, this verified the county inspector's January analysis of the role of Daly and the composition of the city Volunteers, as did comments made by Patrick Pearse. Pearse and Roger Casement addressed the Athenaeum meeting and reported favourably to Tom Clarke on the response of those present.[8] Pearse told Daly that he had pitched his speech

> ... in a key intended to find a response in the Home Rule heart as well as in the Nationalist heart, more properly so called. I believe that the rank and file of the Home Rulers are ready, if properly handled, to go as far as you have gone and I hope to go. Here again the Volunteer movement seems to be the one thing that will bring them into line with us.[9]

This is a prime example of what Desmond Ryan referred to as Pearse's 'extraordinary outlook on insurrection in which he believed so strongly that he persuaded himself that everyone must at heart agree with him'.[10]

As in the rest of the country, the Volunteer organization grew rapidly throughout Limerick. The inspector-general pointed out that 'each county will soon have a trained army far outnumbering the police, and those who control the Volunteers will be in a position to dictate to what extent the law of the land may be carried into effect'.[11]

With the outbreak of the First World War in August 1914, the question of who controlled the Volunteers developed along lines amenable to the purposes of the IRB. In the meantime, the Curragh incident in April, the Larne gun-running in May, and the Howth gun-running in July acted as spurs for Volunteer membership. The Royal Irish Constabulary (RIC) recorded the strength of the Volunteers in Limerick before the September split as being 8,235 members in eighty-two branches.[12] David Fitzpatrick calculated that there were fifty-eight members of the Volunteers per thousand of population in Limerick at this time. The comparative figure for Clare was forty-nine.[13]

The strength of the City regiment in September was approximately 1,250 men. When the regiment split over Redmond's war policy, which called on Volunteers to join the British army, 250 men initially remained with the original organization, a higher proportion than in the rest of the country.[14] On 4 October, 208 men attended the first meeting of those who followed Eoin MacNeill. The same number attended on 11 October but from that point on the average turnout was around 100.[15] Some 1,000 Volunteers declared for Redmond. However, this figure disguises the fact that Redmond's endorsement of the war was not greeted with enthusiasm in Limerick. Attendances at drilling had declined substantially after the outbreak of war in August. The county inspector reported that this was partly due to a lack of competent instructors but that the principal factor was that Volunteers believed that they would be required to join the army if they continued to parade.[16] The National Volunteers showed no immediate desire to join the army, according to the inspector general, and a number of farmers' sons emigrated because of a rumour that the Militia Ballot Act was about to be enforced.[17]

Ernest Blythe was occasionally successful in encouraging National Volunteers to secede, particularly where he had the support of the Catholic clergy, and in recruiting farmers' sons of military age, who believed that membership of the Irish Volunteers would protect them from conscription.[18] Liam Manahan, commandant of the Galtee battalion, assessed the split as ultimately beneficial for the Irish Volunteers. He argued that the elimination of destabilizing and demoralizing political rivalries provided the Irish Volunteers with a new unity of purpose and made them a more cohesive military unit.[19] It was certainly the case that the Irish Volunteers now had a more definite goal, that Redmond's influence had been removed, and that this suited the IRB. However, the continuing presence of IRB agents within the Volunteers meant that divisions remained, particularly among the leadership. These divisions were most profoundly manifested in the intrigues and uncertainties of Easter 1916.

The custodians of the weapons which the city Volunteers had acquired before the split followed MacNeill. The threat of the minority element was therefore disproportionately potent. The National Volunteers, despite their greater numbers, had only a fraction of the rifles per capita that the Irish Volunteers had, and 'not much' ammunition.[20] Colonel Moore, the military leader of the National Volunteers, found it almost impossible to procure rifles from manufacturers who were concentrating on supplying the army. At some stage in the first half of 1915 Colonel Moore had gone to Limerick with proposals for reconciliation between the rival Volunteer forces but the 'local extremists' would not entertain him. MacNeill, for his part, would not countenance adopting the insurrectionary methods advocated by subordinate leaders in Limerick as the basis for reconciliation.[21] In December efforts by the rector of Mungret College, Fr Cahill, SJ, to effect reconciliation came to nothing because the National Volunteers refused to compromise on any grounds.[22]

By early 1916 the National Volunteer movement in Limerick existed only in name. The Irish Volunteers, meanwhile, were increasing in strength. There were 689 members in seventeen branches in February and 872 members in twenty-two branches in June, according to the police. They greatly improved their organization and efficiency.[23] This was due in large part to the work of Robert Monteith in the city and east Limerick, and the efforts of Blythe in west Limerick. The Limerick Volunteers were well regarded by their colleagues nationally. In the summer of 1914 the *Sinn Féin* newspaper described the Limerick city corps as 'the best drilled in Ireland'.[24] In February 1915 Pearse wrote: '*Is dóigh le'n a lán gurab é cath Luimnighe an cath is treise dá bhfuil againn. Tá fir maithe in a gceannais, fir nach bhfuil a sárugad in Éireann, ar dílseacht, nár ar calmacht, nár ar stuaim.*' ('There are many who think the Limerick battalion is the best we have. There are good men in command, men whose loyalty, courage and determination are not surpassed in Ireland').[25]

Early in 1915 an inspector from headquarters identified the Limerick regiment as the most efficient in the provinces and as leading Dublin in some respects. A year later, thanks to the competence of its leaders, Limerick was still the best-organized urban area outside Dublin.[26] The circumstances in Dublin, however, were radically different to those in the rest of the country. Communications were better, it was easier to concentrate forces there and the Dublin brigade was better drilled and armed. In addition, Dublin officers were more closely informed of the intentions of the military council and, consequently, were better prepared for the Rising. In August 1915 Monteith left Limerick and made his way to Germany to act as drill instructor to Casement's prospective Irish brigade. Monteith was a serious loss to the Limerick Volunteers. Liam Manahan believed that had Monteith remained in Limerick the Volunteer leadership would have been more disciplined and mature by the time of the Rising.[27] Coupled with the departure of Monteith, the imprisonment and deportation of Blythe was a serious blow to the Limerick Volunteers on an organizational and operational level. Liam Mellows had fallen foul of the Defence of the Realm Act along with

Blythe. His return to Galway before the Rising gave the Volunteers there a significant boost.

On 23 May 1915, Whit Sunday, Volunteer companies from Dublin, Cork and Tipperary joined their Limerick colleagues to parade through the city. Between 1,100 and 1,200 of what the Redmondite *Limerick Leader* labelled as 'pro-German' Volunteers marched. The police estimated that 700 of the Volunteers were armed, and were accompanied by 220 Fianna members.[28] The marchers encountered organized, persistent, and extensive barracking and physical challenges, particularly at the hands of the women of the Irishtown district, many of whom had menfolk serving in the British army. One of the leading republicans in Limerick, Madge Daly, among others, claimed that a representative of the Ancient Order of Hibernians had come from the headquarters of that organization in Dublin to foment opposition to the Volunteer parade and left money in all the public houses in the poorer quarters of the city, such as the Irishtown, where the separation allowance families lived.[29] Michael Hartney stated that the violence was the work of 'an organised gang of hooligans, all members of the National Volunteers'.[30] The Galbally Volunteers discharged shots into the air at one stage and fifty police and a number of priests were required to restore order.[31] The only consolation the Volunteers could possibly have taken from the episode was that they had maintained discipline in the face of formidable provocation, yet the following week Pearse wrote, rather sanguinely, to Madge Daly: 'I hope our visit has helped the Limerick Company. We all felt that the great bulk of the people in the city were sympathetic and that the hostile element was small, though noisy. Personally, I found the whole experience useful.'[32]

The hostile reactions to the Volunteers in Limerick on Whit Sunday and in Newcastlewest on St Patrick's Day, 1916, when they were pelted with rotten eggs, were not isolated incidents. A meeting of the Limerick County Board of the Volunteers on 24 April 1915 made special arrangements for the upcoming Whit Sunday parade. All Limerick units were asked to support the newly formed Irish Volunteers Insurance Society, *An Cumann Cosanta*, 'which insures Irish Volunteers against victimisation, the possibility of which we have learned through experience'.[33] James Gubbins concurred with the police that the persecution that Irish Volunteers were most likely to face because of their political activities was loss of employment:

> Many who attended the inaugural parade did not stay the course. This was not surprising, some were teachers or Civil Servants, whose livelihood would have been jeopardised, had they continued in the movement. Employers at the time wielded a most potent weapon … the weapon of economic pressure, or to use a cruder phrase, the threat of

starvation, and there were some who did not hesitate to use it. One member of the Committee, a married man with a family, was confronted with the blunt choice, 'The Volunteers or your job'. Who could blame him for choosing his job?[34]

Michael Hartney observed that while recruits 'were of the better type, sober, respectable young men', it was, nevertheless, 'tantamount to leaving a job to join, because the employers, in the main, were bitterly opposed to the Irish Volunteers'.[35] The Crowley family of Ballylanders were heavily involved in the Volunteers. The local post office was on their premises and Tadg was sub-postmaster. In March 1915 Tadg received a 'warning letter' from the government in relation to his Volunteer activities. A post office inspector warned the Crowleys that if they did not resign from the Volunteers they would have to give up the post office. On the advice of Michael Colivet, the most senior Irish Volunteer in Limerick, they adopted a less public role in the Volunteers.[36] Alphonsus O'Halloran believed that such economic considerations were a crucial factor in the decrease in Volunteer numbers in the city from over 200 at the first couple of meetings after the split in October 1914 to an average of 100 thereafter. Liam Forde confirmed that 'employees of a considerable number of business concerns were told that they must desist parading with the "Sinn Féin" section of the Volunteers or lose their employment. Consequently, the recorded average attendance at parades fell to about one hundred.'[37]

In January 1916 Redmond won a significant victory in securing Ireland's exclusion from conscription when it was imposed on Britain. In February the *Leader* declared that 'the heart of Limerick remains thoroughly sound and inflexible in its fealty to the leadership of Mr. Redmond'.[38] On 25 January Stephen Quin, a unionist, was elected mayor in the hope that his family connections and personal friendship with the lord lieutenant would allow him to attract industry, in the shape of munitions factories, to Limerick.[39] Councillor Dalton proposed a resolution that the new mayor should not act in a manner 'that might be likely to lower the national dignity of our city'. In an unambiguous indication of a significant shift in the political equilibrium of Limerick Corporation since August 1914, when only two members opposed Redmond's call for Irishmen to join the British army, nine out of thirty-seven members of the corporation, who, to use Councillor Matthew Griffin's expression, considered Quin a unionist 'flunkey', supported Dalton's resolution.[40]

In the wake of the split in the Volunteers Michael Colivet was elected as officer commanding (OC) Limerick city battalion. George Clancy, head-centre of the IRB in Limerick, and James Ledden, another Fenian veteran, became vice-commandant and honorary colonel respectively. Colivet was not sworn into the IRB until December 1915, by which stage plans for an insurrection were well advanced.[41] Colivet was OC of the Limerick brigade at Easter 1916. As was the case with MacNeill and the national leadership of the Volunteers, then, the senior officer in Limerick, if he was as radical, was certainly not as well informed as some of his junior staff. Charlie Wall was not sworn into the IRB until Tuesday 16 April. He was then appointed OC west Limerick battalion and informed of plans for the Rising.[42] In March 1915 Edward Daly, Thomas MacDonagh, Éamon de Valera and Éamonn Ceannt were appointed to command the four Dublin city battalions. Pearse, Plunkett, Hobson and O'Rahilly were appointed commandants on the headquarters staff. De Valera joined the IRB soon after but neither he nor long-term member Hobson were in the confidence of the inner circle. O'Rahilly did not join the IRB. Thomas Ashe, as OC of the 5th battalion of the Dublin brigade, was also working on plans for the Rising since early 1915.

On 15 November 1915 Terence MacSwiney lectured to the Limerick Volunteers on 'the spirit of Mitchel's teachings and its application today'. He chose this subject because he believed that 'too many of them [the Volunteers] expect to be alive after the business is all over, and I hope to show that Mitchel teaches something else'.[43] In December the police learned from an informant that 'prominent extremists and Irish Volunteers recently met at Limerick to discuss the proposal to strike a blow for Irish Independence'. They were apparently awaiting the opportunity which they believed the conscription scare would afford them in the form of popular support.[44] Clarke and MacDiarmada spent Christmas 1915 at Daly's and it may well have been during this visit that Easter Sunday was decided on as the date of the Rising. In his last public speech, delivered to the west Limerick Volunteers at Newcastlewest on St Patrick's Day 1916, Seán MacDiarmada repeatedly referred to the need for sacrifice and resistance. He urged them to vow that 'the hillsides of Ireland would be dyed with their blood before they gave up any arms'.[45]

The Irish Volunteer units in Limerick in 1916 were comprised of the Limerick city, west Limerick and Galtee battalions and a battalion in the Doon–Castleconnell area. These four battalions, together with four more in Clare led by Captain Michael Brennan, constituted the newly formed Limerick command under Michael Colivet. A full-strength battalion should have 500 soldiers. None of these eight battalions ever mustered much more than 200 men. The city battalion was the best armed yet not every city Volunteer had access to a rifle.[46] Between 150 and 400 west Limerick Volunteers, for instance, many of whom had no firearms, assembled at Glenquin castle on Easter Sunday under the command of Charlie Wall. The last instruction that they received was MacNeill's countermanding order at 3 p.m. before disbanding around 8 p.m.[47] Again, between 150 and 400 Volunteers from Ahane, Doon, Cappamore, Killonan, Caherconlish and Killaloe mobilized in Castleconnell but were dismissed.[48] The British forces in the city alone consisted of 800 infantry, a battery of artillery, and 100 constabulary. By Easter Monday afternoon 2,000 infantry with two batteries of artillery had taken complete charge of the city, holding all the roads and bridges. The local RIC judged that only the prompt arrival of the military had averted violence in the city.[49] Inspector-General Chamberlain formed the opinion that if Casement had not been arrested and the arms had landed, the Volunteers in every county would have risen.[50]

Until the Tuesday before Easter, Colivet was working from ambiguous instructions to take Limerick and hold the line of the Shannon in the event of a rising. It was only then that he learned of the expected arms landing in Kerry (the military council had known since the end of 1915 and Austin Stack, in charge of operations in Kerry, had been informed in February). His plans to hold the north shore of the river and retire into Clare if necessary were now obsolete. He met Pearse in Dublin on Wednesday and was tasked with taking delivery of the German arms at Abbeyfeale and forwarding the surplus to Galway while also attacking police and military barracks and disabling telegraph, telephone and rail communications. This was to be initiated before the arrival of the German arms in Abbeyfeale, in order to create a diversion which would ensure their safe passage. Colivet was also under the impression that a German expeditionary force was expected. When he had taken control of Limerick he was to relieve Dublin. In relative terms, a numerically weak, poorly equipped, inexperienced, embryonic army was being asked to go on the offensive against well-armed, experienced opponents in strong defensive positions.

Contrary to Terence MacSwiney's expectations, and to MacDiarmada's hopes, there was no violence in Limerick at Easter 1916.[51] Patrick Whelan returned from Tralee with news of the capture of the *Aud* and the arrest of Casement and of Stack on Saturday. This prompted Colivet to send James Gubbins and Liam Forde to Dublin to ask for instructions and to suggest that the Rising should be postponed. Gubbins stated that after meeting MacDiarmada he sent a coded telegram to Limerick that the Rising was on, but Colivet does not appear to have received it. When Colivet had not heard anything by Saturday evening, he provisionally cancelled all operations planned in the Limerick command for Sunday. This nullified the impact of MacNeill's countermanding order to such an extent that it was already something of a dead letter when The O'Rahilly arrived with it on Sunday morning. The real significance of the countermanding order in the Limerick context lay in the fact that it was Colivet's first inkling of the divisions in headquarters. He was clearly not in the confidence of the military council. Thus, the IRB infiltration scheme was not fully effective. Colivet reiterated his orders cancelling manoeuvres for outlying units but decided to take the city battalion on its usual march to Killonan in an effort to maintain the pretence of normality.

On Sunday afternoon Colivet received a coded message from Fitzgibbon in Dublin that the Rising was off. Forde returned at midnight with a message from Pearse that everything was postponed for the present but to await further orders. Gubbins returned on Monday with a message from MacDiarmada that the Rising would still go ahead and to resist arrest. Patrick Whelan returned from a second mission to Tralee on Monday morning with the news that Monteith had counselled against action. Agnes Daly brought a dispatch from Pearse to Colivet in Killonan at 2 p.m.: The Dublin brigade was going into action at noon and Colivet should carry out his orders of the previous Tuesday. Circumstances had changed drastically, however, and the orders no longer seemed relevant to the officers present.

On Tuesday, 25 April, Colivet convened a meeting of senior officers at which, by a majority of ten to six, it was decided that nothing more could be done. On Friday, 5 May, after it was learned that the British were set to raid for arms, the Limerick Volunteers, through Colivet, and with Bishop O'Dwyer acting as a facilitator, surrendered their guns to Mayor Quin, who passed them on to Sir Anthony Weldon, commander of the British forces in Limerick. Limerick Volunteers surrendered a total of 253 rifles, 105 shotguns, twenty-eight revolvers, twenty-six sword bayonets, three swords and 13,228 rounds of various types of ammunition.[52] Monteith claimed that the Volunteers actually retained their working rifles and revolvers and substituted unserviceable weapons for them. Madge Daly and James Gubbins claimed that most of the men destroyed their weapons before surrendering them.[53] Whether or not surrendered weapons were destroyed is something of a moot point, however, because they were no longer in Volunteer hands.

The issue of the surrender of arms was crucial for two reasons. Firstly, it created dissension in the ranks. Secondly, the retained arms remained available for use at a later stage. If the surrender of arms was partly an attempt to pre-empt arrests and deportations it was largely successful in this regard, although Colivet reported to the Volunteer executive that 'contrary to common report, no engagement whatsoever was given, or sought, that there would be immunity from subsequent arrest'.[54] Most of the fifty people who were arrested in Limerick after the Rising were released after a few days.[55] The relatively benign reaction of Colonel Weldon, who was an 'Irishman and a Home Ruler' according to James Gubbins, meant that the Volunteer organization in Limerick remained basically intact after the Rising.[56] In fact, the police became aware of almost immediate efforts on the part of the 'Sinn Féin revolutionary movement' in Limerick to sustain and build subversive momentum at underground meetings and through the Irish National Aid League and Irish Volunteers Dependents' Fund.[57]

The point has also been made that had the authorities not generally refrained from aggressive action when they found themselves in situations such as that which developed at Glenquin on Easter Sunday, when RIC men armed with carbines shadowed the Volunteers, it might have provoked guerrilla fighting in the provinces before the Dublin Rising was defeated.[58] Police and military correspondence reveals a great deal of uncertainty among the authorities about how to react to the Volunteer renaissance so soon after the apparently terminal defeat of Easter week. However, a report written by Colonel Weldon on 18 January 1917 seems to indicate that, sometime earlier in the month, Colivet had assured him that there would be no further drilling. Weldon, under the impression that Colivet did not approve of the resumption of Volunteer activities and that he would try to curtail drilling, recommended a restrained course of tolerance. County-Inspector Yates, on the other hand, pressed for Madge Daly to be court-martialled for allowing her premises to be used by the Volunteers.[59]

Uncertainty reigned in south Limerick. Commandant Liam Manahan received MacNeill's order cancelling the 'manoeuvres' planned for Easter Sunday shortly before noon that morning from The O'Rahilly. He paraded in Galbally nonetheless (Manahan had had interviews with Tomás MacDonagh in Dublin during the previous weeks and knew that MacNeill was not fully aware of the gravity of the situation) and did not dismiss his men until 6 p.m. that evening by which time MacNeill's order had been repeated to him no less than five times from Charleville, Limerick and Tipperary. It was not until the early hours of Tuesday morning that vague information arrived that fighting had started in Dublin. He received no further orders but notified the companies of the Galtee battalion to remain on stand-by. On Wednesday Batt Laffan, among the most senior Volunteers in Limerick city, sent word that there was no likelihood of any action taking place in the city because of the reinforced military presence there. At 10 p.m. on Wednesday Seán Treacy of Tipperary brought verbal confirmation that there was fighting in Dublin and urged Manahan to take action against the local RIC barracks. Manahan ordered immediate mobilization but the battalion's dispatch riders had been dismissed and Captain Tom Murphy of Ballylanders had used all his riders to mobilize his own company. This meant that it was after midnight on Wednesday when Manahan's orders for remobilization were received by Galbally, Mitchelstown, Anglesboro, Kilfinane and Ardpatrick.

By 6 a.m. on Thursday morning only Ballylanders and Galbally had fully mobilized and were in a position to implement Manahan's plan. The late arrival of his orders had made it impossible for the other companies to mobilize and procure arms. Word had also come from Cork that there was no possibility of military action there. Manahan then decided to demobilize and await definite orders but the next news was of the surrender in Dublin on the following Sunday. According to Manahan, it was on the advice of officers from the city and without his knowledge that Volunteers under his command relinquished their arms to the British late in the week following the surrender in Dublin. Seán Meade of Ballylanders company and Edmond O'Brien of Galbally company confirmed that the order to surrender arms came from Colivet rather than Manahan.[60] On the second Sunday after Easter the RIC warned Manahan that if the Ardpatrick company, who still retained their weapons, did not hand them over they would be arrested and deported. Manahan gave the Ardpatrick men the choice of giving up their arms. Some Volunteers took this option.[61]

IRB man Donal O'Hannigan took command of the Louth Volunteers at the start of April. O'Hannigan answered to Pearse and did not demobilize in response to MacNeill's countermanding order. He left Dundalk with 160 men on Sunday morning but only twenty-eight remained mobilized on Monday evening. Twelve RIC men surrendered to them in Lurgan Green and they arrested a number of British officers. They commandeered several cars and carts, wounding one incompliant farmer in the process, and captured another ten policemen at Castlebellingham and a Lieutenant Dunville of the Grenadier Guards. In a subsequent scuffle Dunville was wounded and Constable Magee fatally shot. O'Hannigan attempted to rendezvous with the Fingal battalion on Sunday but Thomas Ashe had surrendered.

Liam Mellows, who had been deported with Ernest Blythe in March, only resumed his command in Galway on Easter Monday night after returning from England in disguise. He was another IRB agent on the Volunteer executive but not in the confidence of the military council. After the disorder of Sunday 1,000 men mobilized around the county in response to Pearse's remobilization order on Monday, and between 500 and 600 bivouacked with Mellows. They were poorly armed and their orders to hold the line of the Shannon were based around the receipt of 3,000 German rifles.[62] After unsuccessful raids on police barracks in Oranmore, Craughwell and Gort on Tuesday morning Mellows moved to Athenry. Following skirmishes with the RIC he moved south to Moyode castle on Thursday. The departure of 200 Volunteers from the camp on Friday prompted Mellows to move towards Clare with the intention of making contact with the Limerick Volunteers. The Galway insurgents eventually disbanded in the early hours of Saturday.

As elsewhere, there was much confusion in Wexford until Vice-Commandant Paul Galligan arrived with orders from Connolly on

Wednesday night to cut rail networks. There was no move against the rail lines but 100 Enniscorthy Volunteers took possession of that town in the early hours of Thursday morning. They did not perceive themselves to be sufficiently well armed to attack the RIC barracks. A smaller force set out for Dublin but retreated on meeting troops in Ferns. Enniscorthy held out until Monday, 1 May, when they got confirmation of the surrender from Pearse. There were no serious casualties in Galway or Wexford. The most innovative Volunteer exploit of Easter week was that of the 5th (Fingal) battalion of the Dublin brigade in north Dublin and Meath under Thomas Ashe and Richard Mulcahy. It was also the action that most closely prefigured the guerrilla tactics and barracks attacks of the 1919–21 campaign. Some 120 men mobilized on Sunday but dispersed that night. Approximately half that number reassembled on Monday. Though poorly armed, they were mobile, as all had bicycles. Their modus operandi was offensive rather than defensive. On Tuesday they lost twenty men to the GPO but on Wednesday the RIC in Swords and Donabate surrendered with minimal resistance. On Thursday they found Garristown RIC barracks largely abandoned. As they negotiated the surrender of Ashbourne barracks on Friday a police column of fifty-five men in seventeen cars came upon them. After five hours of fighting, two Volunteers had been killed and five wounded. Eight RIC men were dead and fifteen wounded. The motorized column and the barracks surrendered to Ashe. The Fingal battalion surrendered, under orders from Pearse, on Sunday, 30 April.[63]

The Volunteers in Louth, Wexford, Galway and north Dublin, then, certainly occupied the opposition forces in their localities to various extents but had little or no direct impact on events in Dublin. They showed that the failure of the arms landing, conflicting orders and isolation from other active units were not insuperable impediments to action. Conversely, no countermanding order was necessary to cause inaction in Ulster. Pearse and Connolly had planned for the Belfast Volunteers to march across Ulster without engaging in action and to rendezvous with the Tyrone Volunteers on the way to Galway. The Tyrone men, however, simply refused to leave their own county and the plan disintegrated. Denis McCullough would not commit the Belfast Volunteers to action without the support of the Tyrone men, and that was the end of the Rising in Ulster.[64]

In early 1917 the executive of the Volunteers authorized an inquiry into the action of the Limerick units (as well as Cork and Kerry) during Easter week. Having investigated the dispatches alleged to have been received by Limerick from Dublin and Kerry, they submitted their findings in March 1918:

Some of these dispatches, [Limerick] did not, in our opinion, receive at all and those they did receive were so conflicting that we are satisfied no blame whatsoever rests on the officers and men of Limerick. With regard to the surrender of arms, it is to be deprecated that at any time arms should be given up by a body of men without a fight.[65]

While the report acknowledged that the loss of the arms ship coupled with conflicting and contradictory orders had contributed to the fiasco in Limerick, and that no blame could be attached to the battalions or their OCs, it also looked unfavourably on the surrender of arms. Colivet wanted a direct verdict as to whether or not the surrender of arms was justifiable in the prevailing circumstances, but none was forthcoming. Kathleen Clarke cast doubts on the competence, if not the commitment, of the Limerick leadership. She was highly critical of the indecisiveness of Colivet and Clancy. Clarke's sister, Madge Daly, believed that the Limerick officers did not possess the necessary military experience or acumen to deal capably with the situation that confronted them and claimed that the more influential older men overruled the younger men who were most keen for action.[66] Daly's claim seems to be substantiated by the record of voting. The six members of the local leadership who wanted to commence hostilities on 25 April but were outvoted by ten of their colleagues were Captains Liam Forde, Michael Brennan and James McInerney, Lieutenant John Lane, Section-Commander John McSweeney (who was IRB centre for a circle in the city) and Seán Ó Muirthuile, who was attached to the Limerick city regiment at the time. Michael Hartney also cast doubt on the willingness of the local leadership to fight, suggesting that they were more concerned with politics than revolution.[67]

It should also be pointed out that approximately 140 out of the 200 or so city Volunteers turned out at Easter. This was a comparatively high ratio and it is likely that all would have had rifles at their disposable. Some were on duty elsewhere: Forde and Gubbins were in Dublin, Whelan was in Tralee, James McInerney had been assigned to Newcastlewest to oversee operations there, and John Grant, riding a motorcycle, was acting as liaison officer between the various units in Limerick. Not more than 100 Volunteers, however, and perhaps as few as eighty, spent Easter Sunday night at Killonan.[68] This somewhat mediocre response from the rank and file may have been partly attributable to Colivet's cancellation order of Saturday evening and MacNeill's countermanding order but it may also have been reflective of the leadership provided by senior local officers. The theory that the prevalence of revolutionary violence in the 1917–23 period was solely a function of the presence or absence of strong-willed individual leadership has been challenged by the statistical analyses of David Fitzpatrick, Peter Hart and Erhard Rumpf and A.C. Hepburn.[69] However, Easter week 1916 was a significantly different enterprise to the extended campaigns of the Tan and

Civil Wars. To a large extent, the provincial Rising turned on what local commanders knew of the military council's plans. Yet the Galway Volunteers, from an almost identical state of affairs, produced a very different result to Limerick. Whatever about providing inspirational leadership, Colivet certainly did not improvise in the imaginative manner that Mellows did in Galway or Ashe and Mulcahy did with the Fingal battalion.

The first accounts of the Rising to emerge in the Limerick local press concentrated on the German link and civilian casualties. On 27 April the *Limerick Chronicle* reported the attempted arms landing in its 'The War' column under the heading 'German Descent on Irish Coast'. The importance of the German connection was exaggerated at the time. On 4 May the *Chronicle* claimed that the rebels had fired indiscriminately at traffic and on 5 May the *Leader* described the number of casualties as 'appalling'. Initial public reaction seems to have been one of curiosity as to the causes of the rebellion combined with indignation. The climate in Limerick was very much one of staunch support for the IPP. The *Leader* claimed that the country was 'unquestionably behind the Irish leader' and identified a choice for nationalists between 'futile revolution and disaster' or 'constitutionalism and success'. Its editorial of 10 May did, however, warn against the tension being exacerbated by vindictiveness on the part of the military authorities. On more than one occasion, the executive of the city National Volunteers recorded its 'implicit confidence' in Redmond's leadership.[70]

The prior of the Franciscan order in Limerick was a brother of John Dillon and, according to Madge Daly, 'a fanatical pro-Britisher'. One Franciscan preached a sermon denouncing the Volunteers and condemning the Rising as a sin.[71] The county inspector commented that the insurrection was 'generally denounced as an insane act ... done by those getting German money and that these people had to show something for what they got' but he did note an undercurrent of sympathy with the rebels. The inspector-general identified that sympathy as being most pronounced in Limerick, Cork, Kerry, Clare and Galway.[72] Limerick County Council, while renewing its confidence in Redmond, expressed 'regret that the military authorities should have acted so severely' and appealed to the government to deal leniently with 'our misguided fellow countrymen'. The council also congratulated Bishop O'Dwyer on his response to

> ... the solicitation of General Maxwell when he endeavoured to get his Lordship on his side at a time when he was engaged in directing that heroic Irishmen be shot down after surrender and further directing that the arrest and deportation of thousands of Irishmen and Irish women without charge or trial not to speak of the effort to victimise two patriotic clergymen in his Lordship's diocese.[73]

O'Dwyer's defiance of General Maxwell, who wanted the bishop to take disciplinary action against two priests for their nationalist activities, and his glorification of the rebels coincided with and closely reflected, if not directed, a drastic transformation in the tenor of public opinion on the Rising. He was one of the first prominent figures to publicly voice what was to become the popular attitude to the rebels and the executions. While most of the IPP (with the exception of John Dillon), newspapers and Catholic hierarchy condemned the rebels, O'Dwyer praised the 'purity and nobility of their motives ... and splendour of their courage' and condemned the executions and the 'history of the mismanagement' of Ireland by Britain.[74] On 6 June Prime Minister Asquith told his cabinet that O'Dwyer's letter to Maxwell was one of five factors that had contributed to the reverse in opinion on the Rising and raised anti-British fervour.[75] The Limerick RIC shared this opinion:

> The consequence of the rebellion and the subsequent executions have been an increase of disloyalty and disaffection and a more bitter feeling against England and the British Government than has ever before been experienced. The R.C. Bishop and some of the clergy have to some extent voiced the feelings of the people in this respect.[76]

The failure of the Limerick Volunteers to realize their military potential in 1916 was to have significant implications for the organization of revolutionary forces in the county in subsequent years. Post-1916 the IRA in the city was split into two adversarial factions, as was the IRA in the Galtee battalion area. The divisions in what was to become the east Limerick brigade revolved around efforts by the IRB to secure its dominance by undermining Liam Manahan, who opposed its influence. The situation in the city was more complex. Alphonsus O'Halloran described how, in May 1917, the Roger Casement Sinn Féin Club in the Irishtown district decided to form a Volunteer company from its own members and applied to the authorities of the battalion for a drill instructor. When this request was refused on the basis that a company already existed in the area the Casement Club resolved to form a unit independent of the 1st battalion. Other new companies soon organized in the area and linked up together under the designation of the 2nd battalion. It was a source of tension that some of those who became prominent in the new battalion were former Redmondite National Volunteers and had been bitter adversaries of the 1st battalion since the 1914 split. O'Halloran was skirting around the real issue, however. James Gubbins reasoned simply that 'The trouble started because no fighting took place in 1916.'[77]

Some members of the 1st battalion were dissatisfied because no action had been taken during Easter week, and Lieutenant Arthur Johnson and a small number of the rank and file seceded and joined the new unit. Liam Forde recalled that 'the officers of the 1st Battalion were severely criticized for not having joined in the fight'. David Dundon and his colleagues in the new battalion 'resented very much the fact that although trained and equipped prior to 1916 the 1st Battalion did not engage in the fight'. Michael Hartney, who transferred from the 1st to the 2nd battalion, emphasized the military rationale behind the development. He recalled that there was

> a feeling in Limerick that the existing Volunteers would not fight, owing to the officers in charge being more interested in politics than revolution, and it was decided to start a second battalion ... The 1st Battalion did not function and some of them transferred to the 2nd Battalion.

Peadar McMahon, in conversation with Richard Mulcahy, recalled that when he arrived in Limerick:

> There was a company that met but didn't drill, didn't read any military manuals, didn't talk about military matters at all and on one occasion when you [Richard Mulcahy] were in Limerick ... you gave them a description of the battle of Ashbourne and I thought that might get them going but it didn't ... Later on a few of us came together and started a second battalion in Limerick. Dunne was Commandant there and I was Vice Commandant. Colivet was in charge of the first battalion.

George Clancy was another member of the 1st battalion who did not favour activity according to McMahon, and the 1st battalion was only stirred to meet by the formation of the 2nd.[78] George Embush told Ernie O'Malley that 'Neddie Punch and a few men wanted to do something or other, but the others didn't want to do anything ... the raids for arms were undertaken by small groups. When things got too hot the First Battalion didn't work.' Michael Stack's understanding of events was that the surrender of arms after the Rising had caused a lot of resentment and that this was largely responsible for the creation of the new unit. When Michael Brennan returned from internment in January 1917 he found 'great bitterness against the local leaders, more for surrendering their arms than for not fighting'. According to Patrick Whelan, 'dissatisfied members of the existing battalion, on the inspiration of Ernest Blythe, Peadar McMahon, Seán Ó Muirthuile and other Volunteer organisers, were responsible for the split'. Madge Daly and Peadar Dunne, who was appointed OC 2nd battalion and later OC mid-Limerick brigade, were also involved. James Gubbins told Ernie O'Malley that 'the row was first started through the Daly sisters'.

The Dalys apparently 'did everything to stigmatise the officers of the local Bn. They had Ernest Blythe with them in that'. Blythe 'identified himself with the Second Bn ... Blythe took an active part in the Limerick situation ... he was a satellite of the Dalys'. Thus, as O'Halloran emphasized, there were two independent Irish Volunteer battalions in Limerick city, 'each claiming to be in control, and though there was no real friction between them, relations were not good, since the spirit of co-operation was lacking'. Gubbins stated that 'the 2 BNs never worked side by side'. Brennan recalled 'quite a lot of bitterness between the two outfits and neither would march under the command of the other'. Richard O'Connell felt that 'no one took any notice of the 1st' because it was not active.[79] Éamon Dore of the 1st battalion also confirmed that the cleavage and the ill-feeling between the two contingents originated in the circumstances of the formation of each unit:

> The 1st Battalion was the unit which existed from the Redmondite Split in 1914, while the 2nd was formed after 1916 and was mostly composed of men who, up to the Easter Week executions had been very hostile to our movement and had been followers of the political party of John Redmond. It was men such as those who afterwards formed the 2nd Battalion who were foremost in the assault upon the Dublin Brigade when the latter came to Limerick on a recruiting parade on Whit Sunday 1915. This fact was not forgotten by those who composed the 1st Battalion, and was the chief cause of the bad feeling between these units.[80]

The two battalions did not fully reunite until March 1921.

Hart has made the case that the division between the two battalions was based on a social barrier rather than simply evolving from the circumstances of their respective origins. Hart has shown that IRA units were often formed around a particular workplace, but that any kind of stratification or segregation between companies was very rare.[81] However, Hart identified the Limerick city IRA as an exception. That the Limerick Volunteers fell out after the Rising was not unusual, but the consequences were. The split was not merely personal or political, but social, according to Hart.[82] The 208 MacNeillite Volunteers who paraded on 4 October 1914 included

> ... a typical cross-section of the inhabitants, such as could be found in any urban area. Tradesmen, clerks, shopkeepers, teachers, shop assistants and labourers were all represented ... Players and former players of the game contributed to the ranks of each of the four companies, in particular to A Company, where they provided more than half the personnel. At the start, three of the four companies had Rugby men as captains. The GAA representation was relatively weak.[83]

The post-Rising 1st battalion, criticized for its inactivity at Easter 1916, 'was nearly confined to the rugby clubs in the city', according to James

Gubbins, while the 2nd battalion 'were more working men' according to George Embush.[84] The five companies which comprised the 2nd battalion were organized around a number of junior hurling teams that had formed after the Rising.[85] Peadar McMahon was of the opinion that

> The 2nd Battalion were a different type of people – decent fellows but they were all working people. The 1st Battalion were all white collar workers … that was one of the reasons the 1st Battalion didn't like them – the fact that they were all working men.[86]

That elements of the working class in Limerick were hostile to the Irish Volunteers had been borne out on Whit Sunday 1915. Skilled workers and the lower middle class were in a dominant majority in the ranks of the Limerick Volunteers before 1917, just as they were in Cork. Unskilled and semi-skilled workers were even less well represented in Limerick than they were in Cork.[87] The rift between the 1st and 2nd battalions, then, had its genesis in the split of September 1914 and the inaction of Easter week, but it was also reflective of the increasing involvement of members of the working class in militant nationalism from 1917. The 2nd battalion was 'manned largely by young fellows who had not anything to do with Bn 1', according to Gubbins.[88] In this sense, the reorganization of the city IRA into two battalions seems to have been as much an extension of the republican movement as it was a fissure within the movement.

It is reasonable to argue that, even at the most generous of estimates, the Volunteer forces in Limerick, in terms of both numbers and arms, were far below what was required to carry out any version of Pearse's orders to the letter. Communications were poor. The loss of the *Aud* meant that the existing plans became redundant. Nonetheless, the Volunteers of Galway, Wexford, Louth and Fingal showed that it did not have to be possible to carry out orders to the letter in order to go into action. Their efforts remained localized, however, because they lacked support. The choice by Colivet and his colleagues not to go into action was rational, but out of tune with the spirit of the IRB's intentions. Colivet, however, was not completely familiar with the intentions of the IRB because of their subterfuge. All Volunteer officers, on the other hand, were acquainted with that organization's policy of not surrendering arms.

The decision to stage the Rising on Easter Monday, forced on the rebel leaders by MacNeill's countermanding order, meant that it was impractical to expect the country at large to rise to any significant extent. Not only were communications inadequate but the chain-of-command had been severely compromised. The orders distributed to selected officers on Monday could not counteract the effect of repeated eleventh-hour volte-face. The provincial Volunteers were unsure about which orders to follow or what was happening in Dublin, and they did not have the arms they were told they would receive. It is unlikely that MacNeill's countermanding order alone stopped many Volunteers who wanted to fight from participating in the Rising. This was certainly the case in Dublin, and, in the context of Colivet's cancellation order of Saturday night, also applied to Limerick. MacNeill did not sink the *Aud* or corrupt the chain-of-command but his countermanding order did grievously undermine the already tenuous plans for a nationwide rebellion.

NOTES

1. *Report of the Royal Commission on the rebellion in Ireland. Minutes of evidence and appendix of documents*, H. C., 1916 (Cd. 8311), pp. 10, 39, 55. I wish to acknowledge funding received from the Irish Research Council for the Humanities and Social Sciences.
2. *Report of the Royal Commission on the rebellion*, p. 1.
3. Indicative of the danger of infiltration by spies and informers was the fact that a friend of the Daly family was supplying information to the police. See Note 44 below.
4. For full explorations of these issues see Maureen Wall, 'The background to the Rising, from 1914 until the issue of the countermanding order on Easter Saturday 1916' and 'The plans and the countermand: The country and Dublin', as well as G.A. Hayes-McCoy, 'A Military History of the 1916 Rising', in Kevin B. Nowlan (ed.), *The Making of 1916* (Dublin, 1969); see also Kevin B. Nowlan, 'Tom Clarke, MacDermott and the IRB' and T. Desmond Williams, 'Eoin MacNeill and the Irish Volunteers', in F.X. Martin (ed.), *Leaders and Men of the Easter Rising: Dublin 1916* (London, 1967).
5. National Archives Ireland [herein NAI], Bureau of Military History (BMH), Witness Statement (WS) 1420, Patrick Whelan, pp. 1–2.
6. County Inspector (CI), Limerick, Monthly Report [herein MR], November and December 1913, Colonial Office (CO) 904/91.
7. CI, Limerick, MR, January 1914, CO 904/92.
8. *Limerick Chronicle*, 27 January 1914; Michael Brennan, *The War in Clare, 1911–21* (Dublin, 1980), p. 8; For more on the infiltration of the Limerick Volunteers by the IRB see NAI, BMH, WS 1710, Liam Forde, pp. 2–3; Tom Clarke to John Daly, 26 January 1914 (University of Limerick Special Collections [herein ULSC], Daly Papers [herein DP], Box 2, Folder 47); NAI, BMH, WS 1700, Alphonsus J. O'Halloran, pp. 1–4.
9. Pearse to Daly, 29 January 1914, in Louis le Roux's unpublished biography of John Daly, 'The life and letters of John Daly', Chapter 13, p. 4 (University of Limerick Special Collections, Daly Papers, Box 3, Folder 73). It was around this time that Pearse was sworn into the IRB.
10. Desmond Ryan, *The Rising: The Complete Story of Easter Week* (Dublin, 1949), p. 83.
11. CI, Limerick; Inspector-General [herein IG], MR, May 1914, CO 904/93.
12. CI, Limerick, MR, September 1914, CO 904/94.
13. David Fitzpatrick, *Politics and Irish Life, 1913–21: Provincial Experience of War and Revolution* (Dublin, 1998), p. 133.
14. Somewhere in the region of 13,000 of the 180,000 Volunteers followed MacNeill. The figures cited by the various authorities often differ but the orders of scale are generally consistent. See Joe Lee, *Ireland, 1912–1985: Politics and Society* (Cambridge, 1989), p. 22.
15. NAI, BMH, WS 1700, Alphonsus J. O'Halloran, p. 8; Madge Daly Memoirs (hereafter MDM), p. 50 (ULSC, DP, Box 3, Folder 77); Mannix Joyce, 'The story of Limerick and Kerry in 1916', *Capuchin Annual* (1966), p. 330.
16. CI, Limerick, August and December 1914, CO 904/95.
17. IG, MR, October 1914, CO 904/95.
18. CI, Limerick, MR, March 1916, CO 904/99.
19. Liam Manahan (ULSC, Liam Manahan Papers (hereafter LMP), Book 3, pp. 15–17).
20. CI, Limerick, MR, October–December 1914, CO 904/95; The chief secretary put 176 rifles in the hands of 437 Irish Volunteers but only 65 rifles in the hands of 7,081 National Volunteers. At the start of 1916 police figures documented the National and Irish

Volunteers as being in possession of 243 and 195 rifles respectively. Breandán MacGiolla Choille (ed.), *Intelligence Notes, 1913–16* (Dublin, 1966), pp. 80, 110–12, 178–9.

21. Precis of information received by the Crime Branch Special [herein CBS], June 1915, CO 904/97.
22. CI, Limerick, MR, December 1915, CO 904/98.
23. IG, MR, October 1915; CI, Limerick, MR, November 1915, CO 904/98; February–June 1916, CO 904/99–100; MacGiolla Choille (ed.), *Intelligence Notes*, pp. 149, 215, 222.
24. Sinn Féin, 4 July 1914.
25. Quoted in NAI, BMH, WS 765, James Gubbins, pp. 8–9.
26. *Irish Volunteer*, 13 February 1915; 16 January 1916.
27. Liam Manahan (ULSC, LMP, Book 3, pp. 18–20).
28. IG, MR, May 1915; Precis of information received by the CBS, May 1915, CO 904/97; MacGiolla Choille (ed.), *Intelligence Notes*, p. 222.
29. *National Volunteer*, 29 May 1915; *Limerick Leader*, 26 May 1915; *Irish Volunteer*, 29 May, 5 June 1915; MDM, pp. 87–9 (ULSC, DP, Box 3, Folder 77); NAI, BMH, WS 1700, Alphonsus J. O'Halloran, pp. 9–17; Joyce, 'The Story of Limerick and Kerry in 1916', pp. 333–5.
30. NAI, BMH, WS 1415, Michael Hartney, p. 2.
31. *Limerick Chronicle*, 25 May 1915; See also NAI, BMH, WS 456, Liam Manahan, pp. 3–4.
32. Patrick Pearse to Madge Daly, 28 May 1915 (ULSC, DP, Box 1, Folder 29).
33. *Irish Volunteer*, 15 May 1915.
34. Precis of information received by the CBS, June 1915, CO 904/97; NAI, BMH, WS 765, James Gubbins, pp. 5, 9–10.
35. NAI, BMH, WS 1415, Michael Hartney, p. 1.
36. NAI, BMH, WS 737, Seán Meade, p. 2; *Report of the Royal Commission on the Rebellion*, p. 62.
37. NAI, BMH, WS 1700, Alphonsus J. O'Halloran, p. 8; WS 1710, Liam Forde, pp. 3–4.
38. *Limerick Leader*, 11 February 1916.
39. Judith Crosbie, 'The Era of Radicalism: Limerick's Mayors during World War One', in David Lee (ed.), *Remembering Limerick: Historical Essays Celebrating the 800th Anniversary of Limerick's First Charter Granted in 1197* (Limerick, 1997).
40. *Limerick Chronicle*, 25 January 1916.
41. NAI, BMH, WS 1420, Patrick Whelan, pp. 4–5; WS 765, James Gubbins, pp. 6–8.
42. NAI, BMH, WS 164, Charles Wall, pp. 1–2.
43. Terence MacSwiney to Madge Daly, 23 October 1915 (ULSC, DP, Box 1, Folder 39); Terence MacSwiney to Madge Daly, 1 November 1915 in MDM, p. 83 (ULSC, DP, Box 3, Folder 77).
44. IG, MR, December 1915, CO 904/98. This was presumably the same informant who, a year earlier, was able to tell Constable James J. O'Mahony of William Street barracks with whom John Daly was in correspondence as well as who he was regularly meeting with in Limerick. However, O'Mahony did write that he also had 'other sources' of information on the Dalys. County Inspector Gates also referred to O'Mahony garnering information from 'other sources'. The information provided by the informant in early 1915 does not seem to have been very revealing and he was 'afraid to be inquisitive fearing they might become suspicious, for he says they are aware that letters coming through the post are under observation'. Censorship of Daly's post from November 1914, including his correspondence with MacDermott and Tom and Kathleen Clarke, had been unproductive and at the end of January 1915, by which stage it had become obvious to the police that this circle operated an alternative system to the general post for sensitive correspondence, the censorship was ended. These reports on censorship and the Limerick informant were all marked 'Secret' and presented to the Crime Special Branch of Dublin Castle between November 1914 and February 1915. CO 904/164.
45. *Weekly Observer*, 25 March 1916.
46. Liam Manahan claimed that on St Patrick's Day 400 men of the Galtee battalion, in full uniform and nearly all armed with some kind of weapon, paraded in Ardpatrick. NAI, BMH, WS 456, Liam Manahan, pp. 7, 18. If 400 men were actually armed it is likely that many would have been carrying 1798-style pikes. The RIC reported that 300 Irish Volunteers, 140 of them armed, marched in Ardpatrick on St Patrick's Day. Some 208 Irish Volunteers reportedly marched in Newcastlewest, 155 of them armed. Police accounts of the city parades vary. Four hundred National Volunteers 'jeered' between 150 armed Irish Volunteers and fifty Fianna, and 240 Volunteers, 179 of them armed. 'Sinn Féin Movement', CO 904/23; CI, Limerick, MR, March 1916, CO 904/96. According to Undersecretary Matthew Nathan, on 31 March 1916 the Volunteers in Limerick were in possession of a total of 457 firearms,

specifically 161 Lee-Enfield, Lee-Metford and other .303 magazine rifles, twenty-five Martin-Enfield and other .303 single loaders, twenty Mauser and Mannlicher rifles, two other unidentified rifles, 205 shotguns and fifty-four revolvers and pistols. See *Report of the Royal Commission on the Rebellion*, p. 123. By Nathan's figures only Kerry, Cork and Tyrone had more firearms than Limerick. He did not provide statistics for Dublin city.

47. Wall recalled the presence of 150 Volunteers. Michael Collins of Monagea company estimated 400. NAI, BMH, WS 164, Charles Wall, p. 2; WS 1301, Michael Collins, pp. 1–2.
48. William McCarthy estimated 150. Seán Ó Ceallaigh estimated 400. NAI, BMH, WS 1453, William McCarthy, p. 2; WS 1476, Seán Ó Ceallaigh, p. 4.
49. MacGiolla Choille (ed.), *Intelligence Notes*, p. 215.
50. IG, MR, April 1916, CO 904/99.
51. Galbally Volunteers did cut the telegraph wires in Ballylanders. NAI, BMH, WS 597, Edmond O'Brien, p. 12.
52. CI, Limerick, MR, May 1916, CO 904/100.
53. See Robert Monteith, *Casement's Last Adventure* (Dublin, 1953), p. 198; MDM, p. 147 (ULSC, DP, Box 3, Folder 77); NAI, BMH, James Gubbins, WS 765, p. 31.
54. BMH, Contemporaneous Document 145, Michael Colivet.
55. MacGiolla Choille (ed.), *Intelligence Notes*, pp. 240–1; CI, Limerick, MR, May 1916, CO 904/100; *Limerick Chronicle*, 11 May 1916.
56. NAI, BMH, WS 765, James Gubbins, p. 30.
57. IG, MR, August; CI, Limerick, MR, May–August 1916, CO 904/100.
58. Wall, 'The Plans and the Countermand', p. 213.
59. Report by Colonel Weldon, 18 January 1917 (National Archives UK, WO 35/94).
60. NAI, BMH, WS 737, Seán Meade, p. 3; WS 597, Edmond O'Brien, p. 13.
61. NAI, BMH, WS 456, Liam Manahan, pp. 8–17.
62 The Galway rebels had twenty-five rifles, sixty revolvers, sixty pikes and 300 shotguns, according to Fergus Campbell, 'The Easter Rising in Galway', *History Ireland*, 14, 2 (2006), pp. 22–5. They were young Catholic males from small farm, labouring and artisan backgrounds. Most of them were members of a secret agrarian society that had been active in Galway since 1907 and had been sworn into the IRB. Few of them had benefited from land purchase legislation and they had economic as well as political motivations for fighting.
63. Charles Townshend, *Easter 1916; the Irish Rebellion* (London, 2005), Chapter 8; Ryan, *The Rising*; Hayes-McCoy, 'A military history of the 1916 Rising', pp. 298–303; the *Capuchin Annual* of 1966 included accounts of Easter week 1916 in Ashbourne, Enniscorthy, Galway, Limerick, Kerry, Cork and Belfast, as well as Dublin; C. Desmond Greaves, *Liam Mellows and the Irish Revolution* (London, 1971), Chapter 5.
64. Denis McCullough, 'The events in Belfast', *Capuchin Annual* (1966), pp. 381–4.
65. Quoted in James A. Gubbins and A.J. O'Halloran, 'Limerick's projected role in Easter week 1916', in Jack MacCarthy (ed.), *Limericks Fighting Story from 1916 to the Truce with Britain* (Tralee, 1965), p. 39.
66. Kathleen Clarke [Helen Litton (ed.)], *Revolutionary Woman: An Autobiography* (Dublin, 1991), pp. 71–3; MDM, pp. 113 and 145–6 (ULSC, DP, Box 3, Folder 77).
67. NAI, BMH, WS 1415, Michael Hartney, p. 4.
68. NAI, BMH, WS 765, James Gubbins, p. 25; WS 1700, Alphonsus J. O'Halloran, p. 22.
69. For a breakdown of the myriad factors which determined the geography of Irish nationalism, republicanism and revolutionary activity see David Fitzpatrick, 'The Geography of Irish Nationalism, 1910–21', *Past and Present*, 78 (1978), pp. 113–44; Peter Hart, 'The Geography of Revolutionary Violence in Ireland, 1917–23', *Past and Present*, 155 (1997), pp. 142–73; Erhard Rumpf and A.C. Hepburn, *Nationalism and Socialism in Twentieth-Century Ireland* (Liverpool, 1977).
70. *Limerick Leader*, 28 April, 1, 10, 12 May, 19 July 1916.
71. MDM, p. 117A (ULSC, DP, Box 3, Folder 77).
72. CI, Limerick, MR, April 1916, CO 904/99; IG, MR, July 1916, CO 904/100.
73. Limerick City and County Archives (LCCA), LCC minutes, 6 May, 8 July 1916.
74. *Limerick Leader*, 29 May 1916; *Limerick Chronicle*, 3 June 1916.
75. Leon Ó Broin, *The Chief Secretary* (London, 1969), p. 189.
76. MacGiolla Choille (ed.), *Intelligence Notes*, p. 215.
77. James Gubbins' interview with Ernie O'Malley is in University College Dublin Archives (UCDA), Ernie O'Malley Notebooks, P17b/129.
78. Conversation between Peadar McMahon and Richard Mulcahy, 15 May 1963 (UCDA,

Richard Mulcahy Papers, P7b/181, pp. 7–8, 10).

79. NAI, BMH, WS 1700, Alphonsus J. O'Halloran, pp. 25–6; WS 1710, Liam Forde, pp. 15–16; WS 1415, Michael Hartney, pp. 4–5; WS 525, Michael J. Stack, p. 1; WS 1420, Patrick Whelan, p. 14; WS 656, Richard O'Connell, pp. 5, 8, 9; Brennan, *The War in Clare*, pp. 21, 37; David Dundon, written statement, circa February 1926 (NLI, Ernie O'Malley Papers, Ms. 10,973/17).

80. NAI, BMH, WS 515, Éamon Dore, p. 5.

81. See Peter Hart, *The IRA at War, 1916–23* (Oxford, 2003), Chapter 5 – 'The social structure of the IRA', especially p. 120. See also Michael Hopkinson, *The Irish War of Independence* (Dublin, 2004), p. 118.

82. Hart was not the first to point to this apparent anomaly, however. During his interviews with his former colleagues in the late 1940s and early 1950s Ernie O'Malley 'noticed that there was a good deal of working men in the 2nd Bn and I think this was a kind of distinction between these 2 Bns'. See O'Malley's interview with James Gubbins (UCDA, EOMN, P17b/129, p. 58).

83. NAI, BMH, WS 765, James Gubbins, pp. 4–5.

84. James Gubbins (UCDA, EOMN, P17b/129, p. 57); George Embush (UCDA, EOMN, P17b/130, p. 18).

85. NAI, BMH, WS 1710, Liam Forde, p. 15.

86. Conversation between Peadar McMahon and Richard Mulcahy, 15 May 1963 (UCDA, Richard Mulcahy Papers, P7b/181, pp. 7–8).

87. See Tom Toomey, 'The Rise of Militant Nationalism in Limerick city, 1912-17' (MA, University of Limerick, 2006), pp. 29-35, 38; Peter Hart, *The IRA and its Enemies* (Oxford, 1998), pp. 155–8.

88. James Gubbins (UCDA, EOMN, P176/129, p. 56).

2

Vanguard of the Revolution? The Irish Citizen Army, 1916

Ann Matthews

There is a significant historiography on the revolution that began in Dublin on Easter Monday, 24 April 1916, but comparatively little on its origins. Easter 1916 is usually referred to as the 'rebellion' or 'rising' but James Connolly's writings anticipated a 'revolution'. In February 1916, *Irish Worker* carried an advertisement for a Liberty Hall concert which was billed as the 'most exciting event of 1916 except the revolution'.[1]

This chapter analyses the issue of class in Ireland in terms of the relationship between the Irish Volunteers and Irish Citizen Army (ICA). Much valuable information has been gleaned from the 'witness statements' collected by the Bureau of Military History. Launched in 1947 by Minister for Defence Oscar Traynor, the bureau amassed 1,744 statements, including 150 from women. For the period in focus, 130 men submitted details of their activities in the Irish Volunteers, as did twelve ex-members of the Irish Citizen Army. There are also twenty-three statements from members of Cumann na mBan, five from the women associated with the ICA, one from Mary McLoughlin of the Clan na Gael Girl Scouts and one from Annie Mannion, matron of the South Dublin Union.

McLoughlin stated that 'Clan na Gael girl scouts was formed in 1910 under the auspices of the Hibernian Rifles … to cater for girls in Dublin, who were excluded from membership of na Fianna.'[2] However, Belfast girls were welcomed into Na Fianna, not least Nora Connolly and her sister Ina who were both members of the Betsy Gray branch. Helena Molony attributed this situation to Countess de Markievicz who she claimed 'never liked girls', and often exclaimed, 'they always confuse me those dreadful girls'.[3]

Witness statements have strengths and weaknesses. They contain significant problems of chronology and major differences of perspective on some events. There is evidence of collusion, collaboration and redrafting, and many appear to have been later versions of pension applications. Such factors compound errors arising from subjectivity and bad memory.

However, when it comes to the issue of social status, memories are very clear. The inbred and subconscious sense of place within society reveals much of Ireland in the early twentieth century, where, it has been observed, 'there were as many classes as there were castes in India'.[4] Before 1916, this class bias was palpable in the relationship between the two major nationalist separatist volunteer armies, the Irish Volunteers and ICA.

In 1936, Ernie O'Malley, from a comfortable middle-class background, explained his perception of social life in Ireland in his autobiography, *On Another Man's Wound*. He described members of his Volunteer company as 'the professions, university students, government clerks, business men, skilled labour, unskilled labour, news-boys and at the very bottom there were the out-of-works [unemployed] and the guttees [sic]'.[5] He recalled his years in the local parish primary school, where 'we learned to mix with guttees in primary school and also sit beside patched home dignity, and thrift or carelessness'.[6] His sister in boarding school was taught how to enter and leave a carriage, the flouncing courtesy, recitations for company, and art as applied with needles in a ladylike way. He also recorded that with his siblings he 'spent many happy hours talking or listening to the servants', of whom he said 'that except for nanny … were in a rank of servitude and looked upon as a third sex'.[7] This perspective was not considered insulting and accords with details of servant girls in Cumann na mBan sources.

Some biographers of Countess de Markievicz refer to her by her first name, Constance, or even 'Connie', which creates a retrospective illusion that she perceived herself as one of the masses in Liberty Hall 1914–16. However, many witness statements note her insistence in being addressed as 'madame'. Kathleen Behan, in her autobiography *Mother of all the Behans*, had a unique perspective on women within the nationalist movement who used the nomenclature of madame. This is ascribed by Behan to one of the rules of Inighinidhe na hÉireann that required members to adopt Gaelic names for use within the association. Inighinidhe na hÉireann was founded in 1900 by a committee of over seventy women involved in the cultural nationalist movement. It was the first female organization of its type and, according to Molony, sought to teach children 'from the slums' about their Irish heritage.[8] The use of English expressions such as 'miss' or 'mrs' ceased and this apparently created problems for married women. Behan observed:

> We had a lot of gentry on our side – the nationalist side … they did not want to use English expressions like Mr. and Mrs. On the other hand, if they used the Gaelic versions Mrs. McBride would come out as Bean McBride, which means McBride's woman, that would not do for them it was too common. So all these grand ladies were Madame this and

Madame that as though they were French. The working classes did not bother with such nonsense. Mrs. Furlong or Mrs. Behan was good enough for me.[9]

The Irish Volunteers and ICA also operated within the class structure of the time and the relationship between them was often, to say the least, fraught. The ICA was founded during the Dublin Lockout in November 1913 and was conceived as a means of defending the workers from the Dublin Metropolitan Police. The Irish Transport and General Workers' Union was at the heart of the conflict and catered mainly for unskilled labour. These men represented a group regarded as being at the very bottom of the social stratum. One civil servant with the Department of Lands described the membership of the ICA as 'a group of the roughs of the city who under Larkin and Connolly had banded themselves into a citizen's army'.[10] This view was prevalent in 1916.

The Irish Volunteers was founded on 25 November 1913 at the Rotunda in Dublin, three weeks after the formation of the ICA. This was a self consciously respectable affair where a 'special platform had been reserved for the ladies'.[11] This was repeated when the Cork branch was founded at Cork city hall. Clearly, the social mores of Victorian society prevailed. In this instance, a rule of etiquette forbade unmarried females appearing in public unaccompanied, or in the company of a male without a chaperone. This may explain why the Irish Volunteers did not admit women members.

Other very serious class issues pertained at the Rotunda when members of the ICA entered the meeting and objected to the presence of Laurence Kettle. When Kettle, a member of the Irish Volunteer provisional committee, rose to speak, the ICA men voiced dissent and shots were fired.[12] The protest stemmed from the fact that Kettle's father, a farmer, was involved in a labour dispute with his workers. Áine Ceannt noted from the ladies' platform: 'Captain Jack White of the Citizen Army went onto the platform and addressed the meeting, which brought calm to the situation.'[13] Unsurprisingly, the behaviour of the ICA alienated many of the Volunteers present and the relationship between the organizations remained strained.

Five months later, in April 1914, the female auxiliary organization of the Irish Volunteers was formed. It was named Cumann na mBan (the Irish Women's Council) and its first branch, located in Dublin, was known as the árd croabh (Central branch). They met at the headquarters of the Irish Volunteers, 206 South Brunswick Street. The Irish Volunteers and Cumann na mBan attracted the range of the middle classes, higher, middle and lower, as well as shop assistants, clerks, and working-class artisans. Many artisans did not wish to be associated with unskilled labour.

Elizabeth Somers, a founder member of the Central branch, left a good record of its activities. Her mother was postmistress of Dalkey when

Elizabeth was observed by the police 'and members of the public collect-
ing money on behalf of the Irish Volunteers during 1914'.[14] However, her
use of the post office as a point of distribution for Cumann na mBan
leaflets led to the sacking of Mrs Somers. It was claimed that 'the authorities were concerned that Elizabeth had access to information passing
through the post office'.[15] Mrs Somers became the first civil servant to
lose her job owing to an association with separatist nationalist activities.
In an effort to save her mother, Elizabeth disclosed:

> The women who joined this branch at its inception were from every
> class and all shades of politics … it was non political and non-sectarian
> and it meetings were agreeable social gatherings where professionals
> and business women, university students, civil servants, and women
> of the highest social standing met for first aid classes, concerts, lec-
> tures, conversations, etc, etc.[16]

Somers described raising funds to equip the new Volunteer army. The
Central branch began a series of weekday and Sunday collections during
which she was accompanied 'by a chaperone and five or six others as they
raised money at a football match in November 1914'.[17]

By early 1915, the Central branch moved to Parnell Square and, arising from the Cumann na mBan convention that year, two new branches
were formed on the north side of the city. The Fairview branch met at the
Father Mathew Park and the Colmcille branch in Blackball Street. There
was no sense of solidarity between the Cumann na mBan, ICA or Irish
Women Workers' Union owing to the class differences between the members of the three organizations.

When Cumann na mBan was founded in April 1914, Inighinidhe na
hÉireann was still in existence. However, it was then a small group of no
more than fifty women and had long deviated from the ethos of the original organization founded in 1900. In 1914, Countess de Markievicz
acted as president, with Helena Molony second in command. Evidently,
they simply took over an organization in terminal decline. In addition,
members of Inighinidhe na hÉireann did not join or affiliate with
Cumann na mBan; instead they remained active at Liberty Hall and
developed a working relationship with the Irish Citizen Army.

The connection with Liberty Hall led to the opening of a cooperative
shop which gave employment to the female workers in lieu of strike pay.
Jinny Shanahan headed the venture, which produced children's under-
clothing and workmen's shirts.[18] The cooperative was located in an Eden
Quay building with internal access to Liberty Hall and became a cover for
political activists who wanted to visit Connolly without drawing the
attention of the police. Consequently, young girls and women employed
in Eden Quay were drawn into the activities of the ICA, and political

intrigue became a part of everyday working life. There were, however, four women involved in Liberty Hall whose origins were not working class. Countess de Markievicz had an aristocratic, Anglo-Irish background, Dr Kathleen Lynn was the daughter of a Church of Ireland rector, Madeline Ffrench Mullen was the daughter of a Royal Navy officer and Nellie Gifford the daughter of a barrister.[19]

By 1915 Cumann na mBan still had just two branches in the city of Dublin. A third was formed later in the year and given the long name 'the Inighinidhe na hÉireann branch Cumann na mBan' in order to differentiate it from the original organization.

TABLE 1 CUMANN NA MBAN BRANCHES, 1914–1916[20]

	Branches	Area
1	Ann Devlin Glasgow	Scotland
2	Ard Padraic	Limerick
3	Athy	Kildare
4	Belfast	Antrim
5	Caitlín Ní Houlihan	Cork
6	Carrigaholt	Clare
7	Central Branch Parnell St	Dublin
8	Clonmel	Tipperary
9	Colmcille Branch Blackhall Place	Dublin
10	Cork City	Cork
11	Fairview	Dublin
12	Galway city	Galway
13	Inighinidhe na hÉireann Sth Dublin	Dublin
14	Kildysart	Clare
15	Kilkee	Clare
16	Liverpool	England
17	London	England
18	Maryborough	Laois
19	Tipperary Town	Tipperary
20	Waterford	Waterford

Meanwhile, there was virtually no cooperation at rank and file between the ICA, Irish Volunteers and Cumann na mBan. However, in June 1914 a tentative relationship was encouraged when the Wolfe Tone committee invited the Irish Volunteers and ICA to participate at the annual demonstration at Bodenstown, county Kildare. While not exactly brothers in arms, this event brought the two organizations closer together. Sean O'Casey remarked: 'It was the first time they had stood side by side, and took orders from a common commander, and this drawing together was possibly a symbol of a union that would be finally cemented together with the blood of both organisations.'[21]

The ICA roll book for early 1916 shows that the organization had 334 registered members, only one of whom was female, Countess de Markievicz. This indicates that the other women involved at Liberty Hall were not official members of the ICA. James Connolly is registered as commander-in-chief and Michael Mallin as his second-in-command. The ICA is invariably perceived as a mass of men who operated between Liberty Hall and their training ground at Croyden Park, Fairview. However, the organization was actually divided into twelve sections located throughout the city of Dublin and its environs (see table 2). Each section had a commander and, in some cases, other officers.

TABLE 2 SECTIONAL STRUCTURE OF THE IRISH CITIZEN ARMY 1916[22]

Army Section number	Section Name	Commanders	members
1	High St.	George Oman, Martin Kelly, Edward Burke,	30
2	Aungier St	n/s	21
3	Sth. Circular RD.	James Kelly	14
4	Capel St	John Kelly	33
5	Gloucester St	John Reilly	34
6	North Strand	George Norgrove, Thomas O'Donoghue	23
7	Baldoyle Co Dublin	Not stated	15
8	Dorset Street	Owen Carton	24
9	Church St.	n/s	16
10	North Wall	John Mahon	30
11	Inchicore & Crumlin	Daly, Peter Kinsella	11
12	Townsend St	Terence McGuire	19
13	Section not stated		64
	total		334

In late 1915 and early 1916 it was claimed that members of the Irish Volunteers 'in Scotland and England moved to Dublin'. Seamus Robinson of the Glasgow Volunteers recalled that 'there was a general impression in our garrison from the time we left Scotland that a fight was bound to come'.[23] They settled at Larkfield House in Kimmage, county Dublin, where the Plunkett family owned an estate of twenty acres, a house, several outhouses and a disused mill. The buildings included the Larkfield Chemical Company Limited, which manufactured carbolic acid, and provided cover for their presence and movement. Robinson estimated that there were around ninety men at Larkfield. They used the mill building for training and became known as 'the Kimmage Garrison'.[24]

For several months before the rebellion, twenty-eight men of the Glasgow Volunteers and two women of the Ann Devlin branch, Cumann na mBan, travelled constantly from Glasgow to Dublin with guns and ammunition. The women were Margaret Skinnider, branch captain, and a 'Miss O'Neill'. A third member, Lizzie Morrin, was a dressmaker who made waistcoats and jackets with hidden pockets to conceal the munitions.

Skinnider also carried 'detonators for bombs in her hat with the wires wrapped around her beneath her coat'.[25] The men at Kimmage spent their time in preparation by making buck shot for cartridges and home-made bombs using billycans. A candlelit shooting range was established on a lower floor of the mill.

The RIC in Belfast observed the activities of Lillie Connolly. They noted: 'Her family have always taken an active part in the extreme move-ment, such as attending meetings of Cumann na mBan, Gaelic League, Irish Volunteers, etc; her house had been the meeting place of leading Sinn Féiners and such persons as the Countess de Markievicz, O'Rahilly, Sean McDermott and Denis McCullough.' The RIC believed that arms, ammunition and explosives were moved from Motherwell to Dublin through Belfast and that the individual carrying the material stayed in the Connolly household.[26]

By March 1916 cooperation between the leadership of Irish Volunteers and the ICA enabled them to present a united front on the issue of revo-lution. This harmony, however, was much less in evidence among the grass roots of either organization. Three weeks before Easter Sunday, the ICA was mobilized to protect Liberty Hall from a police raid. Rosie Hackett recalled that 'the men responded to the mobilisation instantly, with many of them reporting to Liberty from their workplaces'. She noted 'Citizen army men, in their working clothes, coming from all directions of the city'.[27] James O'Shea was more descriptive: '... men in all conditions of dress some with whips hanging from their belts, others in smocks all full of grease, mud and coal and cement, showing the various jobs they did; Sean Connolly who came from City Hall was apparently the only one respectably dressed'.[28]

After this mobilization, many of the men and women slept on the premises. During Holy week, the preparation of the food supply and medical necessities fell to the women. Molony stated that there were 'large quantities of provisions ordered in to make rations for the men ... We bought the supplies of meat, bread, butter, tea, and sugar and we cooked it in Liberty Hall.'[29] Two men made a bread-cutting machine to make the task easier. The women used the machine to supply the men 'with two days' rations'.[30] Women who had received first-aid classes rolled bandages for first-aid kits. During this time the Belfast RIC observed Lillie Connolly and one of her daughters buying supplies of lint and bandages which were sent on to Dublin.[31] Similarly, the women of Cumann na mBan prepared bandages and first-aid kits at the Irish Volunteer HQ in Dawson Street.

On Easter Monday, 24 April 1916, the vanguard of the revolutionary forces gathered at Liberty Hall. At 11.15 a.m. fifty-six men of the Kimmage garrison assembled and marched out with George Plunkett to Dolphins Barn and onwards into the city by tram. Joe Robinson from

Glasgow recalled: 'We were a unique body of soldiers going into action in a tram.'[32] Plunkett insisted they pay their fare and marched them down Abbey Street to Liberty Hall. On arrival, Margaret Skinnider told Seamus Robinson: 'It's on.' The ICA and Kimmage group formed into three bodies in Beresford Place outside Liberty Hall.[33] Matthew Connolly of the ICA recalled: 'As we lined up on the street in front of Liberty Hall, the sun was shining, and the Custom House clock told us it was twenty minutes to twelve.'[34] He watched the arrival of Plunkett's contingent and was handed two home explosive devices by James Connolly.[35]

The leadership element gathered in Liberty Hall comprised Patrick Pearse, James Connolly and the staff of the Irish Volunteers. There were 194 members of the ICA, fifty-one of the Kimmage garrison and thirty women. Of those present, only Winifred Carney belonged to Cumann na mBan. A member of the Belfast branch, Carney acted as secretary to James Connolly.[36] The first group to leave for the General Post Office, HQ of the revolt, included Pearse, Connolly and the senior Volunteers officers. They were accompanied by fifty-nine ICA and up to seventy men attached to the Kimmage grouping, as well as Carney, whose typewriter was conveyed to the GPO in an ammunition cart. They moved along Eden Quay and turned into Sackville Street where Séamus Robinson and five men took over a building on the Bachelors Walk corner of the thoroughfare. According to Robinson, the six were armed with an ICA-owned rifle, two shotguns, two small arms, plus 'a fair supply of home made (billycan) grenades'.[37] The remainder proceeded to the GPO where 'Pearse nominated Volunteer Paddy Morrin, a steeplejack from Glasgow, to hoist the flag of the Irish Republic on the flagpole of the GPO'.[38]

The second group to leave Liberty Hall was the City Hall garrison, which marched off across Butt Bridge and up Tara Street into College Green and Dame Street. Thomas Kain, secretary of the ICA during Easter week, placed the roll book inside his coat to prevent it being found by the British.[39] This garrison comprised twenty-eight men and eight women of the Citizen Army; their commander was Sean Connolly. Matthew Connolly, a member of this garrison, recalled:

> We were moving along Dame Street, and groups of people in holiday mood were moving about. A voice from the footpath remarked 'here's the Citizen Army with their pop guns' ... Another said 'there goes Ireland's only hope'. And they laughed at their own jokes. Little did they know? ... The angelus bells were ringing out from across the city churches.[40]

A common thread running through the ICA accounts is the memory of the ringing Angelus bell. Many working people did not own watches and the Angelus served as a marker of time, as well as a call to prayer.

The third and last group to leave Liberty Hall was the St Stephen's Green garrison under Michael Mallin. He led 101 men and fifteen women to the south side of the River Liffey. James O'Shea recalled crossing Butt Bridge and continuing via Tara Street and College Green into Grafton Street. Hackett and O'Shea concur on this route, although Frank Robbins averred that Mallin went up Eden Quay to cross O'Connell Bridge en route to Grafton Street. Robbins noted the time on the Ballast Office clock as being 11.55. Hackett, a member of the same group, was beyond the Clarendon Street turning on Grafton Street when the Angelus sounded. Just afterwards, O'Shea's section moved out of Grafton Street and sighted a policeman who 'passed a remark about playing soldiers ... He got an awful shock when he saw us marching straight into St Stephan's Green'.[41]

There is a significant body of primary source evidence to challenge the prevailing orthodoxy that Cumann na mBan was not mobilized at Easter 1916. The witness statements make it clear that they were kept as informed of developments as the men. Furthermore, it can be established that Cumann na mBan was, in fact, mobilized in two areas in the city. On the south side, members of the Inighinidhe na hÉireann branch Cumann na mBan, under Captain Rose McNamara, obeyed orders to mobilize at the Weavers Hall in Cork Street at 10 a.m. Some 'twenty-five members turned out' and marched to Emerald Square to join the 4th battalion, Irish Volunteers, under the command of Éamonn Ceannt. They marched behind the men to a distillery building at Marrowbone Lane.[42] Moreover, on the north side of the city, 'the women were ordered to mobilise at Palmerston Place, which was in the vicinity of the Broadstone Railway station'.[43]

Apparently, the only garrison that did not accept women was that located at Boland's Mill. The commander, Éamon de Valera, refused to allow women work in the sector under his control. De Valera's actual HQ was in the Health Dispensary, Barrow Street, where he led his unit on Easter Monday. The dispensary contained the living quarters of Dr Healy, his wife and their servant, all of whom left at the point of a gun. At that time, it would have been social death for an unmarried female to be in such close quarters with men in such a situation, as de Valera would have known. In the Jacob's factory garrison, women were confined to the 'main hall during the hours of darkness'.[44] Women in the GPO, similarly, were allocated a separate room at night which was guarded by Brian O'Higgins.[45] While de Valera's refusal to accept women within his garrison has often been singled out, the same situation existed in the South Dublin Union and the Mendicity Institute.

There has been confusion about the presence of women in the South Dublin Union arising from an erroneous claim in the *Catholic Bulletin* in

1916 that nurse Keogh, fatally wounded at the hospital, was a member of Cumann na mBan. Keogh was simply a member of the nursing South Dublin Union.[46] If Keogh had also been a member of Cumann na mBan her name would have featured prominently in the propaganda of the organization. In actuality, the rank-and-file membership of Cumann na mBan had remained aloof from the women of the ICA circle right up to and including 1916. At Easter, however, many were thrown together in the chaos of the rebellion and had no choice but to cooperate.

Nora O'Daly of the Fairview branch Cumann na mBan arrived at St Stephen's Green late on Monday evening and was disappointed to find that the ICA were in control. According to O'Daly, she and other members of Cumann na mBan were greeted by Countess de Markievicz who informed them 'if we cared, we could throw in our lot with theirs ... this we eventually did as no other course seemed open to us and after all, we were fighting for the same cause ... I admit for one that I was disappointed at having to make this decision'.[47] O'Daly's middle-class sensibility was troubled at having to talk to people to whom she had not been properly introduced, especially if they were working class. She said: 'Here all were strangers (except de Markievicz) and somehow one cannot feel the same confidence in people previously unknown.'[48] She remained unhappy until she met Madeline Ffrench Mullen: 'I remember distinctly how all my doubts and anxieties were dissipated in a moment when I caught sight of this plucky lady.'[49]

At Marrowbone Lane Lily O'Brennan discovered she was isolated from her friends in Cumann na mBan (Central branch) and joined up with the Inighinidhe na hÉireann group. O'Brennan claimed: 'None of them knew me nor did I know them, though the majority of them were inhabitants of Dolphins Barn where I was living.'[50] Inighinidhe na hÉireann recruited working-class girls and women in the area whereas O'Brennan lived in Dolphins Barn with her married sister, Áine Ceannt, her brother-in-law Éamonn Ceannt, their son David, and a servant. On a social level, O'Brennan would never have mixed with these women. This divide was perpetuated during the fighting, and O'Brennan commented: 'Being in a way an alien amongst them I thought the best thing I could offer to do was to keep a diary, so any bits of news were passed to me.'[51]

City Hall garrison was the first to fall, and by Tuesday morning it was in the hands of the British army. Among the prisoners taken were Dr Kathleen Lynn, Madeline Ffrench Mullen and Helena Molony, an actor. Lynn's account of their imprisonment is interesting, and even here the finer points of social stratification were observed. The three women shared a cell and were given one basin of water a day for washing. Lynn recorded: 'I being the doctor used it first, Miss Ffrench Mullen second, and Miss Molony was last. We all had some sort of a wash, so that was something.'[52]

While the accepted social order was maintained at the washbasin, the revolution was on the receiving end of hostility around the country.

In Cork city, the initial reaction to news of rebellion on Monday was an assumption that the ICA had decided to go it alone. A Cork Volunteer recalled: 'Suddenly like a bolt out of the blue came accounts of the Rising in Easter week 1916. The reactions of a good many people, myself included, were 'what fools they were, to think they could fight England'.[53] This attitude was echoed in particular in the *Cork Examiner*, which 'branded the Rebellion a communist disturbance'. J.J. Lee's survey of provincial newspapers during Easter week discerned that the Rising was typically misinterpreted as either a German invasion or an act of subversion perpetuated by Irish socialism. Meanwhile, it became clear within hours in Dublin that the effort was not solely an ICA initiative and many additional Irish Volunteers joined in.[54]

Tensions, which may be attributable to class conflict, surfaced during the surrender. When Elizabeth O'Farrell of the ICA carried the order of surrender to the garrisons, she had difficulty when dealing with Éamon de Valera and Thomas McDonagh. Following the surrender of the GPO and St Stephen's Green garrison, she was brought by Major de Courcy Wheeler to Butt Bridge to begin the journey to the Boland's Mills garrison. She walked to Barrow Street where she encountered Volunteers she knew, and enquired of them where she could find de Valera. They told her he was 'at the Grand Canal Dispensary'. When O'Farrell located the building it was so heavily barricaded that she had to be lifted inside. De Valera was shaving and came to talk to her with the towel still around his neck. O'Farrell recalled that when 'de Valera came to me, at first I think he thought the thing was a hoax, but by the time some of my volunteer friends came in he realised I was to be trusted'.[55] However, he refused to accept the order to surrender because he would only take orders from his immediate superior officer, Thomas McDonagh. At Jacobs's factory, McDonagh also refused to obey the surrender order on the grounds that he did not recognize Connolly, a signatory, as a leader of the revolution. The same issue arose at Church Street, part of the Four Courts garrison.[56]

According to Fr Augustine and Fr Aloysius, Franciscan friars who described themselves as chaplains to the rebel army, there was a clear distinction made by Connolly about the original surrender document. Fr Augustine recalled that at 7 a.m. on 30 April 1916 he and Aloysius 'went to Dublin Castle to seek a permit from Brigadier General Lowe the commander of the British Forces' so as to enable them to visit Patrick Pearse who was being held at Arbour Hill military prison. Lowe received them very courteously and promptly granted them the permit. He also suggested to them that they should see James Connolly, who was being held in the castle in the Red Cross hospital. Both men agreed, and Augustine said of the meeting in Connolly's room: 'Approaching his bedside I asked him if the surrender document said to have been signed by Pearse was genuine, and he assured me in the affirmative. "Did you also sign it," I then asked. He said "Yes". Then as I turned to leave him, he said: "But only for the men under my command." These words are indelibly imprinted on my memory.... The General was a gentleman: he recognised the delicacy of the situation.'[57]

Aloysius concurs with this story to a large degree and added his perception of Connolly's words, which were that 'in our presence (General Lowe) asked Connolly if his signature to the letter advising surrender was genuine. Connolly's reply was "yes, to prevent needless slaughter".... He added that he spoke only for his own men'. Both men were then taken to Arbour Hill to meet with Pearse, who told them he had already signed a new surrender document for another friar named as Fr Columbus. However, he wrote yet another surrender document for the two men for the garrison at Jacob's factory, where the surrender was finally completed.[58]

When the Irish Volunteers and the Irish Citizen Army came together at Easter 1916 and launched the revolution, they produced a proclamation that promised a significant social transformation. This was largely influenced by the socialist ideology of equality of class, religion and gender as advocated by James Connolly, the leading proponent of this ideology in Ireland. He brought together, in his extensive writings, the rhetorical ideal of a republican and socialist Ireland. For a brief point in time, the dream of a united struggle across the ranks of class division led Connolly to align the ICA with the conservative separatist nationalist Irish Volunteers. For Connolly, aware that he faced execution, the issue was not about how the revolution would end; it was, rather, about a new beginning. With Connolly's death, the dream of a new nation based on equality ended, his writing consigned to the margins. In the aftermath of 1916, Connolly's aspirations were ignored, and the significant role of the ICA as a vanguard of the revolution pushed aside. In Dublin on Easter Monday 1916, however, the Irish Citizen Army were a major force.

NOTES

1. *Irish Worker*, 6 February 1916, p. 2.
2. Bureau Military History (BMH), Mary McLoughlin, National Archive of Ireland (hereafter NAI), BMH papers, WS 934, p. 1.
3. BMH draft copy of statement by Helena Molony, Kilmainham Gaol Museum, Molony papers, p. 64.
4. Lady Gordon, *The Winds of Time* (London, 1934), pp. 165–6.
5. Ernie O'Malley, *On Another Man's Wound* (Dublin, 1936), p. 46.
6. Ibid., p. 19.
7. Ibid., p. 10.
8. BMH statement by witness, Helena Molony, NAI, BMH papers, WS 391, p. 2.
9. Kathleen Behan, *Mother of All the Behans* (Dublin, 1994), p. 48.
10. Department of Lands day book, 26 April 1916, Mr F.W. Taylor, Kilmainham Gaol Museum, Old Register no. 264.

11. BMH statement by witness, Áine Ceannt, NAI, BMH papers, WS 264, p. 9.
12. Ceannt, BMH.
13. Ceannt, BMH.
14. RIC police report, 3 April 1915, Public Records Office (hereafter PRO), CO papers, 904-215-412.
15. RIC police report, 3 April 1915, PRO, CO 904-215-412.
16. RIC police report, 26 January 1915, PRO, CO 904-215-412.
17. RIC police report, 26 January 1915, PRO, CO 904-215-412.
18. Mary Jones, *These Obstreperous Lassies* (Dublin, 1988), p. 15.
19. BMH statement by witness, Dr Nancy Wyse (NAI, BMH papers, WS 541), pp. 11–12.
20. Bloxham and Wyse Power, BMH, Cumann na mBan concert programme, 16 April 1916 and *Irish Freedom*, 22 August 1914.
21. Seán O'Casey, *The Story of the Irish Citizen Army* (Dublin, 1919), p. 34.
22. William O'Brien papers, BMH.
23. Seamus Robinson, University College Dublin Archives Department (hereafter UCDAD), Coyle papers, p61/13 (15).
24. Seamus Robinson, UCDAD, Coyle papers, p61/13 (9).
25. Margaret Skinnider, *Doing My Bit for Ireland* (New York, 1917), p. 9.
26. RIC police report, 9 June 1916 (PRO, CO 904-215-408-249).
27. BMH statement by witness Rosie Hackett, Military Archive, WS 546, p. 3.
28. BMH statement by witness John O'Shea, Military Archive, WS 733, p. 26.
29. BMH draft copy of statement by witness Helena Molony (Kilmainham Gaol Museum, Dublin), p. 34.
30. BMH statement by witness James O'Shea, Military Archive WS 733, p. 41.
31. RIC police report, 9 June 1916, PRO, CO 904-215-408-249.
32. Joe Robinson, UCDAD, Coyle papers, p61/13 (30), p. 5.
33. Seamus Robinson, UCDAD, Coyle papers, p61/13 (14).
34. BMH statement by witness Matthew Connolly (Military Archive, WS 1764), p. 4.
35. The grenades were made from tin canisters or milk cans, with a small stump of fuse projecting from one end, on which a blob of sulphur was daubed, like the end of a match. They weighed four or five pounds and were crudely soldered. The men had been told in training to strike the sulphur on a wall or stone, count one, two, three, and then throw. The devices were manufactured in Larkfield and at St Enda's, Rathfarnham.
36. BMH statement by witness Jerry Golden (Military Archive, WS 521), p. 14.
37. Seamus Robinson, UCDAD, Coyle papers, 61/13 (16).
38. Ann Devlin branch, Glasgow 1916–22, UCDAD, Coyle papers, 61/4 (67), p. 1.
39. In 1927 Kain retrieved the roll book from its hiding place in Castle Street. He gave it to William O'Brien, who photographed it and returned the original to Kain. The copy was placed in the Bureau of Military History in the 1940s. BMH, William O'Brien papers, Contemporaneous Documents, 154/1; see Appendices.
40. Connolly, Military Archive WS 1746, pp. 4–5.
41. BMH statement by witness James O'Shea, Military Archive, WS 733, p. 43.
42. BMH statement by witness Rose McNamara, NAI, BMH papers, WS 482, p. 5.
43. BMH statement by witness Eilís Bean Uí Chonaill (Ní Riain), NAI, BMH papers, WS 568, p. 6.
44. BMH statement by witness Robert Holland, Military Archive, WS 280, p. 23.
45. Gertie Colly Murphy memoir, Kilmainham Gaol Museum, p. 3.
46. BMH statement by witness Annie Mannion, Military Archive, WS 297, p. 3.
47. Nora O'Daly, 'The Women of Easter Week', *An tÓglach*, (Irish Defence Forces Journal), (3 April 1926), p. 4.
48. Ibid.
49. Ibid.
50. Lily O'Brennan, 'We Surrender', *An Cosantóir*, VII, 6 (June 1947), pp. 303–8.
51. Ibid.
52. Ibid.
53. BMH statement by witness J.J. Bradley, Military Archive, WS 190, p. 3.
54. J.J. Lee, Ireland 1912-1985 (Cambridge, 1989), pp. 33-7.
55. Elizabeth O'Farrell, 'Events of Easter week', Catholic Bulletin, VII, 4 (April 1917).
56. BMH statement by witness Fr Aloysius, Military Archive, WS 200, p. 6 and Fr Augustine, WS 920, p. 11.
57. Ibid.
58. Ibid.

3

A Land Beyond the Sea: Irish and Scottish Republicans in Dublin, 1916

Máirtín Seán Ó Catháin

The founder and leading light of an obscure militant Scottish nationalist militia of the 1930s, the Scottish Defence Force (SDF), Séamus Reader once declared: 'As long as I can remember, from my earliest years I had a good national background.'[1] As a Glasgow-born activist in the lead-up to the 1916 Easter Rising, it is, however, unclear what 'national background' Reader was referring to. His father was a Glaswegian ironworker of Anglo-German-Scots parentage and his mother a daughter of the peculiarly English puritan sect, the Congregationalists. He himself came to Irish nationalist politics through the unlikely avenue of following the trials and tribulations, as well as the actual parade routes, of Glasgow's Irish flute bands, though from his earliest political involvement Reader was one of a small band of Scots who appear to have been convinced of the regenerative qualities of an Irish nationalist insurrection on Scottish nationalist fortunes.

The pre-modern, pre-nationalist neo-medievalism of Pearse and his associates found a keen reverberation in the extra-nationalist ideas of Reader and company. His and their endeavours as Irish republicans served as a committed expression of their pan-Celticism and as a prelude to further Scottish–Irish nationalist solidarity. These Gaelic revolutionaries found within the exiled Irish republican movement in Glasgow a welcome home for their pan-Celtic ideas amidst the old Fenians, Catholic socialists, suffragists and ordinary Irish nationalists who made up the eclectic components of that movement. Most importantly, their politics were given added impetus and status as a result of their being the most adept and active element of Irish republicanism in Scotland in the period leading up to the Rising in the face of the failures of both the Irish Republican Brotherhood (IRB) and the Irish Volunteers in Scotland.

It is only in the last few years that the participation of the Irish abroad in the 1916 Easter Rising has been addressed, though in the 2006 state commemoration of the event it merited no special attention, beyond some scattered references to Scots-born Margaret Skinnider of the Irish Citizen Army garrison in St Stephen's Green.[2] Connolly's involvement, as a son of 'Auld Reekie', rarely if ever pays much attention to his birthplace, while fellow socialist, Charles Carrigan from Denny in Stirlingshire, who was killed in the evacuation of the GPO, is almost completely unknown. These individuals and others like them who came to Dublin in 1916 from various parts of Scotland reflect many of the changes and difficulties increasingly faced by Edwardian Scottish society in the twilight of the liberal ascendancy. They also, however, tell us much about the Rising and its appeal outside the confines of petit-bourgeois romantic separatist circles. Here was a prized moment for a small but significant number of revolutionaries in the Irish and British archipelago who held forth a variety of promises and could be seen to encapsulate a whole host of causes, illusory or otherwise, besides that of militant Irish nationalism. Elsewhere in Europe, it may well have appeared the last kick of the conventional nineteenth-century urban insurrection, embracing an older and decrepit form of self-determination unappealing as sure as it was to be unsuccessful.[3]

There has never been any exploration or analysis of Scotland's contribution to the Easter Rising, although a recent work on the Irish in Britain drew attention to this neglect, and the release in the last few years of the Bureau of Military History witness statements (or 'miser's hoard', as Charles Townshend called it), covering the period 1913–21 helps shine a light into the gloom surrounding that contribution.[4] Most accounts commonly agree there were around forty to fifty participants in the Rising who came from Scotland. The majority and core group were made up of members of Na Fianna Éireann, the militant Irish boy scout organization of Countess Markievicz and Bulmer Hobson, founded (or re-founded) in 1909. The second largest group comprised the Irish Volunteers of Glasgow and surrounding districts and lastly, the smallest component of the Scottish contingent included Cumann na mBan and Irish Citizen Army members, some of whom had been in Dublin for some time. Within these categories, however, there were further sub-groups each with a different relationship not only to their comrades and the overall 'British' contingent but also, and more importantly, with the various elements in the IRB military council which planned and ultimately executed the insurrection.[5]

The Irish in Scotland's involvement with the Rising began in a dramatic manner. At one of the regular quarterly meetings of the supreme council of the IRB held in Clontarf town hall in the autumn of 1914, a decision was taken to stage a rising before the end of the war. It was not, however, one that met with unqualified approval by all there, and Scotland's representative, a south Derry man living in Glasgow named

John Mulholland, opposed the decision. This was possibly on moral grounds but more probably for reasons connected to the IRB's constitution post-1867. If so, Mulholland's position mirrored that of Bulmer Hobson, who also believed that an insurrection should not take place without popular support. This was hardly at a premium in the pre-war atmosphere of 1914.[6] Mulholland, however, was also president of the IRB overall and chair of the supreme council, so his decision had potentially massive ramifications rarely accorded anything more than a brief mention by most historians. The Tom Clarke–Seán MacDiarmada strategy, which was apparently premised on weighting the supreme council with those likely to support an insurrectionary effort in the coming war, saw them bring Mulholland in as supreme council president to offset the power such an Irish-resident chairman might have had on their plans. This policy of offering the post to outsiders, thus reducing the presidency to a titutlar and largely anodine command, had apparently been drawing together for a number of years before the prospect of war became more prescient, and may reflect the organizational decrepitude of the IRB's governing body at this time or perhaps the judgement of the militants on the ineffectual chieftaincy of the Fred Allan years as much as their trust in some of their contemporaries. Mulholland returned to Glasgow, called a meeting of all the district centres to explain his decision, resigned and promptly left the organization, and left it in some disarray from which it never really recovered until Joe Vize's overhaul (under Michael Collins' orders) in 1918.[7]

Mulholland's replacement, Charles Carrigan, was in post for less than a year when, being Glasgow-born, he was forced to resign and leave for Ireland after he faced conscription.

The post-Rising autopsy and arguments over 'who was out' often alluded to the allegation that many of the Irish in Britain who took part in Easter week were in Dublin as a result of the threat of conscription. This notion of having fled to Ireland was perpetuated even by Séamus Robinson, later kingpin of the south Tipperary IRA, and employed in his invective against Collins during the Treaty debate in the Dáil. Robinson, completely disingenuously, stated that far from some IRB master stroke, the deployment of the Irish in Britain came about after the British introduced the Military Service Act in 1916. The 'refugee' epithet, however ungrounded, nonetheless stuck, and as many of the English-Irish (as opposed to the Irish in Scotland) stuck with their man Collins after the Treaty, it formed a central plank of the anti-Treatyite propaganda with 'refugee' serving as a cipher for 'shirker'. Carrigan's replacements, Dan Branniff and then in quick succession, Patrick McCormick, gave confused orders over the mobilization of the Scottish division, contributing to a split which intensified when it became clear that the Glasgow IRB leader Tom McDonnell from Tempo in Co. Fermanagh was actually in

Dublin during the Rising but failed to take part and subsequently lied about his involvement on his return to Glasgow.[8] Continuous investigation in Scotland and Dublin after the Rising failed to provide the inconclusive proof needed to oust McDonnell (he eventually became the recipient of a state pension, though his memoir of 1916 is unsurprisingly oblique). The leftovers created a rift in the IRB exacerbated by the cabalistic activities of Collins' strategy, and there existed rival brotherhoods long before the Treaty split.

A more coherent, or at least less divided, organization and in many ways the most persistently Quixotic and occasionally downright bizarre was Na Fianna Éireann. Established in Glasgow in April 1910 and led by a fairly prominent Fenian from the north of the city, Tom Gillespie (indicating it was under IRB tutelage from its inception), the Fianna soon flourished, attracting around fifty members soon after its foundation and launching a second 'slua' or branch (actually 'troop') in Govan soon after.[9] A number of the members were young apprentices in Glasgow's various heavy industries and had skills which were put to an imaginative use far from those originally intended in their group and in the Rising itself. The organization was addressed by the group's original founders and patrons Bulmer Hobson and Constance Markievicz and in many ways, in spite of its initially humble aims, expanded and sustained the other constituent elements of Scotland's expatriate Irish republican movement. Its activities mirrored the early Baden Powell scout movement from which some of the young men were drawn and involved route marches, signalling, map-reading, drill and mock battle manoeuvres.[10] This highly militaristic routine was broken up by an equally strong social and cultural emphasis which encapsulated Irish classes, céilidh dancing, 'seilgí' or outdoor trips and picnics, lectures both literary and historical, and concerts. One leading member, the aforementioned Séamus Reader, was attracted by the claim of his brother Alex that the Fianna, unlike the Baden Powell scouts, had swords, an image as calculated to get a response from a twelve-year-old aspirant soldier as any post-Mafeking Glasgow youth.[11]

The Fianna comprised those drawn from the regular scouting bodies in Glasgow and the irregular, for example, the vaguely Scottish nationalist 'Fingallians' and the socialist 'Clarion Scouts'. It was probably this variegated Glasgow radical composition that created the peculiar political mix of Irish and Scottish individuals committed to overlapping ideologies that delivered a hybrid Scoto-Irish socialist republicanism. There was also, however, a strongly 'actionist' ideology at the heart of the Fianna that went beyond semaphore lessons into the territory of armed raiding parties that pillaged a heavily militarized Clydeside in the lead-up to the Rising for weapons and explosives.[12]

The Fianna's leading figure was undoubtedly Séamus Reader

(1899–c.1971), who occasionally Gaelicized his (actually east Prussian) surname Ó Rídire. It is difficult to discern Reader's main other Scots-born, and possibly Scots nationalist, compatriots in the Fianna, though certain names such as Alexander Carmichael, William Oswald, Charles Strickland and Charles (or Cormac) Turner were probably among them. Some of these young men were also later to follow Reader's odyssey into a Scottish republican Fianna, Fianna na hAlba, and the highways and byways of an increasingly obscurantist Celtic nationalism.[13] He rose quickly in Na Fianna Éireann both as a result of his previous scouting experience and his well of enthusiasm, and also joined the IRB and the Volunteers. The Belfast brothers, Séamus and Joe Robinson, who had been members of the original 1902 Fianna in that city, had overall command of both the Volunteers and the Fianna in Glasgow, and a number of others were also Belfast men, which led in some measure to a complicated relationship with the Dublin leadership, complicated by the Glasgow IRB, as the Glasgow–Belfast link often took precedence.[14]

A further note of complication was added through Reader's contacts with Markievicz and Connolly. Reader served as a conduit for Connolly's contacts with his leftist supporters in Glasgow, including the Red Clydesiders, Willie Gallacher and Arthur McManus (who became first chairman of the Communist Party of Great Britain). For what purpose these contacts were ongoing cannot be accurately ascertained, though it is interesting to speculate from Young's research and the more recent work of Donal Nevin that Connolly may have entertained a simultaneous Celtic socialist uprising in Glasgow and Dublin.[15] This, if true, would cast Connolly's ideas and motivations around the time of the Rising into quite a different light than has hitherto been the case.

The real question is to what extent Connolly's Glasgow contacts knew of the Rising. Definitely the Irish among them – McManus, Regan and Gallacher – had some indication of previous intention from Connolly, but to what extent and, perhaps more centrally, to what purpose? Reader was certainly supplying arms for the Irish Citizen Army, some of which appear to have come from Connollyite supporters in Scotland prior to the Rising (and Connolly's involvement in the military council from January 1916) and possibly in contravention of his primary loyalty to the Fianna and Volunteers. Reader affirms he was also warned off his contacts with Markievicz, with whom he appears to have established a strong bond, and told never to discuss IRB business with her. He continued, however, to act in what seems to have been an entirely non-partisan manner, though it is clear from his memoirs and statements that most of the cache of revolvers, detonators and explosives brought over from Scotland by Reader and his Fianna boys went to what he termed the 'Surrey House clique' around Markievicz and Connolly.[16]

At a meeting of the Old IRA (Scottish division) held in Eustace Street in Dublin in December 1934, and with the benefit of hindsight, it was recorded that the company of Volunteers sent over to Dublin from Glasgow before Easter week were known as the Scottish division, making up part of the Kimmage garrison attached to GHQ and comprising 1st battalion, 'A' company, numbering around fifty to sixty men. Their commandant was Joseph Robinson and his fellow officers were Liam Gribben and Bernard Friel. All three were also members of the Fianna and had only in the months before the Rising become Volunteers. Robinson was arrested with Reader at the end of January 1916 charged with smuggling explosives and imprisoned, the only two arrests, important though they were, to disrupt Scottish preparations prior to the Rising.[17] Support, however, was readily forthcoming from John Maclean in the Clyde Workers' Committee, as well as from the Young Scots League and Scottish Home Rule Party, further indicating the elongated lines of solidarity the republicans had drawn out. This is all the more remarkable given the hostility of Maclean and his colleagues in the Socialist Labour Party (SLP) to ideas of an insurrection by nationalists and the virulent strains of sectarian and anti-Irish sentiment that were present in Scottish nationalist circles. Reader records that these ties were maintained after his arrest and that information regarding Scotland was passed to Pearse and Connolly via several IRB contacts and a leading member of the Clyde Workers' Committee, Tom McGill.[18]

The Volunteers who ended up in Dublin in 1916 were, many of them, skilled workers whom it was felt by the military council could obtain work and support themselves prior to the Rising. This position was considerably different from that of the Fenians who departed Scotland for the ill-fated 1867 Rising and were conspicuous by their unemployment as they were unwelcome lodgers among the movement that had to support them.[19] John McGallogly's experience was not untypical of the Volunteers from Scotland. Born in a bleak Lanarkshire miners' row in 1898 and encouraged by his elder brother's example, he joined the IRB and Volunteers in Glasgow in 1915. He took part in raids for explosives and left for Belfast with his brother to avoid police follow-up operations on the Glasgow–Dublin route after the arrests of Robinson and Reader. In Belfast they met with three of the Fianna, one of whom was also a Volunteer officer, and decided to make for Dublin, even though IRB orders had encouraged the Glasgow men to wait in Belfast where they would take part in the rising in Ulster, something made clear to Reader in his discussions with Seán MacDiarmada prior to his arrest.[20]

This problem continued up to Easter week itself when two leaders of the Scottish IRB found themselves marooned in Belfast awaiting Scottish Volunteers who never arrived. According to Séamus Robinson, early IRB orders from the unfortunate Tom McDonnell had encouraged Volunteers with engineering experience to report to Dublin and he was part of the second batch that easily evaded the attentions of the RIC detectives at the ports, who they knew, and headed for George Plunkett's Larkfield home and the Kimmage garrison, comprised of the 'British' contingent for the Rising. This was also where the McGallogly brothers eventually ended up after wandering the streets of Dublin in a fruitless search for Tom Clarke's shop in Parnell Street (which they didn't know was actually officially named 'Great Britain Street'), and eventually obtaining lodgings with a Volunteer in Dundrum after a Pythonesque series of events.[21]

Conditions in Kimmage camp were quite basic. Robinson recorded: 'Our life in the garrison was only mildly exciting. There were no baths and few disinfectants. Existence became most uncomfortable; a dry shampoo against a wooden stanchion was not much of a palliative. It did, however, turn some backbiters into bosom pals.' The Volunteers from Scotland herded and slept together at Larkfield and were only divided up among the English Volunteers on the Monday morning. The main batch with John McGallogly of about fifty-six men left the camp and boarded a tram at Harold's Cross: 'Each man had a different kind of kit. No two had it affixed in the same way and probably no-one could have put it on in the same way twice. I was armed with a shotgun and a .22 automatic. We dismounted at O'Connell Bridge and marched to Liberty Hall.'[22]

A number of the Liverpool and Glasgow Irish manned the bottom of Sackville Street at the bridge (a fact apparently confused by Townshend, who in his recent work on the Rising notes that an important defensive point would have been O'Connell Bridge, states that this was effectively ignored but gives evidence of its defence). Undoubtedly, it was a strange experience for native Dubliners to be chased off the bridge and quays by men with Glaswegian, Liverpudlian and Cockney accents who took up positions in the two corner buildings of Hopkins and Hopkins' jewellers and Kelly's gun shop. Most of the rest of the English and Scots were based in the main GPO garrison, though there were a few scattered across the city in other garrisons.[23]

The final segment of the Scottish contribution were the women of Cumann na mBan and the Irish Citizen Army volunteers. This was definitely the smallest contribution, though because of her autobiographical account published in 1917, Margaret Skinnider's name and role occasionally stands out.[24] It's unclear whether any other Cumann na mBan women from Glasgow travelled with Skinnider when she made her final visit before the Rising, joining up with the Irish Citizen Army (ICA) in St Stephen's Green, where she was shot and seriously wounded during the Rising. Skinnider had a background in supporting the suffragist movement and as a fiercely independent individual had used the proclamation as evidence in her argument with ICA commandant, Michael Mallin, that women should be allowed to fight on the same terms as men. She, like the Fianna, whom she joined on a previous visit to Dublin disguised as a boy, had smuggled explosive material from Glasgow to Dublin, and had set up a marksmanship class for women in Glasgow.[25]

Her motivation to become involved came not through any sibling rivalry or inspiration, unlike the Robinsons, Readers, Rices, Carmichaels and McGalloglys but through a childhood memory of the class divisions marked out in the landscape of her ancestral Monaghan, an instinctual loathing for the 'big house' versus cottage hovel dichotomy. Even as her nationalist reflexes and upbringing began to apportion blame for this structure on the British administration, her republicanism remained largely undefined, stressing national pride and economic rejuvenation over ideas of Gaelic cultural renaissance, blood sacrifice or febrile Jacobin conspiracy. A naivety, common to other Rising participants and born out of the optimism of the pre-war generation, and which both historians and commentators seriously underestimate, shines from the pages of Skinnider's testimony. Her genuine dismay at the reality of urban warfare, the disinterest of Dubliners, the brutality of combatants, and the ultimate collapse of the Rising speak about more than the over-inflated hopes of a twenty-four-year-old maths teacher. They show a woman experienced in the bear-pit of Glasgow politics as much as in the rifle club, but someone who nevertheless for all her admitted 'hard-headedness' remained a revolutionary novice, investing the Rising as many of her comrades from Scotland did, with a panoply of visionary and ultimately futile aspirations never to be realized in her lifetime, never mind a week in the spring of 1916.

With her in the Green was Captain Joseph Byrne, a Glaswegian former British soldier who had been called up by his regiment at the outbreak of the war and sent to France; though on a short home leave soon after he decided to abscond and did so after boarding his troop ship at Liverpool. Back in Glasgow, Byrne involved himself with various socialist groupings, though like several of the Fianna and Volunteers, appears to have been drawn to the Catholic Socialist Society of John Wheatley, founded in 1906. It is not known when or where he joined the ICA but he escaped arrest (as did Margaret Skinnider) after the Rising and returned to Glasgow. Glasgow did, however, have an ICA unit in later years and so it is possible that there was one prior to the Rising.[26] A citizen's army had been mooted in Glasgow previously among socialists and it was believed, with Defence of the Realm Act-related repression and the ratcheting up of tensions as the war got underway on Clydeside, that some sort of dual Dublin–Glasgow strategy of resistance and, possibly, insurrection might well be inevitable, particularly, as Young has shown, following the arrest of John Maclean in February 1916.[27]

What then from these collages of allegiances, cross-channel alliances and republican associations can we discern about those who left Scotland to take part in the Easter Rising of 1916 in Dublin? In many senses they were typical of Edwardian Scotland on the eve of the war: overwhelmingly young, keen and morally righteous for the coming fight, militaristic and naïve, liberal in their politics with leftist tinges, and above all, intensely patriotic. These were not values at all out of keeping with their genera-tion and other Scots, but the direction of these characteristics and their expression made the difference and serve to underline the unevenness of immigrant integration in the early part of the twentieth century as well as the unevenness of Scottish society in general. Moreover, the genuine attractiveness of the Irish revolutionary cause and its occasionally amoe-bic shape enthused others as well as the refusenik Irish. Skinnider's involvement, for example, as her book clearly shows, was born out of two perceived layers of injustice: one which prevented her as a woman from certain areas of life and one which prevented her 'country' (though not as she stated her 'home') from releasing itself from a historic, social and political injustice.

Others, such as Reader, were burning with the ardour of young men unwilling to give loyalty to the British empire after having been raised in the sectarian street politics of west central Scotland and eager for an out-let for that frustration. But they were also people, influenced by Connolly's Celtic communism and the patriotic fervour of the Young Scots and Scots National League with which they identified the Irish question, who made little or no distinction between Scotland and Ireland. Whether this pan-Celtic idealism was a reflection of a knowledge or an ignorance of Scotland's historic and often controversial role in Ireland is difficult to say and should also not be too readily expanded to the entire expatriate Irish republican movement in Scotland. After his arrest, John McGallogly had baulked at an Irish soldier, albeit in a British uniform, referring to him as a trouble-making 'Scotch bastard'. During her recuperation Skinnider had been questioned by a detective who revealed what was probably a more representative take on contemporary Irish attitudes towards the Scots when he informed her that her opinions didn't go with her accent. Indeed, Skinnider alluded to this point else-where in the memoir, affirming that she was glad of her accent's attribu-tion of loyalty on many occasions both during and after the Rising.[28]

What is clear is that the Scottish division, including the Volunteers and Fianna, only made up part of the Kimmage garrison and, while as active in the Rising as their compatriots from England, only suffered one fatality, Charles Carrigan, whereas the contingent from England (who appear never to have identified themselves in that or subsequent years as the 'English division') lost five or six Volunteers and had a further three or four injured. The entire Scottish division in total only appears to have numbered the fifty-six or so individuals put forward by McGallogly, and of this only a handful were arrested. The mistakes of the IRB contributed to this small number, but the recalcitrant attitude of the Fianna in choosing Dublin over Belfast, the confusion and dispersal that happened after the arrests of Joseph Robinson and Séamus Reader, and the quite separate arrangements of Cumann na mBan and the Irish Citizen Army, as well possibly as the Hibernian Rifles, all made an impact on the Scottish participation. The overall profile of the contingent appears far more cosmopolitan that any other segment involved in the Rising, which in itself makes an interesting case for how different the Irish in Scotland were from the Irish in the rest of Britain. In addition to this there is the possibility that Scotland holds the key to fully understanding the role of its more senior representative in Connolly. Whatever the summation of his role, it can scarcely be denied that the pastiche of previous overtly single-purpose and slightly deterministic interpretations of individual motivations has to be re-assessed in the context of a re-examination of concepts, identities and psychologies.

NOTES

1. Military Archives of Ireland (MAI), Bureau of Military History (BMH), Witness Statements, WS/627, statement of Séamus Reader, p. 1; Risteárd Ó Glaisne, *Cad a Deir Tú leis na hAlbanaigh?* (Indreabhán, 1978), pp. 105–8.
2. Michael Foy and Brian Barton, *The Easter Rising* (Stroud, 2004); Tim Pat Coogan, *1916 The Easter Rising* (London, 2003), p. 30. Coogan repeats the error of citing Connolly's birthplace as Monaghan rather than Edinburgh; Shane Hegarty and Fintan O'Toole, *The Irish Times Book of the 1916 Rising* (Dublin, 2006); Sinéad McCoole, *No Ordinary Women: Irish Female Activists in the Revolutionary Years* (Dublin, 2004), pp. 42, 73; *Irish Independent*, 13 April 2006.
3. Donal Nevin, *James Connolly: A Full Life* (Dublin, 2005), pp. 3–7; John Newsinger, *Rebel City: Larkin, Connolly and the Dublin Labour Movement* (London, 2003), pp. 144–5; Jonathan Githens-Mazer, *Myths and Memories of the Easter Rising: Cultural and Political Nationalism in Ireland* (Dublin, 2006), pp. xiv–xv, 110–13.
4. Brian Dooley, *Choosing the Green? Second Generation Irish and the Cause of Ireland* (Belfast, 2004); *Irish Times*, 28 March 2005; Charles Townshend, *Easter 1916: The Irish Rebellion* (London, 2006), p. xvii.
5. Iain D. Patterson, 'The Activities of Irish Republican Physical Force Organisations in Scotland, 1919–21', *Scottish Historical Review*, LXXII, 193 (April 1993), p. 49; Máirtín Ó Catháin, *Irish Republicanism in Scotland, 1858–1916* (Dublin, 2007). There was also a sole participant of the Easter week Rising in Enniscorthy who came from Glasgow, named Matt O'Brien; see *Irish Weekly* (Belfast), 30 December 1961.
6. Diarmuid Lynch, *The IRB and the 1916 Insurrection* (Cork, 1957), pp. 23–9; F.X. Martin, 'McCullough, Hobson, and republican Ulster', in F.X. Martin (ed.), *Leaders and Men of the Easter Rising* (London, 1967), pp. 102–4, and Kevin B. Nowlan, 'Tom Clarke, MacDermott, and the IRB' in Martin (ed.), *Leaders*, pp. 114–18; Keith Jeffery, *Ireland and the Great War* (Cambridge, 2000), pp. 30–1.
7. MAI, BMH, Witness Statements, WS/828, statement of James Byrne, pp. 1–2, WS/777, statement of Patrick Mills, pp. 1–2, WS/627, statement of Séamus Reader, p. 8; Owen McGee, *The IRB: The Irish Republican Brotherhood from the Land League to Sinn Féin* (Dublin, 2005), pp. 349–51. McGee posits a situation of general disarray and lack of organizational strength in the IRB at this time, which may be a more likely cause of the complex internal politics and jockeying for influence that was taking place.
8. National Library of Ireland (NLI), MS. 15,337, statement of Patrick McCormick, p. 1; MAI,

BMH, Witness Statements, WS/272, statement of Daniel Branniff, pp. 1–2; Private papers of Éamonn Mooney, commandant, Scottish brigade IRA (1919–25), Minutes of Scottish Brigade, Old IRA Association (1947–55), in possession of Mrs Cathleen Knowles-McGuirk. I am extremely grateful to Stephen Coyle and Cathleen Knowles-McGuirk for access to and use of these valuable papers.

9. MAI, BMH, Witness Statements, WS/627, p. 3; *Glasgow Observer*, 10 July 1915; Private papers of Éamonn Mooney, commandant, Scottish brigade IRA (1919–25), list of Fianna boys in Glasgow 1908–21.

10. *Glasgow Observer*, 30 January, 6 & 20 March, 15 May and 7 August 1915. The biggest event for the Irish National Boy Scouts in this period appears to have been their parade in full regalia to St Agnes' Church in Lambhill in Glasgow for a service in honour of the Irish miners killed in the 3 August 1915 Cadder pit disaster; Patterson, 'Activities', pp. 48–9. Patterson fails to assign any importance or significance to the role of the Fianna in the events leading up to 1916, something which is also a factor in other studies of the Rising in general and was recognized by F.X. Martin as far back as 1967. Martin (ed.), *Leaders*, p. 101.

11. MAI, BMH, Witness Statements, WS/627, statement of Séamus Reader, p. 2.

12. David Prynn, 'The Clarion Clubs, Rambling and the Holiday Associations in Britain since the 1890s', *Journal of Contemporary History*, 11, 2 (1976), pp. 67–8; MAI, BMH, Witness Statements, WS/ 627, statement of Séamus Reader, p. 2; NLI, Frank Gallagher MS. 21, 265, account of Séamus Robinson, p. 60, and in appendix letter from Mrs Kathleen Kincaid, nee Keating to the editor, *Sunday Press* dated March 1954.

13. New Register House (NRH), Registrar General's Office (RGO), Register of Births, Deaths and Marriages (Scotland), Marriage Certificate (1898), Registration District 644/5, Enumeration Book 7, and Census of Population (Scotland) 1901, district 644/3, p. 74; Private papers of Éamonn Mooney, commandant, Scottish brigade IRA (1919–25), list of Fianna boys, Glasgow 1912–17; Hugh MacDonald, 'Amlaibh MacAindreas: Another Scots Fighter for Ireland', *Scottish Workers Republic* (undated), kindly donated by Stephen Coyle, Glasgow; *Scots Independent*, 8 November 1969; Peter Berresford Ellis, *Scotland Not Only Free But Gaelic: A Tribute to Séumas Mac a'Ghobhainn* (Glasgow, 2000).

14. NLI, Frank Gallagher MS. 21, 265, account of Séamus Robinson, pp. 58–9; NLI, MS 15,337, statement of Patrick McCormick, pp. 7–8; MAI, BMH, Witness Statements, WS/272, statement of Daniel Branniff, pp. 3–4.

15. William Gallacher, *The Last Memoirs of William Gallacher* (London, 1966), p. 171; Thomas Bell, *Pioneering Days* (London, 1941), pp. 50, 94–5; James D. Young, *The Rousing of the Scottish Working Class* (London, 1979), pp. 194–5, 205–8; James D. Young, 'The Irish Immigrants' Contribution to Scottish Socialism, 1880–1926', *Saothar*, no.13 (1988), pp. 94–5; James D. Young. 'John Maclean, Socialism, and the Easter Rising', *Saothar*, no. 16 (1991), pp. 25–7; Nevin, *Connolly*, p. 320; Peter Berresford Ellis, *A History of the Irish Working Class* (London, 1972), p. 217; C. Desmond Greaves, *The Life and Times of James Connolly* (London, 1961), pp. 356, 368–9.

16. Greaves, *Connolly*, pp. 389–91; MAI, BMH, Witness Statements, WS/627, statement of Séamus Reader, pp. 7–8, WS/1767, statement of Séamus Reader, pp. 1–2, 6–7, 16–20; Margaret Skinnider, *Doing My Bit for Ireland* (New York, 1917), pp. 57–60.

17. Private papers of Éamonn Mooney, commandant, Scottish brigade IRA (1919–25), Minutes of Scottish Brigade, Old IRA Association (1947–55), December 1934 monthly meeting; MAI, BMH, Witness Statements, WS/1767, pp. 21–9; Breandán Mac Giolla Choille (ed.), *Intelligence Notes 1913–16* (Dublin, 1966), pp. 161–2.

18. MAI, BMH, Witness Statements, WS/1767, pp. 6–7, 33–4; Young, 'Maclean', pp. 23–4; Peter Berresford Ellis, *The Celtic Revolution* (Ceredigion, 1985), p. 46; Greaves, *Irish Working Class*, pp. 255–6.

19. Máirtín Ó Catháin, 'The Fenian Movement in Scotland, 1858–1916', unpublished PhD, University of Ulster (2001), pp. 109–15.

20. University College Dublin Archives (UCDA), P60, McGallogly statement, pp. 1–3; Uinseann MacEoin, *Survivors* (Dublin, 1980), pp. 198–201.

21. NLI, Frank Gallagher MS.21, 265, account of Séamus Robinson, p. 60; UCDA, P60, McGallogly statement, pp. 4–6.

22. NLI, Frank Gallagher MS.21, 265, account of Séamus Robinson, pp. 61–2; UCDA, P60, McGallogly statement, pp. 6–7; Peter Hart, *Mick: The Real Michael Collins* (London, 2006), pp. 81–90.

23. Private papers of Éamonn Mooney, commandant, Scottish brigade IRA (1919–25), statement

of service of the late Seumas [sic] McGallogly (from 1913–1924), dated 6 March 1956; UCDA, P60, McGallogly statement, pp. 7–10; Townshend, *1916*, pp. 101–2, 158, 210; Joe Good, *Enchanted By Dreams: The Journal of a Revolutionary* (Dingle, 1996), pp. 23–32.

24. National Archives of Ireland (NAI), Crime Branch Special (CBS) reports (precis), report dated 29 August 1904 from county inspector of Fermanagh to inspector-general, Dublin Castle re. Captain James Maguire of Hibernian Rifles; *Glasgow Observer*, 26 February 1910 for spread of American Alliance Ancient Order of Hibernians in Scotland; *Hibernian*, 28 August and 4 September 1915 for later links to Scotland.

25. Skinnider, *Doing my Bit*, pp. 9–10, 64–5; MAI, BMH, Witness Statements, WS/627, statement of Séamus Reader, p. 6; Private papers of Éamonn Mooney, commandant, Scottish brigade IRA (1919–25), Máire Bean Nic a'Ghalloglaigh notes October 1953.

26. Skinnider, *Doing my Bit*, pp. 8–10, 20–7, 142–3, 179–80; Frank Robbins, *Under the Starry Plough* (Dublin, 1977), pp. 154–5; Brian Hanley, 'The Irish Citizen Army after 1916', *Saothar*, no. 28 (2003), pp. 37, 47; Patterson, 'Activities', p. 50. There is also some evidence that Dublin docker, Jim Fearon, who had been based in Glasgow, took part in the Rising with the Irish Citizen Army; see *Irish Weekly* (Belfast), 30 December 1961.

27. James D. Young, *The Very Bastards of Creation: Scottish International Radicalism 1707–1995: A Biographical Study* (Glasgow, 1996), pp. 192–200. There is some evidence that Young may have revised his interpretation of Maclean in recent years, but his view that Maclean had no interest in, sympathy for or intrigue with republicans before 1920 does not stand up to close scrutiny; Untitled and undated article by Stephen Coyle on Irish-Scottish networks in the 1916 to 1922 period, p. 2, kindly donated to the author by Stephen Coyle, Glasgow; Emanuel Shinwell, *Conflict Without Malice* (London, 1955), p. 43.

28. UCDA, P60, McGallogly statement, p. 12; Skinnider, *Doing my Bit*, pp. 130, 194.

4

The British Labour and Socialist Movement and the 1916 Rising

David Granville

The relative paucity of information and analysis with regard to the response of British socialists and trade unionists to the events of Easter 1916 implies that, with a few notable exceptions, this has been one aspect of the Rising which has not over-exercised the minds of historians on either side of the Irish Sea.[1] Given the role of James Connolly and the Irish Citizen Army, widespread labour movement support for home rule and the proximity of the Dublin Lockout, a struggle which generated considerable support among British workers, it appears odd that the response of the British movement has not provoked a closer and more detailed examination. This is all the more surprising given that the Rising posed a major threat to British colonial rule at a time when the empire was involved in an inter-imperialist war raging throughout Europe and the Near East. There was also growing labour unrest in Britain, particularly in Scotland. From a British labour history perspective, the Rising barely attracted more than a mention in a number of works regarded as standards on the Labour Party or trade unionism in Britain.[2]

Where references to Ireland appear, most concentrate on the 1913–14 Dublin Lockout or on the influence of syndicalist ideas on British socialists and the trade unionists.

GDH Cole's *A History of the Labour Party from 1914*, published in 1948, is one of the few books to mention 1916 within the main body of the text. In a chapter dealing with the party and opposition to British participation in the First World War, Cole notes: 'Hard upon the Clyde deportations followed the Easter Rebellion in Ireland, which cost James Connolly, Sheehy Skeffington and other socialists their lives.'[3] No further explanation is deemed necessary.

The 1920 edition of Beatrice and Sidney Webb's history of British trade unionism included a lengthy footnote on trade unionism in Ireland. This not only referred to the Dublin strike of 1913–14 but also acknowledged 'the great transformation' in Irish trade unionism brought about by the 'foundation and remarkable development of the Transport and General Workers' Union'.[4]

However, despite going on to cite Connolly as one of the 'heroes' of the Irish trade union movement, the Webbs, prominent Fabian socialists, made no direct reference to the events of Easter 1916. The note does, however, include an oblique criticism of Irish labour's involvement in the Rising by suggesting that the Irish trade union movement had, during the first two decades of the twentieth century, 'become fired with nationalist spirit and almost revolutionary fervour'.[5]

This somewhat muted criticism of Connolly and the Irish labour movement for being, simultaneously, 'too nationalist' and 'too revolutionary' was nevertheless in line with the cautious reformist approach to securing political advance and improved conditions for working people adopted by groups such as the Fabians, the Independent Labour Party (ILP) and the trade union hierarchy. Labour Party conference and Trades Union Congress (TUC) debates in the months following the Rising also steered clear of either commenting on or discussing what had occurred in Ireland. This downplaying, or in some cases silence, is undoubtedly a reflection of the Labour Party's decision to join the coalition government in 1915. At the time of the Rising, Labour Party leader Arthur Henderson was a British government minister and a member of the cabinet. Although not a member of the inner war cabinet, Henderson and other Labour ministers were directly implicated in the government's decisions to bombard Dublin and to execute Connolly and the other leaders in the rebellion's aftermath. As Brian O'Neill notes in his book, *Easter Week*, published in 1936: 'It was difficult for it [the labour movement in Britain], therefore, to protest against either, and it made no protest.'[6]

The Marxist historian T.A. Jackson echoes O'Neill's point in *Ireland Her Own*, stressing that while the 'English labour movement' was sympathetic to the Irish demand for home rule, at the time of the Rising, its 'orthodox upper strata' was 'co-operating cordially in the prosecution of the war'.[7]

At odds with the anti-war left in Britain, both pacifist and revolutionary, Jackson concludes that it was, therefore, hardly surprising that the very same labour leaders who rejected the rebels' anti-imperialist strike for Irish freedom found little difficulty in accepting the pro-war Irish Nationalist Party view of the rebellion as being 'totally unrepresentative of the main body of Irish opinion'.[8]

On Britain's entry into the First World War on 5 August 1914, both the Labour Party executive and the parliamentary party had reiterated the party's position of opposing the government's policy of boosting Russia in Europe and Asia at Germany's expense – a policy, Labour leaders argued, which had been responsible for bringing about the war.[9]

However, as soon as Prime Minister Asquith asked parliament to grant an initial war credit of £100,000,000, it became clear that Labour was seriously divided and that party leader Ramsey MacDonald was unable to command a majority.[10]

MacDonald resigned and was replaced as chairman and leader of the Parliamentary Labour Party by Henderson, who only days earlier had addressed a rally in Trafalgar Square denouncing the war and demanding that the British government refuse to take part.[11]

The policy of the Socialist International, to which the Labour Party was affiliated, had been agreed at the Stuttgart congress of 1907 and confirmed subsequently at Copenhagen (1910) and Basle (1912). In response to events or crises which threatened world peace, it was to be the duty of workers and their parliamentary representatives 'to exert all their efforts to prevent the war by means of co-ordinated action'. In the event of war breaking out it was to be their 'duty to work for its speedy termination, and to exploit with all their might the economic and political crisis created by war to arouse the population and to hasten the overthrow of capitalist rule'.[12] The Labour Party's anti-war campaign lasted barely a handful of days. By the end of August 1914 the party, now led by Henderson, had voted for war credits, given its support to the government's military recruitment campaign and, in conjunction with the trade union leadership, effectively declared an industrial truce.[13]

As Connolly was to write in the *Irish Worker* in September 1914, with the honourable exception of the Independent Labour Party and the Socialist Labour Party, 'the organised and unorganised Labour advocates of peace [in Britain] swallowed the bait and are now beating the war drums and hounding their brothers on to the butchery of their German comrades – and hounding them on with the cant of fraternity on their lips.'[14]

By mid-May 1915, Labour had accepted Asquith's invitation to join a coalition government alongside the Liberals and Conservatives. Henderson was appointed president of the Board of Education, while two other Labour MPs, William Brace and G.H. Roberts, joined him as undersecretary for home affairs and junior lord of the treasury respectively. Having forsaken the policy of the Socialist International and donned the belligerent, jingoist mantle of the British ruling class, it was a short step from here to denouncing the Easter Rising as an act of treachery at a time of war, deserving of a harsh and uncompromising response. Years later, contributors to the letters pages of the socialist press were continuing to remind Henderson that he had cheered the rebels' execution when they had been announced in the House of Commons.[15]

There is, however, some evidence which suggests that not all of Labour's forty MPs were prepared to go along with the general party consensus and openly condemn the Rising. Speaking during a censure motion debate in the House of Commons on 16 October 1916, the Irish-born

Labour MP for Leeds East, James O'Grady, a former president of the Trades Union Congress who knew Connolly from his own time as a union organizer in Belfast, criticized the executions. He emphasized the sincerity of those who had taken part in the rebellion and chastised fellow MPs for their lack of understanding of Ireland:

> I knew some of the men who were, unfortunately, executed by the British government. I knew them to be absolutely sincere. They always declared themselves to be what they were – the enemies of English rule in Ireland, and they died enemies of that rule in Ireland. I always thought that it was one of the characteristics of the British race to have some regard for a man who has the courage of his convictions, and that in circumstances like these they would have taken the human view ... would not have gone to the extent of executing these men... Englishmen never can and never will understand Ireland. It is a question of psychology, as well as a question of politics and justice. You have never attempted to understand Ireland.[16]

O'Grady's contribution to the debate on a Nationalist Party censure motion condemning the continued application of martial law in Ireland was far from being a ringing endorsement of the Rising. A staunch supporter of Britain's participation in the war, he tempered his contribution by reassuring the government that the Labour Party would 'not do anything to prevent or to embarrass this government in carrying on the war'.[17]

O'Grady, a backbencher, may have spoken up for the integrity of the men and women who had taken part in the Rising, but there was to be no sympathy at leadership level. In fact, there was to be very little said about Ireland at all until the issue of home rule came to the fore once more towards the end of the 1914–18 war.

Another Irishman who was active in the British labour movement was the playwright and Fabian-socialist George Bernard Shaw. Like O'Grady, Shaw neither agreed with nor supported the rebellion. However, he understood Irish frustrations and anger concerning the non-implementation of home rule and condemned the executions as wrong and politically counter-productive. In the *Daily News* of 19 May 1916 Shaw wrote:

> My own view is that the men who were shot in cold blood, after their capture or surrender, were prisoners of war, and that it was, therefore, entirely incorrect to slaughter them... Until Dublin Castle is superseded by a National Parliament and Ireland voluntarily incorporated with the British Empire as Canada, Australasia and South Africa have been incorporated, an Irishman resorting to arms to achieve independence of his country is doing only what Englishmen will do, if it be their misfortune to be invaded and conquered by the Germans in the course of the present war.[18]

In his capacity as the chairman of the Fabian Research Department, Shaw had contributed an interesting essay to the 1916 *Labour Year Book*, a publication which recorded developments within the party over the previous twelve months. Addressing himself to the question 'Why a Labour Year Book?', Shaw wrote: 'The world is full of books telling us what we do not want to know; the ideal of the editors of the *Labour Year Book* is a book that will tell its purchasers what they do want to know and what no other book will tell them.'[19]

The 1917 *Labour Year Book*, which covered the period of the Easter Rising and included a report of the party's annual conference held in January 1917, dealt with the Rising and its aftermath in a single sentence: 'Still another attempt has been made to solve the Irish problem. It is true to say that the parties came closer together than ever before during this long and bitter controversy, but the attempt proved to be abortive. *There was the calamitous outbreak in Ireland followed by a reign of martial law, and the outlook became bleaker*' (my emphasis).[20]

It would appear that the 'ideals' of the book's editors did not stretch to informing party members of its leaders' response to the Rising – or they had come to the conclusion that they did not want to know.

The implementation of home rule and support for the Nationalist Party were to remain the main planks of party policy so far as Ireland was concerned, as was confirmed at the party's annual conference held in Manchester in January 1917 where delegates endorsed, 'by general assent', a resolution deploring 'the failure to give legislative effect to the temporary settlement of the Home Rule controversy recently arranged by the Secretary of State for War between the two chief Irish parties and desires to express its entire sympathy with the National Party in the repeated postponement of plans intended to realise their national aims'.[21]

Despite the executions of James Connolly and his ICA deputy Michael Mallin, the bombardment of the ITGWU Liberty Hall headquarters and the deaths, injury and internment of a number of Irish trade unionists, the British Trades Union Congress was, if anything, even more reluctant to discuss the Rising than had been the Labour Party.[22] While the TUC's parliamentary committee responded to the death of Lord Kitchener on 5 June 1916 by passing a series of resolutions 'expressing profound regret and sympathy', as the report of that year's annual congress, held in Birmingham in September, recorded, there were to be no motions of sympathy or obituaries for the executed Irish labour leader Connolly, or for the other Irish trade unionists who had lost their lives in the Rising.[23] In fact, there was to be no debate on the situation in Ireland at all until congress met in Derby in September 1918, two months prior to the ending of the First World War.

At the Derby congress, a resolution urging the implementation of home rule 'under the most generous and free conditions of democratic self-government' was moved by dockers' leader Ben Tillet and carried by general assent.[24] The resolution's focus on home rule and its appeal to Irish workers to support the British war effort 'to help us win the war for peace and peoples, and for the establishment of democracy and the subjection of militarism' confirmed that a majority of British trade union leaders continued to support Redmond's Nationalist Party and its assessment of the situation in Ireland. In moving the successful 1918 TUC resolution, Tillet, a one-time anti-war pacifist and militant syndicalist turned pro-war 'patriot', was nevertheless forced to acknowledge that other forces had come to the fore and that independence rather than home rule was fast becoming the new context within which the 'Irish question' was now being framed.[25] The extent to which this had become true would be obvious to both TUC and Labour Party leaders alike by the end of the year.[26]

While there were clear reasons why Labour Party and TUC leaders had not wanted to debate the Rising, the same could not be said of the various socialist parties and publications which abounded at the time. Most were either overtly critical or uncomprehending of how a socialist like Connolly could 'abandon' his past 'socialist' beliefs to throw in his lot with a group of nationalists in an irresponsible and flawed military adventure that was always doomed to failure. Connolly had been involved, in one capacity or another, with the Independent Labour Party, a key affiliate of the federal British Labour Party, since its foundation by Keir Hardie in 1893. It was not always a comfortable relationship as the acrimonious debate in 1911 between Connolly and Belfast ILP leader William Walker, which stemmed from an appeal by Connolly for socialist unity in Ireland and an independent Irish labour party, amply demonstrated.[27]

Despite having considered resigning from the party immediately prior the start of the First World War,[28] Connolly praised the ILP in the *Irish Worker* in September 1914 for having joined the Socialist Labour Party in Britain in opposing the war.[29] The ILP's position, however, was not based on revolutionary socialism and anti-imperialism but on anti-militarism, pacifism and a gradualist approach to achieving socialism in Britain, and the party's response to the Irish Rising reflected this. The major strands of the ILP's analysis of the Rising appeared in *Labour Leader*, the official weekly organ of the ILP, within days of the rebellion taking place.

The paper's 'Review of the Week', almost certainly penned by editor Fenner Brockway, a leading figure within both the ILP and the No-Conscription Fellowship, regretted 'the scenes of violence which have occurred in Dublin' and went on to remind readers of the ILP's opposition to armed force, even where this was 'under the control of a labour organisation'.[30]

The report continued: 'but it should be remembered that the Irish

Volunteers and the Irish labour movement are only following the example set by Carson and his Ulster Army. Violence begets violence, and the
policy of the Iron Heel pursued by the authorities in Ireland, intensified
as it has since the outbreak of the war, has encouraged reliance upon
armed force.'[31] The paper was to restate and amplify these basic themes
throughout May and to sharpen its condemnation of the rebels, Carson
and British government policy:

> We condemn as strongly as anyone those who were immediately respon-
> sible for the revolt, but it is not upon them that the heaviest respon-
> sibility rests. They were animated by a deep sense of the wrongs
> Ireland has suffered at the hands of Britain, and those who have been
> responsible for those wrongs are the real authors of the terrible blood-
> shed which has occurred. More responsible than anyone is Sir Edward
> Carson. It was he and his fellow loyalists of Ulster who taught the
> extreme nationalists and Labourists of Dublin to arm, and the
> impunity with which the British Government allowed them naturally
> encouraged Sinn Féiners and Larkenites to follow their example,
> whilst the Dublin strike and the employment of troops against work-
> ers deepened the sense of revolt and drove men like Jim Connolly to
> espouse the policy of violence. We think they have been terribly and
> criminally mistaken, but we hope the British people will realise that
> unless our asserted sympathy with small nations is the most absolute
> cant we must pursue a policy in Ireland which will allow the people to
> realise their high National aspirations.[32]

By the time the following edition of the paper had gone to the printers,
the authorities had executed around a dozen of the rebel leaders, a development which the paper viewed with 'horror and shame'. Britain's 'murder in cold blood' of 'men who were led by righteous indignation of the
wrongs of their country and a holy zeal for its liberation is an act which
will stain our national character throughout history and lower it in the
esteem of all civilised peoples', the paper advised its readers before concluding, prophetically, that Britain's 'savage tyranny' was 'having the
effect of tremendously increasing the sympathy of Irishmen with those
who led the rebellion' and that this would lead to a 'new chapter of
bloody revolt and cruel suppression extending over many years...'.[33]

The *Labour Leader* made no reference to the execution of Connolly
and the paper published neither obituary nor tribute. Only in the case of
the murdered Irish socialist and pacifist Francis Sheehy Skeffington was
such honour extended.[34]

Apart from the condemnation of militarism, from whichever source it
originated, and support for home rule, the paper largely confined itself to
humanitarian concern for those adversely affected by the rebellion and

the government's brutal response, publishing an appeal by the Irish National Aid Association at the end of June 1916.[35]

Tribute was, however, eventually paid to both Connolly and Sheehy Skeffington in the report of the ILP's National Administrative Council, presented at the party's annual conference in Leeds towards the end of April 1917.[36] Delegates also endorsed a strongly worded resolution condemning 'the crimes committed by the authority of the Government against small nationalities and subject races'. Agreed without discussion, the resolution made particular reference to Ireland, protesting against 'the hurried trials ... and the infliction of the death penalty upon men whose honesty of purpose in taking up arms in what they believed to be the service of their country has not been questioned'.[37]

The ILP's bi-monthly *Socialist Review* echoed the party's disapproval of the Rising and its opposition to militarism, from whatever source it originated. However, its main commentary on the rebellion, published three months after the events of Easter 1916, was provided by Eva Gore Booth, the sister of Constance Markievicz. A radical suffragist, Gore Booth had settled in Salford towards the end of the nineteenth century and had become an important figure in the suffragette, peace and women's trade union movements.[38]

While a strong supporter of Irish freedom, as a staunch pacifist she had mixed feelings about the Rising, as is clear from her poetry.[39] Concluding that it had been 'a blow to all those who had hoped for a gradual lessening of hostility', she attempted to place the Rising in the context of Ireland's centuries-long freedom struggle, while explaining to her British labour movement audience the malign impact that British rule and capitalist exploitation had had on the lives of ordinary Irish people: 'her rule in Ireland seems to be followed too often by the old round of misery, poverty, destitution, dirt, disease, starvation, strikes, despair, rebellion, executions, and everlasting bitterness.' Given such a background, and the experience of the recent Dublin transport workers dispute, which had been ruthlessly 'crushed by the starvation of three-quarters of the population', was it 'any wonder', she mused, 'that such desperation should have found an outlet in rebellion?'[40]

The ILP was far from being an homogenous political entity and it contained within its ranks a substantial minority influenced to one degree or another by Marxism and revolutionary socialism. Among these, Shapurji Saklatvala and J.T. Walton Newbold, both of whom were subsequently elected to the House of Commons as Communists in the 1920s, are known to have expressed their support for the Rising.[41] As did the south Wales miners' leader Arthur Horner, who avoided conscription and travelled to Dublin to join the remnants of the Irish Citizen Army.[42] However, while Horner refers to widespread sympathy for the rebels within the

Welsh movement in his biographical writings, it is difficult to assess to what degree such sentiments were prevalent among the ILP rank-and-file as a whole.[43]

More visible, through the party's various publications, was to be the outright condemnation of ILP leaders such as Ramsey MacDonald, at that time well to the left of the Labour Party leadership, or the despairing consternation expressed in Scottish ILP circles, where Connolly had been particularly well known. Tom Johnston, the editor of the independent left-wing journal, *Forward*, declared Connolly's involvement to be 'totally inexplicable' and the 'mysterious and astounding part of the insensate rebellion'.[44] The following week, the paper's 'En Passant' column gave its support to Redmond's plea for clemency for the rebel leaders while condemning the 'military, political and moral folly' of 1916.[45]

A further appeal for clemency appeared in John Wheatley's 'Catholic Socialist Notes' in which he condemned the 'cold blooded execution of the rebel leaders' as 'a black spot on Britain's shield' and pleaded for the government 'to be chivalrous to their enemies' whose bravery 'had reached a point of high nobility'.[46] By mid-June, Wheatley, who greatly admired Connolly and had long struggled to spread socialism among Scotland's Catholic community, many of whom were of Irish descent, had begun to notice a new receptiveness towards Connolly's ideas. Wheatley concluded that Connolly's participation in the rebellion and subsequent execution had removed 'a mountain of prejudice against socialism'.[47]

The Plebs, the journal of the movement for independent working-class education in Britain, saw no such benefit and took a despairing view of Connolly's participation in the rebellion. Edited by J.F. Horrabin, the June 1916 edition carried a memorial for Connolly in which the unnamed author expressed the difficulty as 'an outsider' of understanding either nationalism or how 'a man of Connolly's type and calibre' came to 'play a leading part in so hopeless a business'.[48] The journal concluded that 'the tragedy of the revolt, from a socialist point of view,' was 'that "romantic nationalism" was largely the inspiration of it; and that Connolly – the industrial unionist, the sane writer and thinker – should have been goaded by circumstances into sharing it'.[49]

Writing in the same issue, Grace Neal, an English trade unionist living in Dublin, lays the blame for the Rising at the door 'of the same class who are ultimately responsible for this horrible war – this war in defence of small nationalities!'[50] Like the author of *The Plebs* memorial article, Neal was unable to analyse, politically, why it was that 'the saner leaders of the recent Rising' had become involved in the Rising. Her only explanation was to conclude they had 'been blinded and maddened by their hatred of injustice and oppression'.[51]

An appreciation of Connolly by the Irish labour leader's political mentor

and friend John Leslie was published on the front page of *Justice*, the official organ of the British Socialist Party (BSP), on 18 May 1916.[52] Strongly
critical of the Rising, which Leslie described as 'sad, bad and mad', and of
labour's part in it, Leslie provided a personal assessment of how a socialist
of Connolly's 'keen intellect' and 'analytical ability' had come to be
involved with militant Irish nationalists 'many of whom, if not most', were,
in the view of Leslie, 'the merest reactionaries'. Rejecting the idea that
Connolly had been 'deluded' into joining the Rising, Leslie claimed to have
recognized 'a growing Irishism' in Connolly's outlook, which he wrongly
put down to the influence of Sinn Féin, and suggested that his despair at
the attitude of the British movement was the key factor:

> Knowing the man, I say it is possible that, despairing of effective assis-
> tance from that quarter [the British movement], and indeed believing
> that it would act as a drag upon his efforts to form an Irish Socialist
> Party, he determined at all costs to identify or to indissolubly link the
> cause of Irish labour with the most extreme Irish nationalism, and to
> seal the bond of union with his blood if necessary.[53]

As his contributions to the *Irish Worker* and other socialist publications
from the outbreak of war in August 1914 onwards demonstrate, Connolly
had indeed become openly frustrated with and critical of the leaders of
the British labour movement. This was particularly true with regard to
the transformation of so many from enthusiastic endorsers of the internationalist anti-war position of the Socialist International into chauvinistic
cheerleaders for their own capitalist class once Britain had joined the conflict. Leslie makes no reference to this in his *Justice* article, although it is
unclear whether this is a reflection of his own thinking or an omission
related to the fact that the paper, edited by H.W. Lees, was under the
control of the chauvinistic, pro-war minority faction of the BSP, led by the
party's then leader, H.M. Hyndman.

At the time of the Rising, Hyndman, the foremost figure within
British Marxism for nearly three-and-a-half decades, was on the verge of
leading his followers out of the BSP, following their defeat at the party's
annual conference in Salford, which had begun on Easter Sunday.
Hyndman, who went on to form the National Socialist Party, made his
own position on the Rising clear in early May. Writing in *Justice*, his major
concern was the incompetence of the British authorities in assessing the
threat of rebellion and in allowing Dublin 'to be delivered defenceless
into the hands of a small body of reckless fanatics at a most serious crisis
in our foreign and domestic affairs'.[54]

The Clarion newspaper, edited by Robert Blatchford, a prominent
Hyndman supporter, ignored the rebellion in the editorial pages of the
paper. Blatchford did, however, proffer a resolute defence of the paper's

pro-war stance: 'This is no time to talk of the wrongs of the poor and the emancipation of the workers,' Blatchford urged *Clarion* readers. 'We must save the State.'[55] Comment on the Rising was to be confined to the paper's letters' page where one Englishman resident in Belfast criticized the government's lack of consistency when dealing with Carson's Ulster rebels.[56] While another reader, a rifleman in the Royal Irish Rifles, writing from the front line in France, mourned the death of Connolly while 'deploring his actions and connection with the Sinn Féiners'.[57]

In his brief and polemical history of the Irish Citizen Army, published in 1919, Sean O'Casey refers to 'the earnest sympathy expressed towards the Irish people by many of the leaders of thought among the English people, subsequent to the sad events of Easter week'.[58] Although he only gives one example, it is an important one as far as the question of the British labour movement and Ireland is concerned. Recalling a 1917 rally at the Albert Hall in support of the Russian revolution, O'Casey records that the left-wing Labour figure George Lansbury reminded his audience that it was only three years previously that he had shared a platform at the Albert Hall with Connolly and that: 'he (Connolly) and his dead colleagues ... were just too soon, that is all'. Lansbury went on to insist that 'we British people have got to clear the Irish question up, because until we do it, it is not for us to celebrate other people's triumphs over reaction.'[59]

Made a year after the Rising, with the benefit of hindsight, Lansbury's comments nevertheless echoed the Russian revolutionary leader Lenin's assessment of the Rising made in July 1916.[60] However, an examination of *The Herald*, at that time a weekly independent labour newspaper edited by Lansbury, does not reveal overt support for the rebellion, though a succession of contributors, including Harold Laski, Dora Sigerson Shorter and Lansbury himself, were unequivocally condemnatory of the British government's policy and Carson's Unionist rebels.[61] For Laski, writing in the 27 May edition of the paper 'the moment chosen for its outburst was mistaken' but explainable, with any guilt for the 'massacre' resting upon 'Sir Edward Carson's hands; and, in a lesser degree, Mr Asquith'.[62]

In the 8 July edition of the paper, Lansbury devoted over two-and-a-half pages to Ireland, including his entire editorial comment. In an article entitled 'Ireland's Appeal to Britain', Lansbury gave his support to the campaign to reprieve Roger Casement and quoted extensively from Casement's treason-trial speeches.[63] For Lansbury, although Ireland was 'still under martial law, and ... held in subjugation', her struggle for freedom was bound to continue. The imperative for English people, he argued, was to find an honourable and just 'way out'. The obvious solution, Lansbury suggests, being home rule for Ireland, undivided – 'the right of self-government on lines such as exist in Canada, Australia, and South Africa'.[64]

He was to expand his arguments further in the paper's editorial under the headline 'The Only Cure For Ireland', in which he argued that the 'Irish question' was, in fact, an 'English question ... the age-old and persistent fact of English tyrannical interference with, and distortion of, the life, individuality, and development of Ireland'.[65] Freedom was the only cure for Ireland's ills, he informed *Herald* readers, going on to warn them that 'England (or that section arrogating to itself the right to act for England and Britain) cannot employ repressive force and destructive restriction without lowering and poisoning its own nature, and so spoiling its own freedom and growth. Let England be courageous and try justice.'[66]

Five months later, the paper was to publish Desmond Ryan's fulsome appreciation of Connolly, in which the writer explained the Irish labour leader's decision to join the rebellion within the context of the policy of the Second International and 'with the teachings of a lifetime which identified political independence with social freedom'. Implicitly criticizing socialists who had claimed not to understand Irish labour's participation in the Rising, Ryan noted that, for anyone familiar with Connolly's writings in *Workers' Republic* or with *Labour in Irish History*, it could not have been 'anything unexpected'.[67] Where were the voices of the revolutionary left at the time of the Rising?

In Scotland, where the Clyde had become 'a seething cauldron of unrest and clashing ideas',[68] many militant and politically advanced labour leaders and anti-war agitators, pacifist and revolutionary alike, found themselves before the courts charged under the draconian Defence of the Realm legislation and subjected to imprisonment or deportation. Press censorship was equally draconian and the confiscation and suppression of socialist publications was widespread, as the authorities struggled to quell militant anti-war and labour agitation in an effort to prevent it undermining Britain's imperialist war efforts.[69]

BSP internationalists John Maclean and Willie Gallagher, the latter a key figure in the Clyde Workers' Committee (CWC), were among those imprisoned for sedition, while a number of other prominent Clydesiders, including the Socialist Labour Party's Arthur MacManus, were removed from Glasgow to Edinburgh. Sentenced to three years' penal servitude and frequently held in solitary confinement, it would have been remarkable if Maclean, a man dedicated to the cause of revolutionary socialism, had found himself able to comment on the events of Easter 1916 at the time. He did not. It was not until a series of articles in 1919 and 1920 in *The Worker* and *Vanguard*, and in his 1920 pamphlet *The Irish Tragedy: Scotland's Disgrace*, that Maclean's views appear in print.

It is clear from these that Maclean had retained an admiration of Connolly and recognized that the fight for Irish freedom and economic justice were complementary. 'I was naturally desirous at the most suitable opportunity of visiting it to see the results of Easter week 1916 and the fighters who participated in it for Ireland's freedom from Britain and for Labour's emancipation from capital,' he wrote in *The Worker* in August 1919, following a visit to Ireland.[70]

Importantly, Maclean also recognized that Ireland's freedom struggle posed a particular threat to British imperialism and that its success was essential to the success of British labour. Writing in August 1920 on the significance of the Connaught Rangers' mutiny in India, Maclean looked forward to India's independence as 'the only atonement Britain can make for the slaughter and injury ... at Amritsar' and criticized those on the left who had failed to recognize the anti-imperialist implications of Ireland's freedom fight. 'The Irish situation ... is the most revolutionary that has ever arisen in British history, but unfortunately lads who fancy them-selves the only revolutionaries are too stupid or too obsessed with some little crotchet to see the tight corner the Irish are placing Britain in,' wrote Maclean in *The Vanguard*.[71]

Two years later, in his 1922 election address, Maclean was to suggest a link between events in Scotland during the war and the 1916 Rising: 'When Jim Connolly saw how things were going in Edinburgh he resolved on the Easter Rebellion in Dublin, the beginning of Ireland's new fight for freedom,' he declared.[72] Connolly was certainly aware of the great upheavals taking place on the Clyde and had strong contacts with social-ists throughout Scotland as a result of many years of socialist activity on both sides of the Irish Sea. Some writers have even suggested that the Socialist Labour Party, of which Connolly had been a founder member in 1903, was involved in preparations for the Irish Rising, though how far this extended beyond the clandestine printing of the suppressed *Irish Worker* for a few months in 1915 is disputed.[73]

Maclean's inevitably belated endorsements of Connolly's involvement in the Rising have led the Scottish labour historian James D. Young to argue that Maclean's 'retrospective' support for the Rising represented a shift in the Scottish labour leader's position.[74] While lack of evidence resulting from Maclean's confinement makes any clear-cut assertion impossible to prove either way, there is certainly no doubt of Maclean's support for Ireland's freedom struggle from 1919 onwards or that the Irish struggle was absolutely crucial for Maclean, strongly influencing his own individual synthesis of Scottish nationalism and revolutionary socialism.[75]

Young's assertion that Maclean's use of an ultra-pacifist defence at his trial for sedition in 1915 supports his argument for Maclean's 'retrospec-tive' endorsement of the Rising is particularly questionable. Speaking in court in his own defence, it is undeniably true that Maclean stated his opposition 'to the present military system' and his conscientious objec-tion to settling 'national disputes' by military means.[76] However, it is far from clear that this reflected his thoughts on anti-imperialist struggles in the colonies, which he clearly saw as vital in undermining British imperialism. It appears just as likely that his remarks were directed primarily at the inter-imperialist war then raging – and, importantly and understandably, at securing an acquittal, which on that occasion he did.

One of the more curious responses to the Rising was to come from Connolly's former comrades in the once strongly syndicalist Socialist Labour Party of Britain. Connolly had been a founder member of the party in 1903 and although political differences with American SLP leader Daniel De Leon had resulted in a breakdown in relations, a lessening of the British party's tendency towards sectarianism since the start of the war, which the party resolutely opposed, and support for the Irish transport workers in Dublin during the lockout had helped to overcome these divisions.

Leading SLP figures such as Tom Bell and Arthur MacManus had known Connolly for many years and were particularly close to the Irish labour leader. Both had been involved in organizing the clandestine production in Scotland, on SLP presses, and shipment to Ireland of the *Irish Worker* in early 1915. Both were also, along with William Paul and John S. Clarke, part of a small group of SLP militants responsible for producing the SLP's official organ, *The Socialist*.[77]   In his brief history of the Communist Party of Great Britain, published in 1937, Bell stresses the influence the Irish Rising had on the development of the revolutionary movement in Britain: 'The heroic and revolutionary example of Connolly enabled the workers to see with startling clarity the contrast between the devotion, loyalty and self sacrifice of a true son of the exploited class, and the corrupted leaders of the Labour aristocracy.'[78]

It is surprising, therefore, that the first reference to the Rising did not appear in *The Socialist* until June 1916. Even then, it is only mentioned in passing in a short article, the main point of which was to emphasize the state's use of military to defend capitalism, at home and abroad:

> Many young soldiers felt very keenly that they had to fight the Britishers in Dublin. Leaving the merits or demerits of the revolt aside, it will now be realised that armies are the force used by capitalist States to maintain their undisputed sway. Armies are not only used against 'foreigners', they are used against any section that oppose the production of dividends, or cause any friction in the making of profits. Hence armies sent to France, Dardanelles, Persia, Ireland, or the Clyde.[79]

The August edition of the paper continued the theme in a satirical article ('Pro Patria') attributed, possibly pseudonymously, to Henry Lynch. Written in the form of an imagined dialogue between 'a stranger from Arcady' and two representatives of the British ruling class, the writer attempts to expose the latter's idea of patriotism, which the stranger equates to 'defence of British rule' and the financial interests of British capitalism. The 'Sinn Féin' rebellion had to be crushed because it didn't suit 'our English traders', argues the secretary of an imaginary 'Patriotic Club', while his associate, 'Overfed', concludes: 'Ireland could be an independent nation, but so long as the Labour people there were kept under we could always arrange matters with the capitalist class there. That shows the wisdom of shooting as many of the Labour people as possible.'[80]

The most significant reference to the Rising in *The Socialist* was a reprint in its September edition of a damning commentary on Maxwell's official government report into the revolt, which had originally been published in *New Ireland* on 29 July. A footnote from 'The Editor' explains that the report has been included 'in fairness to the Irish rebels' and that the paper's own position on Ireland appears in 'another column'. Unfortunately, there is no trace of this other column in the paper.[81]

Another regular contributor to *The Socialist* was the journalist and historian Richard Michael Fox. Although he went on to write a number of important books about Ireland's freedom struggle, including a history of the ICA and a biography of Connolly, none of the small number of articles mentioning Ireland or the Rising which appeared in *The Socialist* throughout 1916 are attributed to him. However, in his 1937 autobiography, Fox suggests that the Rising had a major impact on his circle of radical London socialists: 'We in North London hailed the Irish Uprising as the first crack in the as yet undisputed rule of the imperialists.'[82] Other revolutionary socialists, including Maclean, had reached a similar conclusion.

There are a number of possible reasons why, despite Connolly's closeness to key figures within the SLP, *The Socialist*'s coverage of the situation in Ireland in the months immediately following the revolt was scant and unsympathetic towards the Irish rebels. The paper's militant labour tendencies and anti-war agitation meant that it was constantly under threat from the authorities, which dismantled and confiscated its presses on a number of occasions and attempted to arrest its main contributors.[83] In the month prior to the Rising, MacManus was one of a number of CWC leaders exiled to Edinburgh. Shortly afterwards Clarke, realizing that it was only a matter of time before he was arrested, went on the run to England. For much of the period between the Irish Rising and the end of the war, the paper was effectively produced clandestinely.[84]

There was also the question of hostility to the nationalist content of the Easter Rising within the SLP, for whom the capitalist class worldwide were the only enemy and industrial unionism the key to socialist advancement. In common with a majority of British socialists, many SLPers lacked a thorough Marxist understanding of the national question, and in particular its relationship to the struggle against British imperialism. That the struggle for national democracy in Ireland was not on the party's political radar was apparent from the SLP's *Manifesto on State Socialism*, published in September 1916, which identified the Belfast working class as 'British'.[85]

Such criticisms could not have been attached to Tommy Jackson, who had become close to the SLP by 1916 after several years as a freelance speaker and Marxist propagandist. Jackson had originally gained an interest in Ireland through his contact with a former comrade of Connolly's, Con Lehane, whom he had met when both had been founder members of the Socialist Party of Great Britain (SPGB), a tiny Marxist sect, which had split from the Social Democratic Federation (SDF) in 1904.

According to the late C. Desmond Greaves, who knew Jackson well, and who contributed an epilogue to the 1971 edition of Jackson's history of the Irish struggle, *Ireland Her Own*, Jackson was 'one of the very few' socialists to understand the significance of the Rising.[86] A regular speaker at the Town Hall Square in Leeds throughout 1916, news of the execution of Connolly spurred Jackson on to mount an emergency platform, from which, in what Greaves describes as 'the most fiery speech of his life', he denounced Connolly's murder: 'I was as good as insane with grief and rage – and, as I still think, justifiably so,' Jackson recalled in his autobiography.[87]

It was to be a far cry from the combination of hostility and lack of interest in the Rising expressed by Jackson's former comrades in the primarily London-based Socialist Party of Great Britain. Born in mid-1904, the party eschewed industrial action while prioritizing electoral activity and Marxist education as means to overthrow the existing system. The party's journal, *Socialist Standard*, had little to say about the Rising. However, it criticized both the 'futility' of the rebels' 'narrow nationalist aims' and the 'utter hopelessness of such a revolt against the mighty organised force of the State'.[88] Socialism alone was worth fighting for, the SPGB journal proclaimed, informing readers that the Rising was 'yet another illustration ... that the organised socialist conquest of the political power of the State is the only way, and that mere mob violence plays into the hands of the oppressor and strengthens the gyves that fetter us'.[89]

The SPGB's analysis stood in stark contrast to the overwhelmingly sympathetic response to the Rising which was to appear in *The Call*, the journal of the anti-war internationalist majority within the BSP, edited by E.C. Fairchild. Although the paper's first edition of May 1916 proclaimed that it was refraining from 'making any exhaustive comment on this latest phase of the war for liberation' (in Ireland), it showed no hesitation in 'fixing the full responsibility for the antecedents of the affair on the shoulders of successive British governments'.[90] However, unlike those socialists who had argued similarly but who then went on to condemn the rebellion, the paper instead demonstrated an understanding of Ireland as a separate nation struggling to free itself from the yoke of imperialist domination, and sought to explain to its readers the link between 'generations of deliberate and ofttimes bloody repression of a freedom-loving people' and 'a hatred of all things English', which 'the average Englishman taught at school to regard Ireland as part of the "United Kingdom" utterly fails to realise'.[91]

The paper's 18 May edition went even further, seeking to explain the rise of Irish nationalism, in its various manifestations, 'as the voice of the most oppressed of modern nations, struggling to be free'. In emphasizing the legitimacy of Ireland's freedom struggle, the paper confronted the arguments of those who had condemned the Rising for being national democratic rather than socialist: 'We do not as Social Democrats here discuss the practical impossibility of the self-contained nation in the capitalist world. Ireland, when she at last becomes a self-directed community, will find the solution to her economic problems. The suppression of Ireland for centuries past is the great outstanding example of an organised attempt to stamp out nationhood.'[92]

To rise without adequate force may have been 'foolish', 'driven by desperation' and 'doomed to failure', but it was, for the BSP internationalists, completely understandable: 'We who are charged, however, with caring nothing for nationality can understand this effort of the Irish people to throw off the alien yoke ... How far from Britain must a nation be in order that the Coalition Government and its supporters shall defend its rights and liberty.'[93]

A week later, the paper declared its support for maintaining the territorial integrity of the Irish nation, arguing that 'no sound argument can be adduced in favour of the exclusion of Ulster'. It also delivered a prescient and dire warning concerning the likely impact a policy based on 'terror and oppression' would have on Britain:

> Martial law in Ireland, though curtailed after a few days' unlimited authority ... will destroy every remnant of regard for the British people held by the Irish. Since England cannot afford to have near her shores a subject colony seething with discontent, all her interests demand the immediate removal of the terror and oppression that found their culmination when men, who should have been regarded as prisoners of war, were shot in cold blood.

Like Maclean, BSP and CWS militant Willie Gallagher was imprisoned at the time of the Rising. Unfortunately, Gallagher's 1936 autobiographical account of the upheavals in Glasgow during the war years, *Revolt on the Clyde*, gives no indication of his response to the events of Easter 1916. It was to be a decade later, in a second autobiographical volume, *The Rolling of the Thunder*, that Gallagher was to write of his 'friendly association' with both the labour and nationalist sides of the Irish movement. It was this relationship which led him to be sent by the Communist Party of Great Britain to warn de Valera and the other Irish leaders that an agreement to divide Ireland was about to be signed by British and Irish representatives negotiating in London. However, although he recalled that 'Collins and the other nationalists had looked to the shop steward movement on the Clyde as allies in their struggle for independence', he provided no further details in his autobiographical works.[94]

Some of the most sympathetic coverage of the rebellion was to be found in the columns of the *Women's Dreadnought*, the suffragette journal edited by Sylvia Pankhurst.[95] A left-wing socialist and suffragette, Pankhurst was a friend and admirer of Connolly's and had shared a number of political platforms with him in both Britain and Ireland. At the outbreak of the Rising, she dispatched Patricia Lynch, a young Cork-born suffragette, to Dublin to report on events. Her eyewitness accounts, published originally in the *Dreadnought*, and later in book form with a preface by Pankhurst, were openly sympathetic to the rebels and exposed British brutality. They were also a journalistic scoop.[96] The paper's coverage was such that it drew the attention of British intelligence, which noted with concern that the 6 May edition of the paper contained 'objectionable matter in favour of the Irish rebels and against conscription'. On the following day it was also noted that 'Miss Lynch ... has declared that she intends to organise a branch of the WSF [Workers' Suffrage Federation] in Ireland'.[97] Two years later, the seven-point programme adopted by the WSF at its annual conference in 1918 would include self-determination for India and Ireland.[98]

Throughout history, British socialists' understanding of, and sympathy for, those Irishmen and women whose objective has been to 'break the connection' with Britain, and who have dedicated themselves to ensuring that Ireland takes its place in the community of nations as a sovereign, independent and united country, has been, at best, faltering and partial. The Irish rebellion of Easter 1916 was to be no exception. That considerable evidence exists to support the commonly held view that many British socialists greeted the events of Easter 1916 with a combination of hostility and bewilderment is not in doubt. However, their reasons for reacting thus were far from uniform and reveal a more complex picture than some historians would have us believe.

While the influence of pacifism among anti-war socialists, and a general hostility towards nationalism across the British left, lay at the heart of much of the condemnation of the Rising and to confusion concerning the participation of Connolly and the Citizen Army, other factors were also at play. Labour Party and trade union leadership support for Britain's war effort between 1914 and 1918 was particularly relevant, as was the inability of all but a small minority of the revolutionary left to see the Irish rebellion as a significant blow against British imperial rule and integral to the struggle for socialism in Ireland.

Although home rule was widely supported throughout the British movement, and condemnation of government policy towards it often unstinting – particularly with regard to the failure of successive governments to implement home rule or to face down Carson's Unionist rebels – it is clear that many British socialists had yet to adopt a thoroughly anti-imperialist critique of British imperialism. For the most part they were also either unaware of, or actively opposed to, Connolly and Lenin's theories, markedly similar but arrived at separately, on the national question. As a result, while home rule was seen as both desirable and acceptable by many British socialists, separation, independence and a break with the empire was not what they had in mind when advocating 'the rights of small nations'. Even among radical and militant socialists, any notion that the national question was integral to the struggle for working-class state power and socialism was not widely accepted by British socialists at the time of the Rising.

For the leadership of the Labour Party and other pro-war elements of the British left, matters were more straightforward. It saw the rebellion as an act of treachery. Its condemnation was an inevitable consequence of its abandonment of the policy of the Socialist International, its embrace of national chauvinism, and its support for Britain's participation in the war. It is hardly surprising, therefore, that the Labour and trade union leaderships went to considerable lengths to ignore the Irish rebellion, so far as that was possible, rather than place themselves in the invidious position of having to justify their actions to a working class which, while not necessarily understanding or supporting the participation of Irish socialists, felt nothing but revulsion at their government's response, in which their leaders were thoroughly implicated.

However, hostility towards nationalism or support for British imperialist objectives was far from being confined to the mainstream of the Labour Party or the pacifist left, as the rampant jingoism and pro-war stance of the BSP leader, Hyndman, clearly indicated. Others from within the British Marxist tradition, such as Connolly's political mentor, Leslie, were among those who rejected Connolly's linking of the fight for social and economic justice with the struggle to free Ireland from British rule.

The attitude of Connolly's former comrades in the Marxist SLP is less clear. This may, at least in part, be explained by the government's use of repressive measures in response to militant labour and anti-war agitation, particularly in Scotland. Although the SLP's newspaper, *The Socialist*, continued to appear regularly, the deportation of its editor and the imprisonment of its business manager highlight the difficult circumstances under which it was produced in this period. However, the absence of any significant commentary on the situation in Ireland in the months following the Rising, or an obituary or appreciation of Connolly, certainly suggest that those responsible for the paper's production in this period were either not overly sympathetic or regarded the Rising as an irrelevance to the class struggle, in which, for the SLP, militant industrial trade unionism remained the priority.

It was among the most staunchly internationalist and anti-imperialist sections of the movement that sympathy and support for the Rising was strongest, although, for objective reasons, including British government attempts to suppress militant labour and anti-war agitation, it was, in some cases, years before this support was publicly recorded. The imprisonment of Maclean and Gallagher, both of whom were on the internationalist wing of the BSP and implacably opposed to Hyndman's pro-war jingoism, effectively prevented them from contributing a contemporary assessment of the Rising – though both were to endorse it retrospectively. Whatever doubts exist as to their exact thoughts on learning of the Rising while in prison, there can be no doubt that *The Call*, the paper of the internationalist wing of the party, came closest to demonstrating that Ireland's struggle to free itself from British imperialism did not represent a negation of the struggle for socialism and working-class state power but was, indeed, integral to that struggle.

Other left-wing internationalists, both inside and outside the Labour Party, including George Lansbury and Sylvia Pankhurst, reached similar conclusions – though possibly more intuitively than through any advanced theoretical understanding of British imperialism or the national question. It was with remarkable clarity that Lansbury reminded British socialists that the 'Irish question' was, essentially, an 'English question' and that the repressive nature of British policy in Ireland would have a corrosive impact on democratic freedoms in Britain. However arrived at, Lansbury's assessment was to retain its relevance throughout the twentieth century and continues to impact on the lives of British and Irish people alike right up to the present day.

NOTES

1. See C. Desmond Greaves, *The Life and Times of James Connolly* (London, 1961); T.A. Jackson, *Ireland Her Own: An outline history of the national struggle for freedom and independence* (London, 1946); W.K. Andersen, *James Connolly and the Irish Left* (Dublin, 1994); Raymond Challinor, *The Origins of British Bolshevism* (London, 1977); Seán O'Casey, *The Story of the Irish Citizen Army* (Dublin, 1919); Brian O'Neill, *Easter Week* (London, 1936); R.M. Fox, *James Connolly: the Forerunner* (Tralee, 1946); Young, 'Easter Rising and Clydeside socialism', in Robert Duncan and Arthur McIvor (eds), *Militant Workers: Labour Class Conflict on the Clyde, 1900–1950* (Edinburgh, 1992); David Howell, *A Lost Left: Three Studies in Socialism and Nationalism* (Manchester, 1986); Donal Nevin, *James Connolly: A Full Life* (Dublin, 2005); Peter Berresford Ellis, *A History of the Irish Working Class* (London, 1972);Geoffrey Bell, *Troublesome*

Business: the Labour Party and the Irish Question (London, 1982).
2. Sidney Webb and Beatrice Webb, *The History of Trade Unionism* (London, 1920); Herbert Tracey (ed.), *The Book of the Labour Party: Its History, Growth, Policy and Leaders* (3 vols, London, 1925); G.D.H. Cole, *A History of the Labour Party from 1914* (London, 1948); Francis Williams, *Fifty Years' March: the Rise of the Labour Party* (London, 1950).
3. Cole, *A History of the Labour Party*, p. 29.
4. Webb and Webb, *The History of Trade Unionism*, pp. 472–4.
5. Webb and Webb, *The History of Trade Unionism*, p. 473.
6. O'Neill, *Easter Week*, p. 87.
7. Jackson, *Ireland Her Own*, p. 401.
8. Ibid.
9. Tracey (ed.), *The Book of the Labour Party*, vol. 1, pp. 202–3.
10. Ibid., p. 203.
11. Palme Dutt, *The Internationale* (London, 1964), p. 131.
12. Quoted in Walter Kendall, *The Revolutionary Movement in Britain, 1900–21: The Origins of British Communism* (London, 1969), p. 50.
13. A.L. Morton and G. Tate, *The British Labour Movement 1770–1920* (New York, 1957), p. 256.
14. *Irish Worker*, 26 September 1914, quoted in Nevin, *James Connolly*, p. 517.
15. *Forward*, 4, 11 & 25 September 1920.
16. Hansard, 1916, vol. 86, cols 626–7. Quoted in Bell, *Troublesome Business*, pp. 34–5.
17. Ibid., cols 734–5. Quoted in Bell, *Troublesome Business*, p. 36.
18. *Daily News*, 19 May 1916, quoted in Berresford Ellis, *A History of the Irish Working Class*, pp. 231–2.
19. *Labour Year Book*, 1916.
20. *Labour Year Book*, 1917.
21. *Labour Year Book*, 1917.
22. Michael Mallin, Connolly's ICA deputy and a former secretary of the Silk Weavers' Union, was executed on 8 May. Peadar O'Maicin (Painters' Society and vice president of Dublin Trades Council), Richard O'Carroll, Ernest Cavanagh and Sean Connolly were among those who died during the fighting. Another ITGWU and ICA stalwart, William Partridge, court-martialled and sentenced to fifteen years' imprisonment, was released from Dartmoor prison, suffering from Bright's disease, in April 1917. He died on 26 July 1917. Thomas Foran, Cathal O'Shannon, P.T. Daly, William O'Brien and Michael Mullen were among those to have 'served long or short terms of imprisonment or internment after the insurrection'. W.P. Ryan, *The Irish Labour Movement from the Twenties to Our Own Day* (Dublin, 1919), pp. 248–50.
23. 1916 Trades Union Congress report, pp. 181–2.
24. 1918 Trades Union Congress report, pp. 290–4.
25. See Brock Millman, *Managing Dissent in First World War Britain* (London, 2000), pp. 111–12.
26. 1918 Trades Union Congress report.
27. *Forward*, 27 May–8 July 1911.
28. Letter to William O'Brien, quoted in Nevin, *James Connolly*, p. 505.
29. *Irish Worker*, 26 September, 1914, quoted in Nevin, *James Connolly*, p. 517.
30. *Labour Leader*, 27 April 1916.
31. *Labour Leader*, 27 April 1916.
32. *Labour Leader*, 4 May 1916.
33. *Labour Leader*, 11 May 1916.
34. *Labour Leader*, 18 May 1916.
35. *Labour Leader*, 29 June 1916.
36. Independent Labour Party Annual Conference Report, 1917.
37. Independent Labour Party Annual Conference Report, 1917.
38. *Socialist Review*, August–September 1916.
39. Hyland, Eva Gore Booth, 'Irishwoman in Manchester', *North West Labour History*, no. 16 (1991–2).
40. *Socialist Review*, August–September 1916.
41. Sehri Saklatvala, *The Fifth Commandment* (Salford, 1991), p. 89; Joyce M. Bellamy and John Saville (eds), *Dictionary of Labour Biography* (vol. X, London), pp. 150–6.
42. A.L. Horner, *Incorrigible Rebel* (London, 1960), pp. 25–6.
43. Ibid.
44. *Forward*, 6 May 1916.

45. Ibid., 13 May 1916.
46. Ibid.
47. Ibid., 17 June 1916.
48. *The Plebs*, vol. 5 (June 1916).
49. Ibid.
50. Ibid.
51. Ibid.
52. *Justice*, 18 May 1916.
53. Ibid.
54. Ibid., 4 May 1916.
55. *The Clarion*, 31 March 1916.
56. Ibid., 26 May 1916.
57. Ibid., 9 June 1916.
58. O'Casey, *The Story of the Irish Citizen Army*, p. 65.
59. O'Casey, *The Story of the Irish Citizen Army*, p. 65.
60. Published originally in *Sbornik Sotsial-Democrata*, no. 1 (October 1916); see also Lenin, *Collected Works*, vol. 22, pp. 353–8; D.R. O'Connor Lysaght (ed.), *The Communists and the Irish Revolution* (Dublin, 1993), pp. 61–5.
61. *The Herald*, 13 May–2 December 1916.
62. Ibid., 27 May 1916.
63. Ibid., 8 July 1916.
64. Ibid.
65. Ibid.
66. Ibid.
67. Ibid., 2 December 1916.
68. Morton and Tate, *The British Labour Movement*, p. 260.
69. For a detailed account see Millman, *Managing Dissent*.
70. *The Worker*, 23 August 1919. Quoted in Nan Milton, *John MacLean: In the Rapids of Revolution* (London, 1973), p. 161.
71. Quoted in Milton, *John MacLean*, p. 177.
72. Quoted in ibid., p. 74.
73. See Thomas Bell, *Pioneering Days* (London, 1941), p. 38; Challinor, *The Origins of British Bolshevism*, p. 127; and Young, 'Easter Rising and Clydeside Socialism', pp. 165–6.
74. Young, 'Easter Rising and Clydeside Socialism', pp. 155–75.
75. For example, see Howell, *A Lost Left*, pp. 211–16.
76. Quoted in Milton, *John MacLean*, p. 93.
77. Raymond Challinor, *John S. Clarke: Parliamentarian, Poet, Lion-Tamer* (London, 1977), p. 37.
78. Tom Bell, *The British Communist Party: A Short History* (London, 1937), p. 34.
79. *The Socialist*, June 1916.
80. *The Socialist*, August 1916.
81. *The Socialist*, September 1916.
82. R.M. Fox, *Smoky Crusade* (London, 1937), p. 216.
83. Challinor, *John S. Clarke*, p. 37.
84. Ibid.
85. *The Socialist*, September 1916.
86. Greaves, *The Life and Times of James Connolly*, p. 423.
87. T.A. Jackson, *Solo Trumpet: Some Memories of a Socialist Agitator and Propagandist* (London, 1953), p. 127.
88. *Socialist Standard*, May 1916.
89. Ibid.
90. *The Call*, 4 May 1916.
91. Ibid.
92. Ibid., 18 May 1916.
93. Ibid.
94. William Gallagher, *The Rolling of the Thunder* (1947), pp. 54–6.
95. Quoted in Challinor, *The Origins of British Bolshevism*, p. 168.
96. Mary Davis, 'Class, Race and Gender', Sylvia Pankhurst Memorial Lecture, 2003.
97. National Archives: Secret Service files KV2/1570/88656 & KV2/1570/108227.
98. *Workers' Dreadnought*, 1 June 1918. Quoted in Tony Cliff, *Class Struggle and Women's Liberation: 1640 to today* (London, 1984).

5

Who Fears to Speak of Easter Week? Antipodean Irish Catholic Responses to the 1916 Rising

Rory Sweetman

News of the Easter Rising came as a terrible shock to the Irish abroad. In the midst of the Great War Irish rebels had apparently stabbed the British empire in the back by launching a rebellion with German aid. In the antipodes, leading Catholics rushed to deliver horrified public denunciations of the 'made-in-Germany rebellion', its treacherous leaders and their deluded followers. However, six years later New Zealand Catholics were to adopt a very different stance when one of their own leaders was put on trial for his allegedly seditious opinions on the Rising. During his offending speech, on St Patrick's Day 1922 in the Auckland Town Hall, Bishop James Liston spoke of 'that glorious Easter' and lauded those Irishmen who he claimed had then and since been 'murdered by foreign troops'.[1] Following an overwhelmingly hostile public outcry the Catholic community rapidly mobilized in Liston's support, even threatening to offer physical resistance should he be convicted and jailed. This chapter attempts to explain that dramatic change in attitude by assessing how the largely Irish-descended Catholics in the southern hemisphere coped with the fallout from the Irish revolution.

The meaning of the 1916 Rising in Australian Catholic history has been skilfully teased out by Patrick O'Farrell in his various writings.[2] There was regular conflict over matters Irish in nineteenth-century Australia between the Catholic community and a colonial establishment that O'Farrell has described as anti-Catholic and anti-Irish. He identifies the tactic usually adopted by the Catholics as minimizing, forgetting or evading the Irish issue. So it was again after the Rising, he argues, with a reluctant and indifferent Catholic laity forced to cope with the accidental and misleading prominence of Ireland. In fact, their real concerns were local and immediate, while the major questions at issue were Australian ones.[3]

Why the Irish issue became so prominent despite this policy of non-provocation was partly a result of woolly thinking by those who assumed a close connection between Irish and Australian events (principally the Easter Rising and the defeat of conscription) because of simple chronology. Ireland was also invoked by those seeking to inflate the importance of petty local concerns, and by others who genuinely believed that Irish issues mattered in antipodean politics.[4] But, for O'Farrell, it was largely due to pushy Irish priests, most fairly recent immigrants, personified by the dominant and inescapable Daniel Mannix, Catholic archbishop of Melbourne (1917–63). Provoked in turn by Mannix, there were some who found Ireland a useful stick with which to beat their Catholic enemies.[5]

This refusal by both friend and enemy to allow antipodean Catholics to evade or minimize the Irish issue had an interesting consequence. The combination of local questioning of Catholic loyalty, repressive British policies in Ireland and the forceful lead offered by Daniel Mannix and his New Zealand equivalent, Dr James Kelly, led eventually to a belated and reluctant embrace of the advanced Irish nationalist case. On both sides of the Tasman Sea the 1916 Rising was reinterpreted by an increasingly alienated Catholic body as a symbol of their current dilemma, wrestling with minority status in an hysterically pro-British colony.

The Irish issue was a perennial difficulty for the Catholic Church in New Zealand given its strong Irish identity and the divisive effect of Irish politics.[6] The din of battle in Ireland in the nineteenth century was often heard at the antipodes. A comic opera 'Fenian Rising' took place on the west coast of New Zealand's South Island in 1868, while the violence associated with the Irish Land War in the 1880s divided even the Catholic community.[7] Making up only one-seventh of New Zealand's population, and mostly Irish by birth or descent, Catholics were in a vulnerable position in the furthest flung of Britain's colonies.[8] They were to be found largely in the humbler occupations and had few representatives in positions of authority. From the turn of the century their leaders decided that gentle persuasion, rather than aggressive demand, was the order of the day in pursuing Catholic social, political and educational rights.[9] The Catholic bishops supported compulsory military training, condemned socialism, and trumpeted their imperial loyalties.

The foremost exponent of this art of accommodation was Henry William Cleary, editor of the sole Catholic journal, the *New Zealand Tablet* (1898–1910) and subsequently bishop of Auckland (1910–29).[10] Wexford-born, with Australian pastoral experience, Cleary was well suited to cope with the thorny Irish issue. He had shown marked skill as a controversialist in his early career.[11] Always careful to stress the unifying potential of Ireland's national struggle, he organized the commemoration of the centenary of the 1798 rebellion, encouraging the enthusiastic participation of Irish Protestant clergymen. Cleary wanted unity in Irish ranks at home as well as abroad. In December 1898 he wrote to the Irish politician John Dillon of the need to 'put an end to a disunion which has been the despair of our people in these colonies for many years past ... I have not permitted the insertion [in the *Tablet*] of any letters, news, or correspondence that could create divisions on the question of Irish politics.'[12]

Such policies helped to soothe colonial fears of the threat to imperial unity posed by Irish home rule. The friendly reception accorded to successive Irish parliamentary delegations in 1907, 1911 and 1914 was in stark contrast to the hostility that greeted the Redmond brothers in 1883.[13] The visitors, generally on fund-raising tours, were careful to cut the cloth of Irish political ambitions to a colonial measure. With the re-emergence of home rule as a live political issue after the elections of 1910, Ireland again dominated the cable news. Each act in the lengthy drama was closely followed in New Zealand. The coincidence of Irishmen – William Ferguson Massey (Reform) and Sir Joseph Ward (Liberal) – leading New Zealand's major political parties led to a careful choice of words.[14] There was vocal and influential colonial backing for the Ulster resistance to home rule, but when real war broke out in August 1914 the local partisans quickly sank their differences in a chorus of patriotic harmony.[15]

Support for Irish home rule allowed antipodean-born Catholics to reconcile their dual loyalties, to embrace both the British and Irish cultural traditions in which they had been reared. They saw a future self-governing Ireland as happily integrated into the British empire. While the great celebrations planned to welcome the arrival of Irish self-government were postponed indefinitely, the passage of the Third Home Rule Act in September 1914 allowed its colonial supporters to add their collective voice to the praise of empire. Indeed, there were widespread predictions that the Irish question would be solved on the western front as the adherents of Orange and Green fought side by side. The First World War gave the colonial Irish the perfect opportunity to prove the worth of their loyal professions, and the New Zealand Catholic community went to war with gusto.[16] Its leaders spoke in favour of conscription, once they were assured of the effective exemption of their clergy and religious.[17] Bishop Henry Cleary spent the grim winter of 1916–17 in the Flanders trenches as an army chaplain and wrote lyrically of the unity he witnessed there between Irish Catholic and Protestant, nationalist and unionist.[18]

As in Britain, the first anniversary of the declaration of war saw the creation of a coalition government in New Zealand, with Sir Joseph Ward (a Catholic) restored to power as Massey's deputy.[19] Until 1916, Ward's outspoken imperialism and the well-advertised response of the Catholic community to Britain's cause were more than sufficient to offset the contagion of alleged Irish and Catholic disloyalty overseas. However, as in Australia, the material for a future conflagration was all there. By late 1916 resentment at the Catholic Federation's aggressive campaign for state funding for private schools, suspicions of papal neutrality or even pro-Germanism, and of Catholic disloyalty in Australia and Canada meant that community camaraderie was wearing thin.[20] As war weariness grew and casualty lists lengthened, a search for scapegoats began. The *New Zealand Tablet* was kept busy refuting claims of inadequate Irish recruiting figures, while the visit of a papal delegate provoked the first outburst of local bigotry that would scar the New Zealand body politic for the next decade.[21]

After the Easter Rising the Irish issue was added to a long list of alleged misdeeds by Catholics against the British empire. The *Bible Standard* spelt out some of these in November 1916. 'It is sufficient to call attention to the open rebellion in Ireland, in which priests figured as leaders of disaffection, to the fact that the South of Ireland is far behind Ulster in the proportion of volunteers for service, and to the further fact that the Clerical Party in Canada openly counsels the French-Canadians against enlistment, and ... is openly fomenting rebellious sentiments ... [to see that] Popery is pro-German and anti-British at the present crisis.'[22] That same month saw Archbishop Patrick Delany of Hobart describe the changed atmosphere that had developed in Australia to his friend Henry Cleary.

> At first the war seemed to have the effect of cooling domestic friction. Now it would seem as if the nervous tension occasioned by the state of war was seeking relief in a recrudescence of home quarrels. I think the Orange and Protestant Alliance parties are if anything more bitter than before. The wish to see Ireland and the Holy See shown up in the most unfavourable light is ever more and more in evidence.[23]

All this helps to explain the public fury at the news of the Easter Rising and the shocked response of antipodean Catholics. At a stroke the Irish issue was revived in all its nineteenth-century divisiveness. The result was an isolated and embittered Catholic body, stung by a colonial establishment which discounted its loyalty. Despite recent claims that the First World War 'served firmly to incorporate ... [the] Irish into the New Zealand nation', the stresses of world conflict not only ruined the chances of a peaceful resolution to the Anglo-Irish problem but also left those who sympathized with Irish national aspirations in Britain's colonies feeling alienated and deeply aggrieved.[24]

While early reports of the 1916 Rising in the New Zealand newspapers referred dismissively to the outbreak of 'riots' in Dublin, the note of condemnation grew much shriller as the extent of the violence and of German involvement became clear. The overseas cables linked Zeppelin raids and a planned naval assault on England with the capture of 20,000 German rifles off the Kerry coast as part of a co-ordinated enemy attack. There were also stories of 'Sinn Féiners' shooting at unarmed civilians, including women and children, on the streets of Ireland's capital. The public outrage that such reports evoked was well reflected in the stance adopted by most newspaper editors. According to the *New Zealand Herald*, the rebels were

> manifestly without any idealistic inspiration ... The wholesale robberies, the callous murders, show us what sort of men were engaged in this mad outbreak ... [The Rising] was destructive, not constructive; the craving for loot, and not the love of freedom, evidently sustained its instigators and inflamed its dupes.[25]

The *Dunedin Evening Star* denounced the Rising as a 'villainous stab in the back', and noted of the executed rebel leaders: 'so may all traitors perish'.[26] To the *Otago Daily Times* the insurrection represented 'black treachery almost at the very heart of the Empire', carried out by men who should have 'betaken themselves to some other part of the world, and to the refuge of some citizenship other than British'.

> Far better it had been that these Sinn Féiners and their dupes had been openly serving in the armies of Germany than that in this treacherous manner, while enjoying all the privileges of British rule, they should have fallen upon and shed the blood of countrymen of themselves and of the soldiers who have been contributing to their immunity from attack and from servitude from a foreign yoke.[27]

The severe tone of New Zealand's dailies reflected the hostile and somewhat confused cable news, which drew deeply on British conservative press sources.[28] The label 'Sinn Féiner', though inaccurate, was, as O'Farrell notes, 'an ideal term of abuse, with its foreign sound and connotations'.[29] James Connolly's involvement meant that the Rising could be portrayed as a socialist or syndicalist outbreak, tainted by the anarchism of the Dublin labour troubles of 1913. Nevertheless, there was a widespread refusal to believe in fundamental Irish disloyalty to the empire. The Anglican primate, Bishop Nevill, made sympathetic references to Irish patriotism at the general synod at Christchurch, while Prime Minister Massey, after expressing 'shock and disappointment' at the Rising, insisted that 'the huge majority of the Irish are intensely loyal, and will prove their loyalty before the trouble goes far'.[30]

The hostile public response to the Rising was echoed in the Catholic community. Gathered in Auckland for their annual general meeting, the leaders of the Hibernian Australasian Catholic Benefit Society greeted news of the outbreak with surprise, confusion and horror.

> On one of the cross roads a member of the party read out from the evening paper the deplorable news. The faces of those present were a study, each one betraying intense emotion. It was resolved before they left the spot on the cross roads that the first business to be transacted,

when the conference reassembled in the evening, would be to draft
and forward a cable message of support to Mr John E Redmond.[31]

There followed the litany of reactions that O'Farrell has identified in
Australian Catholic circles – disgust, shame and a sense of personal
betrayal, culminating in an anguished repudiation.[32] Leading New Zealand
Catholics clamoured to condemn the rebels and to reaffirm their belief in
Irish constitutionalism. Loud assertions of loyalty to Britain were accompanied by an insistence that the real Irish patriots were to be found in France
and Flanders.[33] Some commentators even tried to turn the Rising into proof
of Irish Catholic loyalty to the British empire. Was it not 'the splendid loyalty and steadfastness of the Irish people that really saved the situation and
proved the complete undoing of German hopes and schemes?'[34]

Unlike the Australian Catholic bishops, who trenchantly denounced
the Rising, the hierarchy in New Zealand was silent on the subject.[35] Not
so the *New Zealand Tablet*, the church's 'sole organ', which immediately
condemned the 'made-in-Germany rebellion' as an 'insane plot' led by
nonentities, with the deluded 'Sinn Féiners' as its 'tools and victims'. It
was at pains to stress that Sir Roger Casement, 'the *fons et origo* of the trouble', was a Protestant ('not a follower of the dominant religion of Ireland')
and had been a perennial troublemaker in Irish nationalist circles. 'This
wretched being', clearly 'an out-and-out traitor', was probably insane.[36]

The *Tablet*'s other main scapegoat, James Connolly, had also been
allegedly infected by revolutionary American ideas (syndicalism) and was
dismissed as 'a bitter assailant of the Catholic Church'.[37] Nor were the rank
and file considered to be any more impressive or representative. 'The misguided movement had behind it neither the spirit of Irish nationality nor
of Irish faith.' Had not the Sinn Féiners constantly 'thwarted and opposed,
and bitterly and venomously denounced, the Nationalist Party'? The *Tablet*
was utterly baffled by the Rising. 'Insane in its leader, it was insane also in
its conception, possessing no definite objective, and having, of course, no
possibility of success.'[38] It took comfort in the disclaimers of the Irish overseas, especially the condemnations by the Australian bishops.[39]

Monsignor James Coffey, the senior priest of Dunedin diocese, was most
outspoken in his censure of the 'riotous outbreak'. In his Sunday sermon on
30 April he denounced the Sinn Féin movement as anti-clerical and anti-
national, predicting that 'no man of standing or influence in the country
would be found in the ranks of the rioters'.[40] A day earlier at a public meeting of 'representative Irishmen' in Dunedin, the Tipperary-born Coffey had
thrown his considerable weight behind John Redmond and called for
increased volunteering in New Zealand by his fellow-countrymen 'to show
that the hearts of Irishmen throughout the Empire were sound'. Other
speakers at the meeting regretted 'the criminal and insane action of the
Sinn Féiners and their dupes', whose only result was 'to bring their country

into disgrace'. The Rising was minimized as 'an insignificant, though ugly, speck on the face of that magnificent pile of patriotism which the true Irish nation has built up during this war'.[41] There was plenty of evidence to confirm O'Farrell's view that Catholic resentment in New Zealand, as in Australia, arose largely from concern about the local implications of the Rising, which had painted all Irish colonials as potentially disloyal.

How to explain so similar a response? At the start both Catholic and non-Catholic readers were drawing from the same sources, largely the confused and fragmentary cable news. While this would change, as the Irish Catholic overseas press reported events more fully and as letters and newspapers arrived from Ireland describing the reality of the situation, the initial antipodean Catholic hostility to the Rising accurately reflected attitudes in Ireland.[42] There was also a deep colonial investment in Irish constitutional nationalism, a belief in what Redmond saw as the 'union of hearts' between Ireland and Britain, and a determination to win the war 'in defence of right, of freedom and religion'.[43] In July 1916 pride in the Catholic war sacrifice was deepened by the heavy losses in the Battle of the Somme. New Zealand Catholics did not need reminding of the price of their loyalty, as the faces of their dead sons stared out of each weekly issue of the *Tablet*.[44]

Nevertheless, by late 1916 there was a distinct shift in antipodean Catholic attitudes. O'Farrell deems it anachronistic to attribute decisive importance to the Rising in this transformation, as until at least 1918 it was seen as a clear failure.[45] However, glorious failure was an Irish nationalist tradition; also, it was not so much the Rising that soured colonial Irish opinion as the subsequent British repression. Few argued that the principal rebels did not deserve their grisly fate, but the nature and extent of the British execution policy caused considerable disquiet. Once the Rising's leaders were shot there came a search for someone else to blame. While this did not mean approval of the rebels or their actions, Catholics grew increasingly critical of British policy before, during and after the Rising. The Asquith government's initial failure to challenge Ulster Unionist resistance to home rule became a focus of Catholic commentary, as did the numerous acts of crown brutality during the suppression of the Rising.[46]

The long-drawn-out executions and numerous arrests and deportations of suspected rebel sympathizers were deeply unpopular; still more so the brutal murder by British forces of the pacifist Francis Sheehy Skeffington and several civilians in North King Street, Dublin.[47] There was justice in John Dillon's bitter complaint in the House of Commons that the government's policy was 'washing out our whole life work in a sea of blood'.[48] Meanwhile, Irish journals had begun to report on the piety and pure lives of the rebel leaders and the heroism with which they met their death. Henceforth colonial attacks on the rebels would draw a defence fuelled by reports of a sea change in Irish opinion. Catholic indignation in New Zealand was sharpened by Bishop Henry Cleary's detailed eyewitness accounts of post-Rising Dublin, published in the *New Zealand Tablet*.[49] Cleary described the rise of Sinn Féin sentiment in Ireland and the growing public realization of the Redmondites' failure, not least in seeming to endorse the partition of Ireland in the abortive post-Rising negotiations over home rule. One can chart the change in attitude in the cable sent to Ireland by New Zealand Hibernians in September, which protested about British policy in Ireland and demanded immediate Irish home rule.[50]

The role of the Catholic clergy in the rebellion became a matter of dispute in late May 1916 after reports that priestly sympathy for Sinn Féin was behind much of the trouble in Ireland.[51] At the public meeting of 'representative Irishmen' held in Dunedin, Monsignor Coffey made it clear where the local Catholic clergy stood on the Rising.

> All the priests here regretted exceedingly that this thing had happened, and though they could not be present, they were in accord with the spirit of the meeting. Every priest in Dunedin, except two, had brothers at the front, where they were doing their duty either as chaplains or as combatant soldiers – and the two exceptions had no brothers.[52]

However, his fellow priests soon made Coffey aware of their unhappiness with the 'jingoistic' approach of the *Tablet* and its editor on the Irish question.[53] With a studied disregard for the censor, Fr James Prendergast (Palmerston North) poured out his feelings on the dead rebels in a letter to John Dillon. 'These fellows laid down their lives for a cause, no matter how mistaken they were. We only judge their motives and their name and fame will never die in Ireland's memory. I can't get their deaths out of my mind, even so far away.'[54] Other Catholic priests could not suppress their indignation with British policy. When Dean Patrick Power (Hawera) declared in the *Taranaki Daily News* that the British government had to 'repair the havoc wrought by English Huns in Dublin', he sparked off a furious press debate and found himself reported to the Defence Department for disloyalty.[55] Power was informed by an angry correspondent that Irishmen had 'something to wipe off the slate' after the insurrection by 'the irresponsible Dublin mob … [with] pockets filled with German gold'.[56]

As managing director of the *Tablet*, James Coffey had to cope with an increasingly hostile New Zealand press, puzzled and outraged in equal measure by the rise of Sinn Féin in Ireland. Immediately after the Rising, Coffey had expressed appreciation of 'the just and liberal spirit of the press in not stirring up ill-feeling or striving to make political capital out of a very regrettable incident'.[57] This initial press reticence was partly due to Prime Minister William Massey's habitual circumspection on the

Irish issue, in sharp contrast to his Australian counterpart, William Hughes, who led what amounted to a personal crusade against Sinn Féin.[58] It was not long, however, before the columnists and correspondents began to take aim at nationalist Ireland. As Coffey later explained to Bishop Cleary: 'Any attempt to explain the rising of Easter or any kind word for the poor fellows who were driven to their death was scoffed at and ridiculed. No man could keep his patience under such taunting.'[59]

This sort of provocation was deeply offensive to many New Zealand Catholics, already aggrieved over the public reluctance to recognize their war sacrifice, the brusque rejection of their claims for educational state aid, and a general sense of social exclusion. The refusal to tolerate any deviation from the narrow definition of loyalty prescribed by the Anglophile establishment was demonstrated by the argument in Christchurch over the Dublin Relief Fund. Set up in late 1916 to collect money for alleviating the distress caused by the Irish insurrection,[60] the fund's patronage by Bishop Brodie drew the fire of the *Christchurch Press*, which denounced it as unnecessary and pernicious.[61] Brodie responded with a defiance that delighted his new flock. A protest meeting was held at which he called for a Catholic boycott of the offending organ. While his argument with the *Press* was against what he saw as that paper's 'oppression of the poor', rather than any defence of Irish rebellion, the support Brodie received revealed the Catholic community's shift in attitude over the Irish issue.[62]

O'Farrell has noted how various Australian groups attempted to use the Irish issue for their own purposes; this was equally true of New Zealand. As Redmondism lost momentum, its former colonial supporters began to respond to those expressing more radical Irish views, notably the newly-formed New Zealand Labour Party, the burgeoning network of Maoriland Irish Society branches, and a coterie of Irish-born priests led by the irrepressible Dr James Kelly, nephew of the archbishop of Sydney.

In Australia, Irishness and Catholicism had long been identified with left-wing politics. While the New Zealand Labour Party (NZLP) had strong evangelical roots, its birth in the middle of the Great War contributed to the party's early sympathy for radical Irish nationalism. The bitterly-fought wartime issues of conscription, sectarianism and Ireland soon helped to forge an informal electoral alliance between the Catholic community and the NZLP, latent in 1919 but fairly overt by 1922. Labour's organ, the *Maoriland Worker*, was exceptional among the New Zealand press in its refusal to condemn the Easter Rising.[63] Its editor and the NZLP's first leader, Harry Holland, then published a year-long series of articles attempting to explain the historical background to the insurrection.[64] He was impressed by the heroism of James Connolly, and by the promise of social reform carried by both the proclamation of the Irish republic and Sinn Féin's 'Democratic Programme'. From 1917, Holland regularly toured the country lecturing on the Irish question, while Labour politicians attended and spoke at Irish gatherings like the Dublin Relief Fund meeting in Christchurch.

While O'Farrell is unsure whether Harry Holland first took up the Irish issue with an eye to the votes it would attract, Richard Davis has argued persuasively that militant Labour had adopted this very tactic before the war.[65] There were good reasons to do so; the Irish Catholic community was largely working class with a strong group identity, particularly on the west coast and in the cities where the infant Labour Party had its roots. For the NZLP, Ireland was at once an advertisement for the evils of imperialism, the hypocrisy of the Allied war aims, and the need for national self-determination. Its opposition to conscription in New Zealand could be defended by reference to the 100,000 British soldiers stationed in Ireland. Over the next few deeply troubled years the NZLP was encouraged to support Sinn Féin by the example of its Australian and British counterparts.[66]

After 1919, facing a Liberal Party without its long-time Catholic leader, the NZLP clearly felt that by vigorously supporting Irish self-determination, and by advertising its rival's failure to follow suit, it would draw the Catholic vote to itself on a permanent basis.[67] The *New Zealand Tablet* was delighted by the NZLP's approach to the Irish question, having frequently condemned Ward's 'faineant silence' and declaring him to be 'almost as culpable as Mr Massey' for ignoring the call to promote Irish self-determination.[68] Labour was prepared to do what Ward would not.

> Holland and Fraser could be always trusted to stand up and speak out for one of the small nations for which so many brave boys were sent to die. If we have not commented oftener on what they have done for the Irish cause it is not due to any lack of appreciation and gratitude. We are their debtors, as is every Irishman, and every man of Irish blood in New Zealand, and we do not forget it.[69]

Others felt differently about Labour's Irish policy. When questioned on his attitude towards Ireland during the 1919 election campaign, C.F. Bennett, the Reform candidate, replied that he was 'standing for the loyal electorate of Auckland West and not for Cork or Tipperary'.[70] The Reform member for Roskill, W.H. Potter, declared that the British government had been too lenient on the 'murderous and rotten crowd' of Sinn Féin.[71] Some local councils refused to allow the use of their public halls by the itinerant Labour lecturers. After Peter Fraser had held a meeting in Hawera in March 1921, the secretary of the local Political Reform League informed Prime Minister Massey of widespread resentment at 'the base tactics adopted by the Labour Party in dealing with the Irish question'.[72] To further infuriate such critics, reward for the NZLP's 'Irish campaign' soon came in the shape of Catholic votes, which helped to return Labour members in increasing numbers at both the 1919 and 1922 elections.

In the final months of 1916 the establishment of a number of Irish clubs, which federated as the Maoriland Irish Society, was another Catholic expression of concern with the unhappy state of Irish affairs.[73] The society's newspaper, the *Green Ray*, voiced republican sentiments for eighteen months before its suppression by the government in mid-1918. Dunedin-based, and a lay rather than clerical initiative, the *Ray* boasted of its non-sectarian stance.[74] Its occasional criticism of Catholic bishops for being insufficiently vocal on the Irish issue did not prevent the *Ray* from building a close working relationship with those priests who led the cheering for Sinn Féin.[75] (One can contrast the Sydney-based Irish National Association, which was kept at arm's length by the Catholic Church.)[76] The *Ray*'s strong Labour orientation backs up O'Farrell's claim that militant republicanism drew most support from the Irish-born, especially the more recent immigrants, and from the working class.

From March 1917, with the appointment of Dr James Kelly as editor of the *New Zealand Tablet*, the traditional clerical lead in antipodean Irish affairs was resumed. The Wexford-born priest would become the chief means whereby Catholic indignation over the treatment of Ireland was communicated to the New Zealand public. Kelly was a reluctant emigrant, an Irish Irelander deeply involved in the cultural resurgence associated with the Gaelic revival.[77] During 1915–16 he had been assisting the ailing *Tablet* editor, John Askew Scott, although as he noted wryly to an Irish friend: 'They will not allow me to write on the war owing to my having revealed tendencies to show fair play.'[78] While Kelly was one of the very few people in New Zealand who saw that there was another side to the war, it was his trenchantly expressed Irish political views that immediately drew public attention. For Kelly, Irish history was 'one long arraignment' of England, a country that Irishmen had 'every reason to curse'.[79] He was to re-fight all of nationalist Ireland's lost battles in his editorial columns: the Treaty of Limerick, the Famine, Fenianism and the Land War were his constant points of reference. In early 1918 his feelings on the bloody geography of Irish history were expressed in a moving tribute to Thomas Ashe, the Sinn Féiner who died on hunger strike.

> We have personal knowledge of how vividly the wrongs of Ireland have sunk into the souls of the people as a consequence of years of inhuman persecution. We have lived in a county where the name of every townland was a reminder of a burned chapel, of a murdered priest, of massacred children, or of violated women. The memories of these crimes have been too well accentuated to allow them to die.[80]

Kelly had initially dismissed the Easter Rising as 'mad, bad and sad', although adding that 'Maxwellian monstrosities made heroes of those who were only fools.'[81] However, the second *Tablet* issue under his editorship contained a defence of the 1916 leaders, who 'died like men, bearing the punishment for the faults of all'.[82] This redemptive interpretation was to become familiar to *Tablet* readers over the next five years. Pearse, Connolly and their colleagues were not rebels, 'for the simple reason that no Irishman is loyal to England'.[83] Rather, Kelly maintained, they were 'brave men who gladly laid down their lives to regenerate Ireland'.[84] Their executioner, General Maxwell, had 'fashioned a shrine in the heart of every true Irishman'.[85] The Sinn Féin party, as legatee of those who 'saved the soul of Irish nationality', was to be encouraged to take up its inheritance.[86]

Kelly came to Dunedin determined to change the policy of the 'sole organ of the Catholic Church in New Zealand'. His opinion of his predecessor was predictably severe. 'Before I came here the *Tablet* was edited by a convert and his Imperialistic views and general indifference to Irish questions did the paper much harm.'[87] He was also keen to pay back those responsible for the sniping press attacks on Ireland, the pope and Catholic loyalty since the war began. The sneers of Ireland's enemies demanded an equal assertion of Irish rectitude.[88] He soon took aim at the local columnists 'Civis' (*Otago Daily Times*) and 'Ariel' (*Dunedin Evening Star*), conducting a vicious slanging match with the former. When 'Civis' described Sir Roger Casement as 'Judas Iscariot', Kelly replied with a reference to Queen Victoria as 'a certain fat, old, German woman'.[89] Kelly's anti-British diatribes were so savage that after only nine issues from his pen New Zealand's solicitor-general advised his government to suppress the *Tablet* and prosecute its editor for sedition.[90]

Some historians have interpreted Kelly's appointment as evidence that the hierarchy intended to provoke a collision with the state.[91] In fact, by early 1917 the bishops were urging caution in Catholic public utterances, and specifically the avoidance of intemperate attacks on the government.[92] They were becoming (rather belatedly) aware of the danger of appearing to put sectional interests before the national good and to take advantage of the war crisis. Given this background, the hierarchy blundered badly by entrusting its newspaper to an Irish priest for whom the idea of conciliating the enemies of Ireland and Catholicism was a 'heresy'.[93] This is not to suggest that Kelly was completely unrepresentative. As soon became evident, he had a strong group of clerical and lay supporters, some of whom had lobbied vigorously for a change of *Tablet* policy. James Coffey later explained to an irate Bishop Cleary that ' before he [Kelly] came down here he was urged by the vast majority of the priests to adopt a strong aggressive policy. In fact they told him as some of them told myself that if the *Tablet* did not drop its jingoism they would turn it out of their parishes.'[94]

Who were these priests? Michael Sheahan, a prominent Auckland Hibernian reluctant to desert Redmondism, described them as young, recent arrivals from Ireland.[95] While the brief colonial experience of the Irish clergy was a factor in their response to the thwarting of their political desires, both in Ireland and New Zealand, they also included many senior priests who could boast a long colonial residence.[96] The identity of Irish and Catholic interests was axiomatic for these men, their Irish patriotism 'almost a second conscience'.[97] In his call to arms Kelly made no differentiation: 'As you are Irish, as you are Catholics … there must be no sin of patience and no scandal of content so long as the wrongs of Ireland or … of our Church remain unrighted. These two causes must come first … for God's sake and for Ireland's.'[98]

What motivated these men and their supporters? O'Farrell is convinced that Ireland was more a symbolic than a real issue, and that Australian Catholics used its emotional potential 'to attach feelings of additional passionate intensity to causes much closer to home – the place of Catholics in the community, the state recognition of Catholic educational claims, the conduct of the war effort'. Ireland itself was not at stake, he insists.[99] Ireland may indeed have become the symbol of local Catholic grievances in New Zealand, but James Kelly deliberately fomented and agitated these grievances in order to recruit support for Irish national self-determination. His early sympathy with the rebels and anger at British policy in Ireland soon turned into an uncritical commitment to Sinn Féin. The future of Ireland was very much at stake for Kelly, whose primary goal was to enlist antipodean Catholics in her national struggle.

He did this by exploiting bitter local arguments over conscription, education and sectarianism. The crisis over clergy conscription, which blew up just as Kelly took over as *Tablet* editor, was the perfect issue with which to radicalize his readership, to hammer home the need for unity and defiance against the enemies of Catholicism and of Ireland – 'which is the same thing', Kelly asserted.[100] He interpreted the government's mishandling of clerical exemption from conscription as deliberate persecution and was blunt in threatening all manner of opposition. 'We have protested and if necessary will prove our earnestness in a manner this Dominion will never forget … The priests will not go; and our people have a habit of defending their priests.'[101] When the exigencies of the conscription issue demanded a switch from indignation to diplomacy, the bishops were to find that it was no easy task to control their tyro editor.[102]

Kelly's highly coloured version of Irish history shaped his understanding of current events in Ireland and the lessons he drew from them for the readers of the *Tablet*. 'Remember that at the root of the wrongs of Ireland is the same cause to which we owe our wrongs here; hatred for

Catholics that stops at no injustice, and shrinks from no dishonour.'[103] He consistently read New Zealand events in Irish terms.

> For us the lesson comes from Ireland: Ourselves Alone! Catholics have long endured their wrongs in silence, being urged thereto by politicians for ends best known to themselves; and we know with what fruits! We believe that the heresy of conciliation is as dead in New Zealand as it is in Ireland or Australia and that Catholics will henceforth fight for their rights. There is no other way left.[104]

For Kelly, the post-1916 fight for Irish independence was 1798 revisited, with the vital difference that this second conflict would dissolve the legislative union between Ireland and England so shamefully created by the first. Familiar with the Sinn Féin movement since its inception, Kelly was delighted to witness its supercession of the Irish Parliamentary Party. The series of Sinn Féin victories in by-elections during 1917 began with the return of Count Plunkett at North Roscommon just after Kelly was appointed as editor.[105] Most subsequent *Tablet* issues contained material explaining the Sinn Féin view on Irish politics, often drawn directly from Irish publications.[106] 'Knowing Ireland and being in constant touch', Kelly was able to interpret the complexity of Irish political developments for his colonial audience.[107] He presented Sinn Féin's success as both a legitimation of the Easter Rising and a response to historic British repression.

> Again, we are told to forget the past. The past! We might forget the Treaty Stone, or the roasting of Father Murphy, but the deeds of the Scottish Borderers in 1914 and the unpunished murders of Colthurst are too close to warrant any hopes on our part that the policy has altered.[108]

Kelly was ecstatic over Sinn Féin's electoral victory in December 1918. 'The end of the year has brought our justification. The lying press that told its readers constantly that the Sinn Féin movement did not represent the Irish people has had its answer now.'[109] He grew increasingly furious after Dáil Éireann was suppressed and Ireland began to slide into the violence of the Anglo-Irish War (1919–21). Irish realities were finally catching up with Kelly's imagination – a brutally repressive Britain and a local administration that was targeting Catholic interests.[110] Whatever consolation he took from the fact that Irish events had turned out as he predicted, conferring what O'Farrell calls 'the accolades of according with Irish reality',[111] was offset by the maddening indifference of his colonial audience.[112] Kelly's passionate desire to play a part in the Irish struggle was matched by a determination that New Zealand Catholics should recognize their obligation to follow suit. He wanted to stir up sufficient anger at British 'perfidy and oppression' among his readers to move them to united action. 'Do not weep for Erin,' he urged, rather ask 'what are we going to do to save her?'[113] American and Australian events set Kelly a pattern and a model. He cited the numerous demands from organizations and public meetings throughout the British empire for an end to martial law and an immediate grant of home rule, furious that alone of the self-governing dominions New Zealand had failed to raise its voice.[114] In mid-1921 he expressed the fear that 'the last Black and Tan will have been driven out of Ireland while we are dreaming and we shall have had no share in the deliverance'.[115]

Kelly was no diehard republican. On his arrival at the *Tablet*, he wrote that 'even now, if the Irish got Home Rule they would be the most loyal subjects in the Empire'. Until 1921 he repeatedly insisted that Ireland had not yet been offered dominion home rule. Kelly occasionally adopted the tactic of Tighe Ryan, editor of the *Catholic Press* (Sydney), in blaming a Tory reactionary clique in Britain for the Irish imbroglio, but was much closer to the approach of Daniel Mannix, arch provocateur on Irish issues. Mannix and Kelly represented the radical new thinking that had emerged in nationalist Ireland as home rule was outmanoeuvred by Ulster and British politicians. In 1913, they had both left a resurgent Catholic Ireland for what they regarded as a benighted British Protestant colony, in which their co-religionists were apparently enduring second-class citizenship. Both men were eager to challenge this dispensation. Mannix perfected his own forms of provocation, referring to the European conflict as a 'sordid trade war', opposing conscription, and openly supporting Sinn Féin. His speeches were given full space in the *Tablet*. Indeed, Mannix was Kelly's shield against his Catholic critics, the archbishop of Melbourne being 'found as unpatriotic and undignified as ourselves'.[116]

O'Farrell has noted 'the decisive influence of the Australian Catholic episcopacy on Irish nationalist organisation and commitment'. While Mannix stimulated Irish republican sentiments in Victoria, his counterpart in Sydney, James Kelly's uncle Michael, had a 'vigorously repressive effect' on them in New South Wales. However, 'once liberated and encouraged [in Victoria] … they were impossible to repress totally elsewhere'.[117] Without Mannix's lead, O'Farrell argues, the Irish independence issue 'would have received small attention in Australia'.[118] The same could be said of James Kelly and New Zealand. From late 1917, moreover, every step that Kelly took to raise Catholic support for Sinn Féin in New Zealand was fiercely resisted by his fellow-Wexfordman, Henry Cleary, who preferred his priests and people to pray for Ireland rather than campaign for her. He ordered that no flag, emblem, symbol or motto 'calculated to cause ill-feeling' was to be displayed at any Catholic concert, procession or sports meeting in Auckland. The clergy were instructed to ensure that the national anthem ('God save the King') be played at every Catholic function.[119] Cleary also attempted to 'sanitize' the St Patrick's Day celebrations by avoiding the passage of fiery resolutions on Ireland.[120] The climate created by Kelly's furious denunciations of *seoninism* forced Cleary to adopt devious tactics to insulate his diocese from the divisive effects of Irish politics.[121] Kelly refused to appreciate the prudential reasons that motivated Cleary, commenting tartly: 'We want no traitors in the movement.'[122]

Despite such opposition, under James Kelly's able generalship the New Zealand Catholic community stood up to be counted for Ireland. Although never able to force through a parliamentary resolution in favour of Irish self-determination, Kelly managed to orchestrate an impressive number of inspired resolutions and well-attended meetings. Some £6,000 was dispatched back to Ireland. He helped to radicalize the Hibernians, the Catholic Federation, the Irish Self-Determination League, and a legion of St Patrick's Day celebration committees. The new sense of defiance felt by the Catholic body was reflected in booming *Tablet* subscriptions, and the flood of supportive letters received by Bishop Liston after his St Patrick's Day speech in 1922 on the Irish question.[123] The bitter argument up and down New Zealand over his use of the phrase 'that glorious Easter' revealed the gulf in understanding between Catholics and their fellow New Zealanders and was as much a tribute to Kelly's success in educating his Catholic readers as it was an indication of his failure to persuade the wider community of the legitimacy of Irish nationalist claims.

Far from being 'incorporated into the New Zealand nation',[124] the Irish Catholic community emerged from the world conflict as an embittered and isolated faction, disappointed by lack of recognition of its wartime blood sacrifice, in retreat from organized anti-Catholicism, and fearful of the depredations of a hostile government. But many of its leaders believed that the same spirit that saw Irish-descended Catholics stand up for Irish self-determination would ensure the survival and progress of their minority faith, adrift in a sea of Protestantism half the world away from Ireland.

NOTES

1. Rory Sweetman, *Bishop in the Dock: The Sedition Trial of James Liston in New Zealand* (Dublin, 2006).
2. Patrick O'Farrell, *The Irish in Australia* (Sydney, 2006); *Vanished Kingdoms: Irish in Australia and New Zealand* (Sydney, 1990); *The Catholic Church and Community in Australia* (Melbourne, 1977); 'The Irish Republican Brotherhood in Australia: the 1918 Internments', in Oliver MacDonagh, W.F. Mandle and Pauric Travers (eds), *Irish Culture and Nationalism 1750–1950* (London, 1983), pp. 182–93.
3. O'Farrell, *The Irish in Australia*, pp. 252–64.
4. Ibid., pp. 270–3.
5. Ibid., pp. 260–1. See also O'Farrell, *The Catholic Church and Community*, Chapter 5.
6. Rory Sweetman, 'The Furthest Outpost of an Irish Empire: Catholicism in Colonial New Zealand,' in Colin Barr (ed.), *Creating Ireland's Empire: the Catholic Church in the English-speaking World, 1830–1921* (Dublin, forthcoming).
7. David McGill, *The Lion and the Wolfhound* (Wellington, 1990). But see *New Zealand Listener*, 21 January 1991, p. 82.
8. Donald Harman Akenson, *Half the World from Home: Perspectives on the Irish in New Zealand 1860–1950* (Wellington, 1990), Chapter 3.

9. Rory Sweetman, '"How to behave among Protestants": Varieties of Irish Catholic Leadership in Colonial New Zealand,' in Brad Patterson (ed.), *The Irish in New Zealand: Historical Contexts and Perspectives* (Wellington, 2002), pp. 89–101.

10. Rory Sweetman, 'Cleary, Henry William, 1859–1929', *Dictionary of New Zealand Biography, vol. 3 (1901–1920)* (Auckland, 1996), pp. 101–3.

11. His first book, *The Orange Society* (Melbourne, 1897), went through eleven editions on its publication. He refuted well-worn tales of 'Irish outrages' in *An Impeached Nation* (Dunedin, 1909).

12. Cleary to Dillon, 21 December 1898, Dillon papers, Trinity College Dublin (TCD).

13. Richard Davis, *Irish Issues in New Zealand Politics 1868–1922* (Dunedin, 1974), pp. 102–4.

14. Rory Sweetman, 'Massey and Sectarianism', in Lachy Cameron and James Wilson (eds), *Massey: A Reappraisal* (Dunedin, forthcoming). Ward was born in Australia to an Irish mother. Michael Bassett, *Sir Joseph Ward: A Political Biography* (Auckland, 1993).

15. Prominent citizens in Wellington cabled their sympathy to Carson. *New Zealand Tablet*, 5 October 1916.

16. Monsignor James Coffey (Dunedin) had great hopes of this flowering of Catholic loyalty to the empire. He wrote of 'the silver lining that may be seen through the dark war cloud which hangs above. The patriotism of Catholics is clearly seen in ... their willingness to fight for a King who is a Protestant while the Protestants say they would dethrone their King if he became a Catholic ... This is seen and must produce its effect.' James Coffey to P.J. O'Regan, 1 August 1916, O'Regan papers, Alexander Turnbull Library (ATL), Wellington.

17. James Allen to W.F. Massey, 19 December 1916, Allen papers, National Archives [NA], Wellington; *New Zealand Tablet*, 21 December 1916.

18. *New Zealand Tablet*, 20 July 1916, 28 September 1916, 8 February 1917.

19. The two Irishmen were dubbed the 'Siamese twins' so inseparable were they to become over the next four years. Ward's position was a guarantee to the Catholic hierarchy that its vital interests would be protected.

20. Rory Sweetman, 'New Zealand Catholicism, War, Politics and the Irish Issue 1912–22', PhD thesis, University of Cambridge (1991), Chapter 5. See also Hugh Laracy, 'Priests, People and Patriotism: New Zealand Catholics and War, 1914–1918,' *Australasian Catholic Record*, lxx, 1 (January 1993), pp. 14–26.

21. Harold Moores, 'The Rise of the Protestant Political Association: Sectarianism in New Zealand Politics during World War 1', MA thesis, University of Auckland (1966), pp. 114–20.

22. *Bible Standard* (November 1916), cited in Moores, 'The Rise of the Protestant Political Association', p. 139.

23. Delany to Cleary, 18 November 1916, Cleary papers, Auckland Catholic Diocesan Archives (ACDA).

24. Jock Philips, 'Race and New Zealand National Identity', in Neil Garnham and Keith Jeffery (eds), *Culture, Place and Identity* (Dublin, 2005), p. 175.

25. *New Zealand Herald*, 2 May 1916.

26. *Dunedin Evening Star*, 4 May 1916. The *Otago Daily Times* (8 May 1916) agreed: 'These men took up arms in the most treacherous way against their countrymen, carrying their disloyalty to British rule to the most extreme point in co–operation with the active and unscrupulous enemy of their nation. There can be no question of vindictiveness on the part of the authorities in dealing with traitors of this character.'

27. *Otago Daily Times*, 2 May 1916. See Daniel Lark, 'Sectarianism in the South: Dunedin's reaction to Ireland's Troubles', BA (hons) research essay, University of Otago (2006).

28. 'Definite, detailed, and coherent information regarding the actual outbreak and early course of the Irish rising trickles through to us only in very small driblets,' the *New Zealand Tablet* admitted on 18 May 1916.

29. O'Farrell, *The Irish in Australia*, p. 272.

30. *New Zealand Tablet*, 4 May 1916. Massey called for a strong hand to be used in repressing the Rising and for the traitors to get their just desserts. The *Otago Daily Times* (28 April 1916) also did not believe that the existence of a 'nest of traitors' in Ireland indicated disloyalty among the people as a whole.

31. 'The New Zealand Hibernians at their annual conference, now sitting in Auckland, have learned with abhorrence and regret of the disturbances in Dublin; also, they desire to express their deep sympathy with, and entire confidence in you, the Irish Party, and followers.' *New Zealand Tablet*, 4 May 1916.

32. O'Farrell, *The Irish in Australia*, p. 259.

33. 'The world is not likely to forget, as Ireland's set-off, the magnificent loyalty of the Irish peo-
    ple as a whole, nor the glorious valour of her troops on every front on which they have been
    employed.' *New Zealand Tablet*, 4 May 1916.
34. *New Zealand Tablet*, 11 May 1916.
35. O'Farrell, *The Catholic Church and Community in Australia*, p. 323. Henry Cleary, the usual epis-
    copal spokesman on Irish issues in New Zealand, was away in Europe. Bishop Verdon was ill.
    Bishops Redwood, O'Shea and Brodie appear not to have made any public comment.
36. The *Tablet* added a brief account of Casement's pro-German activities and his involvement
    with the Irish-American Clan na Gael. *New Zealand Tablet*, 4 May 1916.
37. *Tablet* editor, John Askew Scott, was virulently anti-socialist.
38. *New Zealand Tablet*, 4 May 1916.
39. Archbishop Carr (Melbourne) also called the Rising 'an outbreak of madness'. *New Zealand
    Tablet*, 4 May 1916.
40. *New Zealand Tablet*, 4 May 1916.
41. Ibid.
42. The immediate response to the Rising by various Irish newspapers was reproduced in the
    New Zealand Tablet, 6 July 1916.
43. *Freeman's Journal* (Dublin), 21 September 1914.
44. The *Tablet* made no charge for preparing photographic blocks for the families of the dead sol-
    diers.
45. O'Farrell, *Irish in Australia*, p. 271.
46. See *New Zealand Tablet*, May–September 1916. Charles Townshend, 'The Suppression of the
    Easter Rising', *Bullán*, 1, 1 (1994), pp. 27–47.
47. The *Tablet* constantly referred to the Sheehy Skeffington case. In his recent study of the
    Rising, Charles Townshend glosses over the North King Street murders as 'perhaps
    inevitable in fighting of such claustrophobic intensity'. *Easter 1916* (London, 2006), pp.
    206–7. New Zealand Catholics were also upset by the suspicious shooting of Fr Felix Watters,
    a Marist priest with a distinguished record of service in the antipodes. *New Zealand Tablet*, 18
    May 1916, 6 July 1916.
48. F.S.L. Lyons, *John Dillon: A Biography* (London, 1968), p. 381. The *Tablet* published a garbled
    version of Dillon's speech on 18 May 1916, and a correct one on 22 June 1916.
49. *New Zealand Tablet*, 21 September 1916, 28 September 1916. Other New Zealand priest vis-
    itors confirmed much of Cleary's analysis of the Irish political scene. *New Zealand Tablet*, 21
    December 1916.
50. *New Zealand Tablet*, 28 September 1916. P.J. O'Regan, a prominent Irish New Zealander who
    felt that the Rising had been 'most unwise and inexpedient in every respect', reminded a
    Hibernian gathering of the pre-war unanimity afforded to Carson and his party. *New Zealand
    Tablet*, 5 October 1916.
51. This stemmed from Augustine Birrell's statement to the Hardinge Commission that 'if the
    priests are anti-Sinn Féiners, Sinn Féinism dies out; if the clergy foster Sinn Féinism, it is
    promoted and extended.' *Otago Daily Times*, 22 May 1916. The *Tablet* had already confidently
    predicted that 'when the full story of the rebellion is told it will assuredly be found that the
    Church has exerted a wholesome and salutary influence throughout the whole of this very
    serious trouble'. *New Zealand Tablet*, 11 May 1916.
52. *New Zealand Tablet*, 4 May 1916.
53. Coffey to Cleary, 24 November 1917, Cleary papers, ACDA.
54. Prendergast to Dillon, 21 June 1916, Dillon papers, TCD.
55. *Taranaki Daily News*, 22 August 1916.
56. *Taranaki Daily News*, 24 August 1916. A police investigation of Power's alleged anti-war ser-
    mons ended with the assurance of Inspector Wilson that the dean was 'a most loyal subject'.
    Wilson to police commissioner, 6 September 1916, 10/4/11, NA.
57. *New Zealand Tablet*, 4 May 1916.
58. Sweetman, 'Massey and Sectarianism'. For Hughes on the importance of the Irish question
    in imperial (and Australian) politics, *New Zealand Tablet*, 2 November 1916. See also John B
    O'Brien, 'The Irish Revolutionary Movement and W.M. Hughes: 1916–1922', in Tadhg Foley
    and Fiona Bateman (eds), *Irish-Australian Studies* (Sydney, 2000), pp. 138–50.
59. Coffey to Cleary, 24 November 1917, Cleary papers, ACDA.
60. Archbishop Walsh of Dublin launched the initial appeal in August 1916, which was taken up
    enthusiastically in Australia and the US. As O'Farrell notes, fund-raising shifted attention
    from the rebellion to the distressful condition of the Irish people through the destruction

caused by the suppression of the Rising. O'Farrell, *Irish in Australia*, p. 266.

61. The *Press* wondered if the funds would be put to disloyal use in Ireland.

62. *New Zealand Tablet*, 2 November 1916. Brodie to P.J. O'Regan, 2 November 1916, O'Regan papers, ATL. Brodie was of Irish parentage and had a full share of patriotic piety, yet he could see the danger to Catholic interests of association with Irish political extremism. Like his mentor, Henry Cleary, Brodie tempered his Irish patriotism with an awareness of what was politically wise. Brodie to Canon Cotter, 30 July 1920, Brodie papers, Christchurch Catholic Diocesan Archives.

63. *Maoriland Worker*, 17 May 1916.

64. *Maoriland Worker*, 24 May 1916 until 2 May 1917.

65. Patrick O'Farrell, *Harry Holland: Militant Socialist* (Canberra, 1964), p. 94. Davis, *Irish Issues in New Zealand Politics*, p. 190.

66. The British Labour Party also conducted a 'Peace with Ireland Campaign' in 1920–21, involving public meetings, questions in the House of Commons, and a Commission of Inquiry to Ireland. D.G. Boyce, *Englishmen and Irish Troubles: British Public Opinion and the Making of Irish Policy 1918–22* (London, 1972), pp. 62–3.

67. Ward lost his seat in the 1919 election. H.E. Holland, *How the Liberals Voted* (Wellington, 1928).

68. *New Zealand Tablet*, 20 March 1919.

69. *New Zealand Tablet*, 24 February 1921. The Scots-born Peter Fraser also took the lead in Labour's 'Irish campaign'. R.P. Davis, 'The New Zealand Labour Party's "Irish Campaign" 1916–1921', *Political Science*, 19, 2 (December 1967), pp. 13–23.

70. *New Zealand Herald*, 3 December 1919.

71. *Auckland Star*, 1 December 1920.

72. Whyte to Massey, 29 March 1921, Massey papers, NA.

73. Davis, *Irish Issues in New Zealand Politics*, p. 196; Sean Brosnahan, 'Shaming the Shoneens: The *Green Ray* and the Maoriland Irish Society in Dunedin, 1916–22', in Lyndon Fraser (ed.), *A Distant Shore: Irish Migration and New Zealand Settlement* (Dunedin, 2000), pp. 117–34.

74. These claims did not fool Acting Prime Minister Sir James Allen, who referred to the *Green Ray* as 'a publication of the Roman Catholics'. Allen to Massey, 6 July 1918, Allen papers, NA. The *Green Ray*'s first issue was advertised in the *New Zealand Tablet* (30 November 1916).

75. Rather than a rival, the *Green Ray* was an additional outlet for James Kelly. This belief worked in the *New Zealand Tablet* editor's favour as the *Ray*'s head was probably offered to placate his enemies. Sweetman, 'New Zealand Catholicism', pp. 205–6.

76. O'Farrell, *Irish in Australia*, p. 257.

77. Born on the banks of the Barrow, in a county scarred by the bloody events of 1798, Kelly saw parallels between that event and the current state of Ireland *(New Zealand Tablet*, 25 October 1917). He was a regular reader of D.P. Moran's *Leader*, which aimed to revive the Irish national spirit and resist the encroachment of Anglicization.

78. James Kelly to John Hagan, 16 February 1916, HAG 1/1916/33, Irish College, Rome [ICR].

79. *New Zealand Tablet*, 26 July 1917.

80. *New Zealand Tablet*, 3 January 1918.

81. James Kelly to M.J. O'Connor, 27 June 1916, HAG 1/1916/86, ICR.

82. *New Zealand Tablet*, 8 March 1917.

83. *New Zealand Tablet*, 25 May 1917.

84. *New Zealand Tablet*, 4 October 1917.

85. *New Zealand Tablet*, 11 October 1917.

86. *New Zealand Tablet*, 24 May 1917.

87. The *Tablet* had been losing money, declining in circulation and, according to Kelly, was 'hardly read at all even by the subscribers'. James Kelly to John Hagan, 16 May 1918, HAG 1/1918/25, ICR.

88. Liston and Coffey later told Cleary how bitter, frequent and unprovoked these had been. Coffey to Cleary, 24 November 1917; Liston to Cleary, 25 November 1917, Cleary papers, ACDA.

89. 'A certain fat old German woman begged her British Ministers to let the Kaiser have Heligoland, and there were tears in her eyes when she prayed that Germany might not be molested when seizing on Schleswig-Holstein. Chickens do come home to roost. War was declared on the twenty-fourth anniversary of the cession of Heligoland.' *New Zealand Tablet*, 1 November 1917.

90. Salmond to attorney general, 9 May 1917, Opinion Book 1917, Crown Law Office, Wellington. The national government did not accept this advice.

91. Davis, *Irish Issue in New Zealand Politics*, p. 204.
92. See Redwood and O'Shea's letters to Monsignor Mahoney, 22 January 1917, Cleary papers, ACDA.
93. *New Zealand Tablet*, 22 November 1917. Bishops Verdon, O'Shea and Redwood had to approve Kelly's appointment. His earlier fiery Irish articles should have been sufficient warning. *New Zealand Tablet*, 27 July 1916, 3 August 1916, 31 August 1916.
94. Coffey to Cleary, 24 November 1917, Cleary papers, ACDA.
95. Sheahan described Kelly as 'an out and out Sinn Féiner who has poisoned the minds' of *Tablet* readers. Sheahan to Dillon, 15 November 1918, Dillon papers, TCD.
96. See Dean Patrick Power's fiery letter on Irish partition, *New Zealand Tablet*, 10 August 1916.
97. *New Zealand Tablet*, 3 January 1918.
98. *New Zealand Tablet*, 26 April 1917.
99. O'Farrell, *Irish in Australia*, p. 253.
100. Kelly to John Hagan, 22 December 1917, HAG 1/1917/95, ICR.
101. *New Zealand Tablet*, 8 March 1917.
102. Kelly confessed rather to 'an unholy joy' at the turn events had taken and was confident that it spelled the end of 'the idiotic policy of conciliation'. Kelly to John Hagan, 14 September 1917, HAG 1/1917/74, ICR. See P.S. O'Connor, 'Storm over the Clergy – New Zealand 1917', *Journal of Religious History*, 4, 2 (1968), pp. 129–48.
103. *New Zealand Tablet*, 3 May 1917.
104. *New Zealand Tablet*, 18 October 1917.
105. For Kelly's jubilant reaction, see *New Zealand Tablet*, 12 April 1917.
106. He regularly cited the *Catholic Bulletin*, *Nationality*, the *Leader*, *New Ireland*, and the *Irish Bulletin*, as well as various American and Australian Catholic papers. He presented a less partial view of the war by using critical British sources like the *New Witness*, the *Nation*, the *Glasgow Observer*, and *Stead's Review*.
107. *New Zealand Tablet*, 8 November 1917.
108. *New Zealand Tablet*, 29 March 1917.
109. *New Zealand Tablet*, 26 December 1918.
110. Massey's Reform Party was returned in the 1919 general election and began to grant a number of the anti-Catholic wishes of the Protestant Political Association. Sweetman, 'New Zealand Catholicism', Chapter 10.
111. O'Farrell, *Irish in Australia*, p. 259.
112. He blamed a 'hireling press' which deliberately hid the truth about Ireland. 'There is a conspiracy against Ireland, and it extends to every daily paper published in this Dominion. We do not mean to say that all the dailies are anti-Irish, but we do say that the cable service doled out to them is rigged by anti-Irish and anti-Catholic agencies. In view of the lies spread here by that means there is hardly a week that it is not imperative to state at length the true facts regarding which garbled versions are disseminated here.' *New Zealand Tablet*, 18 August 1919.
113. *New Zealand Tablet*, 3 May 1917.
114. *New Zealand Tablet*, 21 March 1917. A motion in favour of Irish home rule was passed by the Australian federal parliament in March 1917.
115. *New Zealand Tablet*, 30 June 1921.
116. 'In a word my policy is that of Dr Mannix and the opposition is exactly like that which he met with and from the same sources.' James Kelly to John Hagan, 16 May 1918, HAG 1/1918/25, ICR.
117. O'Farrell, *Irish in Australia*, pp. 260–1.
118. Mannix 'both allowed and forced developments whose relative extremism was abnormal to the Australian situation'. O'Farrell, *Irish in Australia*, p. 261.
119. Cleary to Auckland Catholic clergy, 11 August 1919, Cleary papers, ACDA.
120. Cleary to Auckland Catholic clergy, 14 March 1921, Cleary papers, ACDA. When Cleary appeared on the platform of the visiting Prince of Wales in 1920, Kelly retorted that 'no true Irishman – no matter what his position or obligations – should have taken any part in the celebrations as long as England is carrying out systematic Prussianism in Ireland.' *New Zealand Tablet*, 3 June 1920.
121. Sweetman, 'New Zealand Catholicism', Chapter 11.
122. *New Zealand Tablet*, 15 April 1920.
123. Sweetman, *Bishop in the Dock*, Chapter 7.
124. Jock Philips, 'Race and New Zealand National Identity', p. 175.

6

The Wilson Administration and the 1916 Rising

Bernadette Whelan

Woodrow Wilson's interest in the Irish question was shaped by many forces; his Ulster-Scots lineage, political science background and admiration for British Prime Minister William Gladstone's support for home rule. In his pre-presidential and presidential years, Wilson favoured a constitutional solution in Ireland but did not anticipate having to deal with foreign affairs during his tenure. This chapter assesses Wilson's reaction to the radicalization of Irish nationalism with the outbreak of the Rising in April 1916. It will also examine the response of the State Department and the consequences of the Rising for the Wilson presidency.

On the eve of the Rising, the First World War was in its third year, as was Wilson's neutrality policy. In this decision he had the support of the majority of nationalist Irish-Americans who were not members of Irish-American political organizations but were loyal to the Democratic Party.[1] Until the outbreak of the war in 1914, the main Irish-American political organizations, Clan na Gael (CNG) and the United Irish League of America, had been declining in size. In August 1914, however, CNG, with Joseph McGarrity on the executive committee, shared the Irish Republican Brotherhood's (IRB) view that 'England's difficulty is Ireland's opportunity' and assisted plans for an uprising in Ireland against British rule. Immediately they reverted to their traditional strategy of internationalizing the Irish question and hoped to reap the benefits from strategic alliances with the German-American community and representatives of the German government.[2]

By 1916 the small group of 'professional Irish politicians', as British Ambassador Spring Rice termed men like John Devoy and Daniel Cohalan in New York, Joseph McGarrity in Philadelphia and John T. Ryan in Buffalo (a member of the Revolutionary Directory of CNG), were hopeful that their German contacts would aid the IRB-planned rebellion in Ireland.[3] Certainly they were vocal, unyielding and prominent in their pro-German sympathies, but they were not representative of Catholic

Irish-Americans. Most may not have been pro-British but were not pro-German either, particularly after a U-Boat sank the *Lusitania* in May 1915. While the British and American secret services targeted the radicals' activities, events in Ireland altered the quiescent attitude of the majority of Irish-American nationalists and forced Wilson to clarify his views on Ireland.

The Rising went ahead on 24 April 1916 but it was limited to a few areas, particularly Dublin, due to confusion about mobilization orders. Within five days the leaders had been arrested, along with approximately 3,500 others. An estimated 450 people had died and 2,614 were wounded.[4] Nonetheless, the short and long-term consequences reverberated in different ways throughout US politics, in the press and with the public. How did the State Department respond to these challenges?

There were three US consuls assigned to Ireland in 1916; Edward Adams in Dublin, Hunter Sharp in Belfast and Wesley Frost in the Cork office at Queenstown (Cobh). They were responsible to Consul General Robert Skinner and Ambassador Walter Page based in London.[5] When the Rising broke out in Dublin, not one US consul informed the State Department and it was summer before the matter was investigated in the Consular Bureau. Herbert Hengstler minuted on 21 August that the office had received 'nothing about the Rising' from 'Belfast, Dublin or Cork'. The following day, Bureau Director Wilbur Carr could not understand the failure of the consuls in Ireland to report either to the department or to the London embassy on recent 'occurrences' in their districts. He instructed the consuls to explain their 'failure to report'.[6]

The report on the Rising from Adams was dated 29 November and reached Washington the following month. It indicated that when the fighting broke out on Easter Monday he had been six miles away, at home with his son in Ross's hotel, Kingstown, county Dublin. His vice-consul, John Claffey, lived in Lindsay Road, Glasnevin, which was closer to the city. In the following days, neither man was exempt from the travel restrictions placed on people due to the imposition of martial law. Claffey reached the consular office at 9 Leinster Street on 27 April 'by going from doorway to doorway', and he went there again on 2 May with permission from the military authorities. Yet it took Adams until 8 May to resume work in the office. On 25 April, he was prevented at gunpoint from going into the city to secure a pass to exempt him from the regulations. Twice in the following days he was refused a pass and on 3 May he was even barred from returning home for a short while. Adams did not complain about his treatment to any official but instead patiently waited to get permission. When he obtained a pass on 4 May, some of the soldiers at the checkpoints refused to acknowledge it and to allow him passage into the city centre.[7] By the time his thirty-four-page, factual, day-by-day,

account reached the State Department in December 1916, it was of little use. Adams attributed the delay in sending his report to the work
involved in procuring accurate information, the tardiness in obtaining
official statistics and the burden of 'additional, general work incidental to
the Rebellion and its resultant investigations, correspondence, etc'.[8]

It was clear from the report submitted by Adams that much of it was
culled from official publications and that he had little understanding of
the reasons for the Rising. Indeed, he claimed that the 'behaviour of the
troops ... is exemplary in every respect. Even when suffering from unfair
attack ... the men conduct themselves with remarkable patience and
restraint'. He admitted being frightened by the 'alarming' events, particularly the shooting, fighting, rioting, burning and looting.[9] Adams insisted
that when Claffey reached the office on 27 April, 'naturally, no business
could be transacted' and that during his second visit on 2 May, the vice-
consul telephoned to say that there were 'no important matters for attention'.[10] When Adams finally reached the office on 4 May, he found that
post had not been delivered, the telephone and telegraph service was
under military control and he left for Kingstown.[11] Notwithstanding such
assertions, Adams did in fact conduct diplomatic business during the
Rising which could have been immediately reported to Washington.

The report from Belfast was markedly different. Hunter Sharp told
the State Department on 15 September that, 'not having any knowledge
of the existence of political disturbances in my consular district, during
the period mentioned', he contacted the commissioner of the Royal Irish
Constabulary (RIC). The commissioner confirmed that 'there had been
no political trouble in Ulster' during the previous five months and that
the 'general conditions of the province had been quite normal'. On 26
May Sharp received a query from Ambassador Page in London as to
whether one Peter Fox, a US citizen arrested during the Rising, was registered at the Belfast consulate.[12] Sharp replied that Fox was not on his
register of American citizens but that he had been arrested at
Carrickmore, county Tyrone, as a 'Sinn Féiner and Irish Volunteer'.[13]
Even though the Rising did not spread to Ulster, Fox was one of 1,500
people rounded up by the RIC in Sharp's consular district on Easter
Tuesday, 25 April. Of those rounded up, 300 were arrested, 136 sent to
Dublin prisons and the rest incarcerated in other parts of the country.
The fate of US citizens arrested will be examined later. When, on 22
September, Sharp filed a report titled 'Political conditions in Ireland', it
began with an examination of the failure of the 'disastrous rising'. His
unionist proclivities were signalled by his evident support for the view-
point of Ulster's 'leaders'.[14]

When Wesley Frost in Queenstown got around on 14 October to reply-
ing to Carr's instruction, he explained that, being without a vice-consul,

he was not obliged to submit political reports. Moreover, he had no contacts with the insurrectionary movement and his town was free of 'trouble'. Even so, his eighty-four-page report detailed significant rebellious
activity in his consular district, including observations that a company of
Scots Guards had taken charge of Queenstown rail station. He also noted
that a 'powerful' dreadnought had been brought to Queenstown harbour
and anchored up the River Lee towards Cork 'in readiness to shell the
city if necessary'.[15] He provided personal experience of the 'oppressive'
policing of the country at the time: 'From this window of this consulate
can be seen two plain-clothes men of the force, and another is on duty at
the railway station 200 yards away, while there are always a score of uni-
formed men on duty in this town of 8,000 persons.' He believed that the
rise of the Sinn Féin movement was assisted by a 'ponderable quantity of
Irish-American money' and a 'little German-American money' but the
'stertorous plaint of "American dollars" appears entirely unjustifiable'.
However, it was the section headed the 'Dublin insurrection – execution
of leaders' that was marked in the State Department:

> There was an abundance of explosive material (figuratively, not liter-
> ally) for the insurrection ... The German plan in aid of Casement fur-
> nished the detonating stroke, through the mechanism of the Irish-
> German agencies in America. America's responsibility, while techni-
> cally nil, must from a practical or moral standpoint be recognized as
> having some existence; but the stroke came from Germany.[16]

It was unfortunate that his report had arrived so long after the actual
events of April/May 1916. Nonetheless, he confirmed two vital issues;
firstly, it was the German and not the US government which ignited
events in Ireland and diverted British attention from the European war
theatres and, secondly, it was the British executions of the Rising leaders,
the 'youths who were slain' along with the shooting of pacifist Francis
Sheehy Skeffington, that provoked widespread sympathy for Sinn Féin.
A sympathetic Frost wrote that the Skeffington killing was 'now admitted to be the act of a madman' although 'one not too mad to be retained
among His Majesty's officers'.[17]

All three reports were read in the division of Western European Affairs
in the State Department. William Phillips, third assistant secretary of
state, described Frost's report as 'excellent' and the commendation was
added to his efficiency record.[18] Indeed, without Frost the Rising might
have appeared aimless as his report transformed the 'rebels from victims
to leaders in American eyes, as other events were so transforming them
in England and Ireland'. Frost's explanation also emerged subsequently
in newspaper accounts and provided Sinn Féin with a legitimacy and status previously reserved for Parnell's Irish Parliamentary Party.[19] Yet, in the

days during and immediately after the Rising, the State Department was without a first-hand account of events in Ireland and, therefore, had no background to the events. As will be seen, the three consuls' failure to contact the State Department meant that it was unaware at the time of their efforts to protect US interests in Ireland.

Officials in the State Department would have also expected to receive a report on events in Ireland from the London embassy, even though some wished for nothing less than to 'get' the Anglophile Ambassador Walter Page 'home for a rest, or permanently'.[20] After the Rising, Page expressed the view that it was German-inspired and, although the British had mishandled its suppression and the executions of the leaders, he had little or no sympathy for the insurgents.[21] State Department officials understood this interpretation but at the time were just as surprised by the Rising as the US press and public. The exception was the handful of Irish-American republicans who had been involved in its planning.[22] Once news of it appeared in the US press on 25 April, the immediate concerns for Wilson's administration focused on avoiding any allegations of a US dimension to the event that had momentarily distracted the British authorities from prosecuting the war on the European continent and had compromised US neutrality. There were four issues for the administration: firstly, identifying whether or not Irish-Americans had violated the neutrality laws in planning the rebellion.[23] Secondly, it had to refute allegations that the British interception of the *Aud*, carrying the weapons from Germany, resulted from information leaked by the US administration to the British government on Wilson's orders. Thirdly, it had to monitor the impact of the news on the US public in an election year and, fourthly, it needed to ensure that US interests were protected, not just in Ireland but within the wider context of Wilson's continuing peace-making efforts.[24]

State Department officials were informed by US consuls in Ireland about the shipments of armaments to radicals since 1914. Some were funded by US sources and others by Irish and British sources.[25] Furthermore, six days before the Rising, four US Secret Service agents had entered the New York offices of Wolf von Igel, German commercial attaché, and eight documents were seized. They revealed details of a gun-running mission to Ireland organized by the Germans and rebel leaders in Dublin and in Clan na Gael, as well as evidence of subversion and espionage in the US.[26] Spring Rice was informed by the State Department that funds had been raised for revolutionary purposes but that the actual planning had taken place in Ireland and Germany. The Wilson administration decided to separate evidence of fund-raising for Ireland from plotting of the revolt in order to avoid British accusations of breaches of neutrality. In the State Department, Counsellor Frank Polk told Spring Rice in early June that there was 'no sign of Irish plotting' in the US.[27] In the Foreign Office, Rowland Sperling reflected his colleagues' annoyance at Polk's disingenuous statement:

> There may be a technical distinction between 'plotting' and 'raising funds' but the practical result is the same. That is to say it makes very little practical difference whether the funds raised are remitted to the revolutionaries direct, or are converted into arms and ammunition or passage money for agents. The U.S.G[overnment], needless to say, take a different view where their own interests are concerned. I do not know, however, what evidence we have of Irish activities in the US beyond meetings, press articles and collections nominally for relief purposes.[28]

The US government did not disclose the contents of the von Igel papers until autumn 1917 when the US had joined the Allied cause.[29]

The second concern for the Wilson administration revolved around the rumours immediately circulating in Washington and New York of government collusion in the British interception of the *Aud*. One source of these accusations was the *New York Times* and another was John Devoy, who stated in the *Gaelic American* on 29 April 1916 that it was not Irish informers or British spies who gave the details of the *Aud* to the British 'but that deficiency was supplied by the Washington government'.[30] The British government was not given copies of the von Igel documents but Spring Rice received an indirect warning from an American journalist which he cabled to London on 22 April, two days before the Rising started:

> I hear from a sure source that among papers seized by authorities in New York are indications of plan for gun-running in Ireland to begin not before April 23rd. Detachments of men are subsequently to be landed whilst German fleet and Zeppelins make demonstrations to engage the attention of our fleet.[31]

Hartley suggests that this warning was deliberately leaked by the US administration to thwart the gun-running. Secretary of State Robert Lansing had seen the von Igel papers, which included a cable sent by CNG leader Cohalan to Berlin to delay the gun-running until 23 April, and this probably formed the basis of the journalist's warning. But British authorities in Ireland already had information that a ship with arms and two submarines had left Germany for Ireland.[32] Consequently, the capture of the *Aud* resulted from the unpreparedness of the IRB in Ireland, the presence of the British blockade along the country's south coast and British intelligence. It did not arise from a specific US government warning.

Nevertheless, Foreign Office officials felt there was a sense of 'embarrassment' within the State Department arising from Devoy's allegations.[33]

On 28 April, the administration announced in the *New York Herald* that the few von Igel documents relating to the Rising were not 'sufficiently specific to have enabled the American officials to tell the British anything tangible'.[34] The article did not directly address Devoy's accusation about gun-running and instead deliberately led the public to link the conspiracy with Roger Casement's separate return from Germany. The State Department emphasized that there was no intelligence in the papers that 'could have aided the British government in locating or capturing the Casement expedition'.[35] The matter did not end there and the Committee on Public Information (CPI) investigated the von Igel documents. Finally, in September 1917, the CPI announced that by the time the von Igel documents had arrived in the State Department on 21 April 1916 'Casement had spent several hours in an Irish prison.'[36] As Hartley notes, this line of defence proved to be a 'deliberate and largely successful red herring'.[37] So, while the leaking of the information did not contribute to the British seizure of the guns or of Casement, it was intended to prevent the gun-running and the Rising. The CPI deliberately attempted to obfuscate the administration's role therein but ultimately the US administration cannot be accused of betraying the Rising as there was no hard intelligence available about those events.

The third concern of the Wilson administration in April 1916 related to the US public's response to the Irish Rising and later executions, particularly in an election year. The British government's propaganda office in Wellington House in London concluded that the Rising inspired a hostile reception in western and middle-western newspapers, including the pro-British *Chicago Herald*.[38] The mainstream press such as the influential *New York Times*, *Washington Post*, *New York World* and *Chicago Tribune* regarded it as 'foolish and futile'. Their editorials portrayed Casement as the leader and that funding came from Germany and Irish-American revolutionaries. The *New York World*, which was close to the Wilson administration, described the Rising as a 'German conspiracy'.[39] Yet, the German dimension did not automatically condemn the leaders of the Rising in the eyes of some Americans. Wilson acknowledged 'the great shock opinion in this country has received from the course of the British government towards some of the rebels'.[40] Irish-America split along predictable lines. The near-defunct Redmondite United Irish League met in New York on 28 April, condemned the Rising and pledged its support to Wilson's neutrality policy.[41] Shane Leslie, sub-editor of the pro-Redmond *Ireland* magazine, who was then in the US, confirmed that 'pro-Ally Irishmen ... were calm and sorrowful at the Rising'.[42] On the other side, a Clan rally, also held in New York on 30 April, passed a resolution of sympathy and assistance for the rebels.[43] Spring Rice reported to Grey on 28 April:

> The attitude of public opinion as to the Irish rebellion is on the whole satisfactory. The press seems to be agreed that the movement is suicidal and in the interests of Germany alone. The attitude of the majority of the Irish is uncertain, but if the movement spreads the effect here will be very serious indeed. All are agreed that it will be dangerous to make Casement a martyr.[44]

His caution was wise. Lieutenant-General Sir John Maxwell arrived in Ireland on Friday, 28 April, as commander-in-chief with the brief to quell the Rising. A few hours later on 29 April he received the surrender from Patrick Pearse. On the same day, Maxwell informed Field Marshall Viscount French, commander-in-chief of the Home Forces, that he was arranging for 'all known or suspected Sinn Féiners to be taken to Richmond Barracks' and strongly recommended that they all be interned at Holyhead 'except those who I will deal with'. French congratulated him on 'the good work' and stated that Prime Minister Asquith 'is very pleased with it all', as was Lord Lieutenant of Ireland Winbourne.[45] The selection procedure of prisoners who had played prominent parts in the Rising was carried out in Richmond barracks by soldiers and Special Branch officers of the Dublin Metropolitan Police.[46] Maxwell had hoped to deal with the leaders under martial law but did so under the Defence of the Realm Act even though it did not provide for the case of armed insurrection unless there was evidence of aiding the enemy. Irrespective of this difficulty, his main concern on 2 May when the first trials were held was that the 'politicians will not interfere until I report normal conditions prevail'. He expected to be through 'with this part in a week or ten days'.[47]

As matters transpired, between 2 May and 3 August sentences of death, penal servitude for life or terms of imprisonment were handed down. Simultaneously, the deportation of other prisoners to England commenced.[48] Some 187 civilians were tried by military court, with 119 acquitted and ninety death sentences handed down. It was not until after the first trials on 2 May that Irish-born assistant provost-marshal, William Evelyn Wylie (appointed prosecuting officer at the trials), insisted that the prisoners be asked to provide a defence or produce witnesses. A death sentence required the unanimous verdict of all three judges but it was Maxwell's responsibility to confirm or commute them. He did in all but fifteen cases.[49]

The first three executions took place on 3 May, and on the same day French informed Maxwell: 'The PM has expressed himself as "surprised at the rapidity of the trial and sentences".' Asquith also asked French to warn Maxwell 'not to give the impression that all the Sinn Féiners would suffer death' (emphasis in original). Despite this concern Asquith agreed to leave Maxwell 'alone to your own discretion'.[50] On 4 May, four executions took place, followed by one on the 5th, four on the 8th, one on the 9th and two on the 12th. Among those sentenced to death were Jeremiah (aka Diarmuid) Lynch and Éamon de Valera, while those arrested included John J. Kilgallon, William Pedlar and Peter Fox. All had American connections.[51] The combination of the executions, deportations, Casement's trial and the imposition of martial law led to a change in Irish-American and mainstream US opinion on the Irish question.

During May 1916, Americans were shocked and outraged at the executions and the killing of innocent people in Ireland. Mass meetings were held throughout the US to protest against the British government's actions and to demand clemency for the prisoners. Even the most Anglophile of newspapers, the *New York World*, noted that the executions served 'no good purpose', and the *Washington Post* reported that 'a shock went around the civilized world' when it learned that the leaders of the Irish revolt 'had been tried by drumhead court-martial, found guilty and sentenced in a trice and shot at sunrise against a wall of Dublin castle'.[52] The executions brought the moderate and radical Irish-Americans closer than they had been since the 1880s, and many felt that the Wilson administration should intervene.[53]

In preparation for Casement's trial, Michael Francis Doyle, one of Casement's lawyers and Democratic Party supporter, wrote to his long-time friend, Joe Tumulty, Wilson's private secretary. Doyle enquired on 29 April if Wilson might intervene on Casement's behalf 'on the grounds of humanity'. Tumulty forwarded it for counsel to the State Department where Lester H. Woolsey, assistant solicitor, advised that the US had no legal basis for intervention and that official concern should be limited to the fate of American citizens involved in the Rising. Tumulty forwarded the Casement file to Wilson, including a letter from Agnes Newman, Casement's sister. Wilson replied on 2 May: 'We have no choice in a matter of this sort. It is absolutely necessary to say that I could take no action of any kind regarding it.'[54] Although he would not speak out on Casement's behalf, the involvement of US citizens would merit a reaction. Shortly, before Doyle sailed for Britain, he asked Polk in the State Department for 'help' even though he 'confidently' expected to secure an 'acquittal' for Casement which would be of 'material assistance' to Wilson in the forthcoming presidential campaign. Polk would not provide Doyle with a letter to the Foreign Office but he felt sure that Page would 'be glad to do all that he can for you'. He warned Doyle: 'You, of course, realize that [Page] is somewhat limited in his activities, owing to his position.' Wilson knew about the exchange.[55] Casement was sent for trial on 26 June and Wilson's decision not to intervene was strongly challenged when the death sentence was passed. It was also clear in early June that while Tumulty had brought the matter to Wilson's attention he had not offered advice to the president. He acted only as a conduit. In the interim, Congress had taken up the Irish question and some politicians appealed for Wilson to act on two further issues.

The Rising and British treatment of the prisoners was first raised in the Senate on 4 May. Between 12 and 17 May, three resolutions were introduced to the house requesting the British government to treat the Irish leaders as 'prisoners of war' and not as 'criminals'. Speeches critical of Britain were also heard in the Senate, beginning with that of William Borah (Idaho) on 4 May. On 17 May, John W. Kern (Indiana) introduced a resolution asking that the State Department investigate the 'safety and well-being' of US citizens in Ireland. It was sent to Senator Stone's Foreign Relations Committee and forwarded to the White House and the State Department for an opinion.[56] This request for official action to protect US citizens was accompanied by a request from the county Clare Association of California and the Knights of St Patrick for an official condemnation as well. Both requests came to Polk's attention and he reported to Stone that the Kern resolution seemed 'harmless'. He also spoke to Wilson who 'did not think there was any particular objection to it' but deemed it 'somewhat unnecessary to adopt it'.[57] In other words, they felt that the British government could be trusted to uphold the rights of US citizens. However, Lansing announced that the State Department would 'promptly act, for the protection ... of the persons and property of American citizens in Ireland'.[58] This intervention was not unusual and merely reflected existing US diplomatic policy and practice.

Unknown to State Department officials in Washington, during and immediately after the Rising, US consular officers in Ireland had provided assistance to US citizens who were either deliberately or inadvertently caught up in events. Frost in Queenstown reported a 'number' of cases where individuals asked for consular assistance to ensure proper treatment and a fair trial. In addition to informing the London embassy, he dealt with all in the course of his 'welfare and passport duties' and 'no concrete difficulty arose'.[59] In Belfast, as previously mentioned, Sharp dealt with the case of Peter Fox, a naturalized US citizen who was arrested by the RIC in Tyrone on 8 May. Sharp followed procedure and requested the police commissioner to provide him with details on the charges and the result of any trial. On 12 May, he was informed that Fox was a member of the Irish Volunteers and Sinn Féin, that he was in Armagh prison awaiting trial and that his US documents were with the governor of the prison. Sharp's response to this information was to send all details to Skinner in London, who informed him that he had taken all steps necessary and appropriate. Yet, while he received a letter of intercession from Fox's local clergyman testifying to his good character and innocence, Sharp did not visit Fox in prison, nor did he pursue the commissioner for information even though Fox was held without trial. Instead, he passed the case to Adams in Dublin because Fox was moved to prison there.[60] Adams does not seem to have pursued this case either and Fox was among those prisoners interned in Frongoch prison in Wales. However, H.E. Duke, chief secretary for Ireland, subsequently showed clemency once Fox's US citizenship came to his attention.[61]

Although out of the office during the Rising, Adams had assisted US citizens stranded in Kingstown, county Dublin. He set up a temporary office in his hotel accommodation and notified the local police and military of this arrangement. He reported they sent 'several persons' to him for help and 'consulted with' him regarding others. On 28 April he secured a permit to work for the Associate Press journalist, Dewitt T. McKenzie, when he arrived by boat into Rosslare, county Wexford. On the same day, he was approached by a Catholic priest to help secure the release of a former representative of the US diplomatic service who had been arrested that day on Pembroke Road in the city and was detained in Dublin Castle.[62] The individual was James L. Sullivan, former US minister to the Dominican Republic from 1913 to 1915, who had links to CNG and the IRB but had no part in the Rising. Adams knew him and provided a letter to the clergyman confirming Sullivan's citizenship and requesting an official report from the police on the case. Although Sullivan had immediately upon arrest 'asked to communicate with the American consul', this was refused. Adams was unable, perhaps unwilling also, to travel into the city and reported that, after eight days, the priest secured Sullivan's release through 'the kindly aid' of Major Ivor H. Price, the intelligence officer to the military command. The release might also be explained by the force of US criticism of the treatment of the prisoners, particularly fellow Americans.[63] Despite his failure to meet Sullivan, Adams seemed to comfort himself that his presence in Kingstown and a 'few words of friendly interest' reassured others that 'they had a friend at their elbow'. On Monday 1 May, he received a US deportation officer, Mrs Mary C. Bryan, who was escorting an 'insane' woman and her young baby back to her home place in Ireland.[64]

When Adams resumed normal work on Monday 8 May, he handled 'numerous' requests for assistance from 'arrested persons claiming American citizenship'. He reported that some of them were 'difficult of decision and adjustment'. Dealing with cablegrams from the US seeking news of relatives and friends took up a lot of his time. During the following three weeks, his daily work consisted solely of numerous visits to Dublin Castle, Richmond barracks and Mountjoy prison on 'errands of assistance to men claiming American citizenship' who wanted Adams to ensure fair treatment.[65] Between 8 and 12 May he acted on two other cases; one was on his own initiative and another upon State Department instruction.

A few days before 8 May, Adams was contacted by Sinéad de Valera, who believed that her husband, Éamon, was going to be sentenced to death. De Valera was a member of the Irish Volunteers and during the Rising, commanded the 3rd battalion at Boland's mills in Dublin and was charged with 'armed rebellion and waging war against his Majesty the King'. She asked Adams to intervene in her husband's case on the grounds of his US citizenship and gave him a copy of 'Edward' de Valera's birth certificate as proof of this, although he had not taken an oath of allegiance to the United States government. Meanwhile in America, his mother, Catherine de Valera, and half-brother, Fr Wheelright, initiated a letter-writing campaign to the White House, State Department and Congress.[66] However, Adams received no instruction from the State Department concerning de Valera. His 'intervention' comprised a letter to Sir Mathew Nathan, under secretary for Ireland, pointing out de Valera's citizenship.

Adams did not attend de Valera's trial, which took place on 8 May and was 'short and businesslike'. De Valera was questioned about his nationality and he stated that he understood that he was born in New York but he could not say 'whether his father was a Spanish subject or naturalized American' but he regarded himself as an 'Irishman'. De Valera recalled that, the following day, an officer arrived in his cell and told him that he was convicted and sentenced to death but that it had been commuted to penal servitude for life.[67] Despite de Valera's own uncertainty about his nationality, Adams claimed afterwards that his intervention at the request of de Valera's wife led to the death sentence being commuted.[68] In the absence of the court martial record, it is not known if Adams' intervention was discussed during the trial.[69] However, it is more important to examine whether Adams' information on de Valera's citizenship and his involvement as a representative of the US government had any influence with Maxwell, who confirmed or commuted death sentences after each of the trials.

On 6 May, Asquith and his cabinet agreed 'to leave to [Maxwell's] decision dealing with particular cases' subject to a general instruction that only 'ring leaders and proved murderers' should be executed and that it was 'desirable to bring [the] executions to a close as soon as possible'.[70] The outcry in Britain and the United States continued. On 8 May, Maxwell wrote to Robertson, chief of the General Staff: 'Although this rebellion is crushed, it is folly to suppose that all danger is over', but he acknowledged that 'protestations are pouring in'.[71] It is clear, therefore, that Maxwell was not finished with the executions when de Valera was tried. News of the dawn executions became known the same day and Winbourne complained to Maxwell and Asquith about the shooting of 'unknown insurgents'. He feared of the 'disastrous consequences' if 'nearly a hundred others are liable to the same penalty'. Winbourne concluded: 'Public opinion will not support either here or in England further executions of any save perhaps one or two very prominent [emphasis in original].'[72]

After news of the deaths of the 'unknown insurgents' came through to London, Irish Nationalist leader John Redmond telegraphed his 'earnest protest' to Maxwell. Some time later, Asquith warned Maxwell there was 'grave danger of general and bitter resentment' being prolonged at what seemed to be 'periodical vengeance on comparatively little known insurgents' and that a 'reassuring statement was needed without delay'. Maxwell replied on 9 May that '[James] Connolly and [Sean] MacDermott [MacDiarmada] still remain to be tried to-day and if convicted must suffer extreme penalty. As far as I can state they will be last to suffer capital punishment.' Asquith replied: 'I notice with satisfaction that in your opinion there are now not more than two leaders who must suffer extreme death penalty.'[73] On the same day, Maxwell confirmed the death sentences on the final three prisoners – Thomas Kent, Connolly and MacDermott – which went ahead with Asquith's approval.[74]

De Valera's name does not feature in Maxwell's correspondence on 8 and 9 May, even though he had commuted his sentence at this time. However, Wylie recalled that on 8 May Maxwell had shown him Asquith's telegram and insisted that Connolly be tried, even though he was severely wounded. Maxwell then asked: 'Who is next on the list?' Wylie said: 'Somebody called de Valera, Sir.' The general inquired: 'Who is he?' to which Wylie replied: 'I haven't an idea. I have never heard of him before. He was in command at Boland's bakery and the Ringsend area.' Wylie also recalled that Maxwell queried: 'I wonder would he be likely to make trouble in the future?' Wylie replied 'I wouldn't think so, Sir, I don't think he is important enough. From all I can hear he is not one of the leaders.' Maxwell pronounced: 'All right, stop now except for the public trials and come up and dine tonight. I have another job for you.'[75]

This version, which does not refer to de Valera's citizenship, accords with Maxwell's reassurance to Asquith on 9 May that only two more executions would take place, although he did not mention the Kent case.[76] Another retrospective explanation based on an eye-witness account is that of Sir Alfred Bucknill, deputy judge advocate general of the British forces in Ireland from April 1916 to 1919, who supervised the legal aspects of the courts martial. Although de Valera was known by Dublin Castle special branch to be a commandant and his name had appeared in captured documents belonging to Connolly, The O'Rahilly and Clarke, Bucknill remembered in 1953 that: 'Beyond the proclamation of the Irish Republic which contained the names of 7 signatories, we knew very little of the prime movers in the rebellion.' He believed that de Valera was saved by Asquith's reaction to the criticism particularly surrounding the shooting of Francis Sheehy Skeffington.[77] Indeed during his visit to Ireland between 11 and 19 May, Asquith wrote to his wife: 'There have been fewer bad blunders than one might have expected ... there have been no more executions.'[78]

Although there are inaccuracies in Wylie and Bucknill's eye-witness and retrospective accounts, both men were in daily contact with Maxwell and recalled no American dimension to his decision on de Valera. In addition, the other death sentences handed down on 8 May to Richard Hayes, Frank Lawless, Joseph Lawless and Thomas Ashe for their part in the battle of Ashbourne when two Volunteers and up to fifteen RIC men were killed, were also commuted. Ashe's sister Nora later commented: 'I think at that stage as the executions had aroused such indignations the government did not dare execute any more.'[79] In this context, the commuting of de Valera's sentence was not an exception. He stated in 1969:

> I have not the slightest doubt that my reprieve in 1916 was due to the fact that my court-marital and sentence came late. My sentence came just when Asquith said that there would be no further executions save those of the ringleaders, which, apparently, he interpreted as those who had signed the Proclamation. Only Connolly and MacDiarmada were executed after my court-martial. The fact that I was born in America would not, I am convinced, have saved me. I know of nothing in international law which could be cited in my defence or made an excuse for American intervention, except, perhaps, to see that I got a fair trial. It is, of course, true that my wife was encouraged by friends to make, and did make, representations to the American consul here. He was sympathetic, I understand. Similarly, my mother and American friends ... made representations to Washington ... but I feel certain that the administration took no official action.
>
> By the way, Thomas Ashe was court-martialled the same day as I was. He, too, would have been executed, I have no doubt, had he been tried earlier because of the part he took at the Battle of Ashbourne ... he was not an American citizen, and it could not be suggested, therefore, that it was on that account he was reprieved.[80]

De Valera was probably correct. His life was spared by a combination of luck, timing and indirectly the US factor but only in as much as it formed part of the public pressure on Asquith and his cabinet as distinct from Adams' 'intervention'. The first time that the State Department officially raised de Valera's case with the Foreign Office was on 1 July to inquire if the prisoner could be asked 'whether he claims to be an American citizen, and, if so, on what grounds'.[81] For his part, Maxwell, both as a soldier and father-in-law of Clifford Carver, an aide to Colonel House (Wilson's adviser), was more than sensitive to the importance of securing US entry into the war. Yet, it was not until 20 May that he referred directly to a US factor.[82]

Among the trials that Adams stated that he had attended sometime between 8 and 20 May was that of Diarmuid (aka Jeremiah) Lynch, a naturalized American citizen and member of the IRB supreme council, when he heard a death sentence handed down. As Adams was about to leave the prison he saw Lynch and assumed he was about to be executed. He was later informed of the commutation of the sentence to ten years' penal servitude and visited Lynch in Mountjoy prison. Lynch reputedly 'expressed grateful acknowledgement of the services rendered him'. However, Lynch recalled that while Adams did not attend his trial on 17 May he saw him later that day 'in company with the members of the court'. He believed the commutation to be the result of the 'efforts made by friends in the US'. Thus, irrespective of whether Adams attended the actual trial or merely provided a statement to prosecuting officers, his self-proclaimed role is questioned by Lynch's view and further supported by Maxwell's complaint of being 'bombarded' with appeals for clemency for Lynch, including one from Senator James O'Gorman which Wilson instructed was sent to Ambassador Page in London.[83] On 20 May Maxwell reassured Asquith that 'no sentence of the kind indicated will be confirmed by me without reference to you, although Jeremiah Lynch's court-martial has not yet come before me. On the same day he informed the War Office that Lynch's death sentence had already been commuted.[84] In this case there was no likelihood of Lynch being executed, irrespective of Adams' involvement.

On 5 May, Adams received a cablegram from the State Department about the case of John J. Kilgallon, a US citizen with an address at 31 Broadway, New York. He had travelled in Germany, France and England in 1910 and four years later enrolled as a pupil at Patrick Pearse's school at Rathfarnham in Dublin. An RIC Special Branch report noted that during the Rising he had been seen armed and in the uniform of the Irish Volunteers. He surrendered with the other insurgents and was jailed for 'bearing arms'. Adams met Nathan who gave him a letter for the chief commissioner of police. The latter promised to investigate the case and notify the consulate. However, according to his own record of his actions, Adams could not have met Nathan until after 8 May by which time Kilgallon had been deported to Stafford jail in England and then to Frongoch camp in Wales. Consequently, on 12 May, when Polk requested that all information received on the case be sent to his office, Adams had already passed on the case to the embassy in London.[85]

Unsurprisingly, American newspapers were in no doubt but that Wilson's intervention had saved Lynch's life. Adams staked his claim to a share of the credit for the commutation of the Lynch and de Valera sentences by recording not just his visits but that he had kept in 'constant communication' with the British military leadership in Ireland, and he acknowledged Price and Nathan's co-operation.[86] It is clear that between 3 and 12 May his role was not influential in the outcome of any of the trials. Instead, when the issue of citizenship of prisoners was specifically raised in relation to prisoner treatment, it was not until later in the year. On 8 December, Chief Secretary Duke decided that four prisoners held at Frongoch – J.J. Kilgallon, Michael Joseph Lynch (inadvertently confused with Jeremiah), Peter Fox and William Pedlar – would have to be tried or released if their US citizenship could be proved. A few days later, he indicated to the under secretary of state in the Home Office that he would not 'raise any objection to their release provided … they are sent to America'.[87]

However, American opprobrium contributed to the climate of revulsion against the continuation of the executions. Foreign Secretary Grey and particularly his officials in the propaganda section in Wellington House became increasingly concerned about the reaction in the US. Information gleaned from newspapers, Ambassador Spring Rice and reliable informants such as H.J. Wigham, pro-Allied editor of the Republican magazine *Metropolitan*, indicated that Britain's prestige was at an all time low in the US and the widespread anger would soon be felt in Congress and was likely to affect Anglo-American relations and perhaps the prosecution of the war.[88] Indeed on 22 May, Grey asked Asquith to insist that the military authorities in Dublin refer to London prior to the imposition of the death sentence on any US citizen and fully inform the Foreign Office to allow it to give 'early replies to enquiries from the United States government'.[89]

The US administration was obliged to protect the interests of its citizens abroad, thus allowing Adams, Sharp and Frost to act. It was a different matter when it came to the treatment of Irish citizens and issuing an official condemnation as Senator Phelan requested. Polk explained to Tumulty on 3 June that the government could not protest on behalf of non-American citizens.[90] Despite the unambiguous nature of the situation, Tumulty asked Polk to meet with him before he replied to Phelan because 'there is so much dynamite in it that we ought to proceed with care'.[91] This appeal came just days before Tumulty headed to St Louis for the twenty-second Democratic national convention where Wilson expected to be re-nominated as the Democratic Party presidential candidate. In these pre-convention days any issue that threatened Wilson's chances of re-election had to be attended to. Undoubtedly, Wilson's closest advisers, House and Tumulty, needed a quietening down of the Irish question.[92] There was no reference to Ireland in the platform which emphasized the importance of 'Americanism'.[93]

Wilson's re-nomination intensified the flow of hostility towards him from radical Irish-America. On 24 June, Devoy's *Gaelic American* accused the Democratic Party of being 'ruled by an autocrat whose every whim it obeys' and it backed Charles Evans Hughes, the Republican candidate and a 'man of honour', for the presidency.[94] Irish-American Democrats were critical of Wilson's response to the Rising and executions but not sufficiently so to desert him as their candidate or his foreign agenda. During the summer, the Democrats campaigned on the powerful slogan 'he kept us out of war' but encountered another threat to their Irish-American support base because of British policy on the Casement case and the administration's response.

The death sentence imposed on Casement on 29 June exacerbated Irish-American and broader American indignation.[95] Tumulty acted to the extent of his influence but without appearing to champion Casement's cause.[96] He arranged for Franz H. Krebs, a journalist, to discuss the case with Wilson on 7 July in the hope that he would persuade Wilson to intervene. Wilson gave him a 'most sympathetic hearing' and indicated that 'the general feeling in Washington is that the death sentence will be commuted'.[97] He offered nothing else. Lansing did not approach Wilson either but he did tell Spring Rice that he would unofficially pass on to the Foreign Office letters received from 'persons of prominence' appealing for Casement's life.[98] Tumulty did not know about this move but Lansing's pro-British stance did not deter his efforts to get Wilson to intervene. An appeal to commute the death sentence had been lodged by Casement's legal team and was due for hearing in London on 17 July. Doyle, using Tumulty's good offices, appealed again to Wilson to mediate with Grey or Asquith. The lawyer was convinced that Wilson's intercession would win clemency for Casement.[99] In London the appeal to the Court of Criminal Appeal was dismissed on 18 July.[100] Two days later, Wilson replied to Tumulty: 'It would be inexcusable for me to touch this. It would involve serious international embarrassment.' A few days later, Page was informed that the State Department would take 'no action' regarding the protests against the sentence.[101]

The probable reasons for Wilson's decision not to act can be synopsized in his firm belief in his party's electioneering slogans: 'Americanism' and 'He kept us out of war'. The former ensured that he would not appease any hyphenate groups who put the interests of their native country above those of their adopted country. In the case of the latter, he was worried that his intervention would worsen US–British relations which were already at a crisis point due to the British government's publication of the blacklist on 19 July.[102] In late July and throughout August, therefore, US relations with Britain were already at breaking point.

This raises the question of the role of the State Department. Lansing and Polk had been fully informed by both Spring Rice and Page about the apparent determination of the British government to execute Casement. Polk was convinced that anything less than a reprieve would not 'satisfy the Irish ... rather a hopeless undertaking at present'.[103] Page, in London, counselled against Wilson's intervention and demurred when instructed by Lansing to pass on a message to Casement from his sister in the US on the grounds that it would 'produce a disagreeable impression' and might damage the US 'if all the facts about Casement ever became public'.[104] Page's opposition to the US promotion of the cause of Irish republicanism is evident but so also is his facilitation of the British authorities' smear campaign against Casement.[105] The ambassador used information shown to him from Casement's 'black' diary as another reason to dissuade Wilson from making any plea of clemency for Casement.[106] Thus, he assisted British intelligence chiefs in discrediting Casement and in undermining the US campaign for clemency. Finally, the actions of Page's staff on 3 August, the day of Casement's execution, also revealed a certain partiality for the British position.

While Wilson was unwilling to act, US politicians seeking votes from ethnic communities in the upcoming elections were more than willing to intervene. On 29 July, four days before the execution day, the US Senate passed a resolution requesting Wilson to transmit to the British government its plea for 'clemency in the treatment of Irish political prisoners'.[107] Polk complied with the instruction and had it transmitted to the London embassy on 2 August, where it reached the desk of Irwin Laughlin, chargé d'affaires.[108] By then Laughlin had received another telegram from Polk, sent at 5 p.m. on 2 August: 'Please report immediately if Senate resolution presented to Foreign Office and also any further details on Casement case.'[109] Fortunately for Page, he was by then en route to Washington for 'a rest'. So, it fell to Laughlin to bring the resolution to Asquith's attention. He admitted to Polk that it was in response to the second telegram, with its urgent tone and focus on the Casement case, that he met with Grey at 10 a.m. on 3 August, and 'in a round about fashion' raised the Casement case and handed the resolution to Grey, who asked if he could bring it to Asquith's attention. Laughlin replied that 'this was the desire of his government' and the conversation continued on to other matters. Laughlin then cabled the secretary of state on 3 August at 4 p.m. that he had delivered the resolution but that Grey 'did not promise an answer but said he would communicate the Senate's resolution to the Prime Minister and probably lay it before the Cabinet'. The cable continued: 'Casement was executed early this morning.'[110] Casement had been hanged in Pentonville prison in London, a few minutes after 9 a.m. on 3 August.

The reaction in the US was mixed. Spring Rice believed that influential newspapers had not over-reacted because of the 'timely warnings' which he had given about Casement's character to certain American journalists and to the Catholic Apostolic delegate.[111] Moreover, he reported to Grey that congressional agitation had been 'rather checked by the dread that some publication will be made exposing the private character of Casement'.[112] Nevertheless, mainstream newspapers that had been critical of Casement now revealed sympathy for him. The *Washington Post* described the execution as a 'colossal blunder' and the *Chicago Tribune* concluded: 'England made him; England unmade him.' Moderate nationalist John Quinn wrote in the *New York Times* on 13 August: 'However technically his offence may be phrased, his actual offence, if any, was that he put the cause of Ireland before that of England or even the Allies.'[113] Quinn, who was close to Spring Rice, refused to believe that Casement was 'abnormal or addicted to abnormal practices'. He believed that Casement's life 'was one of absolute purity'. Nor did he accept that Casement 'ever touched a penny of German money'. Other moderates had expected Casement to be imprisoned and not executed.[114] Not surprisingly, the attacks on Wilson from radical Irish-America ranged from venomous to indignant, particularly after the unionist Lord Robert Cecil, parliamentary under secretary at the Foreign Office, revealed that the British government had not received an appeal from the State Department.[115]

US newspapers reported that, although the resolution had been passed in the Senate on Saturday, 29 July, it was not cabled to London until 3 p.m. Washington time (9 p.m. London time) on Wednesday 2 August, and was not delivered to the Foreign Office until 10 a.m. on 3 August, an hour after Casement had been hanged.[116] The White House, the State Department and the British embassy in London were all suspected of deliberately withholding the message until it was too late to save Casement. This was believed by Casement's sister, Doyle, Senators Phelan and Ashworth and James J. McGuire, newspaper publisher and chairman of the executive committee of the Friends of Irish Freedom (FOIF). They demanded an explanation from the Wilson administration for the delay in the delivery of the resolution from the White House to the State Department.[117]

On three occasions between 1 August and 29 September, Doyle requested a copy of the telegram which 'the President had sent to Ambassador Page' requesting clemency for Casement and a copy of Page's reply. He warned Tumulty that the Republicans are 'making a campaign issue' of the delay in sending the resolution and that the 'great bulk of Catholics and those of Irish descent are opposing the President'.[118] Tumulty believed that the Casement matter played a 'prominent part' in the recent New Jersey Democratic primaries by 'bringing many votes' to Senator James E. Martine and not John Wesley Wescott, a Wilson supporter.[119]

Tumulty knew the delay was caused in the White House but nonetheless he set about getting the 'truth' from the State Department. Subsequently he learned that the resolution passed in the Senate on Saturday 29 July was mailed to Wilson at 5.30 p.m. that evening. It arrived at the White House on Monday 31 July. By now Wilson was back in the White House, after a two-day stay on the presidential yacht, USS *Mayflower*. On 31 July and 1 August he wrote correspondence and met visitors, including the suffragist Carrie Chapman Catt. But it was not until between 11 a.m. and 12 noon on Wednesday 2 August, the day before the execution, that Forester in the White House telephoned Polk and stated that the resolution was being sent to the State Department and 'to please have it forwarded as promptly as possible'. The resolution arrived soon after but was not accompanied by a 'letter of transmittal' directing 'the action to be taken', and Polk had to request this from the White House. In the interim, Polk sent off the telegram to the London embassy at 1 p.m. with the resolution only. After he received the instruction from the White House that Wilson wanted Page to transmit it to the Foreign Office, Polk sent a second telegram, later in the day, asking the ambassador to present the resolution 'at the earliest possible moment' and 'to report' back to Washington.

It was clear, therefore, that the State Department's response was correct and that the delay occurred in the White House. Indeed Polk 'understood from Tumulty that the reason for the delay was that there had been some hesitation about sending the resolution'.[120] Both Polk and Lansing were convinced that there was 'no delay' in the State Department.[121] In the face of continuing criticism of the White House and in the hope of shifting the blame to the State Department, Tumulty pursued the matter into September 1916.[122] Eventually Lansing, Polk, Tumulty and Senators Hughes and Phelan agreed on the same interpretation of events and the explanation that the delay did not matter because the British cabinet was made aware of the Senate resolution, which significantly did not mention Casement by name, by Spring Rice long before the actual paper version arrived but decided to disregard it.[123] This view was presented in the Senate on 8 September, sent to Doyle on 14 October and was subsequently published in the *New York Times* on 17 October. It seems, therefore, that Leary's interpretation that the delay was probably caused by 'administrative incompetence' was partially true, but Wilson's hesitation over whether to send the resolution to London also formed part of the explanation.[124] Although there is no record to explain Wilson's inaction, it may have centred on whether he would provide a personal endorsement.

One final aspect of the Casement affair is worthy of note; the extent to which it and the events surrounding the Rising destabilized Wilson's moderate Irish-American support. Dissatisfaction with Wilson must not be taken out of context or exaggerated. Simultaneous with the Casement matter, the Wilson government had intervened positively in Irish affairs. By July the Irish Relief Committee had raised $100,000 in the US to alleviate the 'unspeakable want and distress' created by the Rising in Ireland and, on 8 July, John A. Murphy and John Gill sailed for Ireland to begin aid operations. They were armed with a letter of introduction from Lansing to Page and were followed a week later by Thomas Hughes Kelly, a New York banker and treasurer of the committee, his wife and the Boston editor, Joseph Smith, a Massachusetts journalist and labour leader. All were US citizens and Murphy and Gill were kept under surveillance by the British secret service from the moment they arrived in Ireland to ensure that their activities were of a philanthropic, and not a political, nature. Prior to this, Spring Rice had advised Grey to adopt a benevolent attitude towards the distribution of funds for the 'sufferers of the revolt'. On 14 July, he suggested to Grey that it would be diplomatically useful if Smith and Kelly were also allowed to land. Lord Hardinge, the permanent under secretary, agreed but noted warily: 'The bitterly hostile attitude of Irishmen in America and the suspicion surrounding J.W. Smith preclude the possibility of regarding such persons as messengers of peace.' The Foreign Office feared that the funds would be used to prepare for another Rising in Ireland. The Home Office took the possibility more seriously. Smith was barred from entering Ireland because 'there was good reason for believing that he was engaged in business hostile to this country'. Kelly was barred by reason of association.[125]

When word of the actions reached the US it aroused anger within influential Irish-American circles. A congressional resolution ensued, calling for the suspension of diplomatic relations and a flood of appeals to Wilson and the State Department, including those from Cardinal Farley of New York and Mayor Curley of Boston. According to Tumulty, Wilson instructed Polk to try and persuade the British authorities to permit the relief operations. On 26 July, Polk instructed Laughlin, in the London embassy, to investigate the situation and to assist Kelly and Smith. Wilson's involvement and Polk's personal reference for Kelly, however, could not outweigh the British intelligence which confirmed that, along with delivering the funds, the men wanted to discover if Ireland was ready for another Rising. For the British, domestic considerations, such as securing Ireland, were supreme. In late September, Page explained to Wilson that protests and complaints about British treatment of US citizens had led the Foreign Office to regard the State Department as an 'easy recipient of personal grievances'. He believed requests to transmit

US aid to Ireland were granted and declined according to British notions of 'the degree of harm they would do to their military cause'.[126] Once again, the Wilson government had shown that it was willing to act when US citizens were involved. In this instance they did not prevail and Smith and Kelly returned to the US in late August.

Thus, against a background of deteriorating US–British relations and of the up-coming election, Wilson's practical inaction on the Casement matter can be contrasted with his willingness to intervene to protect US citizens' rights in foreign jurisdictions. Furthermore, while radical Irish-America remained hostile to him, Wilson's neutrality message appealed to the majority of Irish America. Consequently, he was even able to rebut and survive Jeremiah O'Leary's accusations of pro-Britishness in September.[127]

In conclusion, when the presidential election results were finalized Wilson had increased his vote by almost three million since 1912.[128] Although Wilson believed that he had lost the Irish-American vote, Leary concluded that, in six of the nine states with large Irish-American populations, Irish-Americans voted for Wilson 'in as great or greater numbers than they had ever voted for a Democratic presidential candidate in the immediate past'. The reasons for Wilson's victory centred on his economic and social policies, including the Child Labour Law and the Adamson Eight-Hour Law; while Hughes' unspectacular campaign and the promise of continued neutrality were also significant. Ultimately, Wilson's response to the Irish Rising caused him little damage at the ballot box.[129]

Radical Irish-American figures seeking Irish independence sought a vote against Wilson but the more numerous and influential Irish-American politicians within the Democratic Party emphasized Wilson's domestic agenda which directly affected the electorate. The leadership of the labour movement, including a substantial Irish-American presence, came out strongly for Wilson, particularly after he signed the Adamson Act on 3 September. Nor did the Roman Catholic vote desert Wilson, except in Oregon, where his Mexican policy was influential. In general, Irish-America did not rise up against Wilson when the opportunity came on 7 November; instead most weighed in behind him and set aside whatever misgivings they had about the inadequacy of his response to the Rising and the executions.[130] Joyce Broderick, an Irish Roman Catholic in the Foreign Office, concluded: 'The great mass of Irish voters declined to accept guidance in domestic politics from extremists, either because they mistrusted their prophecies or – what is much more likely – because loyalty to the Democrat Party gave them a fairer prospect of personal profit.'[131] A cynical view perhaps, but it is clear that American issues, not Irish ones, influenced Irish-American voters to support Wilson, irrespective of their sympathy for the Irish at home.

NOTES

1. The author wishes to acknowledge assistance received from Neil Cobbett and Eukaria O'Grady, The National Archives, Kew (hereafter TNA), Professor Keith Jeffery, Queen's University, Belfast, and Professor Eunan O'Halpin, Trinity College, Dublin. T.J. Rowland, 'Strained Neutrality: Irish-American Catholics, Woodrow Wilson, and the *Lusitania*', *Éire-Ireland: Journal of Irish Studies*, 30, 4 (winter 1996), pp. 59–60.
2. See Count J. Bernstorff, *My Three Years in America* (London, 1920), p. 47; T.J. Noer, 'The American government and the Irish question during world war 1', *South Atlantic Quarterly*, 72, 1 (1973), p. 97.
3. Stephen Gwynn, *The Letters and Friendships of Sir Cecil Spring Rice* (London, 1929), p. 309, fn. 2. In 1914 and 1915, the American committee of the Irish National Volunteers sent a total of $25,000 to Eoin McNeill; American Irish Historical Society (hereafter AIHS), Daniel F. Cohalan papers (hereafter DFCP), box 1, folder 11; ibid., box 16, folder, 7; Rowland, 'Irish-American Catholics', p. 75; J.J. Splain, 'The Irish Movement in the United States since 1911', in W.G. Fitzgerald, *The Voice of Ireland: a Survey of the Race and Nation from all Angles by the Foremost Leaders at Home and Abroad* (1923), p. 227.
4. National Archives, Ireland (hereafter NAI), Chief Secretary's Office Registered Office Papers (hereafter CSORP), Calendar of papers relating to the Rising. 25275, Irish Office, draft reply to parliamentary question, 6 July 1916.
5. Each consular office was assigned junior officials and clerical staff while there were three consular agents located in Limerick, Galway and Londonderry. See Bernadette Whelan, *United States Foreign Policy and Ireland: From Empire to Independence, 1913–29* (Dublin, 2006), pp. 73–80.
6. National Archives and Records Administration, Maryland, US (hereafter NARA), Records of the Department of State relating to internal affairs of Great Britain, 1910–29, Record Group 59 (hereafter RG59), M580/6, Hengstler, 21 August 1916; ibid., Carr to Hengstler, 22 August 1916. The only material received from the consuls in Ireland around the time of the Rising were six political newspapers sent by Consul Wesley Frost in March 1916. NARA, RG59, M580/6, Frost to Secretary of State, 11 March 1916; ibid., 841.00/26a, Carr to Sharp, 22 August 1916; ibid., Carr to Frost, 22 August 1916; ibid., Carr to Adams, 22 August 1916.
7. NARA, RG59, M580/6, 841.00/33, 'The Sinn Féin rebellion in Ireland, Easter Week, 1916', in Adams to Secretary of State, 29 November 1916.
8. Ibid., 841.00/33, Adams to Secretary of State, 29 November 1916.
9. By way of contrast to Adam's tardy reporting, Charles Bray, the US vice-consul who replaced Claffey, did not arrive in Dublin until June 1916 but within a few weeks he had managed to secure a copy of the 'Sinn Féin rebellion handbook' which he forwarded to the State Department on 21 August 1916. Ibid., 841.00/29, Bray to Secretary of State, 21 August 1916.
10. Ibid., 841.00/33, 'The Sinn Féin rebellion', 29 November 1916.
11. Ibid.
12. Ibid., 841.00/30, Sharp to Secretary of State, 13 September 1916.
13. Ibid., Sharp to Page, 27 May 1916.
14. Ibid., Sharp to Page, 22 September 1916.
15. Ibid., 841.00/32, 'Political disturbances and political conditions in Ireland', 30 September 1916 in Frost to Secretary of State, 14 October 1916.
16. Ibid., Frost to Secretary of State, 14 October 1916.
17. Ibid., 'Political disturbances', 30 September 1916 in Frost to Secretary of State, 14 October 1916.
18. Ibid., comments on Frost to Secretary of State, 14 October 1916.
19. O. Dudley Edwards, 'American aspects of the Rising', in O. Dudley Edwards and F. Pyle, *1916, The Easter Rising* (London, 1968), pp. 173–4.
20. Ross Gregory, *Walter Hines Page: Ambassador to the Court of St James* (Kentucky, 1970), p. 158.
21. Quoted in ibid., p. 164.
22. Horace Plunkett was in Dublin during the Rising and newspaper reports of an attack on him caused Colonel Edward House, Wilson's adviser, some anxiety. Plunkett thought the Rising to be German-inspired and he hoped this would quicken US entry into the war. House hoped that the Rising would 'ultimately be for good rather than for evil'. NLI, HPP, P6584, reel 2 of 2, Plunkett to House, 4 May 1916; Diary 26 April 1916 in M. Digby, *Horace Plunkett: an Anglo-American Irishman* (Oxford, 1949), pp. 210–11; National Library of Ireland (hereafter NLI), Horace Plunkett Papers (hereafter HPP), P6584, reel 2 of 2, House to Plunkett, 11 May 1916.

23. Francis Carroll, *American Opinion and the Irish question 1910–23: A Study in Opinion and Policy* (Dublin, 1978), p. 62.
24. John Devoy, *Recollections of an Irish Rebel* (Shannon, 1969), p. 469.
25. Diarmuid Lynch brought back a draft of £25,000 from Clan na Gael to Irish Volunteers in November 1914 and McGarrity confirmed that £2,300 was sent to Ireland after 10 March 1916. Frost also indicated that US money financed both the gun-running in 1914 and Sinn Féin's organization. NLI, Lynch papers (hereafter LP), MS 11,128, 'The IRB. Some recollections and comments for the Bureau of Military History', March 1947; Seán Cronin, *The McGarrity Papers: Revelations of the Irish Revolutionary Movement in Ireland and America 1900–1940* (Tralee, 1971), p. 60; NARA, RG59, M580/6, 841.00/32, 'Political disturbances', 30 September 1916 in Frost to Secretary of State, 14 October 1916.
26. Rhodri Jeffreys-Jones, *American Espionage: From Secret Service to CIA* (New York, 1977), p. 63.
27. Carroll, *American Opinion*, p. 62; TNA, FO371/2793, Spring Rice to Grey, 6 June 1916.
28. TNA, FO371/2793, Rowland Sperling, 7 June 1916.
29. Jeffreys-Jones, *American Espionage*, p. 65.
30. Devoy, *Recollections*, pp. 469–70. Devoy exonerated Lansing from any blame in the release of the document on the grounds that he was 'normally a very straight man'. Ibid., p. 470.
31. TNA, FO371/2804, Spring Rice to Grey, 22 April 1916.
32. Christopher Andrew, 'Casement and British Intelligence', in Mary E. Daly (ed.), *Roger Casement in Irish and World History* (Dublin, 2005), p. 79.
33. TNA, FO371/2797, Sperling, 15 May 1916.
34. *New York Herald*, 28 April 1916.
35. Ibid. See also Stephen Hartley, *The Irish Question as a Problem in British Foreign Policy, 1914–18* (New York, 1987), p. 53.
36. Alan J. Ward, *Ireland and Anglo-American Relations, 1899–1921* (London, 1969) p. 108.
37. Hartley, *The Irish Question*, pp. 52–3.
38. H.C. Peterson, *Propaganda for War: the Campaign against American Neutrality, 1914–18* (Norman, 1939), p. 241; TNA, Kew, London, Foreign Office (hereafter FO) 394/43, 'American Press Résumé' for the Cabinet, 25 May 1916.
39. Carroll, *American Opinion*, pp. 56–7; Quoted in Hartley, *The Irish Question*, p. 55; see also TNA, FO394/43, 'American Press Résumé' for the Cabinet, 25 May 1916.
40. A.S. Link (ed.), *The Papers of Woodrow Wilson* (hereafter *PWW*), 69 vols (Princeton, 1966–94), 37, Wilson to House, 16 May 1916.
41. William M. Leary, 'Woodrow Wilson, Irish Americans and the Election of 1916', *The Journal of American History*, 54, 1 (June 1967), p. 59.
42. NLI, JRP, MS15236 (14), Leslie to Redmond, 16 May 1916.
43. Leary, 'Woodrow Wilson, Irish Americans and the Election of 1916', p. 59.
44. Gwynn, *The Letters and Friendships of Sir Cecil Spring Rice*, ii, Spring Rice to Grey, 28 April 1916.
45. University College Dublin Archives (hereafter UCDA), Éamon de Valera papers (hereafter EVP), P150/512, Maxwell to French, 29 April 1916, French to Maxwell, 1 May 1916, Winbourne to Maxwell, 1 May 1916.
46. Brian Barton, *From Behind a Closed Door: Secret Court Martial Records of the 1916 Easter Rising* (Belfast, 2002), p. 26.
47. UCDA, EVP, P150/512, Maxwell to Kitchener, 2 May 1916.
48. Leon Ó Broin, *W.E. Wylie and the Irish Revolution, 1916–1921* (Dublin, 1989), p. 4; UCDA, EVP, P150/512, Maxwell to Kitchener, 2 May 1916.
49. Barton, *From Behind a Closed Door*, pp. 28, 32, 35. There is still some dispute as to whether eighty-eight, ninety or ninety-seven sentences of death were handed down. Ibid.
50. UCDA, EVP, P150/512, French to Maxwell, 3 May 1916.
51. The cases of Kilgallon, Smith and Kelly are referred to in Yale University Library, Manuscripts and Archives Collection (hereafter YULMC), Frank L Polk papers (hereafter FLPP), box 11, file 369, Polk to Salmon, 12 May 1916; Ibid., Polk to Page, 26 July 1916.
52. Quoted in Carroll, *American Opinion*, p. 57.
53. The Irish Relief Fund Committee was established following the Carnegie Hall meeting. The president was Dr Thomas Addis Emmet and its three honorary presidents were Cardinals Gibbons, Farley and O'Connell, who John Quinn said were 'horrified' at the outbreak of the Rising but their 'feelings too were turned' after the shootings. Gibbons and Farley insisted that pro-German politics should not be associated with the relief scheme before they lent their names as honorary presidents. NLI, John Quinn papers (hereafter

JQP), MS18436, Quinn, 'In the matter of Sir Roger Casement and the Irish situation in America', 2 June 1916, p. 21; NLI, John Redmond papers (hereafter JRP), MS15236 (14), Leslie to Redmond, 3 July 1916.
54. Quoted in Carroll, *American Opinion*, pp. 72–3.
55. NARA, RG59, M580/6, Doyle to Tumulty, 30 May 1916; Ibid., Tumulty to Polk, 31 May 1916; M590/1, entry 'President 2 June 1916'; YULMC, FLPP, box 11, file 369, Doyle to Polk, 30 May 1916; Ibid., Polk to Doyle, 31 May 1916; NARA, RG59, M580/6, Polk to Philips, 31 May 1916; Ibid., Polk to Tumulty, 2 June 1916; Ibid., Polk to Page, 2 June 1916.
56. G. Haynes, *The Senate of the United States: Its history and Practice*, vol. 1 (New York, 1938), p. 297; YULMC, FLPP, box 11, file 369, Polk to Stone, 27 May 1916.
57. YULMC, FLPP, box 11, file 369, Polk to Stone, 27 May 1916.
58. TNA, FO371/2797, Senate, 64th Congress, 1 Session, 'American Citizens in Ireland', Lansing, 7 June 1916.
59. NARA, M580/6, 841.00/32, 'Political disturbances and political conditions in Ireland', 30 September 1916 in Frost to Secretary of State, 14 October 1916.
60. NARA M580/6, Sharp to Page, 27 May 1916; Ibid., Short to Sharp, 17 May 1916.
61. Chief Secretary to Under Secretary of State, Home Office, 14 December 1916, Colonial Office Record Series, vol. 1, *Sinn Féin and Republican Suspects, 1899–1921*, Dublin Castle special branch files (hereafter CO904) CO904/205/227. (Eneclann, Dublin, 2006).
62. NARA, RG59, M580/6, 841.00/33, 'The Sinn Féin', in Adams to Secretary of State, 29 November 1916.
63. NARA, M580/6, 841.00/33, 'The Sinn Féin'; TNA, WO35/69/7, Arrest and Detention of Mr J.M. Sullivan, 15 May 1916, Laughlin to Grey, 1 August 1916; CO904/215/420, Roe to Secretary of State for Foreign Affairs, London, 18 February 1919.
64. NARA, RG59, M580/6, 841.00/33, 'The Sinn Féin', in Adams to Secretary of State, 29 November 1916.
65. Ibid., 841.00/33, 'The Sinn Féin'; T.P. Coogan, *De Valera: Long fellow, Long shadow* (1993), p. 78.
66. NARA, M580/6, 841.00/33, 'The Sinn Féin'; TNA, HO144/10309, Prison Commission Minute, 15 May 1916.
67. The Earl of Longford and Thomas P. O'Neill, *Éamon de Valera* (London, 1970), pp. 48–9; NARA, RG59, M580/6, 841.00/33, 'The Sinn Féin'.
68. NARA, RG59, M580/6, 841.00/33, 'The Sinn Féin'.
69. Not all of the courts martial records survived. Those that did are located in TNA, WO 35/58 and WO 71/344. According to Iain Goode, Deputy Departmental Records Officer, UK Ministry of Defence, the department does not hold any files relating to de Valera's trial.
70. Oxford University, Bodleian Library (hereafter OU, BL), Asquith papers (hereafter AP), MSS 41–3, Letter to King, 6 May 1916.
71. UCDA, EVP, P150/512, Maxwell to Robertson, 8 May 1916.
72. British Library, MS53872 ff53-60, Bucknill papers, Winbourne to Maxwell, 8 May 1916.
73. Ibid., Redmond to Maxwell, 8 May 1916; OU, BL, AP, MSS41–3, Note, Asquith, 8 May 1916; Ibid., Maxwell to Commandeth [Maxwell] to Cinchomfor [Asquith], 9 May 1916; UCDA, EVP, P150/512, Cinchomfor to Commandeth, 9 May 1916.
74. Ibid., Maxwell to Commandeth [Maxwell] to Cinchomfor [Asquith], 9 May 1916; OU, BL, AP, MSS41–3, Kitchener to Maxwell, 11 May 1916.
75. TNA, PRO30/89/2, Wylie papers, Wylie to Biddy, 26 September 1939.
76. There are questions of veracity regarding Wylie's account as it was written in 1939 and without the benefit of papers and notes. A different version of the Maxwell quotation was given by Wylie to David Grey, US minister to Ireland, on 21 May 1941. Grey recorded in a memorandum for his diary for that date that Wylie replied to Maxwell: 'No, he is a school master who was taken at Boland's Mill.' 'All right,' said Maxwell, 'we will go ahead with Connolly and stop with this fellow.' Franklin Delano Roosevelt Presidential Library and Museum (FDRPL), Papers of David Grey, box 9, file Ireland, 1938–47, memorandum for the diary, Dublin, May 21 1941. Coogan notes that Grey later reproduced this reference in 'Behind the Green Curtain', Ch. 8. There are two versions of this unpublished book. One is located in the Franklin Delano Roosevelt Presidential Library and Museum, New York State, US, and refers to the reprieve but not Wylie. See FDRPL, Papers of David Grey, box 11, 'Behind the Green Curtain'. The other version of 'Behind the Green Curtain' in the American Heritage Center, University of Wyoming (AHCUW), Laramie, Wyoming does not refer to Wylie either. See AHCUW, Papers of David Grey, box 1, 'Behind the Green Curtain'. The author acknowledges the assistance of Matthew Hanson, FDRPL and Shannon Bowen,

AHCUW. The Maxwell Papers in the Department of Rare Books and Special Collections, Princeton University Library do not refer to the encounter either. The author is grateful to Dr Meg Rich in Princeton for this information. Coogan conflates the discussion of Connolly and de Valera into a single conversation and offers a different wording than Wylie's 1939 version; Maxwell asks: 'Is he someone important?' and Wylie replies: 'No, he is a school master who was taken at Boland's mills.' Maxwell says: 'All right, we will go ahead with Connolly and stop with this fellow.' Coogan, *De Valera*, p. 78.

77. See TNA, KV2/514; UCDA, EVP, P150/512, Boland to Nunan, 5 February 1953; Ibid., 'Letters of an English soldier in Ireland', in Boland to Nunan, 5 February 1953.

78. J.A. Spender and C. Asquith, *Life of Herbert Henry Asquith, Lord Oxford and Asquith*, vol. 1 (London, 1932), p. 215.

79. WWW.NLI.ie/1916/pdf/7.12.pdf accessed on 5 November 2007; J.B. Lyons, 'Dr Richard Hayes (1882–1958)', in Jim Kemmy (ed.), The Limerick Compendium (Dublin, 1987), pp. 130–2; NAI, Bureau of Military History 1913–21. Statement by witness document no. 645. Witness Nora Ashe, p. 5. Joseph W. Lawless recalled seeing in Richmond barracks that Ashe, Hayes and the two Lawlesses were 'selected from the general body of prisoners' to join the select band of Ceannt, MacDiarmaid, Heuston, Pearse, O'Hanrahan, Colbert, Clarke, MacBride and McDonagh. Similarly Hayes recalled that four Ashbourne men were lodged together in the prison. NAI, BMH, Statement by witness document no. 1043. Witness Joseph W. Lawless, p. 140; Ibid., no. 876, Witness Richard J. Hayes, p. 1.

80. Ibid., 'Reprieve of Éamon de Valera', Éamon de Valera, 3 July 1969.

81. TNA, Home Office 144/10309, Bell to Moylan, 1 July 1916. De Valera's statement, which indicated that he was born in New York but he had asked his mother to find out if his father, who was a Spaniard, became a US citizen, was passed on to Bell. Ibid., J.P. Moylan to Bell, 12 August 1916.

82. Owen Dudley Edwards, *Éamon de Valera* (Cardiff, 1987), pp. 57–8; OU, BL, MSS43, Maxwell to Bonham-Carter, 20 May 1916.

83. NARA, RG59, M580/6, 841.00/33, 'The Sinn Féin'; NLY, LP, MS11,128, 'Supplementary statement on Easter Week 1916', 28 April 1947; OU, BL, AP, MSS43, Maxwell to Bonham-Carter, 20 May 1916; TNA, WO213/8, Field General Courts Martial 1916, 30 March–1 June 1916, no. 8.

84. NARA, RG59, M580/6, 841.00/36, 'The Irish question at the beginning of 1917', 19 January 1917 in Frost to Secretary of State, 23 February 1917; OU, BL, AP, MS43, Maxwell to PM, 20 May; TNA, FO395/43, Dublin to War Office, 20 May 1916. In 1917 Frost reported Lynch's later movements, including his release under the General Amnesty Act and his return to Ireland where he was jailed again for conspiracy to steal pigs so as to prevent their export. The State Department informed the attorney general's office and that of Representative Henry Flood. Ibid., 841.00/66, Adams to Secretary of State, 14 March 1918; NLI, LP, MS10,652, Governor, Mountjoy prison to Department of Justice, 1 January 1945.

85. NARA, RG59, M580/6, 841.00/33, 'The Sinn Féin'; CO904/205/227, RIC, Crime Department – special branch, 'Interned rebels. Said to be American citizens', 9 December 1916; Yale University Library Manuscripts Collection, FLPP, box 27, file 369, Polk to Salmon, 12 May 1916. While Kilgallon was in prison, his father sent a sum of money to the US embassy in London so that he could buy himself 'comforts in the camp'. However, the embassy did not send on the money immediately. Instead, upon receipt of a second sum of £30 to pay his passage to the US after his release in December 1916, Edward Bell in the US embassy suggested to Waller in the Home Office that the Irish authorities could tell Kilgallon that he would not 'handle' any of the money 'until he is starting' for the US. Kilgallon sailed from Liverpool to the US on 7 April 1917. CO904/205/227, 'Kilgallon', Waller, 17 January 1917; Ibid., Asst head constable, Central Police Office, Liverpool to chief commissioner of police, Dublin Castle, 12 April 1917.

86. NARA, RG59, M580/6, 841.00/33, 'The Sinn Féin'.

87. CO904/205/227, Chief Secretary of Ireland to Under Secretary of State, Home Office, 8 December 1916; Ibid., Chief Secretary to Under Secretary, 14 December 1916.

88. TNA, Foreign Office (hereafter FO) 394/43, 'American Press Résumé' for the Cabinet, 25 May 1916; UCDA, EVP, P150/512, Drummond to Bonham Carter, 15 May 1916; TNA, FO394/43, 'minute by Mr R.F. Roxburgh, Wellington House', 25 May 1916.

89. OU, BL, AP, MS37–8, Grey to Bonham-Carter, 22 May 1916.

90. Quoted in Charles Tansill, *America and the Fight for Irish Freedom, 1866–1922: An Old Story Based upon New Data* (New York, 1957), pp. 218–19.

91. YULMC, FLPP, box 27, file 369, Tumulty to Polk, 9 June 1916.
92. For further information on the influence of Irish-America on the convention see E. Cuddy, 'Irish-Americans and the 1916 election: an episode in immigrant adjustment', in J.D. Walsh (ed.), *The Irish: America's Political Class Selected and Interpreted* (New York, 1976), pp. 228–43.
93. H. Eaton, *A History of Nominating Conventions, 1868–1960* (London, 1964), p. 258.
94. *Gaelic American*, 24 June 1916.
95. Carroll, *American Opinion*, pp. 71–8. The lord chief justice at the trial was Lord Reading, who was appointed by Lloyd George in January 1918 as British ambassador to the US in place of Cecil Spring Rice. Marquess of Reading, *Rufus Isaacs: First Marquess of Reading, 1914–35* (London, 1945).
96. See Whelan, *United States Foreign Policy*, pp. 108–9.
97. Quoted in Tansill, *America and the Fight for Irish Freedom*, pp. 209–10.
98. TNA, FO371/2797, Spring Rice telegram, 4 July 1916.
99. Quoted in Tansill, *America and the Fight for Irish Freedom*, pp. 208–9.
100. Reading, *Rufus Isaacs*, p. 21.
101. NARA, RG59, M580/1, entry 'Great Britain 28 July 1916'; *PWW*, 37, W.W. on Tumulty to Wilson, 20 July 1916.
102. William M. Leary, 'Election of 1916', in Arthur M. Schlesinger, Fred L. Israel, William P. Hansen, *History of American Presidential Election, 1789–1968*, 11 vols (Philadelphia, 2001), pp. 2, 259.
103. Library of Congress (hereafter LC), Robert Lansing papers (hereafter RLP), volume 30, Polk to Lansing, 7 July 1916.
104. B. Willson, *America's Ambassadors to England (1785–1928): A Narrative of Anglo-American Diplomatic Relations* (London, 1928), p. 452; R. Gregory, *Walter Hines Page: Ambassador to the Court of St James* (Kentucky, 1970), p. 161; NARA, RG59, M580/6, 841.00/17a, Lansing to Page, 1 July 1916; Ibid., 841.00/18, Page to Lansing, 3 July 1916.
105. See Hartley, *The Irish Question*, p. 85.
106. Gregory, *Walter Hines Page*, p. 162. Gerard in Germany had met Casement in early 1915 and forwarded 'without comment' letters Casement wrote to Bryan dated 1 February and 8 March 1915, which forcefully asserted that he was not in the pay of Germany, his work was dedicated to aiding Ireland only and he feared for his life from a British-orchestrated conspiracy against him. NARA, RG59, M589/6, 841.00/12, Gerard to Bryan, 8 February 1915; Ibid., 841.00/13, Gerard to Bryan, 9 March 1915. Later on in 1916 and again in 1917, Gerard wrote that Casement visited German prisons where he persuaded men to desert the British army and join the German army. PWW, 36, Gerard to Lansing, 11 April 1916; James W. Gerard, *My Four Years in Germany* (London, 1917), p. 131.
107. NARA, RG59, M580/6, 841.00/20, Resolution, 29 July 1916.
108. *Papers Related to the Foreign Relations of the United States*, 1916 supplement (Washington, 1929), Polk to Page, 2 August 1916; Ibid., Laughlin to Secretary of State, 3 August, 1916; NARA, RG59, M580/6, 841.00/20, Polk to Embassy, 2 August 1916.
109. NARA, RG59, M580/6, 841.00/20a, Polk to Embassy, 2 August 1916.
110. *FRUS*, 1916 supplement, Laughlin to Secretary of State, 3 August 1916. Carroll details the private appeals that were made by individuals, including Cardinal Gibbons, John Quinn, Senator Henry Cabot Lodge, and groups to the British government to save Casement's life. Carroll, *American Opinion*, p. 77.
111. Brian Inglis, *Roger Casement* (London, 1973), pp. 375–6.
112. Hartley, *The Irish Question*, pp. 93–4.
113. Carroll, *American Opinion*, p. 78.
114. NLI, JQP, MS18436, Quinn, 'In the matter of Sir Roger Casement and the Irish situation in America', 2 June 1916, pp. 9, 12. Indeed after Casement arrived in Germany, a report appeared in the *New York World* that he was in the pay of the German government and in early 1915 Casement instructed Quinn to sue for libel which he refused to do as he knew the case would not succeed. Ibid., p. 9. In February 1917, Frost in Queenstown reported that most nationalists believed that Casement was not part of the 'inner councils' in Berlin, he had tried to stop the Rising in Ireland and was 'mad'. Frost agreed with the latter comment, having met Agnes Newman whom he believed to be 'distinctly non compos' (emphasis in original). Nonetheless he was sympathetic to Casement, particularly because of the continuation in position of Captain Bowen-Colthurst after the murder of Francis Sheehy Skeffington. Frost endorsed the Irish nationalists' explanation that 'If you are

going to be mad it is safer to be a Unionist.' NARA, RG59, M580/33, 'The Irish question at the beginning of 1917', 19 January 1917 in Frost to Secretary of State, 23 February 1917.

115. Carroll, *American Opinion*, p. 82; *PWW*, 38, Doyle to Tumulty, 29 September 1916.
116. NARA, RG59, M580/6, Moore to Ashurst, 8 August 1916. A headline in the *Washington Times* on 4 August ran 'Casement appeal arrives too late'.
117. YULMC, FLPP, box 11, file 369, Phelan to Tumulty, 4 August 1916; Ibid., Tumulty to Polk, 5 August 1916. James K. McGuire, chairman of FOIF telegraphed Wilson on 5 August. Ibid., McGuire to Wilson, 5 August 1916; NARA, M580/6, 841.00/23, Ashurst to Lansing, 9, 16 and 25 August 1916.
118. LC, RLP, vol 30, Doyle to Tumulty, 29 September 1916; NARA, M580/6, 841.00/28, Doyle to Tumulty, 28 August 1916.
119. LC, RLP, vol 30, Tumulty to Lansing, 29 September 1916; *PWW*, 38, O'Leary to Wilson, 29 September 1916, fn. 2. US Catholics were already critical of Wilson's 'faltering' Mexican policy. Joseph Edward Cuddy, 'Irish-Americans and the 1916 Election: An Episode in Immigrant Adjustment', *American Quarterly*, 21, 2, Part 1 (summer, 1969), pp. 228–43.
120. NARA, RG59, M580/6, 841.00/23, Polk, 17 August 1916; *PWW*, 37, see pp. 502–14; YULMC, FLPP, box 27, file 370, Polk 6 August 1916; NARA, M580/6, 841.00/28, Lansing to Tumulty, 2 September 1916.
121. Doyle appealed to Wilson also, who requested advice from Lansing on his reply. PWW, 38, Polk to Tumulty, 7 August 1916; NARA, RG59, M580/1, entry 'President 31 August 1916'; Ibid., RG59, M580/6, 841.00/28, Lansing to Tumulty, 2 September 1916.
122. YULMC, PLPP, box 27, file 370, Tumulty to Lansing, 7 September 1916.
123. Ibid., Tumulty to Doyle, 14 October 1916; YULMC, FLPP, Polk to McGuire, 3 October 1916.
124. John M. Blum, *Joe Tumulty and the Wilson era* (Boston, 1951), pp. 108–9; *PWW*, 38, Polk to Tumulty, 7 August, 5 October 1916, Tumulty to Doyle, 14 October 1916; Leary, 'Woodrow Wilson, Irish Americans and the Election of 1916', 62, fn. 22; NARA, RG59, M580/6, 841.00/23, Polk, 17 August 1916.
125. Carroll, *American Opinion*, p. 82; Hartley, *The Irish Question*, p. 109; Ward, *Ireland and Anglo-American Relations*, pp. 128–9; Gwynn, *The Letters and Friendships of Sir Cecil Spring Rice*, ii, Spring Rice to Grey, 16 June 1916.
126. Polk informed Page that Kelly had never been connected with Irish politics and was 'very prominent in Catholic circles ... trustee to St Patrick's Cathedral ... friend of three cardinals'. Smith was known by his 'relation to charity rather than to politics'. Polk asked Page to do everything possible 'to assist these persons' and he also contacted Spring Rice. YULMC, FLPP, box 27, file 369, Polk to Page, 26 July 1916; Ibid., box 34, file 765, Office of the Solicitor to Crane, 31 July 1916; *PWW*, 38, Page to Wilson, c. 23 September 1916, p. 244.
127. *PWW* 38, O'Leary to Wilson, 29 September 1916, p. 285.
128. Leary, 'Woodrow Wilson, Irish Americans and the Election of 1916', p. 64, fn. 29; Tumulty, *Wilson*, p. 214; *PWW*, 38, House to Wilson, 30 September, 1916, p. 317; Ward, *Ireland and Anglo-American Relations*, p. 137.
129. Leary, 'Woodrow Wilson, Irish Americans and the Election of 1916', p. 71; Ward, *Ireland and Anglo-American Relations*, pp. 139–40.
130. Lansing, *War Memoirs*, pp. 163-4; Link and Leary, 'Election of 1916', pp. 2,259-60; David Doyle, 'Irish and American labour, 1880-1920', *Saothar*, 1, 1 (1975), p. 52; E. Cuddy, 'Irish-Americans and the 1916 Election', p. 236.
131. TNA, FO371/2793, Spring Rice, 27 March 1916; Ibid., FO371/3071, Broderick, 19 January 1917.

7

Journées Sanglantes/Days of Blood: The French Press and the Easter Rising

Ian McKeane

At the outbreak of war in 1914 the French press, unlike its British or American counterparts, was at the height of its expansion. The Third Republic up to 1914 had seen the growth of unprecedented press freedom in France and there were some fifty dailies in Paris in early 1914, forty of which presented news as propaganda for a particular political point of view.[1] Their combined circulation had reached nearly 10 million, a figure which has not been significantly surpassed since. The circulation of the four *grands* of the Parisian press – *Le Matin*, *Le Petit Parisien*, *Le Petit Journal* and *Le Journal*, was the greatest in the world.[2] The print media of the Third Republic had been vigorous and had exercised considerable political influence. It had ensured that the various crises of the Third Republic had assumed national characteristics with the result that, by 1914, newspapers were part of every sector of French life and enjoyed a commensurate influence. Great public debates had been conducted in the medium. French newspapers had never been so fully read by so many.

President Poincaré made a call for national unity in the face of the enemy at the outbreak of war. The result was *L'Union Sacrée*, political and moral unity for the war effort which secured widespread patriotic support.[3] Although nearly all the press swung behind the *Union Sacrée* and displayed solidarity with the national will to resist the enemy, censorship was put in place in the run up to hostilities. Thus, political news censorship in France was actually a combination of self-censorship and imposed government control, a control which the government felt was secondary to the self-censorship implied by a paper's support for the *Union Sacrée*. Censorship was criticized on all sides. The journalists felt it was too severe, the politicians felt it was biased and the military thought that it was insufficient. But, all in all, the combination of the appeal to patriotism and the application of censorship was remarkably effective.[4] Morale was maintained and the public successfully kept in the dark about the military defeats, diplomatic disasters, the economic effects and the sheer awfulness of twentieth-century warfare. It fulfilled its essential anaesthetic role of preventing a country, whose nerves were at breaking point, from fully experiencing the brutal realities of the times and this was proved by the fact that the essential was that '*les civils ont tenu*' ('the home front has held').[5] In addition, the French press in the period reflected the French government's political attitudes to the United Kingdom to a remarkable degree. France and its press remained faithful allies of the British despite occasional disagreements.

The weakness of the French papers was that, although they had enjoyed thirty years of unprecedented liberty of expression, this freedom had done nothing to protect them from economic pressures. They never matched the number of pages of the larger British papers. Their overseas news gathering systems were weak and their advertising revenues were pitiful, despite the huge daily sales of certain popular Paris papers.

The first effect of this weakness was the disappearance of certain titles like *L'Aurore*, and many Parisian and provincial small-circulation papers.[6] Advertising revenues, such as they had, dropped rapidly, mainly because of the withdrawal of advertising by the financial sector. The miserable wartime adverts for treasury bonds were no substitute for what had been a good source of income before the war. Nor was an increase in personal advertisements, mainly provoked by the dislocation of populations in the battle zone, an adequate replacement.[7] Unlike the British press, where, during the war, circulation rose and techniques and style evolved, the French press stagnated, due largely to the dual censorship regime and difficulties of distribution in a country which was itself a theatre of war. French newspapers also suffered staffing difficulties as the war progressed. The accounts of the degree of this problem vary but it is clear that, particularly after 1916, when typography ceased to be a reserved occupation, many editorial offices were struggling with a depleted workforce.[8] Also, distribution problems increased for the Parisian press and the major regional papers as the railway system suffered wartime pressures.

Stocks of newsprint were good at the outbreak of war and most paper mills were not affected by the invasion. Nevertheless, the number of pages was reduced by about 50 per cent. But, by the end of 1915, the raw material for newsprint production was becoming rare and expensive. The average cost of newsprint in 1914 was FF 0.313 per kg but, by 1916 it had more than doubled to FF 0.695 per kg.[9] The result was that by April 1916, the majority of the French press were limiting themselves to publishing editions of only four pages. Yet, the total tonnage of paper used continued to rise despite these measures, thanks to the increase in the number of editions published each day.[10]

The telegraph was controlled from 30 July 1914 and long-distance telephone calls forbidden.[11] With the proclaiming of the state of siege on 9 August, the 1849 law came into force, by which the military was given the power to suspend any publication.[12] A *Bureau de Presse* was set up in the War Ministry, charged with the supervision of information, and the government made clear that it counted on the *bon vouloir patriotique* (patriotic goodwill) of the press to refrain from publishing any war news without consulting the *Bureau*. The result was that from the start of hostilities, no real news was given out.[13] When, on 29 August 1914, a report was published indicating that the German advance on the front running from the Somme to the Vosges seemed to have slowed, there was an outcry since this was the first that the population outside the affected *départements* knew of the German invasion of the national territory. As a result, information was subsequently supplied in more detail, although the news was still managed with care.[14]

In the period up to Easter 1916, the French war had broadly two phases. The first was the initial German attack which pushed the French forces back to the Marne in the first weeks of the war and which was then repulsed by the French advance to the Aisne. The second phase then set in, with a broad stabilization of the western front from the sea to the Vosges. French military strategy was essentially defensive and, as such, very successful but this strategy meant the maintenance of military effort without the possibility of a great morale-raising victory. In 1916, plans were laid for a largely co-ordinated series of attacks on the Central Powers by the Allies. The British would attack at the Somme, the French at Verdun, the Russians in Galicia and the Italians in the Veneto. The fortress of Verdun had been tenaciously defended since 1914 and had become a symbol of the French nation's resistance to aggression. Pétain, and later Nivelle, both followed a policy of frequently changing the units defending Verdun so that ultimately over three-quarters of the French infantry battalions in the army actually participated in this national blood sacrifice.[15]

Although international events were reported where they had a bearing on the war, it was unusual to have internal events in the United Kingdom reported in detail, apart from key Commons debates. So, one could reasonably expect the reporting of the events of Easter week in Dublin to be minimal. In fact, this was not the case. Despite the need to balance constraints on reporting Allied military troop dispositions with the need to report events relevant to the war affecting France's closest co-belligerent within the censorship paradigm, the development of the Irish story in 1916 was clearly good copy. Not unexpectedly, there was no mention of the fact that two British divisions were tied up in Ireland as a result.[16]

A further aspect of the background to the reporting of the 1916 Rising was the element of Anglophobia which was part of the journalistic scene.

While relations between units of the French and British armies fighting side by side were generally good, there was a level of distrust of the British by their French allies at a higher level, which was expressed in several ways. From the moment on the Marne in 1914, when Joffre had had to beg Field Marshal French '*au nom de la France*' to agree to participate in the Allied counter attack, British commitment had been viewed equivocally.[17] Even on the British side, the role of the British Expeditionary Force (BEF) at the Marne was seen in different ways. Some chroniclers feel that the small BEF played a key role at the Marne while others hold the opposite view.[18] It is therefore not surprising that the potential hesitation by the British high command in 1914 had been noted by the French. In addition, there was the generally anti-British tone of the reports in the American press from French sources.

By early 1916 the British military were concerned in particular about the reports of anti-British speeches in America by the young politician and journalist André Tardieu. They began to take steps to counter this by establishing a press liaison office in Amiens.[19] Its purpose was to counteract French misconceptions about the scale of the efforts of the British forces on the front where the plans for the battle of the Somme were being laid. Newspaper reporting of the Easter Rising was felt to have fed these misconceptions although, as we shall see, this was more a case of British paranoia. The executions of fifteen rebel leaders in Dublin and Cork between 3 and 12 May were generally felt to have provoked indignation at home and bad publicity for Britain abroad.[20] The French press initially reported the courts martial of the various leaders without adverse comment, although the American press had been loud in its condemnation of the executions and this was later reported in France.

News coverage of the Rising was limited even in the British press, since in Dublin during the week of the Rising only the *Irish Times* was actually published and distribution attempted. Although on the spot, it was unable or unwilling to provide an account of events as they happened and, on 27 April, it described the inability of the public to move safely around the city centre as mere 'enforced domesticity'.[21] When the majority of papers in Ireland reappeared in the first week of May, the unionist *Daily Express* led the general acceptance of the government's view, that the Rising was German-inspired and a prelude to invasion. The rightist papers, both unionist and nationalist, added the ingredient of socialist inspiration to the Rising, unlikely though that might have been if the Germans really were behind the enterprise. Clearly, nobody at the time had an accurate picture of events, or of the different immediate reactions to the Rising by the various elements in the population of Dublin.[22] In this light, the French newspapers seem initially to have been remarkably inventive in their reporting. It also explains why, if any reporting was to be carried out, they would have to rely heavily, at least in the early stages, on the copy to be found in the British press. The Rising was thus initially seen through a British prism.

The first French accounts of events in Ireland appeared in the popular press on Wednesday 26 April under the general heading in *Le Petit Journal*: '*Attaques Allemandes contre l'Angleterre – Un Mauvais coup Boche en Irlande, basé sur la trahison, il échoue*' ('Germans Raid England – Hun Coup In Ireland. Treasonable Base Ensures Failure'). Essentially, this was a report of the British admiralty communiqué about the shelling of Lowestoft and Yarmouth and linked the failed German attempt to land arms on the coast of county Kerry to Berlin's desire to provoke a rising in Ireland. The pre-war division in Ireland between the Orangemen and the nationalists was given as the basis of the German plan. This had been scotched, according to *Le Petit Parisien*, by Irish '*loyauté envers l'Angleterre*' ('loyalty to England') since the outbreak of war.[23] The arrest of Roger Casement during the Kerry mission was also noted as a further disappointment for the Germans.

The earliest French newspaper report of the Easter Rising is contained in a report of the response by the chief secretary for Ireland, Augustine Birrell, to a question in the Commons.[24] He stated that the Rising had broken out on Monday and that five areas of the city were under rebel control. He added that troops had been moved in from the Curragh camp in county Kildare and that the Rising had been subdued (*maitrisé*). Other incidents reported under the same title were the dropping of seventy bombs in a Zeppelin raid on East Anglia and the brief naval bombardment of the Suffolk coast by units of the German navy. This was the final feeble manifestation of what had been a major plan hatched in Berlin which was intended to link German logistic support for a rising in Ireland with a serious attack on the English east coast. This would have had the affect of forcing the withdrawal of many British troops from the western front to counter a possible landing and restore order in Ireland.[25] However, by April 1916 the initial German enthusiasm for this plan had waned somewhat.

Other papers also carried similar reports. *Le Petit Parisien* claimed: '*Un Navire Allemand Tente De Débarquer Des Armes En Irlande*' ('German Ship Attempts Arms Landing in Ireland') and '*En Irlande, Tentative Allemande*' in *Le Figaro* ('Ireland, Germans attempt coup'). Taking three Parisian papers as examples of the reporting of the events of Easter week in Dublin, a common pattern emerges. Broadly, it took forty-eight hours to publish in France the news of the Easter Rising. This was because most sources were in London, adding twenty-four hours to the delay. These three papers had different emphases. *Le Petit Journal* gave the simplest accounts but the most frequent. Its presentational style was superficially similar to that of its main competitor, *Le Petit Parisien*, with a main heading, sometimes across two columns, and then a series of smaller sub-headings over perhaps no more than one or two sentences of text. The front page carried the main news content while page three had the heading *Dernière heure* ('Latest news') which added to, updated or expanded items on the first page. This was also the format for the other papers although the page headings could vary.

Overall in 1916, *Le Petit Journal* carried the most pieces, with sixty-five reports concerning the Rising and Ireland. The totals for *Le Petit Parisien* and *Le Figaro* were sixty and twenty-three respectively. *Le Petit Journal* carried thirteen illustrations, including three maps and two cartoons, while *Le Petit Parisien* carried thirteen illustrations, two maps, a Dublin city plan and one in-depth article. *Le Figaro* did not often indulge in frivolities like illustrations, although John Redmond, leader of the Irish Nationalists in the House of Commons, did merit a photo, an indication of the importance given to the 'loyal' Irish that he represented.

The first thing that strikes one when reading these papers is the variety of terminology for what was happening in Dublin. *Le Petit Journal* had the widest variety, using six different terms: *désordres* ('disorders'), *émeute* ('uprising'), *révolte* ('revolt'), *combat dans les rues* ('street battles'), *insurrection* and *rébellion*. The paper also carried a translation of Redmond's manifesto of 11 May where he renounced *l'agitation folle et sterile* ('the insane and sterile agitation'). The use by *Le Petit Journal* of increasingly powerful epithets as the days went by indicated a perception of the events of Easter week as being more serious than perhaps the British authorities wished to accept. Similarly, the language of the pacification is revealing. Phrases used included: *l'ordre est rétablie* ('order re-established'), *repression*, *état de siege* ('stage of seige'), *rebelles cernés par les troupes* ('rebels surrounded by troops'), *l'émeute enrayée* ('the uprising routed'), *l'écrasement de la révolte* ('the revolt crushed') and *pacification*, most of which underlined the serious effort required to regain control of what was one of the United Kingdom's major cities.

The sudden disappearance of Irish matters from *Le Petit Journal* in late June indicates at the very least that the sub-editorial staff were aware of the likelihood of pressure from the censors at the *Bureau de la Presse* and at most that such pressure had been applied directly. *Le Petit Journal* would not assert its independence by printing empty columns if it could help it. Paper was too hard to come by. In any case it was firmly behind the war effort and *L'Union Sacrée*, and blank spaces would imply disagreement with the policy. This is the most likely explanation given that the spring of 1916 was the period when the joint Allied summer offensive was in preparation. The French government could not, at this particular time, have its popular press full of references to *insurrection* and *rébellion* in its closest ally's back yard. The use of *émeute*, with its overtones of disorganized spontaneity, was much more acceptable.

This theory is reinforced by the fact that *Le Petit Parisien* and *Le Figaro* had already more or less dropped the story with the first executions of the leaders in early May. *Le Figaro* rounded off its coverage by reassuring everyone on 4 May with its two headers: *Dublin a repris son aspect normal* and *Le calme en province* ('Dublin back to normal' and 'Provinces quiet'). This begs the question of how the first could be true after the British bombardment of Lower Sackville (now O'Connell) Street and Liberty Hall but the intention is clear enough. However, both these papers did make more effort than *Le Petit Journal* to provide some initial analysis, and the article in *Le Figaro* on 30 April 1916 is particularly interesting and will be discussed later.

This point touches on a central dilemma of the British government. After martial law had been declared, the government also delegated the political management of the events to the military. What this means is that the government was forced to admit that the Rising was no longer 'a street riot on a grand scale', to use Townshend's phrase, and had to give General Sir John Maxwell full powers.[26] His job was to quell the affair and punish the participants as quickly as possible and this he did. His methods – military repression followed by courts martial and rapid executions, not just of the avowed leaders, but of others including sick and wounded prisoners – threw the whole affair into a higher relief than the government felt comfortable with. It also provoked a negative public response from Ireland, Britain and America which also worked to elevate the events of Easter week to the status of a major event.

Looking at the Rising narrative found in these papers there are broadly two principal themes with a third sub-theme common to both. All three themes were closely interwoven as the story developed chronologically. The 'story' begins with Casement's landing on Banna strand in county Kerry and his arrest on Good Friday, 21 April 1916. The clearest way of examining the first theme is by tracking a selection of the headlines in *Le Petit Journal* in the week following the Rising. The coverage begins under the header *Un Mauvais Coup Boche en Irlande* ('A Low Blow by the Hun in Ireland') and the piece indicates that the Rising was inspired or instigated by the Germans.[27]

Harder news followed under the header *Le Pirate S'est Fait Sauter* ('The Pirate Ship Blew Itself Up'), which referred to the scuttling of the *Libau*, better known as the *Aud*, in Cobh harbour.[28] This was the German auxiliary cruiser which had sailed for Ireland from Germany as a gun-runner in late March 1916. She was disguised as a Norwegian merchant ship while having a German naval crew under the command of *Kapitän* Karl Spindler.[29] This initiative was part of the support negotiated by

Casement in Berlin for Irish resistance to British rule, although he was not privy to the final plans for the actual Easter Rising. The result was, of course, that these arms were lost to the Irish Volunteers.

This is followed by the header *L'Allemagne Avait Promis un Débarquement de Troupes* ('Germany had Promised a Military Landing') and the report made the point that the Rising was a military failure precisely because the German troops had not materialized.[30] A newspaper report of an event which did not happen is hardly news; rather, it is propaganda, but the importance of this item is as an indication of the strategic vulnerability of Ireland, at least at first sight. It also suggests that the report owes its origins to British newspaper reports which were based on the idea of German organization which lay behind the Irish Rising.

A major element in the story of Easter 1916 as reported in the French press was the arrest, trial and execution of Casement. This gained immediate importance to French sub-editors because it presented them with a name of note on which to hang the whole story of the Rising. This technique of personalization is common to all newspaper reporting. Personalities are seen as intrinsically more interesting to the reader than depersonalized events. Casement provides the key to the puzzle of the Easter Rising in the French press.

Casement was a professional diplomat of Anglo-Irish origin who had made his reputation by revealing colonial excesses in the Belgian Congo and the enslavement of native Americans by planters in Brazil and Peru.[31] Before the outbreak of war he had become convinced of the justice of the Irish nationalist cause, and in 1914 was fund-raising in America. He then went to Germany in the autumn of 1914 in the hope of arranging military support for a rising in Ireland. He was partially successful in that a shipment of arms was sent from Germany in April 1916 although, as we have seen, the ship was captured soon after entering Irish waters and scuttled by its crew as it was being escorted into Cobh.[32] He himself was landed on the coast of county Kerry from a u-boat and promptly arrested. Escorted through Dublin at Easter weekend 1916, he was taken to London, tried for treason, found guilty and hanged in early August.[33]

In any analysis of the French coverage of the deaths of these Irish nationalists in the hands of the British, the issue of personalization in those reports is crucial. The subtle interplay of factions and extra-parliamentary groups which constituted the run-up to the 1916 Rising was never explained to the French readership. It was not explained to the British either, since the news media in both countries insisted that the Rising was the result of a German plot. However, there were some attempts at analysis and explanation in France after the events.[34]

Their method was through identification of certain key individuals. Little space was given to the fifteen leaders who were shot. In any case, their names meant nothing to the ordinary reader. On the other hand, Casement's arrest, trial and execution did receive considerable coverage. There are a variety of reasons for this. First, he seemed to embody the premise of German involvement. Secondly, he was relatively upper class and at least a 'gentleman'. Such an individual was understood to embody the cultural norms of 'Englishness' as portrayed by popular writers in France such as Jules Verne and André Maurois.[35] Thirdly, Casement had an international reputation as a campaigner against colonial excesses in the Belgian Congo and in South America and these activities had been covered in the French press in earlier years.[36]

A final factor was that it took the British far longer to dispose of him than the other fifteen leaders of the Rising, who were all court-martialled and shot within ten days of their surrender. This gave more opportunity for lengthy coverage and analysis. To this last must be added the intrinsic interest in the chances and conduct of a man on trial for his life, something which always made for good copy in France. The death penalty in France was still carried out according to the words of the sentence 'on a public square'.[37] However, executions were arranged at times of day and with security measures in place to ensure that few, if any, of the general public would be able to observe the grisly process.[38]

To return to the events of April 1916, the news of Casement's arrest on landing from a German submarine was headed *Sans Moi, dit Casement, La Rebellion N'existe Plus* ('Casement: Without me there is no Rising') and French readers were shown that Casement was linked with the events in Dublin as the presumed leader of the rebels.[39] This cemented the idea in readers' minds that the German high command was behind the Easter Rising. The cunning of the enemy was immediately rendered less menacing by the next report of incompetence by what were described as 'German agents'. The header was *Les Complices* ('The Accomplices').[40] This report covered the incident at Killorglin, Kerry, where three Irish Volunteers, who had intended to contact and liaise with the German arms ship, were drowned when their car ran into the sea. *Des Officiers allemands parmi les morts?* ('German officers among the rebel dead?') headed a note of the rumour in Dublin of actual German military involvement and served to reinforce the idea of German inspiration for the Rising.[41] The ineffective management and execution of the whole affair was described under the heading *La Main de l'Allemagne* ('The Hand of Germany').[42]

Finally, this first theme of the German plot was summed up by the report headed *L'Émeute en Irlande: La Part prise par l'Allemagne* ('The Irish Rising: Germany's Role') with the general conclusion that the results of what could be called the 'German effect' on the Rising were shown to be minimal, thanks to German incompetence. The inference is that eventually Germany will be defeated by the Allies.[43] *Le Petit Journal* thus manages to put the best possible gloss, from its readers' point of view, on the sorry events in Ireland.

The second theme is that of the Rising itself. This can be clearly identified in a sequence of headlines from *Le Petit Parisien*. The first report was headed *Une Émeute Éclate à Dublin. Elle est Aussitôt Maitrisée* ('A Riotous Disturbance Breaks out in Dublin. It is Immediately Overcome').[44] The events in Dublin were described as a local difficulty. They were limited to Dublin itself and the government was rapidly in full control of the city. The fact that the disturbances were limited to Dublin was reinforced under the heading *Les Troubles de Dublin N'ont pas Gagné D'autres Villes* ('Dublin Troubles have not Reached other Cities').[45] It is interesting to note that the '*émeute*' had become '*troubles*' and later a '*rebellion*'. In early May a report appeared headed *Les Dessous de la Rebellion Irlandaise* ('What Lay Behind the Irish Rebellion'), which sought to tie in German Celtic scholars with the Rising.[46] In particular, it accused Professor Zimmer and Professor Kuno Meyer. Despite this, the main conclusion of this report was that the British war effort had not been affected since the whole business was on such a small scale that the British garrison in Ireland had no difficulty in dealing with the problem.

After the Rising, its implications were discussed, superficially at least. *Le Petit Parisien* reported that the vast majority of the Irish at home and overseas condemned the Rising; therefore the Irish units in the army who are fighting alongside the French are totally loyal. This was headed *Les Irlandais du Dehors Expriment leur Réprobation* ('Overseas Irish Show their Anger').[47] This was reinforced by the next heading, *Le Pape Invite le Clergé à Prêcher le Calme* ('Pope Calls on Clergy to Preach Calm') over a report of papal intervention in Ireland and assurances to Asquith that the Irish hierarchy would work for the re-establishment of normality. The end of the Rising was signalled by the heading *Les Forteresses des Émeutiers Tombent une à une aux Mains des Troupes Régulières* ('Rebel Strongholds Fall one by one to Regular Troops').[48] The destruction of Dublin city centre and the rigours of martial law were described as the inevitable result of the military repression of the Rising.

A further theme, common to all the papers examined, is that of personalization through the imagined or actual role of Casement. This has been discussed above. What does emerge from the pages of the French newspapers is the fact that the names of the leadership of the Rising, the members of the Provisional government of the proclaimed Irish Republic, were completely unknown to those outside. This may be surprising to students of the 1916 Easter Rising and its aftermath. Only three of the fourteen leaders executed in Dublin were named in the French papers, since the details of the courts martial and the sentences were of little import to the French.[49]

It fell to Casement to figure as the personality at the centre of the whole story of the Rising.[50] His landing and arrest were intertwined with reports about the events in Dublin. He was not unknown to readers of the French press since reports of his pre-war exploits had appeared in various papers at the time. It was his social status as knight of the realm and establishment figure, yet apparently guilty of treasonable activities in Berlin, which gripped the imagination of readers in 1916. Here was a deeply flawed and tragic individual who clearly faced the death penalty for high treason. The story of the final act of his life intrigued the French readership. He was described variously in French newspapers as 'unique', 'a traitor', 'a sad character', 'a coward' and 'the organizer of the underhand action against Ireland'.[51] What was of interest to the readers of the French press was the personality involved. Casement's bearing and social class rendered his situation even more fascinating for the readers. However, the Belgian press reserved the unique epithet *congophobe* for him as an expression of loyal bitterness.[52] Whatever description was appropriate, he made good copy and provided a means to explain, however inaccurately, the strange events in Dublin.

The 1916 Rising caught everyone unawares, outside a relatively small circle of revolutionaries, and it is, therefore, not surprising that the press in France was unable to present an original view on its political background. Casement's arrest, trial and execution, on the other hand, provided an opportunity for an explanation of the events in Dublin at Easter through the examination of Casement's activities and by concentrating on his personality with its presumed defects which led him to betray his country and her allies.[53] In effect, the human interest aspect of what, to most readers, would be a story of political developments of little intrinsic interest provided a framework for some discussion of the political background. Where there is the possibility of demonization of the individual then the copy can be even better. Furthermore, those of the readership who, at best, had ambivalent feelings towards Britain, and at worst were bluntly Anglophobic, could enjoy the spectacle of the British establishment convulsed by having to try one of its own on a charge of high treason.[54]

Yet, it must be stressed that the political motives that drove Casement were not given the airing in either the British or the French press that they might have gained had his trial been held in peacetime. Had that been the case, his crime would possibly not have had quite the same resonance. This said, the discussion of Casement's character is still in progress nearly a century later.[55] In the atmosphere of the second year of the Great War, Casement's actions and his arrest were inevitably going to lead to prosecution and conviction for high treason followed by execution. How could such a man have betrayed his country and, by extension, its wartime ally, France? So, the press continued to feed the prejudices of their readers by the technique of personalization; presenting the issues in terms of the personality of the chief protagonist of the story.

It is clear that it was felt that there was a need to explain the fact of a rebellion in part of the United Kingdom to the French public. The line adopted from the outset was broadly London's official reaction to the events. This is not to say that what was being presented was pure propaganda, since that might imply that it was factually inaccurate. Rather, it was a set of beliefs and opinions favoured by London which provided an immediate and credible explanation of the events to French readers.

Three additional factors came into play. The first was the fact that the Rising lasted as long as it did. At first sight, it might appear that the French press gave a hostage to fortune by suggesting that the Rising was over almost as soon as it began. Yet, the lack of hard news meant that French newsmen took Secretary Birrell's statement in the Commons on Tuesday 25th at face value. He was not contradicted by aggressive questioning by the opposition, so why not believe him? Secondly, it soon became clear that the events in Dublin were mysteriously not affected by Casement's fate. Unknown to the Rising's actual leaders, who were locked in debate at Liberty Hall, he was taken through Dublin to take the boat for England on Easter Saturday morning, apparently preoccupied with the possibility of eventually getting a good night's sleep.[56] By Wednesday, he was imprisoned in the Tower of London and the development of the Rising was such that martial law had been declared in Dublin.

Thirdly, there is the fact that the French were reporting internal events in a neighbouring Allied country. This ensured that the London administration was to be given, diplomatically, the benefit of the doubt. It took over a week before any analysis was attempted. When it came, it was carefully handled and there was little attempt to attribute responsibility to the British administration.

Given the lack of direct reports from Dublin it is not surprising that during Easter week 1916 there was a tendency to personalize the news by concentrating on the capture of Sir Roger Casement. In any case it was a good story. Here is a member of the British establishment with one of those exotic English titles, who, until the beginning of April, has been in the chancelleries of the enemy. He then travels by submarine to the west of Ireland and is landed in a little rubber boat, captured almost immediately, taken to London and lodged in the tower in a traitor's cell. At the same time, the Germans send an armed merchantman to the west of Ireland and this is intercepted by the Royal Navy and scuttled.

Casement's potted biography under the title *Le Traître Casement* in *Le Petit Parisien* described his diplomatic career as 'brilliant', listing his consular postings to Mozambique, Congo, Haiti and Brazil.[57] His knighthood was elevated to a baronetcy and details of his pension, FF 10,500, were given. His involvement in the foundation of the Irish Volunteers, in response to the activities of Carson and his Ulster associates in 1912, was briefly but accurately stated. His wanderings in 1914 from Ireland to the US and thence to Germany were indicated, stressing the point that he had 'refused to forget, like all the other nationalist leaders, past misunderstandings and face the common enemy'.[58] His unsuccessful attempts to raise an Irish legion, particularly at Limburg POW camp, were chronicled with the added fanciful detail that those who had booed his efforts were denied food and that seventy of them had died of hunger, thanks to the efforts of their evil captors. A photo of Casement, taken in South America some years before, was provided on the first page.[59]

For the ordinary French reader, here was a brilliant and brave member of the British ruling class who had gone wrong. The fact that he had been honoured for specific activities in the Congo and Brazil was submerged by the 'brilliance' of his career, chiefly defined by the exotic places where he had been British consul. Much of the information had been culled from the British press, and the paper felt that he was a *singulier personnage*, although stressing his treason. We can only speculate what the response of the readers of the paper was to this information. Yet the elements that would appeal to them were his title, his class and his obvious treason, which would lead inevitably to the gallows. This was an excuse for open *schadenfreude*.

There is an additional factor, which is the impersonal nature of the fairly static trench warfare which had developed by this time. There was a constant search for the individual in this mass warfare. This is evident in the reporting of the war in general. An example is the article in *L'Illustration* in August about the execution by the Germans of the English Merchant Navy captain, Fryatt, who had rammed an attacking u-boat off the Dutch coast.[60] In a recent paper, Joanna Bourke has examined this theme with reference to the training of troops in hand-to-hand combat, specifically with the bayonet, in a war in which such combat was extremely rare. She suggests that images of such combat, which she calls the bayonet fantasy, dominated practically all the writing of the time.[61] Such a perception of the war was as a triumph of the individual over the anonymity of the reality. Casement filled a need for a name, a character and a story which, in addition, provided extra elements of the unexpected, the exotic and the flawed.

The other leaders of the Rising were presented to the French public, although, not surprisingly, with less journalistic zeal. Although their names are now engraved on the columns of the pantheon of Irish nationalist martyrs, in April 1916 they were quite unknown to most people outside their immediate circle. Certainly, the French public had never heard of them. Short biographical articles about Pearse, Connolly and Countess Markievicz were printed, although there was some doubt about how to spell their names. But their time in the public eye was short, and any further examination and analysis of their actions could have led the French press away from the line of the German plot, although this cannot be proven.

It seems that the only Irish 'agitator' who might have been recognized in France was James Larkin, whose left-wing syndicalist activities in 1912 and 1913 in Dublin had been widely reported. In fact, *Le Petit Parisien* expressed surprise that he was not at the head of the rebels, adding, rather disingenuously, that he was in a mental institution in White Plains in the US. This was not true, although he was apparently depressed at the news of the Rising.[62]

Two articles which sought to give a deeper explanation of the Irish situation appeared in *Le Figaro* in April. The first, called *L'émeute de Dublin*, signed 'A. Fitz-Maurice', was a general tirade laying the responsibility for Irish problems on the Germans and their scheming over the last fifteen years.[63] Fitz-Maurice suggested that ever since the Boer War, the Germans had been stirring up trouble for the British. During that war, they had had De Wet in their pay and now Casement. The writer considered that the Germans were insane to think that a Dublin rising with Casement's connivance could succeed and, had blood not been spilt, then the whole thing would have been laughable. Sinn Féin were described as a small faction of illiterate peasants who had been active since 1913 and who had already demonstrated on the streets earlier in the spring of 1916.

What is interesting about this piece is that it takes Casement's activity more seriously than perhaps the British would have wished. It dismisses Sinn Féin but justifies any space given to them by the potential seriousness of the Casement plan. This must have been written as an initial reaction to the first news from Ireland. Had the Rising been squashed in the first two days then this interpretation would have had more validity. On 30 April 1916, another piece by the same writer was published in *Le Figaro* under the header *Les Sinn Féiners*.[64] This article was more considered and critical of the British administration of Ireland. Fitz-Maurice felt that Chief Secretary Birrell and Prime Minister Asquith had been negligent in failing to maintain Irish internal security in the light of Redmondite nationalist support for the war effort. As other writers have noted, they did have a habit of procrastination in the hope that any action would soon become irrelevant: part indeed of their 'tenor of governance which tended to a languorous mandarin assurance'.[65]

Fitz-Maurice alleges that Birrell spent too little time in the country that he was supposed to be governing and had allowed the advanced nationalist movement to flourish unchecked. This said, the real instigators of the Rising were, allegedly, the Germans, who had 'duped' the young Volunteers into action. He continues to the effect that the real Irish will let this plot wither and die and allow Asquith to concentrate on conscripting enough soldiers to fight alongside the French and address the problem of the British defeat in Mesopotamia. There is clear criticism of the British policy in Ireland and that their control of the country was only saved by the loyalty of the 'real Irish'. Here the sub-text is that, indirectly, the 'real Irish' may have also saved the entire war, since their loyalty enabled the British to concentrate on pulling their weight on the western front. This is particularly neat since the reputation of the Irish troops in the field, at Loos, near Lens, for example, was maintained while giving expression to the general feeling, already described above, that the British were not quite as committed to the defence of France as they might be.[66]

The *Académicien*, Gabriel Hanotaux, historian, politician and foreign affairs expert, contributed a piece in *Le Figaro* on 28 April which discussed the possible effects of the Rising on the diplomatic efforts to obtain America's entry into the war on the side of the Triple Entente.[67] He saw the events in Ireland as further proof of the underhand activities of the Germans before the war. Now several thousand young Irishmen had risked their honour and lives for the puppeteers of Berlin, just as fifteen years before in the Transvaal. Such a rising in so secure a state as the United Kingdom, as a result of German plotting, shows that even the national integrity of America could be equally under threat. President Wilson should take note. '*Que Dublin L'avertisse!*' ('Let him be Warned by Dublin!'), thunders Hanotaux, and he adds that foreign minister Zimmerman and military attaché, von Papen, later to be Hitler's ambassador to London, are up to no good in Washington.

This is an intriguing slant on the Rising and again shows that French policymakers took it very seriously. While seeking to minimize its effects in the popular press, occasional articles like this do reveal a higher level of political concern. As if to complement this article – or perhaps distract the casual reader from it – another under the title *Rocambole* by Alfred Capus, also an *Académicien* and joint editor of *Le Figaro*, appeared on the same page in the next column. This made light of the colossal and despicable German plan to dominate Europe, of which the Easter Rising was a small part. Capus finds the whole Irish business redolent of the *Exploits de Rocambole* one of the *romans-feuilleton*, popular serial novels, by the second-empire pulp fiction writer, Ponson de Terrail.[68] He continued by affirming that, naive though the German scheme might have been, it had its dangers and any partial success would be eventually negated by the need to dominate the US as well. *Le Figaro* was clearly aiming its message at the White House and Capitol Hill.

Finally, a most interesting piece appeared in *Le Petit Parisien* by Charles Le Goffic, a poet and novelist from Lannion in Brittany.[69] Its full title was *Les dessous de la rébellion irlandaise où l'on voit à l'oeuvre les allemands Zimmer et Kuno Meyer* ('The secret depths of the Irish rebellion where the Germans Zimmer and Kuno Meyer are at work'). It was illustrated by a photo of John Redmond, the acceptable face of Ireland's politics. The article opens with an 1899 quote from Professor Heinrich Zimmer about the powerful agitation in the 'Celtic fringe of the United Kingdom's rich overcoat' which, he suggests, will lead to a new European phenomenon of pan-Celticism as important as the actual phenomena of pan-Germanism and pan-Slavism. Zimmer and his successor at Berlin, Kuno Meyer, were both philologists, specializing in the study of the Celtic languages, and the article proceeds to charge them with being instrumental in forging the connection between German imperial ambitions and the Easter Rising.

Pre-war German subversive activity was seen as complex and resourceful and Zimmer and Meyer attracted a 'naive clientèle of Irish students' to their courses, thereby emulating the agents of the *Wilhelmstraße*. Le Goffic asks who would have suspected academic philologists of secret recruitment to the German cause. Nobody; so they were given a free hand. He continues by telling his readers that Meyer taught at Liverpool University for twenty-five years while being involved in the Gaelic revival. Cork and Dublin made him a freeman of their cities and, once back in Berlin, he corresponded with the leaders of Sinn Féin. In 1914 he went to America and is believed by many to have been instrumental in arranging for Casement to attempt to form an Irish legion at Limburg. This is not correct. It was Richard Meyer, no relation to Kuno Meyer, who did so much to facilitate Casement's *entrée* to the chancellery in Berlin in 1914.[70]

The article continues by outlining the failure of these academic undercover agents to realize that things were now much better in Ireland, as indicated by the French scholar Joseph Loth, *Professeur au Collège de France*. According to him, only Connacht now contained areas of extreme poverty. Even here, England, mindful of its debt towards the 300,000 Irish soldiers in its army, would surely not allow the scourge of famine to reappear. Le Goffic, following L. Paul-Dubois, describes Sinn Féin, which, incidentally, he translates correctly as *nous-mêmes* ('we ourselves'), as a collection of retrogrades unworthy of consideration, *ramassés de declasses*. He then touches on the historical links between Ireland and France, recalling the emotional accounts by French visitors of how even the poorest Irish peasants showed a genuine interest in the fortunes of

France in the war of 1870–1.[71] Yet, he asserts, the Irish rebels, by shooting at the loyal English ally, are also firing on the French.

The final part of the article asks if there should be some French
responsibility for this state of affairs given that France was once seen as
'the only sympathetic nation' by the Irish. Le Goffic is on dangerous
ground here. He avoids trouble by wondering if France should have not
left the field free to Zimmer and Meyer and should have done more to
maintain that sympathy to Ireland and other small nations, thereby coun-
tering German influence. He feels that, now, France must counter propaganda with propaganda, since the fire-ship lit on England's flank by the
kaiser burned brightly and the seduction of even a small misguided group
of extreme nationalists was too much.

Again, it is clear that, on reflection, the French took the events of
1916 seriously and, although the direct involvement of Zimmer and
Meyer in the Rising was non-existent (Zimmer had died in 1910 and
Meyer was in California), the influence of continental academics on the
self-confidence of those promoting the Gaelic revival of the 1890s was
considerable. Douglas Hyde in his famous address to the National
Literary Society in Dublin on the necessity for de-Anglicizing Ireland in
November 1892 refers to the interest shown in Celtic studies by such as
Zimmer and the French academic, Henri d'Arbois de Jubainville, who
taught at the Sorbonne.[72] Although Hyde never spoke out for home rule
or Irish independence, his movement, *Conradh na Gaeilge* (Gaelic League)
formally associated itself with the struggle for independence by declaring
in 1915 that its activities had both a political and cultural significance.[73]

Le Goffic's thesis, that any student of these continental academics
would return to Ireland fired up with a desire to resort to arms to gain her
freedom, was exaggerated to say the least. It is also worth noting his
omission of Henri d'Arbois de Jubainville. Biographers of J.M. Synge
paint a picture of the Irish writer as a tweedy student in 1902 sitting,
often as the only student present, in de Jubainville's lectures on Old Irish
at the Sorbonne.[74] Synge, of course, is not remembered as a revolutionary,
but had died five years before the Rising. Le Goffic was correct, though,
in implying that Irish nationalists and intellectuals abroad did tend to
know each other and corresponded from time to time. Casement knew
and corresponded with Kuno Meyer.[75] Larkin met Meyer in America.[76]
Synge knew Yeats and Maude Gonne and was encouraged by them.[77]
Maude Gonne later married John MacBride, another leader of the Rising,
shot in May 1916. Yeats knew the Gore Booth sisters, one of whom,
Constance Markievicz, was with Connolly, once Larkin's deputy, in the
Rising. The network was there but it was certainly not driven by German
gown and dagger men. In fact, French academics and writers, such as
Renan, Loti, de Jubainville and possibly even Le Goffic himself as a

'Celtic' poet, could also be said to have had a degree of responsibility.

This state of affairs is indicative of the success of British cultural propaganda. While the notion of cultural colonialism is still a matter for debate, in imperial days there was a particular perception of Ireland.[78] The imperialist view was that British rule in Ireland had been necessary, since the Irish could not govern themselves. This led to the implicit basis of French analysis at this time. We can see how Ireland was viewed through the, perhaps, distorting lens of its larger eastern island neighbour. Those French writers who had actually been there, from de Tocqueville and Baron de Mandat-Grancy down to Louis Paul-Dubois, gave so much space to descriptions of the quaint poverty-struck peasantry that, despite attempting analysis of the socio-political structure of the place, it was their exotic descriptions of the people and the country that impressed the reader. The French reporters in 1916 had done their homework and so it is not surprising that their view of the events of that year, as reported in the immediate aftermath of the Rising, should be dismissive of its actual Irish input. If these people could not govern themselves then surely they could not be sufficiently self-organized to carry out a rebellion.

French reporters were sophisticated professionals, although they had little notion of the true nature of the small group of socialists and advanced nationalists who had jointly carried out the Rising. Nevertheless, they attempted to explain the rationale of the events from what information they did have. The official British view of a German-inspired coup was entirely credible at the time. They managed to convey subtle messages of criticism of the *allié loyal* without undermining the reputation of Irish troops in the field. But they were labouring under considerable difficulties. Even the British press only had a hazy idea of what was happening in Dublin before the Wednesday of Easter week. The Irish themselves, beyond the relatively narrow confines of the centre of Dublin, were more or less completely in the dark.[79] French reporters gained their information by scouring the British and American press and from the Havas news agency. They were limited by the demands in their papers for space for reports of the other events of the war and restricted by the self censorship which had evolved by then. Above all, they could not offend their ally, against whom the Irish had risen. Despite all this, they stuck with the story, and inspection of the reportage reveals a surprising quality of coverage, given all the difficulties.

The political background to the events of April 1916 in Ireland was explained simply as a German plot without any rational involvement by an Irish political movement. This was the line that the British authorities had taken as soon as they had realized that a rising was taking place in Dublin. It was reasonable, given that they had arrested Casement two days before it broke out.[80] The situation of total war demanded that the enemy be blamed for any such event, and such was the wickedness of the 'boche' that they were surely the prime movers behind the events in Dublin. Certainly, the British were not prepared to admit to widespread political disaffection and it was not in the interests of the French to suggest that their ally's war commitment was anything but politically and militarily totally solid. Furthermore, the French were constantly seeking any further proof of their enemy's dastardly behaviour, so the theory of German machinations in Ireland, behind Britian's back, as it were, was accepted uncritically.[81]

It could be argued that, as there had been considerable press coverage of the activities of the Irish Volunteers and the Ulster crisis just before the outbreak of war, some attempt to link this with the Rising might have been made. However, Redmond, as leader of the Irish Parliamentary Party in the Commons, had proclaimed the duty of every Irishman to enlist in the greater struggle against tyranny, and thousands of his Volunteers had responded positively to his call.[82] Khaki-clad, they were now in the ranks of the British ally fighting alongside their French comrades to drive the invader from French territory. There were, of course, significant numbers of Irish Volunteers in Ireland who were involved in training for unspecified future military activity and had not enlisted in the British army.[83]

This fact was not covered in any detail in the French press. To do so would have impugned the reliability of the great ally whose 'tommies' were holding the line along the front beside the brave French *poilus*. The result was that, by the end of the week, the French reporters were able to convey, with some degree of comment, something of the tragic confusion, danger, death and destruction which marked *les journées sanglantes de Dublin* (Dublin's bloody days).

As the situation in Ireland quietened, as civil rule was re-established and the vast majority of the participants in the Rising imprisoned, the trial of Casement was eclipsed by the great battles on the western front of July 1916. As was the custom in the French press, no hint was given of the tremendous losses sustained by the Allies on the Somme and at Verdun. Reports were constant but invariably optimistic. Eventually, the lack of progress made in throwing back the invader became clear to any careful reader. As July wore on, no criticism of the noble ally could be levelled openly for this lack of progress, but the trial of Casement was to put England quietly in the dock.

NOTES

1. R. Manévy, *La Presse de la Troisième République* (Paris, 1955), p. 142.
2. R. de Livois, *Histoire de la Presse Française: de 1881 à nos jours* (Lausanne, 1965) p. 373.
3. A. Cobban, *A History of Modern France*, vol. III (Harmondsworth, 1955), p. 108.
4. C. Bellanger (ed.), *Histoire de la Presse, Tome 3: de 1871 à 1940* (Paris, 1972), p. 413.
5. Bellanger (ed.), *Histoire*, p. 413 and P.Renouvin, 'L'opinion publique et la guerre 14–18', in *Revue D'histoire Diplomatique* (Octobre–Décembre 1970).
6. *L'Aurore* reappeared after the Great War.
7. Manévy, *La Presse*, p. 148.
8. De Livois, *Histoire de la Presse*, p. 142 and Bellanger (ed.), *Histoire*, p. 410.
9. F. Amaury, *Histoire du Plus Grand Quotidien de la IIIe République: Le Petit Parisien 1876–1944* (Paris, 1972), p. 432.
10. Amaury, *Histoire*, p. 432.
11. Bellanger (ed.), *Histoire*, p. 409.
12. Ibid.
13. Ibid.
14. Ibid., p. 410.
15. M. Ferro, *La Grande Guerre 1914–1918* (Paris, 1969), p. 143; R. Wolfson and J. Laver, *Years of Change: Europe 1890–1945* (London, 1996), pp. 190–1.
16. Ferro, *Guerre*, p. 184.
17. Ibid., p. 101.
18. J-B. Duroselle, 'Les Ententes Cordiales', in F. Bédarida, F Crouzet and D Johnson, (eds), *De Guillame le Conquérant au Marché Commun: Dix Siècles D'histoire Franco–Britannique* (Paris, 1979), p. 318.
19. N. Lytton, *The Press and the General Staff* (London, 1920), p. 56.
20. C. Duff, *Six Days to Shake an Empire* (London, 1966), p. 187.
21. J.J. Lee, *Ireland 1912–1985: Politics and Society* (Cambridge, 1989), p. 29.
22. Lee, *Ireland*, p. 30.
23. *Le Petit Parisien*, 29 April 1916.
24. *Le Petit Journal*, 26 April 1916.
25. M. Girodias, *The Black Diaries of Roger Casement* (New York, 1959), p. 405.
26. C. Townshend, 'The Suppression of the Easter Rising', *Bullán*, 1, 1 (spring 1994), p. 30.
27. *Le Petit Journal*, 26 April 1916.
28. *Le Petit Journal*, 27 April 1916.
29. The story of the voyage of the *Libau/Aud* was made available to French readers in 1929 by the publication of K. Spindler's account in his *Le Vaisseau Fantôme* (Paris, 1929), a translation of K. Spindler, *Das Geheimnisvolle Schiff* (Berlin, 1921).
30. *Le Petit Journal*, 1 May 1916.
31. See *L'Humanité*, 29 July 1912, 'Contre les atrocités au Pérou'.
32. See Spindler, *Fantome*.
33. R. Foster, *Modern Ireland 1600–1972*, (London, 1989), p. 471 and R. Doerries, *Prelude to the Easter Rising* (London and Portland, 2000), pp. 3–24.
34. See *Le Petit Parisien*, 1 May 1916 ; Y. Goblet, *L'Irlande Dans la Crise Universelle 1914–1920*, (Paris, 1921) ; and R. Escouflaire, *L'Irlande Ennemie...?* (Paris, 1918), passim.
35. Several of Jules Verne's principal characters are rather unflappable eccentric English gentlemen, for example Phileas Fogg in *Around the World in 80 Days* and Ferguson in *Five Weeks in a Balloon*.
36. See note 31 above.
37. The formula was quoted by Albert Camus at the end of Section 4 of his book, *L'Étranger* (Paris, 1957), and ends '*(vous aurez) la tête tranchée sur une place publique au nom du peuple français*'.
38. See description of the execution of Landru at Versailles in *L'Humanité*, 20 February 1922.
39. *Le Petit Journal*, 28 April 1916.
40. Ibid.
41. *Le Petit Parisien*, 3 May 1916.

42. Ibid., 1 May 1916.
43. *Le Petit Journal*, 2 May 1916.
44. *Le Petit Parisien*, 26 April 1916.
45. Ibid.
46. Ibid., 1 May 1916.
47. Ibid., 29 April 1916.
48. Ibid., 1 May 1916.
49. These were Pearse, Clarke and MacDonagh, whose sentences and executions were reported under the title: '*Trois chefs de la révolte irlandaise sont condamnés à mort et fusillés*' ('Three chiefs of the Irish revolt sentenced to death and shot'). *Le Petit Parisien*, 4 May 1916. Another name that was discussed was that of 'La Comtesse Markievitch' [sic] who was linked to Jim Larkin, through her friendship with his daughter Delia and not through her political leanings. See *Le Petit Parisien*, 2 May 1916.
50. '*Celui qui Organisa le Mauvais Coup en Irlande*' ['The man behind the Rising'], *Le Petit Journal*, 26 April 1916.
51. '*Singulier Personnage*', '*Traitre*', '*Triste Personnage*', '*Lâche*' and '*Celui qui Organisa le Mauvais Coup Contre l'Irlande*'.
52. The Belgian newspaper, *XX Siècle*, published in Le Havre. The Belgian government, in exile and installed at Sainte Adresse, a suburb to the north-west of the town, attacked Casement using this new word to imply that he was in the pay of the Germans even while in the Congo in 1903. Reported in *Le Petit Parisien*, 26 April 1916.
53. Interestingly enough there was no reference to his diaries which proved allegedly his homosexuality.
54. *Le Petit Parisien*, 26 April 1916.
55. See Angus Mitchell, *The Amazon Journal of Roger Casement* (London, 1997), and Roger Sawyer, *Roger Casement's Diaries – 1910: The Black and the White* (London, 1997), for opposing views on Casement's character.
56. Girodias, *Black Diaries*, p. 423.
57. *Le Petit Parisien*, 26 April 1916.
58. Ibid. '*Au lieu d'oublier, comme tous les autres chefs nationalistes, les malentendus passés pour faire face à l'ennemi commun ...*'
59. B. Inglis, *Roger Casement* (London, 1973), p. 193.
60. *L'Illustration*, 5 August 1916.
61. J. Bourke, 'Irish Tommies', *Bullán*, 3, 2 (winter 1997/spring 1998), p. 21.
62. E. Larkin, *James Larkin: Irish Labor Leader 1876–1947* (Cambridge, 1965), p. 192.
63. *Le Figaro*, 27 April 1916.
64. Ibid., 30 April 1916.
65. C. Townshend, 'The Suppression of the Easter Rising', p. 36, Duff, *Six Days*, p. 83.
66. T.P. Dooley, *Irishmen or English Soldiers?* (Liverpool, 1995), pp. 179–80.
67. *Le Figaro*, 28 April 1916.
68. *Rocambolesque* has now passed into French, meaning farcically extraordinary or incompetent.
69. *Le Petit Parisien*, 1 May 1916.
70. Inglis, *Casement*, p. 280. Kuno Meyer certainly knew Casement, if only initially through their shared friendship with Alice Stopford Green.
71. He refers to Louis Paul-Dubois and Philippe Daryl who recount the Irish sympathy for France in 1870.
72. D. Hyde, 'The Necessity for De-Anglicising Ireland', in S. Deane, A Carpenter and J Williams (eds), *The Field Day Anthology of Irish Writing* (Cork, 1991), p. 529.
73. M. Nic Craith, 'The Symbolism of Language', in U. Kockel (ed.), *Landscape, Heritage and Identity: Case Studies in Irish Ethnography* (Liverpool, 1995), p. 35.
74. D. Greene and E. Stephens, *J.M. Synge 1871–1909* (New York, 1959), p. 125.
75. Inglis, *Casement*, p. 302.
76. Larkin, *Larkin*, p. 172.
77. Greene and Stephens, *Sygne*, p. 67.
78. L. Gibbons, *Transformations in Irish Culture* (Cork, 1995), p. 174.

79. F. Moffett, *I Also am of Ireland* (London, 1985), p. 80.
80. *The Morning Post*, 24 April 1916.
81. Immediately after Casement's execution the Germans obliged the French with the execution of the British merchant officer, Captain Fryatt, who had rammed a u-boat instead of surrendering his North Sea ferry. This event got more coverage in the French press than in such as the *Times*. See *L'Illustration*, 5 August 1916, 'Une Lacheté Allemand'.
82. P. Travers, *Settlements and Divisions; Ireland 1870–1922* (Dublin, 1988), p. 85.
83. See M. A. G. Valiulis, *Portrait of a Revolutionary: General Richard Mulcahy and the Founding of the Irish Free State* (Blackrock, 1992).

8

James Connolly, the Easter Rising and the First World War: A Contextual Study

Priscilla Metscher

Irish historians generally view the Easter Rising as a national struggle against British colonial hegemony. The Rising should, however, be considered within a larger international framework: the period between the last decades of the nineteenth century and the early 1920s. This was an epoch of social unrest and revolution on a global scale. This chapter will re-examine James Connolly in this context with special reference to the First World War, 1914–18. It will consider his decision to participate in the Easter Rising and assess the events of 1916 in terms of the right of nations to self-determination.[1]

The First World War was the impetus for a revolutionary upheaval which reached a peak in 1917 with the Russian 'October Revolution', the first successful socialist revolution in history. Considered in this context, the Easter Rising, occurring one year earlier, is not an isolated event, but a spark in a wider revolution that shook the world. Connolly believed that the anti-imperialist activities of Irish socialists during the war could be the starting point of a movement which would end in the emancipation of the European working class. In August 1914 he wrote: 'Starting thus, Ireland may yet set the torch to a European conflagration that will not burn out until the last throne and the last capitalist bond and debenture will be shrivelled on the funeral pyre of the last war lord.'[2]

When Connolly committed the Irish Citizen Army (ICA) to fight in Easter week 1916, it was not just with the hope of realizing a prerequisite for establishing a socialist republic in Ireland. He saw the Irish struggle as part of the general struggle for socialism in Europe. The war, he believed, could provide the working class of Europe with an opportunity to overthrow the capitalist system. On 16 October 1915 he wrote in optimistic spirit: 'Revolution is no longer unthinkable in Europe, its shadow already looms upon the horizon.'[3] At the Zimmerwald conference in

Switzerland one month earlier, V.I. Lenin had proposed turning 'the war of nations into a revolutionary civil war between capitalists and workers'.[4] In his report on Zimmerwald the Scottish socialist, John Maclean, added enthusiastically: 'We learn that a gigantic political strike has already been declared in Petrograd and other important centres. We wish our comrades every success.'[5] Connolly was of the opinion in 1914 that should the European workers rather than slaughter each other proceed to 'erect barricades all over Europe, to break up bridges and destroy the transport service that war might be abolished, we should be perfectly justified in following such a glorious example and contributing our aid to the final dethronement of the vulture classes that rule and rob the world'.[6]

The Rising is embedded in a whole period of social unrest that began before the outbreak of the First World War. This gained momentum during the second half of the war and accelerated between 1917 and the early 1920s. Several of the struggles are both important and exemplary. In Britain, for example, an upward surge of unionism occurred in the late 1890s in reply to an employer offensive. It was a period where trade unionism became more aggressive and political. Union membership soared and industrial unions were formed which organized skilled, semi-skilled and unskilled workers alike.[7] A wave of mass strikes occurred in Britain and Ireland between 1910 and 1914. In 1909 a strike in the south Wales coal pits spread to the whole Cambrian combine. In 1911 a seamen's strike was followed by a railwaymen's strike, the biggest rail stoppage in history: '1912 saw the greatest explosion of industrial discontent that Britain had ever seen.'[8] In Ireland a series of strikes culminated in the famous Dublin Lockout of 1913.

This was also a period in which the major socialist parties in Europe were founded. In Britain the Social Democratic Federation (SDF) emerged in 1883 and the Independent Labour Party (ILP) in 1893. The German Social Democratic Party (SDP) was founded in 1875 and doubled its electoral strength from 10 per cent of the vote in 1887 to 23 per cent in 1893.[9] By 1911 it had more than a million members.[10] The Second International, founded in 1889 on the centenary of the French Revolution, gave cohesion to the various socialist parties internationally, although the parties themselves were often at loggerheads. They generally stood in a vague sense for social revolution, although the nature of this was by no means a clear issue. Thus, at the outbreak of the First World War in 1914, the majority of socialists in the belligerent countries supported the war effort. Marxists, a relatively small group within the International, represented a coherent viewpoint and opposed the war vehemently from the beginning. Of great importance was the setting up of an International Socialist Bureau in Brussels in 1901 to co-ordinate activity.[11]

In 1905 an insurrection occurred in Moscow. The first Russian revolution was a direct outcome of the Russo-Japanese war which erupted in 1904 over Russian and Japanese influence in Korea and Manchuria. It proved a complete disaster for Russia, Port Arthur falling to the Japanese in January 1905 and the military reverses precipitating open expression of political discontent in Russia.[12] The insurrection was preceded by a number of strikes in St Petersburg and other centres, culminating in a great general strike in October 1905 that spread over the country, with railwaymen and postal workers joining in. The strike was mainly political, demanding a constituent assembly as well as the eight-hour day.[13] In mid-December insurrection broke out in Moscow when barricades were erected and pitched battles fought in the streets. Only a fraction of the workers had arms and after heavy fighting with government troops the rebellion was put down.[14] German-Polish socialist Rosa Luxemburg observed that the Russian revolution of 1905–6 was defeated with German assistance, an intervention she attributed to fears in Berlin that democratic republicanism might spread to both countries.[15]

In a series of articles on revolutionary warfare, published in 1915, Connolly studied the Moscow rising very closely. He concluded: 'Even under modern conditions the professional soldier is badly handicapped in fighting inside a city against really determined civilian revolutionists.'[16] Some of his conclusions obviously flowed into the later planning of the Easter Rising in Dublin. Summing up the lessons on street fighting he wrote: 'The fortifying of a strong building, as a pivot upon which the defence of a town or village should hinge, forms a principal object of the preparations of any defending force, whether regular army or insurrectionary.'[17]

A problem of great urgency and centrality to the Marxist theorists within the International in the period before the First World War and after was the *national question*. There had, of course, been an upsurge of national movements over the previous century, arising from the ideas of the French Revolution. We have only to think of the 1848 revolution in Germany and the movements such as Mazzini's La Giovane Italia in Italy and the Young Irelanders, but this was the first time that socialists generally took the problem of national self-determination seriously, relating it to the question of socialism.[18] Writing in February 1914, Lenin underlined how important the national question and Ireland was to Marx. The later Marx believed that for the English working class it was essential to get rid of its connection with Ireland, as only then could it free itself.[19]

Eric Hobsbawm pointed to the fact that the number of national movements increased considerably in Europe from the 1870s, not only among the Irish and Poles, but the Finns and Slovaks, the Estonians and Macedonians. In Spain the Basque National Party was formed in 1894.[20]

Outside Europe, in China the Boxer Movement was largely a response to the interference of the imperialist powers. It was a mass movement, albeit, according to Hobsbawm, xenophobic and anti-modern, directed against foreigners, Christianity and machines.[21] The uprising of 1899–1900 began originally as a peasant revolt in northern China. During the nineteenth century the peasants' economic situation declined, especially in the northern provinces. Peasant handicraft encountered severe competition from cheap western textiles. Coupled with this the European powers had begun to demand territorial rail and mining concessions.[22]

This unrest was combined with resentment at China being forced to sign treaties with Britain, France, Germany and the United States at her own expense.[23] Apart from this, more and more Chinese territories were being seized by the imperialist powers. A secret society known as the 'Fists of Righteous Harmony', called the 'Boxers' in the Western press, soon attracted thousands of followers. At first their aim was to overthrow the imperial Ch'ing government and to expel all foreigners from China, but the Empress Dowager Tsu Hsi managed to win the Boxers over. The rebellion began in the countryside with attacks on Christian missions before spreading to the cities, to Tianjin, for example, finally concentrating on Beijing where the Boxers together with members of the imperial army attacked foreign compounds within the city. The rebellion was quelled by the sending of an international relief force of soldiers and sailors from eight countries (United Kingdom, Japan, Russia, France, the United States, Germany, Italy and Austria-Hungary). Troops from these nations engaged in plunder, looting and rape. On 7 September 1901 the Ch'ing court was forced to sign the 'Boxer Protocol' by which China had to pay war reparations, and on the instigation of the United States an 'open door' policy was pursued which allowed foreign access to the Chinese market until the Second World War.[24] The crushing of the rebellion resulted in the end of the Chinese empire a decade later. Following developments in South Africa and China Connolly sardonically commented in 1900: 'The Boxers in China have developed a sudden aptitude for war, are prowling around on the hunt for foreign devils, and with a smile that is child-like bland are offering to box all Europe, with Japan and America thrown in as appetisers. Great Britain is in want of soldiers there also. Now it only wants a native rising in India and then would come our Irish opportunity.'[25]

In India the emergence of an autonomous movement led to the foundation of the Indian National Congress in 1885 which was to become the party of national liberation. Moreover, there was the movement of passive resistance initiated by Mahatma Gandhi on his return to India from England in 1915 in which he practised his technique of mobilizing traditionalist masses for 'non-traditionalist purposes'. The Bengali nationalist movement stood left of Congress, combining Hinduism with ideas derived from western revolutionary movements.[26]

In Latin America in the years prior to the First World War serious social revolt took place in Mexico against the dictatorship of Porfirio Días and the feudal rule of the great estate-owners. Led originally by Francisco Madero, a large landowner and mine-owner in southern Mexico who had plans for constitutional government and large projects of social reform, by Pancho Villa and his rebel forces in the northern provinces and by Emiliano Zapata, the head of a peasant revolt of Indians and half-castes in the south, the Mexican revolution in its early phase lasted throughout the First World War until 1920. The strength of the Mexican revolution lay undoubtedly in the persistence of peasant revolt led by Zapata and his ability to bring about land distribution and the destruction of the great estates in the areas under his control.[27]

Basing her analysis of labour unrest on the World Labour Group database, Beverly Silver charted the rise of unrest on the eve of the First World War. This was followed by short-lived declines with the onset of war and major waves of unrest following the war.[28] Left-wing socialists vehemently and unceasingly opposed the war throughout its duration. By 1916 the rank and file of the labour movement was beginning to show not just war-weariness, but hostility to an apparently endless and indecisive slaughter. One of the first major strikes during the war which took place in Britain can thus be regarded as a prelude to the revolutionary wave to come. It occurred in Glasgow, on Clydeside in 1915 in the engineering industry. Out of this evolved the Clyde Workers' Committee which became the basis of the shop stewards' movement, the organization of labour at shop-floor level.[29] In October 1915 a strike against rising house rents begun by the Women's Housing Association was supported by Clyde munition workers, who called a general strike. The government was forced to pass the Rent Restriction Act, freezing rents all over Britain at pre-war level.[30] Industrial action was coupled with anti-war politics (the fight for free speech and the struggle against conscription introduced in 1915) in which the socialists of the British Socialist Party (BSP) in Glasgow were predominantly to the fore. John Maclean was one of the outstanding Scottish socialists of this period.[31] The strike of February 1915 on Clydeside was followed by a stoppage of work in south Wales, an area already established as the most militant of the coalfields. The government was forced to settle, but as troubles in the coalfields continued, the south Wales coalfield was brought under state control in November 1916 and in February 1917 state control was extended to the whole industry.[32]

Starting in 1916 with the Easter Rising in Ireland and escalating between 1917 and the early 1920s, a period of revolutionary activity occurred not only in Europe but throughout the world. The Russian October Revolution of 1917 had repercussions internationally. Revolution in Russia was instigated by growing resentment with the autocracy of Nicholas II, by wide-scale inflation and food shortages, inadequate military supplies, leading to heavy losses in the war coupled with the development of revolutionary ideas and movements. A preliminary to the October Revolution was the February Revolution of 1917, which started as a protest against severe bread shortages. A strike by women textile workers in Petrograd was the beginning of mass strikes throughout the city. The strikers were joined by insurgent soldiers, leading to the collapse of civil authority, the Tsar's abdication and the formation of a provisional government. The effective power of the government was challenged by the Petrograd Soviet Workers' Deputies, which claimed to represent the will of workers and soldiers. In April 1917 Lenin arrived in Petrograd from Swiss exile.

With the Bolsheviks achieving electoral victories in the Moscow and Petrograd soviets, Lenin argued that the Bolsheviks should take power into their own hands. At a meeting of the Bolshevik central committee on 10 October a decision was approved to organize the immediate overthrow of the government. On 7 November 1917 (by the Russian calendar) Lenin led a successful revolt against the ineffective provisional government. Armed workers and soldiers captured key buildings in Petrograd. The Winter Palace was attacked and captured, the prime minister, Kerensky, forced to flee. This finally led to the formation of an all-Bolshevik soviet government (Sovnarkom) with Lenin as chairman. The revolution of 1917 was followed by a civil war which broke out in 1918. The newly founded state had to defend itself against a 'white' counter-revolution backed by Britain, France, the US and Japan. This war lasted until 1922, with the defeat of Japanese intervention.[33]

In Germany, Karl Liebknecht, Rosa Luxemburg and the Internationale Group, later 'The Spartakusbund', had been agitating for an end to the world war through mass economic and political strikes. For Luxemburg, the interaction of political and economic struggle was important. In her 1906 pamphlet *The Mass Strike* she wrote:

> Instead of the rigid and hollow scheme of an arid political action carried out by the decision of the highest committees ... we see a bit of pulsating life of flesh and blood, which cannot be cut out of the large frame of the revolution but is connected with all parts of the revolution by a thousand veins ... Political strikes, economic strikes, demonstrative strikes, mass strikes and partial strikes, general strikes of individual branches of industry and general strikes in individual towns, peaceful wage struggles and street massacres, barricade fighting – all these run through one another, run side by side, cross one another.[34]

In April 1917 and January/February 1918, great strikes occurred in Germany in the armaments industry. The Kiel mutiny that began the German revolution of November 1918 was started by sailors who quickly spread revolutionary action to Hamburg, Lübeck, Bremen, Hanover, Cologne, Brunswick and Leipzig. A short-lived soviet republic was declared in Munich in 1919. Street fighting broke out in Berlin and insurrections took place in major cities. In the Ruhr coalfield area a red army was formed.[35]

In the six weeks between the conclusion of the armistice treaty and Christmas 1918 about five million German soldiers left military service and were followed in January 1919 by another two million.[36] The demobbed soldiers could have formed a revolutionary force, but the will to organize such a force was not present on a large scale. The Spartakusbund was too small and the reformist social democratic leaders from within the labour movement prevented the revolution leading to workers' power. Moreover, the Social Democrats formed the government and the murder of the revolutionaries Liebknecht and Luxemburg was carried out by counter-revolutionary killer troops tolerated by Gustav Noske (SPD), the minister of defence (*Reichswehrminister*) at that time.[37] A wave of mass political strikes and anti-war demonstrations occurred likewise in Vienna, Budapest and the Czech regions, and the Hungarian Soviet Republic of March to July 1919 was brutally suppressed.[38] In Italy a general strike of workers occurred in July 1919 as a protest against the government policy of supporting the counter-revolution in Russia. This was followed in August and September 1920 by a wave of factory sit-ins in which the workers took over control of production. In January 1921 the Communist Party of Italy was founded under the leadership of Antonio Gramsci. In March 1922 Mussolini became head of government, which marked the first step towards a fascist dictatorship.[39]

In Britain again it was 'red' Clydeside that came to the fore. On 27 January 1919 40,000 shipyard workers went on strike for a forty-hour week and to protest against the ending of wartime rent restrictions. Following a mass demonstration on 31 January during which the police charged the crowd, it was decided to send troops to Glasgow with tanks and machine guns. As a result the strike was over within ten days, and the demand for a forty-hour week was dropped. John Maclean contended that the 'Bloody Friday' demonstration and the related strikes held the potential for revolution.[40]

By 1918 the situation in Ireland had changed radically. There was mass popular protest against the implementation of conscription. In the North working-class loyalists protested at a mass meeting on the Custom House steps in Belfast on 14 April.[41] Resistance to conscription was so strong that the government dared not implement it. The general election, held on 14

December 1918, was a huge victory for Sinn Féin, which won seventy-three of the country's 105 seats. Summing up the years 1918–21, Michael Collins wrote that it was 'a struggle between our determination to govern ourselves and to get rid of British Government and British determination to prevent us doing either'.[42] The setting up of Dáil Éireann as the legitimate government of the Irish people was counteracted by the British government sending troops to suppress the republicans. There followed two and a half years of bitter guerrilla warfare in an attempt to save the young republic. In a pamphlet published in 1920 entitled *The Irish Tragedy: Scotland's Disgrace*, Maclean condemned the sending of troops to Ireland. He saw in the Irish situation parallels for Scotland.

Not only did the defeated powers suffer revolutions and state breakdowns; even in those countries that won the war massive social unrest and struggles for national self-determination occurred. Lloyd George summed up the situation in 1919: 'The whole of Europe is filled with the spirit of revolution. There is a deep sense not only of discontent, but of anger and revolt among the workmen against pre-war conditions. The whole existing order in its political, social and economic aspects is questioned by the masses of the population from one end of Europe to the other.'[43]

In other parts of the globe, outside Europe, revolutionary movements also occurred. In the two years following the October Revolution 'soviets' were formed by the tobacco workers in Cuba; the years 1917–19 in Spain came to be known as 'the Bolshevik biennium'. Revolutionary student movements erupted in Beijing in 1919 and in Córdoba (Argentina) to spread across Latin America.[44] In 1917 the local revolution in Mexico entered its most radical phase. The October Revolution made its mark on the Indonesian national liberation movement's main mass organization, 'Sarekat Islam'. In Australia mainly Irish-Catholic sheep-shearers cheered the Russian soviets as a workers' state. In the US, Finns converted to communism wholesale in the mining settlements of Minnesota.[45] Strikes broke out in 1919 and race riots shook cities across the country. In Chicago there were five days of rioting. Following the so-called 'red scare', the attorney general, A. Mitchell Palmer, and his assistant, John Edgar Hoover, launched a crusade against the radical left. Wholesale brutal arrests of socialist leaders occurred, the Palmer raids continuing into 1920.[46]

Mention should be made briefly of the independence struggles in Turkey and Egypt following the end of the war. The break-up of the Ottoman empire and the occupying of Istanbul and Izmir by Allied forces in 1918 prompted the establishment of the Turkish national movement under the leadership of Mustafa Kemal Pasha. By 1922 the occupying armies were repelled and with the abolishment of the sultanate the Republic of Turkey was founded with Mustafa Kemal (Atatürk) as first president.[47] After the outbreak of war Britain declared Egypt officially a British protectorate. The deterioration in the living conditions of the Egyptian people during the war together with the increasing pressure by the British occupiers led to the revival of the liberation movement there. In 1922 Britain was forced to abolish the protectorate and announce the establishment of an 'independent' kingdom of Egypt.[48]

The world war was ended by the mass slaughter on both sides and the military defeat of Germany. The revolutionary events that occurred from 1917 also contributed to bringing an end to international conflict for a number of years, but did not succeed in bringing about a world-wide revolution. There was a lack of co-ordination between states; socialist leaders were in too weak a position to make use of the mass strikes for revolutionary purposes; much of the militant protest was directed against the war and with the achievement of peace the political explosive it contained was largely defused.

CONNOLLY, THE EASTER RISING AND THE WAR

By placing the Easter Rising within the above context one can clearly discern those features which connect the Rising with many of the cited upheavals and those that make the Rising a unique event of the time. There are three aspects which determine its individual historical character. Firstly, it was one of the first risings to take place within a colonial system, one of the leading imperial world powers of the period. In this respect Easter 1916 lies within the context of the general issue of the right of nations to self-determination.

Secondly, the Rising arose from a combination of radical socialist forces and those of 'democratic nationalism', a nationalism that was based on the enlightened republican tradition of the United Irishmen and the ideas of the French Revolution.[49] Connolly's political thought concerning a socialist republic suggested a combination of both these forces. The two currents of revolutionary thought in Ireland, nationalism and socialism, were to him not antagonistic, but complementary. He was influenced by the writings of the radical Young Irelander, James Fintan Lalor. Connolly's revolutionary strategy was underpinned by his belief that the fight for socialism in Ireland should be linked to the struggle for national independence. He also believed that the core impetus for the Irish socialist was the radical republican tradition. Thirdly, the outbreak and progress of the world war was undoubtedly the major factor that triggered off a rising. As we have seen, not only in Ireland but in other parts of Europe and the world at large, the war brought about social upheaval on a grand scale. As is generally known, Connolly was of the opinion that England's wartime difficulty was Ireland's opportunity.

At the Stuttgart conference of the International in 1907 it had been agreed that if a European war should break out it was the duty of the working class in the countries affected 'to intervene in order to bring it promptly to an end, and with all their strength to make use of the economic and political crisis created by the war to stir up the deepest strata of the people and precipitate the fall of capitalist domination'.[50] The questions of a general strike and insurrection were passed over in silence, but were nevertheless implicit. At the Copenhagen conference of 1910 Keir Hardie, with the support of the ILP (Independent Labour Party), the British Labour Party and the French Socialist Party, proposed that, if such an event threatened, there should be a simultaneous stoppage of workers, especially in the industries which supplied instruments of war (munitions, transport etc.). But it was decided to postpone the issue of a general strike for further consideration at a subsequent congress. Despite protests and demonstrations, the socialists did not have the power to avert disaster when it came.

Hugo Haase, chairman of the German Social Democratic Party, assured his fellow members of the International Socialist Bureau that the German socialists would refuse to vote in favour of war credits. Despite his assurances however all socialists in the *Reichstag* except Karl Liebknecht voted solidly for them, thus supporting government policy.[51] In Britain the Labour Party, the trade unions, the Fabians and the right wing of the British Socialist Party under Hyndman supported British government policy on the war. As Connolly commented: 'With the honourable exception of the Independent Labour Party and the Socialist Labour Party, the organised and unorganised Labour advocates of Peace in Britain swallowed the bait and are now beating the war drum.'[52] Hardie's idea of a general strike to prevent movement of troops and war materials as part of a concerted international movement was not even considered. The British socialists who were opposed to the war lacked the power to bring the masses out on the streets.[53] Thus, with the labour movement in Europe generally supporting the war, the Second International ceased to function as a collective expression of international socialist policy. In Germany Rosa Luxemburg commented bitterly on the stand of the parliamentary Social Democrats who generally believed the war to be a question of the self-defence of Germany against foreign invasion, a war of freedom against Russian despotism.[54]

In an article entitled 'Revolutionary Unionism and War' which appeared in the *International Socialist Review* in March 1915, Connolly considered the question as to why the socialist movement in Europe had failed to prevent war. He concluded:

In none of these belligerent countries was there an organised revolutionary industrial organisation directing the socialist vote nor a socialist political party directing a revolutionary organisation ... No socialist party in Europe could say that rather than go to war it would call out the entire transport service of the country and thus prevent mobilisation. No socialist party could say so, because no socialist party could have the slightest reasonable prospect of having such a call obeyed ... The failure of European socialism to avert war is primarily due to the divorce between the industrial and political movements of labour.[55]

On 15 August 1914 Connolly voiced his disappointment that the outbreak of war was not answered by general strikes and uprisings of the forces of labour in Europe. He argued: 'If these men must die, would it not be better to die in their own country fighting for freedom for their class, and for the abolition of war, than to go forth to strange countries and die slaughtering and slaughtered by their brothers that tyrants and profiteers might live?'[56] The signal for war, he wrote, should have been the signal for rebellion. Seen in the context of the later Easter Rising his words are indeed significant: 'Even an unsuccessful attempt at social revolution by force of arms, following the paralysis of the economic life of militarism, would be less disastrous to the socialist cause than the act of socialists allowing themselves to be used in the slaughter of their brothers in the cause.'[57]

It was not just the failure of European socialism that dismayed Connolly but the fact that the labour movement in the belligerent countries with few exceptions fully supported the war effort. Connolly's main attack during the war was focused on British imperialism, believing that the weaker Britain became, the stronger became every revolutionary force. He welcomed German victories: 'We do not wish to be ruled by either Empire, but we certainly believe that the first named (i.e. Germany) contains in germ more of the possibilities of freedom and civilisation than the latter.'[58] He was certain of a German victory: 'German arms will win the war.'[59] A German victory, he believed, would bring socialism nearer as only the full development of the capitalist system would make socialism possible, the British empire standing in the way.[60] In an article entitled 'The War upon the German Nation' Connolly placed the onus for aggression on Britain, German competition in industry was a threat to England's industrial supremacy. 'It was determined that since Germany could not be beaten in fair competition industrially, it must be beaten unfairly by organising a military and naval conspiracy against her.'[61]

Two factors undoubtedly led Connolly to express this view. He saw it as his duty to juxtapose his position to the jingoism and slander against the Germans in the home rule press which, he wrote, 'outjingoes the jingoes – is viler than the vilest rags of England'.[62] Besides, British imperialism had an immediate affect on Ireland for it was Britain which ruled Ireland and

British imperialism which was responsible for its colonial status. It is interesting to consider John Maclean's position on this question. He believed that it was the first business of the British working class 'to hate the British capitalist system'. At the same time, however, Maclean was clear that the motive force behind German aggression was 'the profit of the plundering class of Germany'.[63] While Connolly felt it was his duty to desire the victory of Britain's enemy, Rosa Luxemburg, as a socialist in Germany, clearly laid the blame for the outbreak of the world war on Germany. That country's imperialism, she believed, required unrestricted expansion. It was not a question of peaceful development, but rather of the profits of the German bank in Asian Turkey and the future of the profits of Mannesmann and Krupp in Morocco.[64]

In contrast to Bismarck's policy of pursuing a deliberate restriction of objectives with Germany remaining a land power, the rapid growth of German capitalism at the end of the nineteenth century and the beginning of the twentieth led Kaiser Wilhelm II to demand 'a place in the sun' for his state. Bismarck was dismissed to be replaced by Bernhard von Bülow (1900), an exponent of German expansionist world power.[65] Germany, as a late-comer in the race for colonies, had to go on the offensive to establish itself as an imperial power. The expansion of the German navy was undoubtedly a threat to British naval sovereignty and Britain's already well-established global position. David Lloyd George's assertion that it was a question of blamelessly sliding towards catastrophe relieved all the great powers of the responsibility for the outbreak of war.

This opinion was still shared by West German historians as late as the 1950s. Fritz Fischer was the first in the Federal Republic to see Germany as chiefly responsible for an increase in tensions and for the outbreak of war in theses expressed in an article entitled 'Deutsche Kriegsziele. Revolutionierung und Separatfrieden im Osten 1914–1918', 1959 and in a volume entitled *Griff nach der Weltmacht. Die Kriegszielpolitik des kaiserlichen Deutschland 1914/18*, 1961.[66] This led to a heated controversy at the historians' conference in Berlin in 1964. Fischer by no means denied the imperialist policies of Germany's enemies, but he pointed out that what made Germany's endeavour so dangerous was the late development of imperialism there. Coupled with this was the combination of a highly modern technocracy with a state apparatus that had an aristocratic-monarchical and military stamp.[67] What can be established is that all the imperial powers bore responsibility. None was innocent of pursuing aggressive policies which had the potential of leading to war.

It is not clear how much information Connolly had on the views of German socialists at the time. On several occasions Karl Liebknecht attracted his attention. In 'A Martyr for Conscience Sake', written in August 1914 on the unfounded rumour of Liebknecht's death for refusing military service, Connolly praised the German's stand on the war. Connolly wrote: 'There can be little hesitation in avowing that all socialists would endorse his act, and look upon his death as a martyrdom for the cause.'[68] On another occasion Connolly quoted enthusiastically from a letter by Liebknecht printed in *Labour Leader* concerning the stand of British socialists on the war: 'I am ... particularly proud to send greetings to you, to the British Independent Labour Party, who, with our Russian and Servian comrades, have saved the honour of Socialism amidst the madness of national slaughter.'[69] Again in 'Jottings' in the *Worker*, 16 January 1915, Connolly quotes in translation articles by French socialists on Liebknecht's stand in the German parliament: 'That conception of ours is also that of the working class of England, Belgium, Italy, the United States; from one end of the world to the other it represents the hope of the working class, because it is the only basis for a lasting peace, and can assure the uninterrupted development of democracy on the globe ... Liebknecht, you have been our comforter, we shall be your supporters.'[70]

Before the outbreak of war, Connolly considered seriously the introduction of home rule in Ireland as bringing the possibility of national independence closer. 'As Socialists we are Home Rulers, but ... on the day the Home Rule Government goes into power the Socialist movement in Ireland will go into opposition.'[71] He vehemently opposed plans to partition Ireland as 'this would set back the wheels of progress, would destroy the oncoming unity of the Irish labour movement and paralyse all advanced movements while it endured'.[72] The outbreak of war in August 1914 changed the situation radically. The British government used the opportunity to shelve the question of home rule until after the war. This was followed by the introduction of two Defence of the Realm Acts giving military authorities power to arrest civilians and to try them by courts-martial. Martial law was established, restricting civil rights. A succession of bills followed, authorizing the death penalty for those found guilty by a court-martial of intending to collaborate with the enemy.[73]

This gave rise to a completely new situation, one in which Connolly was forced to consider a different strategy from that appropriate to peacetime. The idea of striking a blow at Britain with the use of armed force in Ireland while Britain was at war became a frequent subject in his writings after 1914. Addressing the Irish workers in an article on 5 September 1914, he wrote: 'You have been told you are not strong, that you have no rifles. Revolutions do not start with rifles; start first and get your rifles after. Our curse is our belief in our weakness. We are not weak, we are strong. Make up your mind to strike before your opportunity goes.'[74] One month later he envisaged the possibility of insurrection: 'If it requires insurrection in Ireland and through all the British dominions to teach the English working class they cannot hope to prosper permanently by arresting the industrial development of others then insurrection must come, and barricades will spring up as readily in our streets as public meetings to-day.'[75] In an article in the *Workers' Republic*, January 1916 he set out his programme: 'We believe that in times of peace we should work along the lines of peace to strengthen the nation, and we believe that whatever strengthens and elevates the working class strengthens the nation. But we also believe that in times of war, we should act as in war ... A defeat of England in India, Egypt, the Balkans or Flanders would not be so dangerous to the British Empire as any conflict of armed forces in Ireland.'[76] Connolly was too much of a realist to envisage that the Irish Citizen Army, the army of the Irish working class, could achieve a successful rebellion on its own.[77] He set about forming an alliance between labour and what he termed 'the forces of real nationalism'.[78]

Shortly after the outbreak of war members of the supreme council of the Irish Republican Brotherhood (IRB) took the decision in principle that they would rise in arms for an Irish republic during the war.[79] They were not averse to an alliance with Connolly and the forces of militant labour. Articles appeared in *Irish Freedom* arguing for a union of forces between nationalists and socialists; an Irish republic would entail a social as well as a national regeneration. Patrick Pearse had certain sympathies with Connolly and the labour movement, as can be seen by his pro-labour stand for the workers during the lockout of 1913.[80] The growth of an identity of interest between militant labour and radical nationalism, leading to an alliance between Connolly and the IRB council, was symbolized by the hoisting of the green flag over Liberty Hall on 16 April 1916, which was commented on by Connolly with the now famous words:

> The cause of labour is the cause of Ireland, the cause of Ireland is the cause of labour. They cannot be dissevered. Ireland seeks freedom. Labour seeks that an Ireland free should be the sole mistress of her own destiny, supreme owner of all material things within and upon her soil. Labour seeks to make the free Irish nation the guardian of interests of the people of Ireland, and to secure that end would vest in that free Irish nation all property rights as against the claims of the individual, with the end in view that the individual may be enriched by the nation, and not by the spoiling of his fellows.[81]

Connolly was well aware that the gaining of Irish independence would not automatically lead to a socialist republic.[82] As early as 1897 he was quite clear what national independence without socialism would mean:

> If you remove the English army to-morrow and hoist the green flag over Dublin Castle, unless you set about the organisation of the

Socialist Republic your efforts would be in vain. England would still rule you. She would rule you through her capitalists, through her land-lords, through her financiers, through the whole array of commercial and individualist institutions she has planted in this country ... England would still rule you to your ruin ... Nationalism without Socialism ... is only national recreancy.[83]

He warned the ICA shortly before the Rising: 'In the event of victory, hold on to your rifles, as those with whom we are fighting may stop before our goal is reached. We are out for economic as well as political liberty.'[84]

Together with the supreme council of the IRB, Connolly planned and carried out an insurrection that lasted one week. Circumstances obviously forced him to revise his original insurrectionary plan in which the ICA, with the backing of the Irish Transport and General Workers' Union, would seize control of docks, shipping, railways and production. This was set out in an article entitled 'What is our Programme?' on 22 January 1916.[85] In the end, it was clear to him that labour was not in a position to play a leading role. The original plan envisaged a nationwide rising with a German-backed invasion: 'Volunteers in many parts of Ireland would destroy transport and communication links, to prevent the movement of British troops and loyalists. Rebels in Dublin would seize key buildings, and would hold out for a week or ten days till the invasion force arrived to relieve them. British military personnel and officials would be arrested, and a military governor would be installed.'[86] Nevin suggested that Connolly was opposed to a national uprising, urging instead the occupa-tion of Dublin and the seizure of principal public buildings. This was the viewpoint of John Francis Byrne in his autobiography, *The Silent Years*.[87]

The final plan combined a national insurrection with Dublin as a cen-tre, accompanied by guerrilla warfare in the countryside: 'Volunteers – who numbered some 3,000 in Dublin, including the 200-strong Citizen Army, and 13,000 in the provinces – were to muster all over Ireland, and a large supply of arms was to arrive from Germany.'[88] Had everything gone according to plan, the British army would have been confronted by a for-midable force. The failure of the arrival of German arms and MacNeill's fatal countermanding order issued to the Volunteers damaged the plan for a nation-wide rising.

Assessing the significance of the Easter Rising remains problematic. In his last statement, issued from Dublin Castle hospital on 9 May 1916, Connolly wrote: 'We went out to break the connection between this country and the British Empire, and to establish an Irish Republic. We believed that the call we then issued to the people of Ireland, was a noble call, a holier cause, than any call issued to them during the war, having any connection with the war.'[89] Shortly after the Rising Lenin attacked those who condemned it as a 'putsch'. Lenin explained:

The centuries-old Irish national movement, having passed through various stages and combinations of class interests, manifested itself, in particular, in a mass Irish National Congress in America (*Vorwärts*, 20 March 1916), which called for Irish independence; it also manifested itself in street fighting conducted by a section of the urban petty bourgeoisie *and a section of the workers* after a long period of mass agitation, demonstrations, suppression of newspapers, etc. Whoever calls *such* a rebellion a 'putsch' is either a hardened reactionary, or a doctrinaire hopelessly incapable of picturing a social revolution as a living phenomenon.[90]

Although the London congress of the International had passed a resolution in July 1896 asserting the right of all nations to self-determination, the colonial question was by no means a clear issue within the International. There were those who accepted colonialism as a *fait accompli*, recognizing the 'civilizing' influence of colonialism.[91] Among the left-wing socialists sharp differences existed on the question of self-determination. In the *Junius Pamphlet* published in 1916, Rosa Luxemburg argued that international socialism recognized the right of free, independent and equal nations, but only socialism was capable of creating such nations and of realizing the self-determination of peoples.[92] National problems which can only be solved by war or revolution can in turn only be solved after proletarian victory.[93] Further, she wrote: 'The small nations are only chess figures in the imperialist game of the great powers and are misused just as the working masses of all belligerent countries during the war and will be sacrificed on the altar of capitalist interests after the war.'[94]

Lenin, in his criticism of Luxemburg's standpoint in the *Junius Pamphlet*, argued that a national war can become imperialist or revolutionary, depending on the circumstances: 'National wars against imperialist powers are not only possible, they are unavoidable, they are *progressive* and *revolutionary*.'[95] Writing on the Easter Rising, Lenin commented: 'The dialectics of history is of such a nature that the small nations which are in themselves powerless as an *independent* factor in the struggle against imperialism, play the role of an enzyme, of a bacillus which help the *true* opponent of imperialism, the socialist proletariat, to come to the fore.'[96] Lenin considered that the failure of the Easter Rising was due to prematurity, as it took place at a time 'before the European revolt of the proletariat had *had time* to mature'.[97] The experience of the imperialist war that began in 1914 proved, according to Lenin, that in the epoch of imperialism the civil war of the proletariat against the bourgeoisie in the industrially advanced countries should be combined with democratic revolutionary struggles in which the national liberation movements of the under-developed, oppressed nations play a considerable role.

The legacy of the Easter Rising lies in the continuing significance of the national question, even in an age of globalization. It demonstrates the profound truth that a humane future society consists in the coming together of both factors which in Connolly's mind were the driving forces of the Rising: socialism and democratic nationalism.

NOTES

1. The term is used with reference to Marx's concept of social revolution, meaning a time of severe crisis brought about by the conflict between the material productive forces of society and the existing relations of production and property. See Karl Marx, *Zur Kritik der Politischen Ökonomie* (Berlin, 1958), p. 13.
2. James Connolly, *Socialism and Nationalism* (Dublin, 1948), p. 134.
3. James Connolly, *Labour and Easter Week* (Dublin, 1966), p. 42.
4. G.D.H. Cole, *A History of Socialist Thought Volume 111: The Second International, Part 1, 1889–1914* (London and Basingstoke, 1970), p. 101.
5. *The Vanguard*, October 1915.
6. Connolly, *Socialism and Nationalism*, p. 133.
7. See Beverly J. Silver, *Forces of Labor, Workers' Movements and Globalization since 1870* (Cambridge, 2003), p. 134.
8. Walter Kendall, *The Revolutionary Movement in Britain 1900–1921* (London, 1969), p. 27.
9. Silver, *Forces of Labor*, p. 135.
10. E.J. Hobsbawm, *The Age of Empire 1875–1914* (London, 1987), pp. 116–17.
11. Cole. *Second International*, Part I, p. 44.
12. Ibid., pp. 445–6.
13. Ibid., pp. 446, 457.
14. Ibid., p. 458.
15. Rosa Luxemburg, 'Die Krise der Sozialdemokratie', in *Gesammelte Werke Bd. 4* (Berlin, 1974), pp. 116–17.
16. James Connolly, 'The Moscow Insurrection of 1905', in James Connolly, *Revolutionary Warfare* (Dublin, 1968), pp. 5–6.
17. Connolly, *Revolutionary Warfare*, p. 33.
18. The form of romantic bourgeois nationalism evolving in the latter part of the nineteenth century which tended to be retrograde in character, non-democratic and as in the case of Ireland and Poland connected to Catholicism was rejected by Connolly, Lenin and Luxemburg alike. Luxemburg was especially allergic to Polish nationalism, the pretensions of the Poles to superiority over other peoples, including the Russians. (See Cole, *The Second International*, p. 501). This contempt coloured her attitude to nationalism in all its forms and led to a controversy with Lenin on the question of the self-determination of nations.
19. See V.I. Lenin, *British Labour and British Imperialism*. A Compilation of Writings by Lenin on Britain (London, 1969), p. 125.
20. Hobsbawm, *The Age of Empire*, p. 145.
21. Ibid., p. 282.
22. See Barrington Moore, Jr., *Social Origins of Dictatorship and Democracy* (London, 1967), p. 218.
23. See Jenny French, 'China and the Boxer Rebellion', in *IIGS Newsletter* (August 1998), p. 1.
24. See J. Buschini, 'The Boxer Rebellion', on website of Small Planets Communications (2000), p. 3.
25. Connolly, *Labour and Easter Week*, p. 31.
26. Hobsbawm, *The Age of Empire*, pp. 78, 288.
27. Cole, *The Second International, Part II*, pp. 839–50.

28. Silver, *Forces of Labor*, pp. 126–7.
29. The National Shop Stewards' and Workers' Committee Movement was established in November and quickly spread throughout Britain. See Kendall, *The Revolutionary Movement in Britain*, p. 143.
30. James Hinton, *The First Shop Stewards' Movement* (London, 1973), pp. 125–6.
31. Maclean was born in Pollokshaws, Glasgow, 14 August 1879. He worked his way through Glasgow University, gained an MA and subsequently became a teacher in the city. His political activity was concentrated on Glasgow's Clydeside. Because of his revolutionary opposition to the war he was jailed three times in 1915, 1916 and then 1918 when he was sentenced to five years' penal servitude. Maclean was a Scottish socialist republican with strong nationalist views strengthened by his contacts with Ireland's independence struggle. He had a vision of a Scottish socialist republic on the lines of what Connolly conceived for Ireland. According to Kendall, Maclean came into close contact with Connolly and Larkin, 'gaining an exceptional appreciation of the revolutionary potentialities of the Irish question which stayed with him until the day he died'. Kendall, *The Revolutionary Movement in Britain*, p. 109. See also Peter Kerrigan, 'John Maclean', in *Marxism Today*, 17, 11 (November 1973), p. 324. The treatment he received in jail undermined his health and he died on 30 November 1923.
32. Kendall, *The Revolutionary Movement in Britain*, p. 151.
33. See Alfred Anderle et al (eds), *Weltgeschichte in Daten* (Berlin, 1973), p. 657.
34. D. Gluckstein, 'Revolution and the Challenge of Labour', in *International Socialism Journal*, 61 (1993), p. 5.
35. See Veit Valentin, *Geschichte der Deutschen* (Zürich, 1981), pp. 540, 546–7.
36. Harald Wessel, 'Wer verschwand im Keller?' in *Junge Welt*, 13/14 January 2007, No. 11, p. 10.
37. Gluckstein, 'Revolution and the Challenge of Labour', p. 8.
38. Eric Hobsbawm, *Age of Extremes. The Short Twentieth Century 1914–1991* (London, 1997), pp. 68–9.
39. *Weltgeschichte in Daten*, p. 678.
40. Trevor Royle, edited extract from *The Flowers of the Forest: Scotland and the First World War* (2006), p. 3.
41. See Liz Curtis, *The Cause of Ireland: From the United Irishmen to Partition* (Dublin, 1995), p. 299.
42. Curtis, *The Cause of Ireland*, pp. 305–6.
43. Silver, *Forces of Labor*, pp. 141–2.
44. The May Fourth Movement 1919 began as a student demonstration in Beijing but spread to China's industrial capital Shanghai where it was widely supported by workers. The week-long strike in Shanghai involving some 60,000 participants immobilized the city. During the First World War Chinese workers, including Shanghai craftsmen, were hired especially by French companies to replace French workers who had gone to the war. Among the overseas workers was a large number of Chinese intellectuals, student-workers, who came from poor and middle-class families. With their assistance a large number of industrial and social organizations were formed for Chinese workers in France. 'When the Chinese were in turn displaced by militant Frenchmen at the end of the war, they headed home well-schooled in tactics of labor strife.' Elisabeth J. Perry, 'Chinese Anniversaries in International Perspective', in *Harvard Asia Quarterly*, III, 3 (summer 1999), p. 4.
45. Hobsbawm, *Age of Extremes*, pp. 65–6.
46. Wendy McElroy, 'World War I and the Suppression of Dissent', on website of The Independent Institute (April 2002), p. 5.
47. See *Weltgeschichte in Daten*, pp. 739–40.
48. Ibid., p. 745.
49. The 1798 centenary celebrations of the rising of the United Irishmen gave Connolly the opportunity to present a series of articles entitled '"98 Readings": The principles and ideas which animated the men of '98'.
50. Cole, *Second International*, Part I, pp. 68–9.
51. Cole, *Second International*, p. 92.
52. Connolly, *Socialism and Nationalism*, p. 152.
53. Cole, *Second International*, Part I, p. 97.

54. Luxemburg, 'Die Krise der Sozialdemokratie', p. 72.
55. Connolly, *Labour and Easter Week*, pp. 58–60.
56. Ibid., pp. 40–1.
57. Ibid., p. 41.
58. Connolly, *Socialism and Nationalism*, p. 144.
59. Connolly, *Labour and Easter Week*, p. 118. Connolly's pro-German stance has also been documented by Manus O'Riordan in *James Connolly Re-Assessed: The Irish and European Context* (Cork, 2006).
60. See Connolly, *Socialism and Nationalism*, p. 143.
61. Ibid., p. 140.
62. Donal Nevin, *James Connolly: A Full Life* (Dublin, 2005), p. 518.
63. John Maclean, 'The War and its Outcome', *Justice* (17 September 1914), p. 4.
64. See Luxemburg, 'Die Krise der Sozialdemokratie', pp. 108–9.
65. *Weltgeschichte in Daten*, p. 494.
66. See Alexander Bahar 'Vom Griff nach der Weltmacht', *Junge Welt*, 11 October 2006 No. 236, p. 11.
67. Connolly, *Labour and Easter Week*, p. 43.
68. Aindrias Ó Cathasaigh (ed.), *The Lost Writings, James Connolly* (London, 1997), p. 157.
69. Ibid., p. 155
70. Connolly, *Socialism and Nationalism*, p. 108.
71. Ibid., p. 111.
72. See ibid., p. 178 and Liz Curtis, *The Cause of Ireland*, p. 263.
73. Connolly, *Labour and Easter Week*, p. 49.
74. Connolly, *Socialism and Nationalism*, p. 172.
75. Connolly, *Labour and Easter Week*, p. 139.
76. Nolan draws on MacNeill's statement that Connolly favoured an immediate insurrection with the Irish Citizen Army rising alone if necessary. This could however have been a policy on Connolly's part to goad the council of the Irish Republican Brotherhood (IRB) and MacNeill into action. See Nolan, *James Connolly*, p. 629.
77. Connolly, *Labour and Easter Week*, p. 124.
78. Nevin, *James Connolly*, p. 600.
79. J. Dunsmore Clarkson, *Labour and Nationalism in Ireland* (New York, 1970), p. 286.
80. See Padraic Pearse, 'From a Hermitage 1913', in *Political Writings and Speeches* (Dublin, 1962), pp. 177–9.
81. Connolly *Labour and Easter Week*, p. 175.
82. Pearse was 'nothing as new-fangled as a socialist or a syndicalist' but 'old-fashioned enough to be both a Catholic and a Nationalist'. Pearse, *Political Writings*, p. 181. Some of the language used in his political statements may have been hard for Connolly to digest, such as 'the old heart of the earth need to be warmed with the red wine of the battle-fields'. Pearse, *Political Writings*, p. 216. Pearse's radical democratic principles, however, are voiced in his writings. In his final article, 'The Sovereign People', Pearse lay down his concept of an Irish republic, drawing largely from the writings of Fintan Lalor: 'Let no man be mistaken as to who will be lord and master in Ireland when Ireland is free. The people will be lord and master.' Pearse, *Political Writings*, p. 345.
83. Connolly, *Socialism and Nationalism*, p. 25.
84. C. Desmond Greaves, *The Life and Times of James Connolly* (London, 1972), p. 403. The source of this quotation is obscure. Connolly may have meant 'hold on to your rifles' in a symbolic sense, referring to the retaining of labour's independent role to achieve socialism.
85. Connolly, *Labour and Easter Week*, pp. 139–40.
86. Liz Curtis, *The Cause of Ireland*, p. 265.
87. Nevin, *James Connolly*, p. 63.
88. Curtis, *The Cause of Ireland*, p. 270.
89. Connolly, *Labour and Easter Week*, p. 177.
90. V.I. Lenin, 'The Irish Rebellion of 1916', in V.I. Lenin, *Collected Works*, vol. 22 (Moscow, 1964), p. 355.
91. Cole, *Second International*, pp. 29, 70.
92. Luxemburg wrote *The Crisis of Social Democracy* in 1915 under the pseudonym 'Junius' when in prison in Germany.

93. Luxemburg, 'Die Krise der Sozialdemokratie', p. 136.
94. Rosa Luxemburg, 'Entwurf zu den Junius-Thesen', in Rosa Luxemburg, *Gesammelte Werke*, Bd. 4 (Berlin, 1974), p. 136.
95. V.I. Lenin, 'Uber die Junius-Broschüre', in V.I. Lenin, *Lenin Werke*, Bd. 22 (Berlin, 1971), p. 318.
96. Lenin, 'Die Ergebnisse der Diskussion über Selbstbestimmung', in Bd. 22, p. 365. (My translation from the German edition.)
97. Lenin, 'The Irish Rebellion', vol. 22, p. 355.

9

A people that did not Exist? Reflections on Some Sources and Contexts for Patrick Pearse's Militant Nationalism[1]

Róisín Ní Ghairbhí

> He wrote, acted and died for a people that did not exist.[2]
> Ruth Dudley Edwards on Pearse

> I am come of the seed of the people
> The people that sorrow
> That have no treasure but hope
> No riches laid up but a memory
> Of an Ancient glory.[3]
> 'The Rebel', P.H. Pearse

> *Mise mé féin agus cé sin?*[4] (I am myself and who is that?)
> Meath proverb, quoted in *An Claidheamh Soluis*,
> 7 September 1907.

Perhaps understandably, the career and philosophy of Patrick Pearse is often examined retrospectively as a prologue to a 'doomed' rising. Pearse's intellectual and cultural life is frequently viewed as a prelude which can throw light on the motivations behind his participation in the Easter rebellion and the proclamation of an Irish republic: not all of that life, however, receives the same attention. Pearse's political convictions in the run-up to 1916 are memorably summarized in his well known poem, 'The Rebel'. In this poem Pearse presents himself as spokesman for a historic nation which has been disenfranchised. For Ruth Dudley Edwards, Pearse's identifying with an historic Irish nation is an act of fantasy. In her 1977 biography, *Patrick Pearse: The Triumph of Failure*, she observed that Pearse 'wrote, acted and died for a people that did not exist'. This takes its cue from Pearse's assertion in 'The Rebel' that he had come 'of the seed of the people', and from his declaration that their masters should now 'beware of the risen people' on whose behalf he was speaking. Since so much discussion of 1916 centres on questions of mandate and motivation it is pertinent to reflect on the rationale behind Pearse's assertions, and on the criteria behind their dismissal by Dudley Edwards.

How well did Pearse know his people? Who were 'the people'? And what did they want? Such questions, when explored, offer insights into the genesis of much of Pearse's imagery, rhetoric and actions. On the other hand, when the 1916 Rising and the 'sacrifice' of Pearse's life are taken as the prism which reflects the essence or culmination of his political project, analysis of the agency of Pearse's political formation and of the various modes of articulation of his political philosophy can sometimes become reductive. A trajectory which has Pearse the Gaelic Leaguer, Pearse the creative writer and Pearse the home ruler become, and then be subsumed by, Pearse the propagandist, the republican and the patriot and/or the ideologue and fatalistic exponent of a blood sacrifice, is common, though not uncontested.[5] This analytical framework for a 'republicanization' of Pearse naturally emphasizes his actions in the years immediately preceding the Rising: his joining of the Irish Republican Brotherhood (IRB), his speech at the graveside of Ó Donnabháin Rossa in August 1915 and the overtly revolutionary tracts issued by him from late in 1915.

Xavier Carthy states that Pearse's 'political path to Kilmainham was traced for him by Theobald Wolfe Tone, Thomas Davis, John Mitchell [sic] and James Fintan Lawlor [sic]'.[6] Brian P. Murphy, likewise, traces the 'story of Pearse the revolutionary' to December 1913.[7] Roy Foster speaks of Pearse's 'notable, though rather obscure, radicalism from 1913'.[8] Dudley Edwards refers to Pearse's 'new religion' of physical force as dating from 1915 and states that he had come to these 'new beliefs' 'at bewildering speed'.[9] Similarly, several commentators imply that Pearse's use of heroic exemplars from history and Gaelic literature in St Enda's and in his creative writing to have been commensurate with an intensification of a (sometimes simplistic) Gaelic nationalism. Various references to 'the cult of Cúchulainn',[10] 'Eamhain Macha, Pearse's fantasy playground'[11] and Pearse's 'emotional addiction to the heroic' present Gaelic culture as an extraneous discourse adopted or appropriated by Pearse in an incapacious manner.[12]

In his 1994 book, *Patrick Pearse and the Politics of Redemption*, Sean Farrell Moran claimed that 'Pearse, like all the artists of the language movement, never escaped the parochial bounds of native Irish culture and the cultish nature of the movement.'[13] This betrays the parochial bounds of his own

Anglocentric frame of reference and he seems unaware that Pearse's nationalism (and literary outlook) expressed themselves frequently in a European and even global context. The index of the Dudley Edwards biography lists 'PP, *glorifies* [my emphasis]', following the word 'heroes'. Foster refers to 'Pearse's obsessional Celtic motifs'.[14] Carthy shows total ignorance of the Ulster cycle's literary importance: for Carthy, Cúchulainn, from 'near Dundalk' 'seems to have been a very nasty little boy'.[15] Commentary which infers that Pearse's identification with a historic Gaelic nation and its literature was somehow morbid or simplistic or deriving solely from some psychological need seldom interests itself deeply in the functions, domains and discourses associated with the Gaelic texts and nation themselves.

An analysis of some of the literary, autobiographical and journalistic writings of Pearse which gives due emphasis to the contexts which informed his writings allows a figure (and a trajectory) that may not be familiar to a number of historians to emerge. Analysis by various scholars of Pearse's journalistic and creative work and of his correspondence has painted a more complex picture of the origins and development of his political stance and idiom, and of the role played by Gaelic literature in informing his political views than accounts by some of the commentators mentioned above would suggest.[16] Sources such as Pearse's shortlived political weekly *An Barr Buadh*, his autobiographical fragment and his numerous (uncollected) essays on culture, nationality and identity in *An Claidheamh Soluis* are underutilized sources. Such sources offer important insights into the different strands that informed Pearse's specific understanding of questions of nationhood and nationality.[17]

Meanwhile, Irish language scholarship offers a more nuanced view of cultural life in Ireland in the nineteenth and early twentieth centuries than the narratives of rupture espoused by some commentators dependent on English language sources. This chapter examines some of these texts and sources, alongside more well-known writings by Pearse, in order to re-evaluate the evolution of Pearse's 'militant' nationalism/republicanism and its articulation. Literary criticism, and in particular a criticism which is informed by post-colonial theory, interests itself in questions of agency, reception and textuality; it questions received ideas about canon and 'centre' and is concerned with the ethics of representation and with the practical, political and economic ends to which these are put.[18] As such, it provides a useful focus for addressing a figure such as Pearse whose achievements and motivations are hotly contested. I will be forgiven some minor forays into what is for me the less familiar ground of historical analysis.

Dudley Edwards does not simply deny Pearse's understanding of the people; for her, 'the people', presumably the historic Gaelic nation which inspired Pearse, do not exist. Her sweeping assertion, which elides both the intellectual basis for Pearse's nationalism and also its perceived constituency in one semantic swoop, has influenced countless readers and commentators. In an otherwise mainly favourable review of her biography of Pearse, Joe Lee lamented that Dudley Edwards had failed to address the question of what Pearse actually meant by 'the people' as a critical concept.[19] Since she consciously alludes to the 'people' evoked in 'The Rebel' when she articulates her judgment on Pearse's motivations, a re-examination of that poem is pertinent. A historian constantly strives (or should strive) to use language in a way which is precise and scientific. For a literary critic, however, the impact of a text is predicated on nuance and echo, and words awake into resonance nuances attached to them in other contexts.[20]

For such a critic the imagery, diction and message of 'The Rebel' are radical and recall several songs associated with socialism which were current in the early 1900s. The 'Internationale', for example, in its English translation, tells the workers to 'arise'. For Pearse, the people had already arisen, presumably through their intellectual awakening. Like 'The Rebel', the 'Internationale' rehearses the oppression of servile masses by 'tyrants'; allusions to chains have a parallel in Pearse's mentioning of 'manacles'. The tone and message of both texts is the same: a warning in declamatory rhetoric that a current oppression can no longer endure and that the people themselves must act to free themselves. James Connolly's 'A Rebel Song', which was first published in *The Socialist* in 1903, is another example of this type of diction. The vocabulary of Connolly's poem (with references to 'tyrants', 'manhood', 'chain', 'serf' 'slave' and the oppression of the 'law') bears a striking similarity to the diction of 'The Rebel' and various other texts by Pearse. An imminent reversal of fortune for 'the serf' and 'slave' is proclaimed in both Connolly's and Pearse's texts.

This is not to suggest that Pearse was referring specifically to these songs: the imagery and prophetic voice of 'The Rebel' has precedents in much Irish-language political poetry from the sixteenth century onwards. Pearse had a close scholarly knowledge of (and as we shall see, a personal engagement with) such poetry. Nonetheless, it seems reasonable that the nuances and contexts which were attached to the vocabulary of socialism and which feature so saliently in 'The Rebel' should be taken into account when discussing the poem. It was composed just three years after the Dublin Lockout: Pearse was well aware of the socialist allusions implicit in his choice of diction.[21] The internationalist tone of the poem should also be noted: nowhere is the poem's message of emancipation confined to an Irish context. The diction of socialist texts such as those mentioned above can also offer insights into possible nuances of Pearse's 'blood imagery'. Connolly's song reminds the listener of the life-giving properties implicit in 'blood'. For him 'wage slav'ry drains the workers' blood'. Another socialist anthem, the famous 'The Red Flag' (composed by a Fenian from county Meath), provides a further reminder that kinship, comradeship and the moral imperative of brave precedent were among the ideas evoked by mention of blood (even when being spilled) in political discourse of the late nineteenth and early twentieth century:

> The people's flag is deepest red
> It shrouded oft our martyred dead,
> And ere their limbs grew stiff and cold,
> Their hearts' blood dyed its every fold.
>
> Then raise the scarlet standard high
> Within its shade we'll live and die...[22]

In 'The Rebel' this further (or fundamental) meaning of blood is paramount: 'I am of the blood of serfs.' The rhythm and cadences of the poem are not most obviously those of the ballads of socialism, or even Fenianism, however. The poem's closest antecedent in that regard would seem to be the famous 'Song of Myself' by Walt Whitman (1819–92). Significantly, Pearse owned a copy of 'Song of Myself'.[23] Both Pearse's and Whitman's poems are mystic tracts. Both poets speak in vatic tones. Sometimes using Biblical diction, they nonetheless identify with a wide cross-section of humankind. Both 'The Rebel' and 'Song of Myself' stress an intrinsic dignity which forms a universal human bond linking hitherto disenfranchised communities.

> I know I am august...
>
> Through me many long dumb voices,
> Voices of the interminable generations of prisoners and slaves...
>
> I am the mash'd fireman with breast-bone broken...
> Tumbling walls buried me in their debris,
> Heat and smoke I inspired...
> I heard the yelling shouts of my comrades...[24] (Whitman)
>
> I am flesh of the flesh of these lowly...
>
> My heart has been heavy with the grief of mothers,
> My eyes have been wet with the tears of children...
> I have yearned with old wistful men...
>
> And now I speak being full of vision...[25] (Pearse)

Whitman is famous in American literary history for his declamatory rhythms and radical democratic message which form a fundamental break with the personal but passive epiphanies associated with Romantic poetry. Identification of Pearse's 'The Rebel' with the style and content of Whitman's 'Song of Myself' allows readers to view Pearse's poem with fresh eyes; to see the poem as having a performative function, whose message of universal democracy allows a subaltern nation to speak. This egalitarian outlook was not a late development for Pearse. A parable on identity, 'Eachtra an Eolais', which was serialized in the *Claidheamh Soluis* in 1907 featured a character whose compound identity was represented by his name, 'Mise mé féin'.[26] 'Mise mé féin' was then referred to as 'an duine agus an daonnacht úd, Mise mé féin' ('that person and humanity, Mise mé féin').[27]

Who formed this 'humanity' or 'people' whom Pearse saw himself as representing? Pearse himself stated in *The Sovereign People* that 'the people are the nation; the whole people, all its men and women'. Pearse's feminism remains underexamined, though texts like his short story 'Na Bóithre' (where a young girl suffers a breakdown when she rebels against the role allotted to her gender), his friendship with Mary Hayden and positive commentary on the suffragettes in the *Barr Buadh* provide ample material for reflection. However, Pearse's main focus in *The Sovereign People* is on the idea of a nation or people which encompasses and enfranchises all classes. While it is true that Pearse himself stated that he was 'nothing so new-fangled as a socialist' in October 1913, he made clear on the same occasion that this denial did not entail any lack of sympathy with the ethos of socialism, stating that his instinct was 'with the landless man against the lord of lands, and with the breadless man against the master of millions' and equating the issues concerning Irish socialists with those concerning Irish nationalists.[28]

'The Rebel', in the Whitmanian reading above, has Pearse offer witness of, and empathy with, ordinary working people who have suffered historic disadvantage. Pearse states in the poem that he is 'come of the seed of the people'. What evidence is there that Pearse really had close connections with the emergent subaltern nation of 'The Rebel', *The Sovereign People* and of the 1916 proclamation? The role played by a family heritage of radical nationalism and indeed republicanism in informing Pearse's political viewpoint has often been downplayed. In particular, the nature of the political discourse to which Pearse was exposed on the Brady side of his family merits further attention.[29]

Pearse tells us in his unfinished autobiography that his grandfather Patrick and his siblings had left Nobber in north county Meath in 1848 along with their father, Walter.[30] Meath was badly affected by the Great Famine: up to 25,000 deaths were attributed to that event in the county; many more emigrated.[31] The population of Nobber declined from 2,112 in 1841 to 1,409 in 1851. Nearby areas like Kilmainhamwood showed similar declines.[32] His grandparents' generation were eyewitnesses to, and presumably suffered from, the trauma implicit in such statistics: Pearse did indeed come of the 'people that sorrow'. Despite the primacy Pearse accorded to family influences in making him an Irish rebel in this unfinished autobiography,[33] Dudley Edwards chooses not to ponder at length on the implications of information provided by Pearse himself. When discussing the outlook of Pearse's mother, Margaret Brady, she notes that two of Margaret's 'ancestors' had 'died' during the 1798 rebellion.[34]Pearse himself recounts proudly that his own great-great-grandfather, Walter Brady, participated in the rebellion. He further recounts that one of Walter's brothers was hanged by the Yeomanry and that another was buried in the Croppies' Grave at Tara.[35]

Such details are missing from Dudley Edwards' account, which presents Brady participation in the 1798 rebellion in vague and passive terms. The 1798 connection should not be dismissed so peremptorily given that family history provides an early source for Pearse's republicanism and its articulation. The battle near Tara, in which Walter's brother presumably participated, is well documented: the site and the Croppy Grave are extant and remembered. French and American ideas about citizenship and equality were grafted onto a native Gaelic nationalism in county Meath. Séamus Ó Loinsigh noted reports 'that in the barony of Meath the Defenders spoke of liberty, equality and fraternity in the most extravagant manner and that the lower classes had their minds disturbed by Tom Paine's *The Rights of Man*, a six penny edition of which was distributed gratis, throughout the county.'[36] It would appear that the Defenders who entered the United Irishmen at Nobber were led by Presbyterians whose conscious republicanism was recognized by the Catholic rector, Dr McKenna.[37]

The next generation of Bradys, who included Pearse's beloved grandaunt Margaret, were also deeply politicized:

> Auntie Margaret spoke of Wolfe Tone and of Robert Emmet as a woman might speak of the young men – the strong and splendid young men – she had known in her girlhood. The Young Irelanders she did not talk so much of, except Mitchel; but she had herself known the Fenians, and of them she had songs full of endearing expressions, and musical with the names of O'Donovan Rossa and the Hawk of the Hill.[38]

Recent scholarship has emphasized the continuity between the various idioms of Gaelic nationalism and those of later republicanism.[39] When Pearse later amalgamated the imagery of both discourses to forge the conscience of his own nationalism he was able to draw on an idiom which had been part of his childhood. He recalled that Aunt Margaret '… sang in her low crooning voice old ballads and snatches of songs in Irish and in

English. Her songs were mostly of men dead, or in exile for the love of Ireland, or of some Royal Blackbird or Green Linnet that was to come from beyond the sea.'[40]

Ciaran Ó Coigligh's Irish language edition of Pearse's poetry shows both 'Oro sé do Bheatha Abhaile' and 'Ó a Bhean an Tí' to be reworkings of political poems which were current in the oral culture of nineteenth-century Ireland.[41] They should therefore be read as conscious adaptations of a subaltern militant nationalist discourse. 'Ó a Bhean an Tí' prophesizes 'deargchogadh ar Ghallaibh an uabhair' ('red war on the arrogant foreigner'), reminding us of the Gaelic sources for some of the specific diction found in Pearse's later writings. Dudley Edwards' reference to Margaret's oral histories as 'half remembered tales about Tone, Emmet and the Fenians' bundles discrete elements of history into a rattlebag of hearsay and mythology. Yet Pearse's mother recalled the 1798 Walter's son, her grandfather. Dudley Edwards surmised that aunt Margaret's histories and songs meant that Pearse 'could now stock his daydreams with "real" people': one wonders why featuring in a ballad or family history should make Jeremiah O'Donovan Rossa or Walter Brady less real than a distant Parliamentarian whose speeches were reported in metropolitan newspapers. It is disingenuous in particular of Dudley Edwards to refer to Margaret's imparting of information about the Fenians as 'half remembered tales', given that Margaret had known the Fenians as a middle-aged woman. Her brother was a Fenian. Pearse lived with this man, his grandfather, Patrick Brady, for a time. Pearse heard in this house a balladeer sing songs of Emmet and Tone and speak of Fenians who had drilled locally.[42]

Pearse was not aware as a child of his grandfather's Fenianism, but knowledge of Patrick Brady's political stance grew in importance as he came to realize that his own political ideas were not those of the Irish Party. In a fascinating 'letter' to the MP William O'Brien, which formed part of a series termed 'Beart Litreacha a Chuaigh Amú', published in *An Barr Buadh* as debate on home rule intensified in the spring of 1912, Pearse alludes to the fact that Patrick had also been a follower of John Blake Dillon in 1848. The letter chides the then current generation of politicians (who were debating the Home Rule Bill) for their failure in progressing the political agenda of past generations:

> Do bhínn-se ag léamh bhur n-eachtra ó's ard do mo sheanathair. Do rinne mo sheanathair beagán ar son na hEireann nuair a bhí sé féin óg. Do bhí sé ar lucht leanamhna athair do charad i mbliadhain a '48. Do bhí sé ina fhinín i mbliadhain a '67. Do chreid sé go gcríochnóchadh sibh-se agus bhur gcompánaigh an obair d'fhag seisean agus a chompánaigh-sean gan chríochnú.[43]

As Pearse himself relates, the Bradys left Meath in 1848, a year of revolutionary ferment in Ireland as elsewhere. Walter Brady (the son of the United Irishman of 1798) and his eight children would have seen agrarian unrest and anger at evictions politicize and radicalize another generation of Meath people, particularly during the late 1820s and early 1830s. Desmond Mooney noted a report that 20,000 labourers had taken part in a peaceful demonstration of disaffection in Nobber at this time.[44] Given his political leanings, it is possible that Patrick Brady participated in the Confederate clubs. These clubs offered a broad range of lectures on ideas of citizenship, equality and culture, and classes in Irish language and literature formed part of the programme. In the years following, the political consciousness and political idiom of the 'people' continued to be formed by petitions and pamphlets, by newspapers like *The Nation* and *The Irish People*, and by countless ballads. All this contributed to the ongoing political education of the general populace and surely impacted on the Bradys. Pearse himself emphasized the impact of Fenian ballads on his own identity. [45]

Patrick Brady was a Fenian in 1867 at a time when Fenianism was a mass movement. In 1867 the IRB's proposed constitution for Ireland drew on American and French ideas of universal suffrage and equality: the 'bloody patriots' also had ideas. It is interesting that Pearse chose to couch his opinions in a 'letter', with all the suggestions of familiarity thereby implied. Pearse's pride in his Fenian heritage and the sense of equality implied in the tone of the address to O'Brien reminds us also of the close connections between those who supported an armed rebellion and the Irish Parliamentary Party in the latter half of the nineteenth century. William O'Brien must be considered as a possible seminal influence on Pearse. O'Brien's book, *Irish Ideas* (1893), was in Pearse's possession and includes essays on Gaelic culture and nationality.[46] This may even have been the book he mentions above as having been asked to read aloud to his grandfather (who may have been ailing as he died the year after its publication). Of particular interest in *Irish Ideas* is the text of a lecture given by O'Brien on 26 September 1893, 'The Future of the Young Men of Ireland', a text which, given one critic's association of Pearse with a 'cult of boyhood', is ironically introduced by a citation of Disraeli's statement that 'the history of heroes is the history of youth'. In this essay O'Brien voiced his aspiration that the young men of Ireland would live not 'as the disinherited cast into the awkward darkness, not as the slaves bowed with other men's business, but as the future citizens, rulers and owners of their own delightful land'.[47]

Dudley Edwards has Pearse 'being fed' a 'narrow and often maudlin nationalism' by his grandaunt Margaret and contends that his mind was 'susceptible' to a philosophy of militant nationalism.[48] The impression is that of a contagion, and the value and integrity of the family history is diminished. Xavier Carthy's bias is more pronounced; he writes of a 'young and impressionable boy' whose Aunt Margaret 'by the fireside, told him stories of bloody Irish patriots'. According to Carthy, this 'was not the civilized, humane approach to Irish history that this old lady instilled in Pat and his brother Willie'.[49] Both accounts could be seen to elide the intellectuality of the political discourse that was taking place in Pearse's home life (and in many others) in the closing decades of the nineteenth century. The approach also downplays the Brady/Pearse family's close connections with both physical force republicanism and radical political theory. In any case, far from being a young and impressionable boy, Pearse was in his mid teens when Margaret died in 1893. He was intellectually precocious; we learn from a later account in the *Claidheamh Soluis* (and Dudley Edwards herself recounts) that he tracked down Hyde's newly published compendiums of oral literature in the National Library a year after his aunt's death in a deliberate attempt to find out more about oral literature she had shared with him. The terminological bias of speculation that her 'death during this time must have made her medicine even more potent' belies again the author's lack of interest in the intellectuality of Margaret's knowledge of history and literature, as well as Pearse's sophisticated response to such material.[50]

Sean Farrell Moran's statement that 'Pearse had long associated life with death' is based on a Freudian reading of an excerpt from Pearse's unfinished autobiography which describes a rocking horse given to him in childhood.[51] Pearse's succinct account of family involvement in militant nationalism in that same source goes unmentioned and unanalysed in Farrell Moran's biography. Clearly, however, Pearse was open to formative influences that might well have made him amenable to militant nationalism from an early age. An anecdote which forms part of Pearse's series 'From a Hermitage' (first published in *Irish Freedom* in 1913) describes such an early sympathy.

While the story is presented as a conversation with an elderly priest on a desert island, the detail makes clear that it is based on a real conversation. Pearse remembers the encounter described as having coincided with the start of the Boer War, c.1899. Though Pearse disagrees with the old man's conservative views on the rights of women, he finds himself in sympathy with his militant nationalism:

> Yet we had one interest in common. There was at the bottom of my heart a memory which a course of Intermediate education (by some miracle of God's) had not altogether obliterated. I had heard in childhood of the Fenians from one who, although a woman, had shared their hopes and disappointment. The names of Stephens and O'Donovan Rossa were familiar to me, and they seemed to me the

most gallant of all names: names which should be put into songs and sung proudly to tramping music... 'Look at the chance we have now,' he exclaimed, 'the British army at the other end of the earth, and one blow would give us Ireland; but we've neither men nor guns. GOD ALMIGHTY WON'T GO ON GIVING US CHANCES if we let every chance slip.'[52]

The story shows Pearse to have deemed himself, at least retrospectively, sympathetic to militant nationalism a mere three years into his involvement with the Gaelic League. An interesting aspect of Pearse's famous short story 'Íosagán' which is often overlooked by critics also shows that Pearse was already or still occupied with the long view of physical force republicanism at the end of 1906, when the story was published.[53] The main thrust of the story tells of an old man's mystical encounter with a little boy, Íosagán, who is Jesus Christ. The old man, SeanMhaitias, does not attend Mass: we are told, almost as an aside, that some of the old people recall that he had sold his soul to a 'big man' on the top of Cnoc an Daimh more than sixty years before, which would place SeanMhaitias' clandestine meeting with the 'big man' in the mid 1840s. The explanation is an obvious reference to historic tensions between the Catholic Church and the oath-bound societies of militant nationalism.

Militant nationalist politics is the central theme of Pearse's 'Brighid na Gaoithe'/'An Bhean Chaointe', the first part of which was published in 1907.[54] Oral memory is the locus for the young protagonist's (Cóilin) learning of the true story behind the mental breakdown suffered by an old woman, Muirne. Cóilin, now a grown man in reflective mood, recalls hearing from his own father of how Muirne's son had died in prison having being accused (probably wrongly) of the murder of a hated landlord. The memory of threatened evictions which brought about the crisis is an obvious reference to the Land War. The information is transmitted not as an official history but as what we might now term subaltern history, from father to son. The young boy learns that his own father was present the night of the murder and the rehearsing of the story brings the current political situation (presumably discussion of home rule) into relief. The full version of the story ends with the grown son's recalling his father's stating that there might soon be cause for 'us all to be making tallyho out of the black soldiers'.

Máire Ní Fhlathúin, noting the similarities between Lady Gregory's *The Jail Gate* (1905) and Pearse's 'An Bhean Chaointe', has emphasized the comparative explicitness of the political view expressed in Pearse's story, where the queen's failure to protect the young man, her subject, is contrasted with the pathetic efforts of his own mother, who has tried every avenue of appeal in order to save his life.[55] In any event, both

'Íosagán' and 'An Bhean Chaointe' undermine the narrative which has Pearse as a 'benign' cultural nationalist in the period in question.

Pearse's journalistic work provides further evidence for an early sympathy with militant nationalism and for an early aspiration to achieve a republic by military means. Again, the diction chosen by Pearse is sometimes telling. The Oireachtas in 1906 allowed for 'a review of the fighting forces at the disposal of the Gael' ... 'a national council of war; a milestone on the march to emancipation'. The Irish version of the same article describes the language procession in terms of a nation's army marching.[56] An extraordinary and highly entertaining article, 'In My Garden', published as a supplement to the *Claidheamh Soluis* in August 1906, provides further evidence of Pearse's agenda. The article mainly takes the form of a historical reflection from an imagined newspaper (*The Daily Claidheamh*): the year is imagined as 2006. Pearse's desire for achieving a republic is implicit in the article's contextualizing of Ireland's imagined self-governance as having been 'the splitting up of the British Empire into independent kingdoms and republics' and by references to the Indian and Russian presidents and the South African republic.[57] That military action might have to be taken is clear from the retrospective whose radical message is tempered in the tone of playful parody in which the entire article is written.

> Almost the first act of the Revolutionary Government of 19- (the figure was unfortunately blotted out) had been to employ a national education system embodying the two principles he had referred to.[58]

A reference to 'the National University (founded by public subscription in 1911) – before the war of revolution, in which, by the way its students played a prominent part' indicates that Pearse envisaged his plans being enacted in the medium term.[59] Pearse explicitly stated that he had his own ideas on home rule but that the time was not right to announce them in an article ('Waiting') which was published later that same year of 1906 and which formed a reaction to a statement of John Redmond's. However, Pearse did state that Irish people would not achieve anything without fighting: the word 'troid' was capitalized.[60] On 8 December that same year, the *Claidheamh* carried an advertisement for Bulmer Hobson's newspaper, *The Republic*, which was announced as 'an organ of militant nationalism'. While Pearse was more circumspect about sharing his advanced ideas on militant nationalism in the years following, a 1908 article on a Scoil Éanna trip ('On Sliabh Rua') referred both to enduring local folk memory of 1798 and the possibility of another armed revolt.[61]

In *Mise Éire*, the nation, for Pearse synonymous with the 'people', derives its fundamental identity from Gaelic sources, Cúchulainn and the Cailleach Bhearra being the particular literary figures chosen to emphasize the longevity of Gaelic civilization. For several commentators, Pearse's identification with a historic Gaelic nation has been that of a naive idealist or even a brainwashed ideologue. Eugene McCabe's recollection of the first time he heard Pearse's *Mise Éire* exemplifies a certain type of reading of Pearse's motivations:

> The effect I remember was very moving.... Is there a word to describe that kind of emotion? Nationalism? Tribalism? Atavism, the father of a great grandfather, from Avus a grandfather, resemblance to a remote ancestor, a reversion to the primitive, an obscure sense of belonging, whatever it means it's something we should be wary of; it can make wise men think and do very unwise things.[62]

Given that several commentators present Pearse's discussion of motifs from Gaelic literature as irrational, and given that those motifs were central to his own exposition of his ideas on nationality, it is clear that the nature and extent of Pearse's interaction with Gaelic civilization merits further exploration. Pearse's own great grandfather, Walter Brady (a son of the 1798 veteran), was a native speaker of Irish from Meath.[63] Pearse's mother proudly recalled him as 'a tall old man who wore knee britches and a silk hat and who spoke Irish'.[64] Though Dudley Edwards notes that Walter Brady was a native speaker of Irish, she does not dwell on the implications of this information. Pearse specifically states that Irish was the language of north Meath during the youth of Walter's children.[65] Pearse knew some of Walter's children well having lived for a time with his grandfather, Patrick. His uncle Christy taught him many Irish words and his aunt Margaret was a frequent visitor to the Pearse home.[66] Given the contested nature of Pearse's use of Gaelic literature in his political discourse, surely the possibility that he had himself experienced in childhood the residual influence of a vibrant Gaelic culture which stretched back almost 2,000 years merits further consideration?

Studies of literary material from the decades before the Famine corroborate Pearse's information, portraying a still relatively vigorous bilingual community in north Meath. Pearse's description of the richness and dignity involved in the north Meath Gaelic tradition which he had witnessed through his aunt Margaret's is evidenced by accounts of the sophisticated cultural context which would have formed her.[67] Various letters pertaining to the ordnance survey in north Meath refer constantly to Irish-speaking informants who are often described simply as 'the Irish'. With the exception of specific parishes, there is no implication that the language is about to disappear.[68] Most sources state that Pearse began learning Irish in 1893 but, significantly, what Pearse himself recounts is that he first *saw Irish in print* that year.[69] What form did Pearse's first interface with Irish language culture take? His witnessing of aunt Margaret's oral transmission of Gaelic literary tradition is described in articles in *An Claidheamh Soluis* and *An Macaomh*, the journal of St Enda's:

> One of my oldest recollections is of a kindly greyhaired seanchaidhe, a woman of my mother's people, telling tales by a kitchen fireplace. She spoke more wisely and nobly of ancient heroic things than anyone else I have ever known.... This was my first glimpse of the Boy Corps of Eamhan Macha.[70]

> We remember as a child sitting by a turf fire and listening to a grey haired woman telling Irish folktales. From that gentle seanchaí we first learned how gracious and noble is Mother Éire, how sweet a thing it is to love her, how proud a service to toil and to suffer for her. In converse with her too, we first realized that Éire has a voice and a speech of her own; from her we first learned to pronounce Irish words; from her we first heard the words of Cúchulainn and Fergus and Fionn, of Grainne of the Fleets and the two mighty Aodhs; from her we first listened to the tale of 'Brian's wisdom, Eoghan's genius, Sarsfield's daring, Emmet's early grave and Grattan's life long epic of devotion'.

> Our texts – it was Junior Grade 1894 – were Laoi Oisín and Diarmuid agus Gráinne. We remember the thrill of pleasure with which we heard the familiar names, the eagerness with which we heard the familiar tales. The turf fire was back and the dead voice was back again.[71]

Aunt Margaret was for Pearse 'the woman to whom I owe all my enthusiasms'.[72] Standish James O'Grady is sometimes cited as the original source of Pearse's knowledge of the Rúraíocht or Ulster cycle (the cycle associated with Cúchulainn) but the evidence points to Pearse having first heard of this material, however tangentially, in childhood. The possibility that Margaret herself was citing O'Grady exists but it is extremely remote: O'Grady's works did not enjoy mass or even wide circulation. Pearse emphatically states that Margaret's recitations formed his '*first* glimpse' of 'The Boy Corps of Eamhan Macha' (a conscious quotation) and that he '*first*' heard of the material summarized as the quotation beginning 'Brian's wisdom' from her also.[73] Pearse remembers Margaret '*telling* Irish folktales', *not* reading them; she is consciously alluded to as a 'seanchaí'. The literary and historical material Pearse recalls hearing shows Margaret to have been a product of an oral culture of high intellectuality. Pearse tells us that Margaret first taught him how to pronounce Irish words, a recollection which suggests that she was literate in Irish. This is highly possible: there are references to large numbers of hedge schoolmasters (who were also poets and scholars) teaching Irish (literacy) in the 1820s and 1830s in north Meath and the wider area.[74] Margaret's historical repertoire corresponds to a large extent to Crofton Croker's 1824 summary of the typical political preoccupations of a 'hedge-school master'.[75] Cúchulainn was only being 'discovered' by (non native Irish-speaking) scholars towards the end of the nineteenth century.[76] While divisions between folk/oral literature and a high-end written literature do not hold for other texts of Irish language literature, Margaret's knowledge of the Ulster cycle is particularly intriguing, as this literature was usually, though not exclusively, associated with the written tradition. It is high-end literature. The scholar Éinrí Ó Muirgheasa drew attention to the enduring intellectuality of the Irish language community in north Meath:

> Even when the last great rout came on the spoken tongue the poets of Meath continued to sing, and the scribes to write their songs ... this is the peculiar glory of the Meath–Oriel district that the literary knowledge of the language accompanied the spoken tongue right down to its grave. In most other places the literary knowledge and cultivation of Irish had disappeared many generations before the spoken tongue died out.[77]

A group of Gaelic poets, which included Michael Clarke (1750–1847) and Peadar Ó Gealacain/Peter Galligan (1792–1860), were based near Nobber when Margaret was a young girl.[78] Galligan taught Irish in many local areas for prolonged periods in the 1820s and 1830s.[79] He was one of the most important scribes working in Ireland in the nineteenth century. His manuscript collection included copies of heroic tales, Fenian lays and original compositions, as well as poems and prayers collected from the local population.[80] Pearse says that from all accounts the Brady household in north Meath was full of 'mirth and kindly cheer and song'.[81] The 'Dán an Chodhlata' collected by Galligan is the same 'Sleep Song' (Déirín Dé) taught by Margaret Brady to Pearse, who later had it published.[82] The excerpts reveal Margaret's awareness of Fenian lays and historical poems and songs. It seems reasonable to imagine the Bradys as part of a similar *milieu* to that depicted by Peter Galligan, whose own songs portray a vibrant Irish language community which used oral poetry for both entertainment and political commentary.[83]

Galligan's notes show that literary manuscripts in Gaelic were much sought after by various people in the Nobber area.[84] Studies of this cultural community offer *inter alia* a glimpse of the cultural *milieu* which provided the architecture of Margaret's nationalism. Walter Ong's observation that oral societies 'think memorable thoughts' is relevant. Galligan could cite his genealogy back to the Cromwellian wars: he knew exactly who he was and who his people were.[85] Galligan transcribed Keating's famous defence of Gaelic civilization, *Foras Feasa ar Éirinn*. His manuscripts include copies of poems by Séamas Mac Cuarta and Art Mac Cumhaidh. Mac

Cumhaidh's *Aisling* includes a motif of ancestral leaders rising from their tombs.[86] It is known that Galligan had for a time in his possession a manuscript belonging to a contemporary poet and scribe from south Armagh in north Oriel, Art Mac Bionaid (1793–1879), a scribe with whom Galligan shared the Belfast-based patron Robert McAdam. A later manuscript of Mac Bionaid's included a copy of *Táin Bó Cuailgne*.[87] To say that Margaret (and hence Pearse) may have witnessed transmission of the *Táin* as part of a living oral/scribal tradition may be conjecture, but enough evidence exists to suggest that the influence of a living Meath/Oriel Gaelic tradition merits serious consideration as the original source and as an illuminating context for Pearse's nationalism. This was, after all, his own contention: outstanding Irish language scholarship by Breandán Ó Buachalla and others provides ample guidance for revised approaches.

Pearse's account of learning from Margaret of 'how gracious and noble is Mother Éire', the idea which formed his nationalism, needs to be viewed in terms of his witnessing personally an unbroken transmission of a 1,000-year-old literary tradition. Many of the events in both the Ulster cycle and the Fenian cycles which Pearse alluded to so often take place in Meath and in Oriel. Not far from Nobber, Tara and the Gabhra valley are associated with the battles, deaths and burials of heroes from the major heroic cycles in Gaelic literature. For Margaret, the placenames and characters cited in these literatures would have had a particular immediacy and familiarity. Cúchulainn was referred to as an exemplar of strength in some of the contemporary material collected by Galligan with the same easy familiarity as occurs in the community poetry of Connemara today.[88] Pearse was party to this easy identification with the salient motifs of a sophisticated literature. Community folklore in the north Meath area also included stories and poems featuring the Cailleach Bhéarra, whose name was commemorated in the ancient burial cairns of Sliabh na Caillí a short distance from Nobber.[89] Indeed, a poem about the Cailleach's long memory, which was known to oral tradition in Meath at the time of Margaret's youth, may have provided (along with the early Irish poem *Mise Eba* which had been translated by Thomas McDonagh) a template for Pearse's *Mise Éire*:

> Mise Cailleach Bheurtha bhocht
> Iomdha iongnadh d'amarcas riamh
> Chonacas Carn Bán 'na loch
> Gidh go bhfuil sé anois ina shliabh.[90]

In 1827 Michael Clarke of the 'Nobber' group of poets and scholars published the translation *Ireland's Dirge* alongside its Irish-language original *Tuireamh na hÉireann*, a political poem which had been composed by the Kerry poet Sean Ó Conaill around 1655.[91] The long list of subscribers for Clarke's edition shows that a wide cross-section of the local middle classes and clergy interested themselves in the printed poem.[92] Many more people would have come across the poem as it was read out from manuscripts or learned by heart: Vincent Morley reports that the poem *Tuireamh na hÉireann* was 'phenomenally popular' in manuscript transmission in Ireland.[93] *Tuireamh na hÉireann* lists the woes suffered by a historical Gaelic nation, invoking the names of leaders banished during the seventeenth century and alluding also to the heroic example of the Fianna and Brian Boru. It is, in Seamas Mac Gabhann's words, 'a roll call of famous names … affording glimspses of former glory'.[94] Morley cites the poem's popularity in its suitability for reciting and believes it formed the basis for much of the nationalist discourse of the nineteenth century.[95] Given the documented popularity of *Tuireamh na hÉireann* in north Meath and particularly given that the poem features the 'two mighty Aodhs', the Fianna and Brian Boru who formed part of Margaret's lore, it seems reasonable to count it among the sources which may have influenced (directly or indirectly) the Bradys' view of themselves as part of a historic Gaelic nation which had been wronged and awaited redemption. The assertion of a deep-rooted Gaelic nationhood which is exemplified by *Tuireamh na hÉireann* provides a frame of allusion for Pearse's 1912 poem 'Mionn' and for his political allegiances in general. 'The Rebel' forms part of his redress of poetry for a historical nation which he knew through its literature, family, friends and informants from Irish-speaking areas throughout Ireland. For McCabe to suggest that references to Cúchulainn and the Cailleach Bhéarra in *Mise Éire* are atavistic is to place a value judgment on a Gaelic literature which Pearse and his relations witnessed as part of a cultural continuum stretching back over 1,000 years. Pearse's statement that he belonged to a 'poor remnant of a gallant nation', a nation whose literature had given birth to Cúchulainn, a nation which was older even than another literary character, the Cailleach Bhéarra, was a matter of historical and geographical fact.[96]

Gearóid Denvir's analysis of the predominant cultural influences of nineteenth-century Gaelic Ireland is instructive:

> The Gaelic poets proclaimed through their art a message of hope and redemption for the underclass, the downtrodden, the 'little people' of Ireland, and they promised heaven on earth to those who listened. And it should be noted that their people did listen. Without any doubt, more people in nineteenth century Ireland listened to Raifteirí and the poets, and recited their poems from memory, than read the novels of Maria Edgeworth or the politico-philosophical treatises of Edmund Burke. Thus the native learning, and in particular the poetry, is the native 'public space' and 'tribal memory' in nineteenth century Ireland, which the poets found, as Raifteirí put in 'scríofa i leabhar na daonnachta' (written in the book of humanity).[97]

This assessment of the domain of popular political identity was anticipated by Pearse:

> It is, in fact, true that the repositories of the Irish tradition, as well the spiritual tradition of nationality as the kindred tradition of stubborn physical resistance to England, have been the great, splendid, faithful, common people – that dumb multitudinous throng which sorrowed during the penal night, which bled in '98, which starved in the Famine; and which is here still – what is left of it – unbought and unterrified.[98]

Xavier Carthy's reference to Pearse's 'love for a country that had never existed' owes much to Yeats and Dudley Edwards (and perhaps O'Casey) and little to historical fact. Pearse's writings should be read in the knowledge of his personal engagement with Gaelic literature. This engagement took place at several levels: as a child witness to his relations' repertoire and as an adult who engaged with Gaelic literature at a high level. His evocation of the Fenian and Ulster cycle heroes in Scoil Éanna, in his drama *Macghníomhartha Cúchulainn* and in the rhetoric used in the *Barr Buadh* and elsewhere reflected the foundation myths and high literature of the Gaelic nation. They formed part of a canon and a discourse whose importance had been emphasized since the seventeenth century by both scribal and oral traditions. Pearse was well aware that the material he had access to was residual and spoke of 'snatches of songs in Irish and in English'.[99] Elsewhere he mentioned 'fugitive love songs of the manuscripts and of the countrysides'.[100] In *Ghosts* he wrote of 'the secret songs of the dispossessed Irish'.[101] Through his scholarly and creative work Pearse brought the marginalized literary themes of his childhood to a wider audience. Meanwhile, his analysis of the influence of thinkers like Tone and Emmet in his later political tracts can be seen as the intellectual culmination of a life-long interest in folk history. Dudley Edwards suggests that Pearse did not understand the people of Connacht, and that he had no understanding of the poverty and fears of famine that forced them to emigrate.[102] Given the important fact that Pearse's own Irish-speaking relations left north Meath as the Famine drew to an end, it might make more sense to state that his interest in the people of Connemara was grounded in a natural empathy. Today's delineation of the Gaeltacht in terms of a geographical area for language planning can distract us from the fact that most of the counties of Ireland included native Irish speakers at the turn of the twentieth century. When Pearse engaged with Gaelic culture, as a publisher and activist, as a poet, as a dramatist and as an educator; when he mobilized 'Gaeltacht' people to organize themselves and express themselves, he was engaging with a contemporary, though marginalized, culture. The discourse that Pearse

engaged in might today be termed subaltern history. It formed the basis
for his ideas on nationalism and for his imagined community of the Irish
nation or people: 'All the time we were learning to realise ourselves as a
child of our Mother and the heir of a tradition.'[103]

Commentary which infers that mention of blood by Pearse in various
writings is indicative of a late fascination with blood sacrifice has had an
immense influence on perceptions of him. The phrase 'blood sacrifice'
has become shorthand for Pearse's later political philosophy in some
quarters. However, his interest in the subaltern literature and history of
a historic nation provides the key to understanding much of his imagery
and rhetoric. Such is also the case when engaging with imagery and rhetoric of his which evokes blood in various figurative senses. In any event,
Pearse evoked blood in its varied meanings in writings completed long
before the Rising. In 'An Bhean Chaointe' the narrator is asked to reflect
on the blood drawn from his own grandmother by foreign soldiers: the
emphasis is on kinship and family loyalty (alluding also perhaps to the
bravery of Anne Devlin) rather than on the spilling of blood itself:

> Cé a mharaigh do sheanathair le fuip? Cé a bhain an fhuil
> dhearg as guaillí mo sheanmhátharsa le lasc? Ce a dhéanfadh
> é ach na Gaill?[104]

Another early mention of blood being spilled in the context of militant
nationalism occurs in a postscript which Pearse added to his 1906 article
'An Act of Faith' in *An Claidheamh Soluis*:

> Beidh an fhairrge n-a thuilltibh
> Dearga is an spéir n-a fuil
> Beidh an saol n-a chogadh craorag ar dhruim na gcnoc
> Beidh gach gleann sléibhe ar fuid Éireann is muinte ar crith.

> O' the Erne shall
> run red with redundance of blood
> The earth shall rock beneath you and
> flames wrap hill and wood
> And gun-peel and slogan-cry
> wake many a glen serene.[105]

The verses quoted by Pearse above are from the popular song 'An Rós
Geal Dubh' or 'Róisín Dubh'. The song, which exists in many versions
and with varied emphases on love and politics, is generally dated to the
years following the battle of Kinsale. In citing this verse Pearse was
reminding readers that a native idiom of militant nationalism (which featured motifs like blood and Ireland as a woman and whose prophecies
were not necessarily to be taken literally) had existed for at least 300
years. The allusion to 'Róisín Dubh'/prophecies of bloodshed should be

read in the wider contest of 'An Act of Faith'. The main focus of the article was on the literary texts and oral histories which Pearse had first heard from his grandaunt Margaret and whose idiom he held to be a formative influence on his own nationalism: It is noteworthy that 'An Rós bheag Dubh/Róisín Dubh' was among the songs collected by Galligan.[106] On 11 August 1906 Pearse published a critique of the woman and child depicted in Oliver Shephard's 'Inisfáil' at the 1906 Oireachtas art exhibition. Pearse mentions blood in the context of his discussion of the nationalist political aspirations he perceives as being evoked by Shephard's work:

> Though the world run red with blood, the cause of that Woman shall triumph. Mark next, him who lies prone, – who has died the victorious vanquished, crowned in death. This is a generation that has fought and fallen – but the woman of Destiny blanches not: 'I have my memories ... and I have my HOPES'.

A number of aspects of this article are noteworthy. Pearse echoes again 'An Ros Geal Dubh' and also Yeats' 'Cathleen Ni Houlihan' in describing Shephard's work. He presumes his audience to be *au fait* with the diction and motifs of Gaelic nationalism: after all he has been expounding on the topic himself in the *Claidheamh*. Pearse's reading of the artwork is also interesting. He sees in the figure of the boy 'the growing of a great resolve ... he will fight the fight – win it, it may be, or failing gloriously, go serenely to his death...'. Yet this article belongs to what is generally regarded as the 'benign' cultural nationalist period of Pearse's life. At the end of his reflections, Pearse again refers the reader back to the earlier precedent for the imagery and sentiment he has just expressed, 'An Rós Geal Dubh':

> The garden in its solemn beauty of decay is like the old Dublin and the old Anglo-Ireland which are passing. Raise your head now and gaze around the room; let your imagination wander across the street to the busy Rotunda, where the competitions are in swing and the Ard-Fheis is intent on its work of nation-making; finally rest your gaze once more [...] in the eyes of the Woman of Sorrows, and of the child who is about to adventure himself for her sake; and your thought will be this:
>
> > A Róisín, ná bíodh brón ort, ná cás anois,
> > Tá do phardún ó Phápa na Rómha agat,
> > Tá na bráithre ag teacht thar sáile, s' ag triall thar muir,
> > 'S ní cheilfear fíon Spáinneach ar mo Rós Geal Dubh.[107]

It is almost as if the contemporary generation must recall the idiom and literature of previous generations in order to enunciate their own as yet unarticulated nationalism. As we have seen, Pearse knew this literature intimately; during his editorship of the *Claidheamh* he published over 300 songs; as a collector of folk material and as the main instigator behind the public events side of Gaelic League activities he also knew personally many of the singers who had learned songs such as 'Róisín Dubh' from oral tradition.[108] Pearse later published 'An Ros Geal Dubh' as part of his 'Songs of the Irish Rebels' series in the *Irish Review*. Notwithstanding his own stated views on the impact of his play, *Cathleen Ni Houlihan*, Yeats has somehow escaped accusations of blood sacrifice; indeed his friendship and collaberation with Pearse are often ignored. Yet it could be plausibly proposed that Yeats may have posed the questions to which Pearse provided answers in his late political tracts:

> Was it for this the wild geese spread
> The grey wing upon every tide;
> For this that all that blood was shed
> For this Edward Fitzgerald died,
> And Robert Emmet and Wolfe Tone.[109]

The folk 'play' *Dúnlaing Óg agus an Leannán Sí* which was staged along with *Íosagán* and *The Master* in early summer 1915, and about which Pearse gave a scholarly talk on that same occasion, provides another example of the type of imagery alluded to by Pearse in the 1906 articles cited above.[110]

> An Leannán Sí (The Fairy Lover):
> Titfidh sibh go léir ar aon rian.
> Is bog dearg bheidh an mhaigh amárach
> Le bhur gcuid fola go morálach.

> (You will all fall together
> The plain will be soft and red tomorrow
> Proudly with your blood.)

> Dúnlaing Óg:
> Má thitfimidne, titfidh Gaill.[111]

> (If we fall, the foreigner will fall.)

Such were the sources which informed the opinions advanced in Pearse's pamphlet *Ghosts* which he finished on Christmas Day 1915. Here Pearse made the context for his citation of blood imagery explicit ('I do not defend this blood-thirstiness any more than I apologise for it. I simply point it out as the note of a literature') – before referring again to the song 'Róisín Dubh' and asking:

> Is it to be supposed that these apocalyptic disturbances are to usher in merely a statutory legislation subordinate to the imperial parliament at Westminster whose supreme authority over Ireland shall remain unimpaired 'anything in this Act notwithstanding'? [112]

The references to blood cited by Pearse in *Ghosts* and the other sources discussed here are explicitly presented as proof of a Gaelic people's deep-rooted desire for comprehensive freedom. Pearse's controversial comment in *Peace and the Gael* (also written in December 1915) that 'the old heart of the earth needed to be warmed with the red wine of the battle-fields' certainly seems intemperate. The quotation needs to be read in the full context of its original citation. Pearse was alluding to the Great War in the contentious sentence. The article continues with a discussion of the hoped-for emancipation of people across many nations in the reordering this war would bring about. Pearse relates this reasoning (not originally or solely his; it was one of the aspirations advanced generally for that war) to the morality of a nationalist uprising in Ireland. Thus Pearse's allusion to blood 'sacrifice' is an (perhaps unwisely-chosen) exemplar which is used to argue the concept of a 'just war' for both the ordinary people of other nations and the similarly oppressed Irish; this idea forms the article's real emphasis. It is a further example of the international context in which Pearse sited his nationalism.

The title of Ruth Dudley Edwards' biography of Pearse equates Pearse with 'the triumph of failure'. The book summarizes Pearse's life-view by quoting a translation of a phrase of Cúchulainn's to which Pearse himself had alluded: 'I care not though I were to live but one day and one night provided my fame and my deeds live after me.' To quote this phrase as representing the essence of Pearse (or indeed of Cúchulainn) misrepresents the statement as cited in its original context. Pearse first quoted this sentence in an article which reported on a speech by George Sigerson on 'The Celtic Origin of Chivalry' in the *Claidheamh Soluis*.[113] Dr Sigerson was a gifted scholar discussing the themes of Gaelic literature in an exciting and accessible manner; Pearse's report of the speech a measured and knowledgeable reflection on Sigerson's discussion. Dudley Edwards chose not to focus on another aspect of Pearse's report/Sigerson's speech which might have offered an entirely different leitmotif for her biography – Pearse's noting of Cúchulainn's determination to protect at all times the lives of women and children and the unarmed. Meanwhile, to note dispassionately, as Pearse also did, that Cúchulainn's death could be seen as an analogy of Christian sacrifice is not the same as believing or advocating such a sacrifice.[114] It proves only that Pearse was a brave exponent of comparative literary criticism.[115]

Pearse the political theorist cannot be properly understood without addressing Pearse the literary critic and creative writer. The idea that politics cannot be separated from culture was a central motivation for Pearse's militant nationalism, memorably summarized in his distinction between a nation and an empire:

A nation is bound together by natural ties, ties mystic and spiritual and ties human and kindly, an empire is at best held together by ties of human interest and at worst by brute force. The nation is the family at large, an empire is a commercial corporation at large.[116]

Commentary which presents Pearse's nationalism as emotional or fanatical generally assumes that a separation between culture and nationalism is possible and ignores the fact that he discussed the psychology, domains, ideas and idioms of Irish nationalism, nationalist historiography and Gaelic literature in a measured, erudite and self-aware manner. The challenges posed by Pearse's sophisticated engagement with the question of what mandated and constituted freedom, nationhood and the 'people' provide the real interest of his writings. Far from writing, acting and dying for 'a people who did not exist', Pearse should be acknowledged for his radical and modern understanding of subaltern history and anti-colonial political theory, which sited itself in an international context. His discussion of the ideological continuum which informed his participation in the Rising was both factual and personally felt. The Fenian graves that he saw ghosting the consciousness of a nation included that of his own grandfather. The dead generations invoked in the 1916 proclamation included those of Walter Brady and his United Irishmen brother. In 'The Rebel' Pearse blends the mystic promises of emancipation found in the Aisling poetry of the Gaelic tradition of his relations with the self-help credo of international socialism. The poem's Whitmanian allusions to an emerging democratic order remind us of the heterogeneous nature of the 'people' as understood by Pearse; an imagined community who were not just a historic Gaelic nation but one which encompassed all people who could imagine themselves, or be imagined, existing freely: the precedent which hastened his execution. In 'The Rebel', Pearse wakes a nation from the nightmare of history into modernity.

NOTES

1. The author would like to thank Mr Luke Griffin, Mr Dónal McAnallen, Mr Cillian Ó Gairbhí and Professor Breandán Ó Buachalla for kindly reading drafts of this article and for their helpful suggestions. Any errors are the author's own. Grateful acknowledgement also to Ruán O'Donnell for his patience and encouragement.
2. Ruth Dudley Edwards, *Patrick Pearse, The Triumph of Failure* (Dublin, 1990) (1st edition, Victor Gollancz, 1977), p. 343.
3. P.H. Pearse, 'The Rebel', in *Plays, Stories, Poems* (Dublin, 1966), pp. 337–9.
4. 'Eachtra an Eolais', *An Claidheamh Soluis*, 7 September 1907.
5. See for example, Desmond Ryan, *The Man called Pearse* (Dublin/London, 1919); Seámas Deane, 'Wherever Green is Read' and J.J. Lee, 'In Search of Patrick Pearse' in Theo Dorgan and Máirin Ní Dhonnacha (eds), *Revising the Rising* (Derry, 1991), pp. 91–105, 122–38; Philip O'Leary, *The Prose Literature of the Gaelic Revival 1881–1921* (Pennsylvania, 1994).
6. Xavier Carthy, *In Bloody Protest: The Tragedy of Patrick Pearse* (Dublin, 1978), p. 66.
7. Brian P. Murphy, *Patrick Pearse and the Lost Republican Ideal* (Dublin, 1991), p. 40.
8. R.F. Foster, *Modern Ireland 1600–1972* (London: Allen Lane, Penguin, 1988), p. 477.
9. Dudley Edwards, *Pearse*, p. 232.
10. Carthy, *Tragedy*, p. 33.

11. Elaine Sisson, *Pearse's Patriots: St. Enda's and the Cult of Boyhood* (Cork, 2003), p. 81
12. Dudley Edwards, *Pearse*, p. 37.
13. Seán Farrell Moran, *Patrick Pearse and the Politics of Redemption: The Mind of the Easter Rising 1916* (Washington, DC, The Catholic University of America Press, 1994), p. 149.
14. Foster, *Modern Ireland*, p. 458.
15. Carthy, *Tragedy*, p. 25.
16. See O'Leary, *Gaelic Revival*; Seamas Ó Buachalla, (ed.), *The Letters of P.H. Pearse, with a fore-word by F.S.L. Lyons* (Gerrards Cross, Smythe, 1980); Ciarán O Coigligh (eag.), *Filíocht Ghaeilge Phádraic Mhic Phiarais* (Baile Átha Cliath, 1981); Séamas Ó Buachalla, (eag.), *An Piarsach sa Bheilg/P.H. Pearse in Belgium/P.H. Pearse in Belgie* (Baile Átha Cliath, 1998); Cathal Ó hÁinle (eag.), *Gearrscéalta an Phiarsaigh* (Baile Átha Cliath, 1979).
17. Pearse's unfinished autobiography is preserved at Scoil Éanna. An edited version was published by Mary Brigid Pearse in *The home-life of Padraig Pearse: as told by himself, his family, and friends / edited by his sister Mary Brigid Pearse; illustrated with family portraits* (Browne and Nolan, 1934).
18. See, for example, Eoin Flannery, 'External Association: Ireland, Empire and Postcolonial Theory', *Third Text*, 19, 5 (September 2005), p. 453.
19. 'A Jacobin after his time' (a review of Ruth Dudley Edwards' *Patrick Pearse; The Triumph of Failure*), *Irish Press*, 21 April 1977.
20. See, for example, George Steiner, *After Babel: Aspects of Language and Translation* (London, New York, Oxford University Press, 1998).
21. It should be recalled that part of his definition of nationhood was predicated on its 'resting on and guaranteeing the freedom of all the men and the women of the nation and placing them in effective possession of the physical conditions necessary to the reality and to the perpetuation of their freedom. *The Sovereign People: Tracts for the Times*, 1916 (Dublin: Whelan).
22. 'The Red Flag', in *Songs of Freedom by Irish Authors*, with an introduction by James Connolly (New York, J.C. Donnelly, 1907), p. 12.
23. Brian Crowley, unpublished list of books from St Enda's. Desmond Ryan drew attention to the Whitman influence in *The Man called Pearse* (Phoenix, n.d.), p. 236.
24. Ezra Greenspan/Walt Whitman, *Walt Whitman's Song of Myself: A Critical Edition and Sourcebook* (New York, Routledge, 2004), pp. 159–76.
25. 'The Rebel', in *Plays, Stories, Poems*, pp. 337–9.
26. 'Eachtra an Eolais', *An Claidheamh Soluis*, 7 September 1907. While this article, which formed part of a serialized parable, was not signed, it bears all the signs of being penned by Pearse, the editor of the *Claidheamh* at this time.
27. 'Eachtra an Eolais', *An Claidheamh Soluis*, 21 March 1907.
28. 'From a Hermitage', October 1913.
29. Brian Crowley's work on James Pearse has drawn attention to his radicalism and personal engagement with contemporary debate on nationalism. Brian Crowley, 'His Father's Son: James and Patrick Pearse', *Folk Life Journal of Ethnological Studies*, vol. 43 (2003–5).
30. Unfinished autobiography.
31. Mentioned in Séamas Mac Gabhann, 'Salvaging Gaelic Identity, Peter Galligan (1792–1860)', pp 70–87, in *Ríocht na Midhe*, Vol. IX, No. 2, 1996, p. 84.
32. 1841 and 1851 Census.
33. Pat Cooke noted that the original summary by Pearse of family influences had him become not 'the strange thing that I am' but an 'Irish rebel'. Pat Cooke, 'The Life and After Life of P.H. Pearse' conference, unpublished paper 'P.H. Pearse, a Victorian Gael', UCD and Scoil Éanna, Spring 2006.
34. Dudley Edwards, *Pearse*, p. 5. Her statement that Pearse 'died' might also benefit from a clarification that he was shot.
35. Pearse, unfinished autobiography.
36. *A candid and impartial account of the disturbances in the County of Meath in the years 1792, 93 and 94, Dublin, 1794* cited by Séamas Ó Loinsigh, 'The Rebellion of 1798 in Meath', in *Ríocht na Midhe*, 3, 4 (1966), p. 341.
37. James Pollock, yeoman, of Mountainstown House, Castletown, Navan to the Chief Secretary, Dublin Castle, 3 January 1797 cited in Séamus Ó Loinsigh, 'The Rebellion of 1798 in Meath, *Ríocht na Midhe*, 4, 2 (1968), pp. 33–49.
38. Pearse, unfinished autobiography.
39. Micheál Mac Craith, 'Foinsí an radachais in Eirinn', and Breandán Ó Buachalla, 'An Culra Ideolaíoch', in Gearóid Ó Tuathaigh, (eag.), *Eirí Amach 1798 in Eirinn*, Cló Iarchonnachta (Indreabhán, Conamara, 1998), pp. 11–28 and pp. 29–40 respectively.

40. Unfinished autobiography.
41. Ó Coigligh (eag.), *Filíocht Ghaeilge*.
42. 'From a Hermitage', pp. 204–5.
43. *An Barr Buadh*, Uimhir 3, 30 March 1912. 'I frequently read your exploits aloud for my grandfather. He himself when he was young did a little for Ireland. In the year of '48 he was among the followers of your friend's father. In '67 he was a Fenian. He hoped that you and your companions would complete the work which he and his colleagues left unfinished.' Translation in Séamas Ó Buachalla (ed.), *The Letters of P.H. Pearse* (Gerrards Cross, 1980), p. 258.
44. Desmond Mooney, 'A Society in Crisis: Agrarian Violence in Meath 1828–1835', *Ríocht na Midhe*, viii, 2 (1988–9), p. 107.
45. See, for example, 'From a Hermitage' and 'The Wandering Hawk'.
46. Brian Crowley, unpublished list of books at St Enda's.
47. 'The Future of the Young Men of Ireland, a lecture given on Sep 26th, 1893', in William O'Brien, *Irish Ideas* (London, New York, Green and Co, 1893), p. 167.
48. Dudley Edwards, *Pearse*, pp. 11, 98.
49. Carthy, *Tragedy*, pp. 19–20.
50. Dudley Edwards, *Pearse*, p. 15.
51. Farrell Moran, *Patrick Pearse*, Appendix, pp. 203–12.
52. 'From a Hermitage', in *Irish Freedom*, December 1913, pp. 189–94.
53. *An Claidheamh Soluis*, 22 December 1906.
54. The longer version of the story was published in *An Mháthair agus Scéalta Eile* (1916).
55. Máire Ní Fhlathúin, 'The Anti-colonial Modernism of Patrick Pearse', in H. Booth and N. Rigby (eds), *Modernism and Empire* (Manchester, 2000), p. 165.
56. *An Claidheamh Soluis*, 17 March 1906.
57. 'In my garden', Duilleacháin an Oireachtais, *An Claidheamh Soluis*, 4 August 1906. While the article is not signed, humorous references to bilingualism in education as well as a reiteration of the article's vision in the *Claidheamh* the following week mean that it is almost certain that Pearse is the author. See also 'Na hIndiacha Thoir', *An Claidheamh Soluis*, 15 December 1906.
58. *An Claidheamh Soluis*, 4 August 1906.
59. Ibid.
60. 'Waiting', *An Claidheamh Soluis*, 20 October 1906.
61. 'On Sliabh Rua', *An Claidheamh Soluis*, 31 October 1908.
62. Eugene McCabe, Introduction, in Dermot Bolger (ed.), *Pádraic Pearse, Rogha Dánta/Selected Poems* (Dublin, 2001), p. 18.
63. Unfinished autobiography.
64. Ibid.
65. Ibid.
66. Ibid.
67. Breadán Ó Buachalla, *I mBéal Feirste Cois Cuain* (Baile Átha Cliath, 1968) and Ciarán Dawson, *Peadar Ó Gealacán, Scríobhaí* (Baile Átha Cliath, 1992); Séamas Mac Gabhann, 'Forging Identity – Michael Clarke and the Hidden Ireland', *Ríocht na Midhe*, IX, 2 (1996), pp. 73–95.
68. Michael Herity (ed.), *Ordnance Survey Letters, Meath* (Dublin, 2001).
69. 'Folklore and the Zeitgeist', *An Claidheamh Soluis*, 19 May 1906.
70. 'By Way of Comment', *An Macaomh* (Nollaig 1909), p. 13.
71. 'Folklore and the Zeitgeist', *An Claidheamh Soluis*, 19 May 1906.
72. *Collected Works of Pádraic H. Pearse (Songs of the Irish Rebels etc.)* (Phoenix Publishing Company n,d.), p. 111 (originally cited in the *Irish Review*).
73. The quotation comes from a poem cited in the Tomás Ó Flanghaile book Pearse was later given as a schoolboy.
74. Breandán Ó Buachalla, *I mBéal Feirste Cois Cuain* (Baile Átha Cliath,1968), p. 125. See Pádraig de Brún, 'The Irish Society's Bible Teachers, 1818–27', *Éigse*, 19, 2 (1983), pp. 281–332, continued in *Éigse*, vols 20–6 (1984–90).
75. See Vincent Morley, 'Views of the Past in Irish Vernacular Literature', p.1. Reprinted from *Unity and Diversity in European Culture c.1800, Proceedings of the British Academy, 134*.
76. O'Leary, *Gaelic Revival*, pp. 255–61.
77. Éinrí Ó Muirgheasa, *Amhráin na Midhe* (Baile Átha Cliath, 1933), p. 9.
78. See Séamas Mac Gabhann, 'Forging Identity, Michael Clarke and the Hidden Ireland', pp. 73–95, *Ríocht na Midhe*, IX, 2 (1996).
79. Ó Buachalla, *I mBéal Feirste Cois Cuain*, (Baile Átha Cliath, 1968), p. 125.

80. Dawson, pp. 62, 94.
81. Unfinished autobiography.
82. National Library of Ireland, MS G200, 314, Catalogue of Irish Manuscripts in the National Library Fasciculus V (ed.). Neasa Ní Sheaghdha, Dublin Institute for Advanced Studies, 1979; *Collected Works of Pádraic H. Pearse*.
83. Dawson, *Scríobhaí*, p. 33.
84. Ibid., p. 28.
85. Ibid., p. 16.
86. Tomás Ó Fiaich, *Art Mac Cumhaigh, Dánta* (Baile Átha Cliath, 1973), p. 111
87. Reamonn Ó Muiri (eag.), *Comhrac na nGael is na nGall Lamhscríbhinn Staire an Bhionadaigh* (éigse oirghialla), pp. 76–8.
88. Dawson, *Scríobhaí*, p. 44.
89. Herity (ed.), *Ordnance Survey Letters, Meath*, p. 38.
90. 'I am Calliagh Vera, poor/ Many a wonder I have seen/ I have seen Carn-bane a lake/ Tho' now a mountain green'. 'Of the Parish of Loughcrew', in Herity (ed.), *Ordnance Survey Letters, Meath*, p. 38.
91. Vincent Morley, *Unity and Diversity in European Culture c1800*, p. 177.
92. *Ireland's Dirge: an Historical Poem Written in Irish Translated into English verse by Michael Clarke*, (Dublin, 1827). The list of subscribers, tantalizingly, includes several Bradys.
93. Morley, *Unity and Diversity*, p.181.
94. Mac Gabhann, 'Forging Identity', p. 77.
95. Morley, *Unity and Diversity*, p. 178.
96. 'From a Hermitage', October 1913.
97. Gearóid Denvir, 'Literature in Irish 1800-1890', in *The Cambridge Companion to Irish Literature*, p. 591.
98. *The Spiritual Nation*, 1916.
99. Unfinished autobiography.
100. 'Some Aspects of Irish Literature'.
101. *Ghosts, Tracts for the Times* (Dublin, 1916).
102. Dudley Edwards, *Pearse*, p. 52.
103. *An Claidheamh Soluis*, 19 May 1906.
104. 'An Bhean Chaointe', *An Mháthair agus Scéalta Eile* (1916). The first part of the story appeared in *An Claidheamh Soluis* in 1907. 'Who murdered your own grandfather? Who drew the red blood out of my own grandmother's shoulders with a lash? Who would do it but the English?' *Collected Works of P.H. Pearse, Plays, Stories, Poems* (Dublin and London, 1917), p. 205.
105. 'An Act of Faith', *An Claidheamh Soluis*, 4 August 1906.
106. Enrí Ó Muirgheasa, *Amhráin na Mí*, (Baile Átha Cliath, 1933), pp. 123–4.
107. *An Claidheamh Soluis*, 11 August 1906.
108. Regina Uí Chollatáin, *An Claidheamh Soluis agus Fáinne an Lae 1899–1932* (Baile Átha Cliath, 2004), p. 104.
109. W.B. Yeats, 'Romance in Ireland'. The poem was first published in the *Irish Times* on 13 September 1913.
110. Notice in *An Claidheamh Soluis*, 22 May 1915.
111. Seán Ó Morónaigh (eag.), *Drámaíocht ó Dhúchas: Ó Bhéalaithris Thaidhg Uí Chonchubhair, An Comhlachas Náisiúnta Drámaíochta* (2005), p. 203. The text was originally published in the *Gaelic Journal*.
112. *Ghosts*.
113. 'Our Heritage of Chivalry', *An Claidheamh Soluis*, 14 November 1908. The original quote from the article is 'I care not though I remain in being but one day and one night so that my deeds and fame live after me.'
114. 'Some Aspects of Gaelic Literature'.
115. See O'Leary, Gaelic Revival, p. 261. For a modern take on this topic see John Moriarty, *Ailliliú na hÉrend/Invoking Ireland* (Dublin, 2006).
116. P.H. Pearse, *The Sovereign People* (Tracts for the Times) (Dublin, 1916).

10

1916: Insurrection or Rebellion? Making Judgements

Peter Berresford Ellis

Historians do not merely record facts, they make moral judgements about the information they record. History becomes a matter of personal perception which often reveals more about the writer than the facts presented. In recent times there has been a particular failing by some 'revisionist' historians to acknowledge this truth. They purport to be unbiased, unlike those they seek to 'revise'. In actuality, such historians usually have axes to grind and are often of right-wing inclinations.

Ireland has long had a problem about how its people and history are depicted. One could argue that this goes back to Strabon (c.64 BC–after AD 24), a Greek who sold his talent to boost Roman imperial propaganda. He assured his audiences that the Irish were 'cannibals as well as gluttons'. Pomponius Mela (c.AD 43) declared the Irish were 'ignorant of all the virtues more than any other people, and totally lacking all sense of duty'.[1] Many centuries later, Ireland was still being presented through the distorted and myopic vision of historians representing the views of the English conquerors. It was in answer to them that Seathrún Céitinn (Dr Geoffrey Keating) wrote his robust response, *Foras Feasa ar Éirinn* ('The History of Ireland'). Keating remarked:

> It is almost in the fashion of the beetle they act, when writing concerning the Irish. For it is the fashion of the beetle, when it lifts its head in the summertime, to go about fluttering, and not to stoop towards any delicate flower that may be in the field, or any blossom in the garden though they be all roses or lilies, but it keeps bustling about until it meets with dung of horse or cow, and proceeds to roll itself therein.[2]

Ireland's long struggle to reverse the English conquest, the struggle to regain her independence and achieve a democracy, has long been a subject where many historians prefer, not only to sift out the dung and roll in it but, when there is no dung to find, to devise their own myths.

In an Irish context, there have always been historians willing to justify foreign invasion and imperialism and to deny the moral right of those beset to fight back. Remarkably, this phenomenon has survived the emergence of the independent Irish state. One might have thought they would be confined to the unionists of the partitioned north-east of the country where the problems of national independence and sovereignty are yet unresolved, or to British historians still wishing to justify the vanished empire. What is surprising is that there are citizens of an independent state who still attempt to denigrate their ancestors' struggle for the rights they now freely enjoy. This is not to say that they should accept the events and motivations of the individuals involved without question or criticism. That, after all, is the historian's role. But it is fascinating to find some still upholding the rights of the imperialist to conquer and despoil the country and to denounce any idea that the Irish people had any moral authority to reject the conquest by any means in their power. Joe Ambrose stated in his introduction to *Dan Breen and the IRA*:

> The Irish are also a post-colonial people, incessantly told what to do and think by international opinion makers working in publishing, broadcasting and the arts. A colourful and curious array of nay-sayers, soothsayers and academics – not to mention pseudo-scholars fighting their own private Wars on Terror – devote entire Amazon rain forests of paper to debunking some simple facts of narrative history concerning Ireland's War of Independence. They've taken to their task with gusto and occasional aplomb, undermining complex mythologies that have grown up around the likes of Breen, Michael Collins and Tom Barry. Trying to dismantle the reputations of these rural lads of humble origin, they have sought to create post-modern mythologies of their own from which 1916–23 guerrilla leaders emerge *as political deviants from some imaginary, civilised, democratic norm, frantically in league with nebulous forces of evil, indifferent to mandate or morality*.[3] (emphasis added)

In 1989 I made my views on such Irish neo-colonial historians known and why I consider the term 'revisionist' to be wrong, for all historians worth their salt are 'revisionist'. The very nature of the work of the historian is to study and revise the evidence of the facts of history, thus enabling people towards a greater understanding. But their job is not to distort the facts, which seemed to be the 'stock in trade' of many of those modern writers falling into the neo-colonial camp.[4]

I have also pointed to certain historical attitudes to the insurrection of 1916 in need of questioning.[5] In fact, even the populist term of 'rebellion' brings into question the concept of what the Irish were actually doing. 'Rebellion' implies a disobedience to legitimate authority. An independent India does not refer to the events of 1857–8 as the 'Indian mutiny' or 'Sepoy rebellion', as described in British history, but rather the 'Indian Rising' or 'first Indian War of Independence'. When historians claim Irish insurgents to be acting 'unconstitutionally' and rebelling against the forces of 'law and order', the question should arise for discussion: under who's law and constitution, enacted by what legitimacy, other than military conquest, did England have a right to rule in Ireland? History demonstrates that at no time, in any generation, did the Irish people accept the 'legitimacy' of the conquerors. Yet, the fact that so very few will call the period 1919–21 a 'war of independence' but rather 'the Troubles' is also an indication of some people's faint-hearted belief that Ireland had a moral right to fight for independence.

Several myths have been created about the insurrection of 1916 that have had their basis in either British propaganda of the time or in misconception and misinterpretation. Amazingly, they are still perpetuated. The four main ideas put forward concern the myth of 'blood sacrifice', the use of the GPO as the insurgent headquarters, Connolly's view that the British would not use artillery in Dublin and the attitude of city people towards captive Volunteers.

In spite of the lecture given by C. Desmond Greaves in 1966, published as *1916 as History: The Myth of the Blood Sacrifice*, the idea of 'blood sacrifice' is still widely propounded.[6] This is the view that the leaders of 1916 conceived the insurrection knowing that they stood no chance of success but in the belief that their 'blood sacrifice' would bring about a change of attitude among the people in support of separation from England. The idea was largely a mystic invention of W.B. Yeats. In his poem 'The Rose Tree', a symbol for Ireland, Pearse and Connolly agree that 'there's nothing but our own red blood that can make a right rose tree'. It is a good dramatic, poetic idea and numerous members of the poetic fraternity seized it at the time. Poetry is not history.

There is no evidence of this 'blood sacrifice' concept except in some dubious remarks afterwards attributed to Patrick Pearse, usually quoted from family reminiscences and repeated in order to build Pearse up as some mystical character rather than a practical thinker. However, Desmond Ryan added a down-to-earth authority to the concept by recounting Connolly's words to William O'Brien just before the Irish Citizen Army (ICA) men left Liberty Hall: 'We are going out to be slaughtered.' While Greaves, as Connolly's biographer, accepted this statement, he feels that 'whereas Connolly had thought the original plan gave chances of success, he now had no hope of victory' following the countermanding orders of Eoin MacNeill. Ryan's claims must be weighed against those of others who spoke with Connolly and were impressed by his confidence in achieving the goals of the insurrection. He did not lead his men out to be defeated.[7]

Éamon de Valera recalled meeting Connolly shortly before the insurrection when 'one of the principal subjects of our conversation was a document which had come into Volunteer hands. It was (on its face) the outline of a plan by Dublin Castle for a swoop on the Volunteers and other national organisations. If the document was genuine its bearing on our movement and on our preparations was obvious … I cannot now recall the details of our conversation, but I have never ceased to believe that he regarded the document as genuine.' De Valera confirmed Greaves' assessment: 'He was concerned above all lest the authorities should move first and the revolution die whimpering amid arrests, ridicule and recriminations.'[8]

There was absolutely no question of a suicidal 'blood sacrifice'. The leaders were practical, political thinkers who believed that their plan could succeed. Connolly had studied military tactics but it is often forgotten that he had served in the British army, most likely in the 1st battalion of the King's Liverpool regiment. He must have learned something about tactics during this time, certainly those of the British military. The ICA, moreover, had been trained by Captain Jack White DSO, the son of Field Marshal Sir George White VC (1835–1912) of Antrim. White was imprisoned in Pentonville with Roger Casement in 1916. The Irish Volunteers and ICA were not merely idealists playing at toy soldiers. Many of them had military backgrounds so military strategy was not beyond their grasp.

The plan for the insurrection was well thought from a military viewpoint. Important material on their intentions was found in German archives in Berlin by Colonel J.P. Duggan.[9] These documents related to the discussions and proposals made by Joseph Plunkett to the German high command in 1915 when he went to Berlin to help Casement present the plans. They involved the landing of German arms and a complex nationwide uprising. There was also a proposal for a German expeditionary force landing in Limerick. Professor F.X. Martin commented: 'Now at last we have evidence of the existence of a plan for an all-Ireland rising that was not hare brained.'[10]

It has been no secret since 1916 that the insurgents were expected to rise throughout the country. The failure to do so has been attributed to the countermanding orders issued by MacNeill, in his capacity as chief of staff of the Irish Volunteers. The orders caused confusion and lack of cohesion across the country. The discovery of the plans in Berlin confirmed the earlier assessment of Colonel Eoghan O'Neill. He argued that the insurgents believed that if Germany could be persuaded to ensure the establishment of an Irish administration in Dublin for a sufficient period, such an administration would be able to claim belligerent rights, and international recognition in the peace conference when the war ended. This accorded with the views of Greaves.[11]

Significantly, in March 1916 the British war cabinet discussed the idea of a negotiated peace with Germany. Lowe and Dockrill record: 'Serious consideration of peace terms in Britain started in 1916 with the growing US pressure on the belligerents to end the war. It was a reflection, partly of the necessity of not offending Wilson, partly of a growing consciousness that it might not be possible to gain a sufficient ascendancy over the Central Powers to impose the peace the British Government wanted.'[12]

Perhaps one of the problems giving rise to the half-hearted German support was the kaiser's earlier interest in supporting the 'loyalists' of Ulster. Irish republicans wanted Germany as allies to establish a sovereign republic whereas 'loyalists' sought German aid if London granted Ireland 'home rule'. They hoped for an invasion force to annex Ireland to the German empire. Edward Carson, the unionist leader who had helped form the Ulster Volunteer Force (UVF) in January 1913, had gone to Germany that summer and in August lunched with the kaiser in Hamburg. On his return in September, a provisional government of Ulster was set up in preparation: 'It may not be known to the rank and file of Unionists that we have the offer of aid from a powerful continental monarch who, if Home Rule is forced upon the Protestants of Ireland, is prepared to send an army sufficient to release England of any further trouble in Ireland by attaching it to his dominion.'[13]

The first batch of arms from Germany for the unionists arrived in November 1913. These were escorted to Larne from Hamburg by Lt.-Col. Frederick Crawford, a founder of the UVF and member of the provisional government. While the German high command also supplied some arms to the Irish Volunteers, it was a token quantity which had to be paid for in advance. The kaiser's interest in the unionist offer of an imperial Germany annexing Ireland remains curiously under-researched, unlike his offer to assist republicans to achieve independence. In the event, in 1916 the Germans dispatched the *Libau* with a cargo of obsolete Russian rifles, ten modern machine guns and explosives, all of which was scuttled off Cobh, county Cork.

In spite of the evidence of the insurgents' plans, Professor Charles Townshend is not convinced that the insurgent leaders had any practical strategy. Even Connolly's very knowledgeable military tactics, as shown in his articles on 'Revolutionary Warfare', are deprecated.[14] Townshend has argued that Michael Mallin's digging trenches in St Stephen's Green, overlooked by British positions, was a mistake exploited to deadly effect. Yet this contravened Connolly's instructions on urban guerrilla warfare. Where his teachings were carried out, it was another matter altogether.[15]

Michael Malone and his men occupied the houses at Mount Street Bridge and defended them in the manner recommended by Connolly. Thus, only seventeen ill-equipped Volunteers were able to hold up the advance of Brigadier Maconchy and the Sherwood Foresters moving against their positions from Kingstown (Dún Laoghaire). These seventeen men inflicted 234 casualties on the British (four officers killed and fourteen wounded, 216 other ranks killed and wounded) and even held up assaults backed by armoured cars at an eventual loss to themselves of five dead. This battle caused a lesson to be learned immediately by the British commanders. While the British troops encircled the GPO and outlying buildings, they did not press any frontal assaults as they had at Mount Street Bridge. Instead, artillery was used to weaken the insurgent positions.[16]

Townshend also questioned why the insurgents established headquarters in the General Post Office building in Sackville Street (O'Connell Street) rather than the more symbolic icon of British rule in Ireland, Dublin Castle. Strangely, T.A. Jackson also claimed that the 1916 strategy had two major faults: failure to immobilize the telephone exchange and to capture the castle. Desmond Ryan explained that Connolly rejected the option of seizing Dublin Castle even if it was feasible. The rationale was that the castle was a long and straggling collection of buildings which would be very difficult to defend. Matters were also complicated by the presence of a Red Cross hospital within the precinct. Townshend evidently believed that the insurgents simply chose a 'soft target' in preference. The main reason, however, was that the GPO was a prime objective due to its status as the country's communications centre.[17]

It seems that the first reference in print to *The Post Office Electrical Engineers' Journal* by E. Gomersall was in my article of February 2006. Gomersall was the GPO's superintendent engineer and had been sent to Dublin to re-establish the communications system during the fighting.[18] His comments put the insurgent strategy into sharp relief. In March 2006 Professor Keith Jeffery of Queen's University Belfast published *The GPO and the Easter Rising* which drew upon Gomersall's account to tell the insurrection story from the viewpoint of the staff.[19]

Since 1904 the GPO building had been in the process of enlargement and work was only completed on 6 March 1915. The building housed not only public offices but the telegraph instrument room, trunk telephone exchange, sorting offices, clerical officers of the secretary controller (postal), controller (telegraphs) and other support offices. In nearby Crown Alley there was an automatic exchange that only had 4,000 subscribers. Gomersall lists the importance of the GPO in fine and technical details. The building had its own central heating, three boilers in the basement, pneumatic power plant and lighting system, with two electric lifts. Not only was this the centre of all communications in Ireland, it was an easily defendable building compared to the sprawling mess of Dublin Castle. There was no building better in Dublin for the headquarters of

the insurgency. Once seized, the insurgents were in charge of communications in Ireland. This is, therefore, a necessary corrective to Jackson's
claim that they failed to immobilize the telephone exchange.[20]

When the insurgents took control on Monday, 24 April 1916, just
before noon, some of the staff and engineers were expelled and replaced
with their own men. Michael Collins himself had worked for the GPO
and knew the systems. Richard Mulcahy actually worked in the
Engineering Department of the GPO in Dublin. In fact, in the aftermath
of the insurrection a total of forty-five GPO employees were arrested,
some imprisoned and some suspended. Further, a total of twenty-six civil
servants dealing with GPO matters were questioned and fourteen dismissed from the service while the other twelve names were noted with
'may be reinstated'. The insurgents knew all there was to know about the
role of the GPO.

Michael Staines led a detachment of insurgents directly to the telegraph instrument room to place their own telephonists and telegraphists
in charge. The supervisor reputedly wanted to finish sending some telegraph death notices before she gave up her position, Staines replied: 'No,
some of my men will do that.' Among the GPO employees arrested were,
indeed, several telegraphers. The declaration of the Irish Republic was
broadcast soon after the insurgents took over and this was picked up in
England and in several parts of Europe. It was also heard by transatlantic
ships, thus taking the news to the US. Pearse ordered three insurgents,
one of whom was a former signaller in the British army, to assemble
another transmitter in the Atlantic School of Wireless situated nearby.
Thus the primary task of any coup was achieved: communications were
in the hands of insurgents and immediately denied to the enemy.

Gomersall stated: 'Telegraphic and trunk communications was essential for military purposes. New telephone circuits had to be provided for
military purposes, and the local telephone systems had to be maintained.
Many members of the staff could not leave the vicinity of their homes.
Many of those who could were unable to reach their normal places of
duty.' From late on Monday night engineers and British soldiers were sent
to points several miles outside Dublin to attempt to re-circuit lines by
cutting into telephone wires. But no sooner were links established than
insurgents cut the line, and this state of affairs continued after
Wednesday. Local lines, used for military purposes, 'had also been cut
down at a large number of places – evidently a characteristic feature of
the operations of the rebels – and the restoration of communication from
these temporary offices had necessary to be preceded by making good the
external plant'.

It is clear from Gomersall's reports that the insurgents had conducted
their strategy with level-headed planning and that the insurgents had

been trained to disrupt communications. Main telephone and telegraph lines around Dublin had been generally cut in two or three places. Telegraph poles were chopped down, wires cut, instruments were removed from offices and apparatus in signal boxes destroyed. Gomersall personally visited some sixty places where major equipment had been damaged to prevent it being used by the British. Even more astonishing was the cutting of underground telegraph and trunk line telephone cables by insurgents who knew exactly what they were doing. According to Gomersall: 'The provision of additional circuits for military purposes was a matter of much difficulty and unusual methods had to be employed … the provision and maintenance of the circuits during the rebellion was both difficult and dangerous.'

When the fighting was over and Gomersall entered the GPO on Tuesday, 2 May, to ascertain the extent of the damage, the magnitude of his task soon became apparent. The British artillery had so destroyed it that 'only the shell of the building remained, and in places the débris was still burning and the surrounding ground was extremely hot'. It was not until 11 May that all the temporary communication systems were finally put in place.[21]

The shelling of the GPO by the British comprises another favourite myth of 1916; that Connolly believed that the British, being capitalists, would not use artillery in Dublin and thereby destroy private property. This viewpoint is accepted by Jackson, whereas Greaves found it scarcely credible. Yet practically every account of 1916, and some of the biographies of Connolly, repeat this *ad nauseam*. Connolly is supposed to have 'optimistically insisted a capitalist government would never use artillery against its own property'.[22] Although proverbial, the story has no indisputable source. It may stem from a pre-Rising comment by Connolly that insurgents 'could only hold out in Dublin so long as the British did not use artillery'. This is a different concept entirely and in keeping with his articles on the subject. In the *Workers' Republic* of 29 May 1915, Connolly assessed the lessons of the Moscow Rising of 1905 and observed that well-armed insurgents might be able to capture field guns for use in a city. This was partly to prevent the opposing force reducing the city along with insurgent positions.[23]

Indeed, the British quickly resorted to field guns, placing two eighteen pounders in Tara Street on the Monday evening to begin a bombardment. Had the Germans really landed an expeditionary force, as had been envisaged, had the entire country risen as planned before MacNeill's countermanding order, the British commander might well have needed his field guns in other areas of conflict, taking the pressure off the insurgent headquarters.

The main bombardment commenced on Wednesday when HMS

Helga steamed up the Liffey to train its guns on Dublin. Had Connolly considered a contingency plan to withdraw out of the city if artillery was used? From various accounts there was certainly talk about such an idea from some commanders but by Wednesday, Brigadier General Lowe had encircled insurgent positions. Any idea of withdrawing into the country or resorting to tactics that were to be used so successfully during 1919–21 was out of the question. Connolly is reported as making light of the predicament when speaking to his men that day. He told them that the use of artillery showed British desperation to end things quickly before insurgent units from other parts of the country joined them. This was probably a bid to boost morale.[24]

A recently discovered copy of the letter from Éamon de Valera to Mrs Ina Connolly tells how de Valera, commandant of a battalion covering the Boland's mills area, discussed strategy with Connolly three times, including the tactics of street fighting. Before the Rising they reconnoitred positions and discussed tactics between Grand Canal Street Bridge and Canal Basin, where the *Helga* was to eventually shell positions. In preparation for just such an eventuality de Valera, on Connolly's advice, decorated Boland's mills with flags and allowed a single Volunteer to remain on the roof to draw the fire of naval gunners. According to de Valera: 'Brief as was my personal intercourse with him, his sincerity and determination made a deep impression upon me. I have no doubt that his influence with Pádraig Pearse and the other co-signatories of the Proclamation of Easter Week was immense.'[25]

What has become firmly set in people's minds is the story that the Dublin people jeered the insurgent prisoners as they were led off into captivity. Even the scrupulous recorder of these years, Dorothy Macardle states: 'The people had not risen. Some had cursed the insurgents. Irishwomen had been seen in the streets bringing food to the British troops.'[26] It is quite a leap from this to the claim by Thomas M. Coffey in *The Agony at Easter*: 'The defeated insurgents quickly learnt how most Dubliners still felt about their rebellion when a raucous crowd came pouring out of the side streets to accost them ... Waving British flags they quickly bore down on the advancing column of prisoners and their heavy military escort ... The flood of insults was so fierce and vitriolic it hit the marching prisoners with an almost physical impact.'[27]

This description of how Dublin viewed the insurrection has become almost written in stone. Naturally, it was certainly a view that the imperial propaganda of the time wanted to impress on everyone, so that even the few accounts sympathetic to the insurgents accept it without question. Newspapers were unlikely to publish anything to the contrary. This perspective became less tenable in 1991 when a long obscure eyewitness account of the period resurfaced.[28]

The source was a Canadian journalist and writer, Frederick Arthur McKenzie, one of the best-known and reputable war correspondents of his day. Among his many books was his account of the Russo-Japanese War of 1904–5 and another on Japan's occupation of Korea. He was no anti-imperialist, as is clear from his history of the Canadian experience during the First World War. Moreover, in 1931 McKenzie became one of the earliest official biographers of Lord Beaverbrook.[29] In 1916 McKenzie was a war correspondent for Canadian newspapers and *War Illustrated*, a British propaganda publication. He was one of two Canadian journalists who managed to get to Dublin with the English reinforcements sent to put down the insurrection. He certainly had no sympathy for the Irish 'rebels' and German sympathizers, as he perceived them. Interestingly, Townshend quoted him briefly on the subject of looting but not with regard to the behaviour of the Dublin crowds.

McKenzie published *The Irish Rebellion: What Happened and Why*, with C. Arthur Pearson in London in 1916. He stated: 'I have read many accounts of public feeling in Dublin in these days. They are all agreed that the open and strong sympathy of the mass of the population was with the British troops. That this was in the better parts of the city, I have no doubt, but certainly what I myself saw in the poorer districts did not confirm this. It rather indicated that there was a vast amount of sympathy with the rebels, particularly after the rebels were defeated.'[30] According to McKenzie:

> As I was passing through a street near the Castle cheer after cheer could be heard. A regiment was approaching. People were leaning from their windows waving triangular flags and handkerchiefs. 'They are cheering the soldiers,' I said to my companion. On came the soldiers, marching very quickly as soldiers have a way of doing when they are liable to be sniped at from any point. The advance guard with fixed bayonets sharply ordered everyone back from the sidewalks. As the main body approached I could see that the soldiers were escorting a large number of prisoners, men and women, several hundreds in all. The people were cheering not the soldiers but the rebels.
>
> The prisoners were mostly in green uniforms. Many of them were wearing slouch caps, others were wearing peaked caps like those of the British army. They walked in military formation, and they were singing loudly, triumphantly, a rebel song. There was a smile on every face. They were not going to show us that they were down-hearted. Tears and grief might come on the morrow, but tonight they would keep a brave front. Some of them carried small bags or boxes. First came a large company of men, then a smaller company of girls in long green dresses, and again a large company of men. Around them, on either side, in front and behind, were the soldiers with loaded rifles and fixed bayonets.

The girls were the most cheerful of all. These were the women's company of cooks and Red Cross nurses who looked after the comfort of the men. 'And begob! They didn't mind taking a shot themselves when they got the chance', one man whispered to me. The prisoners displayed a few signs of the heavy fighting they must have gone through. They marched by with head up, swinging along – swaggering would be the better word. Now the cheers grew louder still. They looked up at the womenfolk hanging from the windows, smiling back the greetings and the blessings showered on them.

I spoke to a little group of men and women at the street corners. 'Shure, we cheer them,' said one woman. 'Why wouldn't we? Aren't they our own flesh and blood?'[31]

This flatly contradicts most of the oft-repeated contemporary accounts. Indeed, McKenzie, in his khaki war correspondent's uniform, was mistaken for a British soldier went he went down a Dublin back street. He recalled: 'Here and there people cursed me openly, frankly, and cursed all like me, strangers in their city.'[32]

There is no doubt that some insurgents were the subject of verbal attacks and abuse. However, in 1999 Michael Foy and Brian Barton also highlighted expressions of sympathy from the people watching the prisoners being marched away.[33] They quoted the diary of shopkeeper John Clarke: 'Thus ends the last attempt for poor old Ireland. What noble fellows. The cream of the land. None of your corner-boy class.'[34] A British officer, J.W. Rowath, had a similar experience to McKenzie and observed that 'crowds of men and women greeted us with raised fists and curses'.[35] When the insurgent prisoners were being marched into Richmond barracks, ICA man Frank Robbins saw a group of Dubliners gathered to cheer them.[36] When de Valera's command surrendered in the Boland's mill sector, crowds lined the pavement in Grand Canal Street and Hogan Place. Some implored the insurgents to take refuge in their houses rather than surrender. Foy and Barton conclude: 'Public attitudes locally were not uniformly hostile in an area which the police had come to regard as increasingly militant in the months before the Rising. Some of the [British] soldiers who fought there noted a strong antipathy towards them.'[37]

There is, as Foy and Barton have demonstrated, indisputable proof that what McKenzie had witnessed occurred in various parts of the city. Major de Courcy Wheeler, at the South Dublin Union, noted that there was no hostility from the inhabitants towards the insurgents: 'It was perfectly plain that all their admiration was for the heroes who had surrendered.'[38] To explain why some of the insurgent prisoners encountered hostility, Foy and Barton felt the contradictions could be modified by other factors. They examined the routes which the British guards took the insurgent prisoners. Michael Mallin's column of prisoners was marched two miles to Richmond barracks through a strongly loyalist and Protestant artisan class district. The area was one from which the Royal Dublin Fusiliers and other Irish regiments of the British army drew their recruits. Similarly, around Richmond barracks dwelt people who were economically dependent on the military base. There was also a degree of hostility from Dublin women whose sons were serving in the army in France. That some priests at Church Street castigated the insurgent prisoners and wounded is certainly true. Even so, the generally accepted account of the population of Dublin being uniformly hostile to the surrendered insurgents is one of the myths repeated so often as to become 'history'.[39]

It becomes clear from considering just these few points about the insurrection of 1916 that there is more to be considered, researched and analysed before we can be certain that it is assessed in its rightful historical context. A suicidal 'blood sacrifice' led by dreamers and poets without a sound military strategy? Leaders who seized a post office as a 'soft target' and had not the slightest idea that they would come up against a modern army that would not hesitate to use all the weaponry at its disposal, including artillery, to quell them? An unpopular rising by a small band who were jeered and insulted on their defeat as they were led off into captivity? These are just a few of the myths that have been propagated. There is a long way to go before the last word can be written on the events of Easter 1916.

NOTES

1.   Philip Freeman, *Ireland and the Classical World* (Austin, 2001), pp. 46, 49.
2.   Seathrun Céitinn DD (Geoffrey Keating DD), *Foras Feasa ar Éirinn: The History of Ireland*, 5 vols. (London, 1903), vol. I, p. 5.
3.   Joe Ambrose, *Dan Breen and the IRA* (Cork, 2005), pp. 7–8.
4.   Peter Berresford Ellis, *Revisionism in Irish Historical Writings: The New Anti-Nationalist School of Historians* (London, 1989).
5.   See Peter Berresford Ellis, 'Easter's Red-Gold Flame', *Irish Democrat* (April 1991); 'A New Light on Easter 1916', *Irish Democrat* (February 1991); 'Seizing Dublin's GPO in 1916 made military sense', *Irish Democrat* (February 2006) and 'Why Connolly's revolutionary role should have come as no surprise', *Morning Star*, 7 April 2006.
6.   C. Desmond Greaves *The Life and Times of James Connolly* (London, 1961), p. 410.
7.   Desmond Ryan, *The Rising* (Dublin, 1949), p. 397.
8.   Éamon de Valera to Ina Connolly Heron, 27 December 1960, Marx Memorial Museum, Islington, London.
9.   *Sunday Press* (Dublin), 31 March 1991. J.P. Duggan had previously written 'German Aid in the 1916 Rising', *An Cosántoir*, vol. 30 (1970), pp.88–99. An account of the papers is given in Andreas Kratz, 'Die Mission Joseph Mary Plunketts im Deutschen Reich under ihre Bedeutung fur den Osteraufstand 1916', *Historische Mitteilungen*, vol. 8 (1995).
10. See F.X. Martin, '1916 Myth, Fact and Mysteries', *Studia Hibernica*, no. 4 (1967), pp. 1–24 and 'The 1916 Rising – A Coup d'État or a "Bloody Protest"?', *Studia Hibernica*, no. 8 (1968).
11. Colonel Eoghan O'Neill 'The Battle for Dublin, 1916: A Military Evaluation of Easter Week', *An Cosántoir*, vol. 26 (1966), pp. 211–22.
12. C.J. Lowe and M.L. Dockrill, *British Foreign Policy 1914–22*, Vol II (London, 1972), p. 238.
13. *Irish Churchman* (Belfast), 14 November 1913. The *Churchman* was a Loyalist journal.

14. Connolly's articles in *Workers' Republic* in 1915 were reprinted as *Revolutionary Warfare* (Dublin, 1968).
15. Charles Townshend, *Easter 1916, The Irish Rebellion* (London, 2005), pp. 112–13.
16. M. O'Dubhghaill (ed.), *Insurrection Fires At Easter Tide* (Cork, 1966).
17. T.A. Jackson, *Ireland Her Own* (London, 1947), p. 399.
18. *Irish Democrat* (February 2006) and *The Post Office Electrical Engineers' Journal*, vol. IX (1916).
19. Keith Jeffery, *The GPO and the Easter Rising* (Dublin, 2006).
20. *Engineers' Journal*, pp. 196, 200.
21. *Engineers' Journal*.
22. Greaves, *Connolly*, p. 414. See also Jackson, *Ireland*, p. 397.
23. See *Workers' Republic*, 29 May 1915.
24. Ryan, *Rising*, p. 141.
25. De Valera to Connolly Heron, 27 December 1960, Marx Memorial Museum.
26. Dorothy Macardle, *The Irish Republic* (London, 1937), p. 191.
27. Thomas M. Coffey, *Agony at Easter: The 1916 Irish Uprising* (London, 1969), pp. 259–60.
28. *Irish Democrat*, February 1991.
29. See *From Tokyo to Tiflis* (London, 1905), *The Tragedy of Korea* (London, 1908), *Canada's Day of Glory* (Toronto, 1918) and *Beaverbrook* (London, 1931).
30. F.A. McKenzie, *The Irish Rebellion: What Happened and Why* (London, 1916), p. 105.
31. Ibid., p. 92.
32. Ibid.
33. Michael Foy and Brian Barton, *The Easter Rising* (Gloucester, 1999).
34. John Clark Diary, National Library of Ireland, MS 10485.
35. Imperial War Museum (London), 80/40/1.
36. Frank Robbins, *Under the Starry Plough* (Dublin, 1977), p. 127.
37. Foy and Barton, *Easter Rising*, p. 206.
38. Army Message Book of Major H. de Courcy Wheeler quoted in Foy and Barton, *Easter Rising*, p. 203.
39. Foy and Barton, *Easter Rising*, pp. 203-9.

11

The Wind that Shakes the Barley: Reflections on the Writing of Irish History in the Period of the Easter Rising and the Irish War of Independence

Brian P. Murphy, OSB

> The foeman's shot burst on our ears,
> From out the wildwood ringing;
> The bullet pierced my true love's side,
> In life's young spring so early,
> And on my breast in blood she died,
> While soft winds shook the barley.
>
> > Robert Dwyer Joyce,
> > 'The Wind that Shakes the Barley'.

The film, *The Wind that Shakes the Barley*, directed by Ken Loach and adapted as a screenplay by Paul Laverty, was shown on Irish cinema screens soon after the ninetieth anniversary of the Easter Rising in 2006. From the very first the film generated a lively, and often heated, debate on the character of British rule in Ireland and the Irish response, during the period that encompassed the Easter Rising, the War of Irish Independence (1919–21) and the Irish Civil War (1922–3). It starts with a group of young men playing a game of hurling on a rough pitch traced out on a hillside in county Cork. They return home, gather outside a farmhouse and are suddenly surrounded by a unit of the police force. Names and addresses are demanded. Answers are prompted by the powerful use of rifle butts and the threatened use of bayonets. Within minutes one of the young men, who persisted in giving his name in Irish, is taken inside and brutally killed. The transformation from peaceful play to violent murder is dramatic.

'Foul!' cried the critics of the film: incidents like this never happened. 'Old-fashioned propaganda' was the term used by the historian, Ruth Dudley Edwards, to describe the film in the *Daily Mail*. She added that it was a 'travesty of history' and asserted that by using 'a melange of half truths, he [Loach] hopes he can persuade British politicians to "confront", and then apologise, for the Empire'. 'As Empires go,' she concluded, 'the British version was the most responsible and humane of all.'[1] Other political commentators, historians and film critics were just as scathing in their criticism: Tim Luckhurst in *The Times* claimed that the film was a 'poisonously anti-British corruption of the history of the war of Irish independence'. Simon Heffer in the *Daily Telegraph* called the film 'repulsive'; Steven King in the *Irish Examiner* of 22 June 2006 described it as 'pure and utter propaganda' and Crispin Jackson in the *Tablet* of 24 June 2006 called it 'absurdly one-sided ... mere propaganda, as gaudy and rickety as a St Patrick's day float'. Stephen Howe, in a review carried by opendemocracy.org, maintained that the film 'does mislead by selection and implication'.

Some historians and commentators, however, wrote detailed reviews in support of the film in early summer 2006, notably Luke Gibbons, Niall Meehan, Brian Hanley and George Monbiot.[2] However, the major contribution on the subject has been the critical voice of the historian Roy Foster. In a lengthy article in the *Dublin Review*, Foster dismisses the film as 'an exercise in wish-fulfilment rather than history'. He even takes the time to find fault with 'the awful dirge' that gives the film its title and to comment that it was sung 'off-key'. He also offers a critique of the film's cinematic qualities.[3]

Unlike Foster, I am not able to say anything about the film as cinema. My only qualification in that regard is that I attended the same school in London as Alfred Hitchcock but he had left before my arrival. Nor am I able to make, as Foster does, any observations about the quality of the singing but, in regard, to the historical content of the film and Foster's treatment of it, certain comments may be made. Incidents like the killing of the young Irish Volunteer did happen. So too did the brutal assassination of British troops by the IRA, which, although portrayed in the film, seem not to have been noticed by Loach's critics. Moreover, these incidents happened in the precise context in which Loach has chosen to set them.

The corporal in charge of the 'Black and Tan' police unit prefaced his interrogation of the young hurlers with the statement that he was acting under the powers of the Defence of the Realm Act (DORA). He added that he was implementing particular orders which prohibited people from gathering together either for playing Gaelic games or for speaking the Irish language. It was after these orders were issued that the young Irish speaker was killed. By stressing the Defence of the Realm Act at the very start of the film, Loach and Laverty, the screenwriter, provide the perfect answer to their critics who claim that they have failed to give any rationale behind the British war effort. If Donal Ó Drisceoil, listed as historical advisor, was responsible for this perceptive start to the film he is to be commended.

Loach makes it clear, in a manner that few historians have done, that DORA, which was introduced in August 1914, was the weapon chosen by the British government to confront Irish republicans. War was never officially declared: the Irish problem was treated as a domestic concern of the United Kingdom government. The Act, supplemented by Defence of the Realm Regulations (DORR), effectively permitted the army to use martial law powers as occasion demanded. In this way the terms Special Military Area (SMA) and Competent Military Authority (CMA) became features of Irish life in the years prior to the Easter Rising of 1916. Under this system and under the direction of Major Ivon Price, the chief intelligence officer at the Irish military command, newspapers were suppressed and persons imprisoned, even deported, without the process of civil law.[4]

In this context, Foster's critique of the film makes strange reading. He asserts that 'Loach's film, by beginning sharply in 1920 with no background information whatsoever, contrives to give a completely misleading idea of the historical situation in Ireland at the time.'[5] In fact, with the mention of DORA, Loach has provided one of the most important single items of 'background information' that is required for an understanding of not only the Easter Rising but also the War of Irish Independence. Significantly, Charles Townshend, whom Foster rightly praises for his magisterial work, *The British Campaign in Ireland*, stressed the importance of DORA from its earliest pages.[6]

Possibly of even more significance, no reference to DORA is to be found in the index of Foster's *Modern Ireland 1600–1972*, although it does appear in the text with specific regard to the 1916 Rising.[7] Possibly, too, this failure to recognize the importance of DORA from its inception has led Foster, in his attempt to provide a more accurate historical background than Loach, to claim that in 1914 the political chains binding Ireland to England were 'fairly light' and that there was 'an exceptionally lively (and uncensored) press'.[8] Faced by such incidents as the Curragh mutiny, the creation of an Ulster provisional government, and the shooting of civilians on Bachelor's Walk, Dublin, all of which took place in 1914, it seems reasonable to question Foster's benign description of the political scene at that time.

Questions must certainly be asked about Foster's description of the press as 'uncensored'. How, if the press was 'uncensored', do we account

for the suppression, on 2–3 December 1914, of *Sinn Féin, Irish Freedom,*
Ireland and the *Irish Worker?* Is suppression not censorship? All of these
journals were, by the way, suppressed under the terms of DORA. Several
other papers were to share the same fate before the Rising started. Even
allowing for his qualification that the situation was changed somewhat by
the First World War, one is left with the distinct, if surprising, impression
that Loach, by following the path mapped out by Townshend, provides a
sounder introduction to the British campaign in Ireland than that prof-
fered by Foster. The same may be said of their contrasting views of the
impact of the crown forces upon civilian life in Ireland.

With the introduction of DORA, the two Irish police forces, the Royal
Irish Constabulary (RIC) and the Dublin Metropolitan Police, became
closely integrated with the army in the administration of a court martial
legal system. Unlike the English police force, they had always been
involved in the detection and suppression of dissident political views.
From August 1914 they operated within a military, as well as a civilian,
structure. The term 'crown forces' is commonly used to describe both the
police and the army in Ireland, and the coming together of both arms of
the law had dramatic and draconian consequences upon civilian life in
the country. These consequences Loach attempted to portray in his film.
In some ways Loach has done no more than to represent the reality that
was recognized on the ground by Erskine Childers as early as May 1919,
long before the accession to the police force of the Black and Tans (c.
January 1920) and the auxiliaries (July 1920). That is to say, long before
the real terror of war had commenced.

Childers, who had fought in the First World War in the ranks of the
British forces, informed readers of *The Times* in May 1919 that 'to the
great majority of Irishmen, Great Britain now signifies "Prussianism"
incarnate, and with good reason ... Great Britain is making war, literally,
on the principle of freedom ... force, simple force, is the reply; a military
terror; machine guns, tanks, bombing aeroplanes; soldiers ignorant of law
dispensing justice by Court-martial; a rigid censorship ... police spies and
informers.'[9] It was in that context, so graphically described by Childers
and so vividly portrayed by Loach, that the police forces came to be
regarded as legitimate targets by the Irish Republican Army (IRA).

From the introduction of DORA, some members of the crown forces
felt that the power of court martial placed them above the law. That, for
example, was the excuse of Captain Bowen Colthurst for shooting dead
three unarmed prisoners, including the pacifist Francis Sheehy
Skeffington, on 26 April 1916. So concerned was Sir John Simon with the
way in which Colthurst had applied General Sir John Maxwell's court
martial decree that he felt obliged to point out, in his Royal Commission
report, that 'the shooting of unarmed and unresisting civilians without

trial constitutes the offence of murder, whether martial law has been pro-claimed or not'.[10]

The Simon Report was published in 1916. In June 1920, the year which Loach's film takes as its starting point, Lt.-Col. G.F. Smyth, divisional commissioner of the Munster RIC, speaking at Listowel, county Kerry, expressed the same sentiments as Colthurst, when he assured the men under his command that 'the more you shoot the better I will like you, and I assure you that no policeman will get into trouble for shooting any man'. He concluded by saying that 'in the past, policemen have got into trouble for giving evidence at coroners' inquests. As a matter of fact coroners' inquests are to be made illegal so that in future no policeman will be asked to give evidence at inquests.' Smyth's orders to his men were given, significantly, in the presence of Major General Sir Hugh Tudor, police adviser to the Dublin Castle administration.[11]

By 9 August 1920 the policy enunciated by Smyth had received official sanction from Lloyd George's government, after a special cabinet meeting, with the introduction of the Restoration of Order in Ireland Act. This Act, essentially an enlargement of the powers of DORA, declared that 'regulations so made are also provided for any of the duties of a Coroner and Coroner's Jury being performed by a Court of Inquiry constituted under the Army Act instead of by the Coroner and Jury'. By this legislation the crown forces were provided with a high degree of immunity from the civil law of the land.[12]

At the same time as this legislation became law, a government publication, the *Weekly Summary*, was issued to the police forces, including Black and Tans and auxiliaries. The first number appeared on 13 August 1920. It inculcated a racist attitude towards the IRA and condoned, even encouraged, the use of reprisals. For example, on 27 October 1920 it published, with apparent approval of the sentiments, an order by the Cork branch of the Anti-Sinn Féin Society which declared that 'if in the future any member of His Majesty's Forces be murdered, two members of the Sinn Féin Party in the County of Cork will be killed. And, in the event of a member of the Sinn Féin Party not being available three sympathisers will be killed.' Inevitably, with a government publication airing views like these, some members of the police forces took the law into their own hands. Such a course of conduct was encouraged by the constant endorsement given to the *Weekly Summary* in the House of Commons by Sir Hamar Greenwood, chief secretary for Ireland.

For example, when Canon Magner, the elderly parish priest of Dunmanway, county Cork, was killed on 15 December 1920, a military court martial dealt with the case. Reporting the incident to the cabinet, Lloyd George stated that Magner's 'sole offence was to have helped a Resident Magistrate to get his car going. And here comes a drunken beast of a soldier who makes him kneel down and shoots him.'[13] The killing may well have taken place against a more sinister background: it may not have been the result of a simple chance encounter, as described by Lloyd George. Local tradition records that Canon Magner had received death threats from the Black and Tans after refusing to toll the church bells, barely a month earlier, on Armistice Day, 11 November 1920.

Commenting on the affair, on 19 December, Mark Sturgis, an official in Dublin Castle, put the blame on General Tudor, police adviser, on the grounds that 'these men have undoubtedly been influenced by what they have taken to be the passive approval of their officers from Tudor downwards to believe they will never be punished for anything'.[14] Ironically, and in a perversion of the judicial system, the procedure of court martial, which was designed to prosecute the IRA, was also used to protect members of the crown forces who had committed crimes. The auxiliary cadet officer who carried out the brutal shooting of Canon Magner was named Harte. He was found guilty but insane and sent to live in Canada – the same finding and the same country of re-location as Captain Bowen Colthurst. Of the court martial verdict on Colthurst, Tim Healy had said that 'never since the trial of Christ was there a greater travesty of justice'. The same judgement might well be applied to the verdict on Harte.[15]

If Loach had wished to be provocative, he might well have selected the shooting of Canon Magner for the start of his film; or possibly the killing of Thomas MacCurtain in his home, surrounded by his family, by a unit of the RIC on 20 March 1920. In this case the coroner's jury declared on 17 April 1920 that 'the murder was organised and carried out by the RIC, officially directed by the British Government; and we return a verdict of wilful murder against David Lloyd George, Prime Minister of England; Lord French, Lord Lieutenant of Ireland' and other named officials.[16]

Foster, by ignoring realities such as these (the names of Smyth, Magner and MacCurtain are not to be found in the index to his *Modern Ireland*), is critical of Loach on the basis that 'the impression created by this film is that Black and Tan rule was the general state of things in Ireland before independence, fully authorised and sanctioned by the authorities – which was not the case.'[17] This view is markedly at variance with that of Townshend, who has stated clearly that 'official reprisals' began in the last week of December 1920, when General Macready 'informed the Cabinet that Military Governors in the Martial Law Area (MLA) had been authorised to inflict punishments after rebel outrages'.[18] Once again Ken Loach, by remaining closer to the historical interpretation of Townshend than that proposed by Foster, has conveyed an authentic account of the war in Ireland. One can only wonder why Foster, having rightly praised Townshend's book as a 'brilliantly forensic analysis' of the period, has chosen to disregard the seminal findings contained in it.[19]

Loach attempts in the film to justify armed opposition to British rule on the basis of the Sinn Féin success in the 1918 general election. He does not elaborate on this electoral mandate for the armed struggle: the lead character in the film (played by Cillian Murphy) simply states, during interrogation, that the seventy-three seats won by Sinn Féin in the December 1918 election justified resistance to British rule in Ireland. For reasons of focus, it made sense that such a basic statement sufficed to justify the IRA's military campaign. However, if Loach had the time to develop this theme of a democratic mandate, several other factors could have been introduced into the debate.

Loach might have mentioned that, in the period prior to the December election, over 200 leading members of Sinn Féin were imprisoned without trial under the terms of DORA, which had been introduced by Lord French in May 1918; that the Sinn Féin election manifesto and its election pamphlets were either censored or suppressed; and that at the first meeting of Dáil Éireann on 21 January 1919, some thirty-six Sinn Féin elected representatives were declared absent and described as 'in the hands of the foreigner'. These important realities, all a direct consequence of the imposition of DORA, find no place in Foster's assessment of the 1918 election result in his study of *Modern Ireland*.

On the contrary, Foster attempted to minimize the election and the significance of seventy-three Sinn Féin seats by raising certain allegations of personation at the polls. These minor charges of malpractice pale into insignificance when compared to the major impact of DORA. Once again, Loach's historical setting, however briefly delineated, is shown to be sounder than that of Foster. If any doubt existed as to the democratic mandate of Dáil Éireann and the IRA, it was dispelled by the municipal elections of January 1920 and the county council elections of June 1920. Both of these elections showed widespread support for Sinn Féin, even in Ulster, despite the government's attempt to lessen their chances by introducing proportional representation into the electoral system.

Loach, understandably, within the constraints of the film, had no time to expand on these democratic credentials. However, they were articulated very clearly at the time by Éamon de Valera in a published appeal, in October 1920, to President Woodrow Wilson of the United States. The pamphlet, entitled *Ireland's Claim for Recognition as a Sovereign State*, printed details of the recent elections in Ireland, not only that of 1918 but also the two local elections of 1920. De Valera concluded that 'to repudiate the evidence of the ballot, the most civilised method of declaring the national will, and to demand that, as a condition of recognition, the bullet be more effectively used, is to introduce into international relations an inhuman principle of immorality.'[20] Loach, to his credit, has effectively conveyed this reality: British rule in Ireland in 1920 attached less value to the ballot box than to the bullet.

In this historical context one can discern a very real, if surprising, connection between Ireland and Iraq – a connection which Loach has argued for, but his critics have dismissed as unsustainable. Foster, for example, states clearly that 'Loach has also drawn parallels with the invasion of Iraq, which hardly fit the case.'[21] The connection with Iraq, however, is firmly centred on the treatment that both countries received at the Paris Peace Conference and the Treaty of Versailles, July 1919. While England's rejection of an Irish republic was to be expected, it was not expected that America would acquiesce in such a decision. Although President Woodrow Wilson had been bitterly critical of Irish-Americans, as hyphenated Americans and as supporters of Germany in the First World War, it had been hoped that the peace negotiations would be based on his 'fourteen point' programme.

One of the points identified by Wilson, as a prelude to world peace, was the right to independence of small nations struggling to be free. This pledge, and the simmering conflict between the United States and England over naval supremacy, appeared to make an accord between the two powers impossible. The emergence of an Anglo-American alliance in world affairs, indeed the present accord between the two countries in the most recent war in Iraq, may be traced to this time and to these particular events. For this reason it merits further attention. There were several reasons for Wilson's move towards an alignment with England. As well as a specifically calculated British diplomatic campaign to win Wilson over to their side, there were two underlying reasons for the accord. Firstly, it marked the culmination of the dreams and aspirations of Cecil Rhodes and Alfred Milner that there should be an Anglo-American alliance in world affairs; and, secondly, it was in harmony with the views of an influential group in American politics which had, over the last twenty years, promoted the expansion of America's own navy and empire.

The vision of Rhodes and Milner was given practical expression in the secret formation of the Round Table association and the public foundation of the Rhodes scholarship scheme. Writing in his *Confession of Faith*, Rhodes confidently asserted: 'Why should we not join a secret society – with but one object the furtherance of the British empire, for the bringing of the whole uncivilised world under British rule, for the recovery of the United States, for the making of the Anglo-Saxon race but one empire?' Lionel Curtis and Philip Kerr, leading figures in the Round Table association, played leading roles in the shaping of the Versailles Treaty and of the Free State settlement in Ireland.[22]

Their imperial aspirations found a sympathetic response among the ranks of those Americans who not only had presided over the recent occupation of Hawaii, Puerto Rico, Cuba, Honduras and the Philippines but also had approved of a world tour of the American fleet, numbering some sixteen battleships, in 1907–9. Commenting on the American move towards empire, Charles Beard wrote: 'Here, then, is the new realpolitik. A free opportunity for expansion in foreign markets is indispensable to the prosperity of American business. Modern diplomacy is commercial. Its chief concern is with the promotion of economic interests abroad.'[23]

In this context the Treaty of Versailles (28 June 1919) marked a triumph for the ideals of Rhodes and the Unionist-dominated British coalition government and also signalled the beginning of a new Anglo-American world order. The hope of Patrick Pearse, expressed in his surrender appeal of 29 April 1916, that the Rising 'has been sufficient to gain recognition of Ireland's national claim at an international peace conference' lost out to the imperial policy of Rhodes. The voice of Ireland was not to be heard at the peace conference.[24] By the terms of the treaty, Great Britain, in return for engaging in the Washington naval talks with America (a treaty was signed in January 1922), was given a free hand to pursue its commercial and strategic interests in such areas as Mesopotamia (modern Iraq), Afghanistan, Palestine, India and Africa.

As a result of the Versailles Treaty, Great Britain was free not only to impose military rule in Ireland but also to wage war in modern Iraq, where mustard gas was used against the Shias in 1920 and indiscriminate mass bombing against the Kurds in 1921. The oil fields of that country, both then and today, were one of the main policy objectives of the British government.[25] The success of British policy, and the attendant failure of Ireland's case for recognition, was commented upon by Childers at the time. Writing publicly on 2 July 1919 in the *Daily News*, he asserted that 'it has not been difficult to stifle the voice of Ireland at Paris. Her independence has no market value, while its repression on the grounds of military necessity was the best of all precedents for similar policies elsewhere.' He concluded: 'The subjection of Ireland is international poison contaminating the politics of the world.'[26]

The same view was later expressed by Robert Lynd, an English journalist and a member of the Peace with Ireland Council, who, reviewing the situation in Ireland in 1920, asserted that the responsibility for the murders 'rests primarily with the immoral violence of a Government which met the dreams of a small nation for self-Government, not with the Fourteen Points, but with the points of a bayonet'.[27] Loach and Laverty, by identifying with the prescient words of Childers and Lynd, have offered insights not only into the war in Ireland but also into the current war in Iraq. They point the way to universal truths in the conduct of human affairs that were also recognized by George Monbiot in his review of the film. In 'Occupations brutalise both the occupiers and the occupied', he stated: 'It is our refusal to learn that lesson which allows new colonial adventures to take place. If we knew more about Ireland, the invasion of Iraq may never have happened.' Significantly, if regrettably, Foster's particular historical focus does not enable him to discern this very real connection between the wars in Ireland and Iraq.[28]

If Loach's emphasis on DORA and the 1918 general election contributed greatly to a sound historical backdrop to the film, so too did his focus at the start of the film on the ban on nationalist organizations. This ban, which was passed under the terms of Balfour's Criminal Law Act of 1887, became law on 10 September 1919 and had grave political, social and economic consequences. As a result of the ban, Dáil Éireann was declared a 'dangerous association' and was suppressed along with Sinn Féin clubs, the Irish Volunteers, Cumann na mBan and the Gaelic League. These firm measures were not occasioned by any major military action on the part of the IRA but rather by the attempt of Dáil Éireann to function as an alternative parliament. The launching of a Dáil Éireann loan on 21 August 1919, in the name of the government of the Irish Republic, while provocative to the Dublin Castle administration was a positive attempt to raise money in order to initiate a programme of social reform. The loan itself was declared to be 'seditious', and many newspapers which carried advertisements for it were immediately suppressed. By adopting such tactics Dublin Castle became engaged in a war of attrition with the Irish people that had significant social consequences.

Loach and Laverty have received much criticism for attempting to address these consequences in their film. Support for their approach, however, is to be found in a most unlikely contemporary source: the writings of the official press censor attached to Dublin Castle, Major Bryan Cooper. He was a Protestant unionist from county Sligo who had fought bravely in the First World War and who acted as the official press censor from the early months of 1919 until September of that year. Commenting on the government policy of suppression, in the month that he relinquished office, he stated publicly that 'it would surely be wise to abandon a procedure which only tends to inflame and exasperate moderate opinion in Ireland'.[29] As the year drew to a close, Cooper became even more critical of government policy, asserting that it was wrong to oppose Dáil Éireann's programme of afforestation and industrial renewal. He concluded that the path which the government was 'now following leads not to peace and contentment, not even to the maintenance of law and order, but the alienation of the sympathies of moderate Irishmen and the strengthening of Sinn Féin'.[30]

Similar support for Loach's focus on social and economic issues – indeed his concern for the impact of war upon ordinary people – may be found in the writings of Erskine Childers. Reviewing the actions of the

British crown forces, both army and police, in the *Daily News* of 19 April 1920, Childers insisted that far more than military matters were at stake. He asserted that 'an attempt is being made to break up a whole national organisation, a living, vital, magnificent thing, normally and democratically evolved from the intense desire of a fettered and repressed people for self-reliance and self-development. This attempt, if we are to give words their right meaning, is the great crime, the fundamental crime.'[31]

Loach addressed some of the social issues at the heart of this 'fundamental crime' by depicting the British army's brutal response to the railwaymen's strike, an event often ignored in many accounts of the war; by portraying the burning of a family farmhouse and the shooting up of a town as reprisal measures; and by staging a debate on the Democratic Programme in a Dáil Éireann court.[32] While Loach has been criticized for showing such incidents, the reality on the ground was far worse. Some forty creameries were burnt to the ground, or badly damaged, between the months of April and November 1920, as reprisals against IRA attacks. These creameries were the brainchild, in particular, of two Protestants, Sir Horace Plunkett and George Russell (AE), who were actively involved in their development as part of the Irish Agricultural Organization Society's work of improving the living conditions of both unionists and nationalists.[33]

'Hit the creamery and you hit the community'; such was the rationale behind the actions of the crown forces, as described by Hugh Martin, the British journalist who travelled throughout Ireland in 1920 and, for his pains, was targeted by the auxiliaries.[34] Faced by British denials, particularly by Sir Hamar Greenwood, of the troops' participation in these attacks, George Russell called for a public inquiry and maintained that 'creameries and mills have been burned to the ground, their machinery wrecked; agricultural stores have also been burned, property looted, employees have been killed, wounded, beaten, threatened or otherwise ill-treated'.[35] Had Loach been solely concerned with painting a totally damning picture of the British military regime in Ireland, as his critics claim, surely he would have featured the burning of these creameries or the burning of Cork city, 11–12 December 1920? That he refrained from doing so says more for the balance of his approach than that of his critics.

With specific reference to those critics who say that social and economic matters received an unwarranted priority in the film, two final observations may be made. Firstly, at the start of the period, in April 1919, a soviet was declared in Limerick city. The method chosen to suppress the soviet was the imposition of DORA: most of the city was defined as an SMA (Special Military Area) and General C.J. Griffin was appointed the CMA (Competent Military Authority).[36] Secondly, towards the end of the period, at the general election of June 1922, seventeen representatives of the Labour Party were elected to Dáil Éireann. Compared to the fifty-eight pro-Treaty deputies and the thirty-six anti-Treaty deputies, the number of Labour deputies was high. Moreover, it has been calculated that the average vote for a Labour candidate was 7,365; for a pro-Treaty candidate, 5,174; and for an anti-Treaty candidate, 3,372, thus providing a forcible reminder that, even at this critical stage in Ireland's political development, social and economic issues were the main concern of many. Taken together, the two events provide further confirmation, if any was needed, that Loach got it spot on, not only for his focus on social affairs but also for introducing his audience to the British forces in Ireland in the context of DORA.[37]

If Loach has been criticized for making too much of social and economic issues, he has also been criticized for showing too little of the IRA's sectarian attacks on Protestants. Foster and other critics complain that, by ignoring the recent writings by Peter Hart on the IRA in Cork, Loach has concealed the religious conflict that permeated the war in that part of Ireland. In general it should be noted that Hart brings to his study of the period many of the characteristics that may be discerned in Foster's *Modern Ireland*. Like Foster, Hart makes no reference to DORA in the index to *The IRA and its Enemies* and, again like Foster, he trivializes the impact of the 1918 general election. While focussing on alleged incidents, in which young Volunteers 'locked old people into their homes', Hart makes no reference to the hundreds of leading Sinn Féiners who were actually behind prison bars under the court martial terms of DORA.[38]

Inevitably, as a result, Peter Hart rejects the idea that the IRA enjoyed any form of democratic mandate for the war that it waged. The ideals of the 1916 proclamation of independence and the expression given to those ideals in the constitution of the reformed Sinn Féin party in October 1917 find little place in Hart's analysis of the IRA. Nor does he give any indication that the armed struggle may have been motivated by any of the profound statements that were issued by Sinn Féin and Dáil Éireann at that time. For example, little or no emphasis is given to the statement against conscription in 1918, the Sinn Féin election manifesto of the same year, the Declarations of Dáil Éireann and the formal appeal to the Paris Peace Conference, both made in 1919. Of the conference, itself, and the Treaty of Versailles, Hart, like Foster, is significantly silent.

The origin of Peter Hart's work has been on a social analysis of IRA membership: this was the subject of his first published study on 'Youth Culture and the Cork IRA' as part of the Trinity College history workshop.[39] This essay, which formed part of his thesis and subsequent book, argued that the social bonding that arose from the association of young men in such traditional groupings as the Wren Boys influenced their joining the

IRA. The emphasis is on the social rather than the ideological; and on a social unity that is coloured by, among other things, boisterous behaviour and cross dressing – nothing to enhance the image of IRA membership!

The Wren Boys, who only engaged in their ritual celebration on one day of the year, the 26 December, St Stephens's Day, were, and still are, represented in England by the Mummers. Both groups celebrated the winter solstice. Questions arise as to the validity of Hart's approach: would it be relevant to research the Mummers in order to assess the social bonding that brought them into the British army in the 1914–18 war? Would it be relevant to research the Wren Boys in the Carcassone region of France, whose ritual ceremonials lasted for a month, in relation to their joining the ranks of the French army? Somehow I do not think so. And, yet, Loach is criticized for not following this pattern of interpretation mapped out by Hart's thesis.

Foster, for one, is quite clear on this point. He laments the fact that the work of Hart, composed with 'skill and empathy' and painting a picture of 'class resentment, religious and ethnic antipathy and local power-struggle', has not been portrayed in the film.[40] Writing earlier and more specifically about the small Protestant farmers, drapers and schoolteachers, Foster noted that they 'became "targets" for reasons which had less to do with political affiliation than atavistic ethnic conflict'.[41] Hart's work, it is claimed, should have led Loach and Laverty to depict the execution of a Protestant landlord in the film as carried out for religious, rather than military, reasons; that he was shot, in other words, because he was a Protestant, rather than because he was an informer. Hart's use of official sources, however, to make this case are so selective as to be unsustainable.

Hart writes, citing the official British *Record of the Rebellion in Ireland 1920–1921*, that 'in the south the Protestants and those who supported the Government rarely gave much information because, except by chance, they did not have it to give'.[42] If this quotation from the *Record* told the whole story, then religious motives, as the thesis of Hart maintains, must have played a part in the IRA's attacks upon Protestants for the simple reason that they had no information to give. In fact, the selective quotation from the *Record of the Rebellion* by Hart does not tell the whole story. The next two sentences from the *Record*, which Hart has omitted, report that 'an exception to this rule was in the Bandon area where there were many Protestant farmers who gave information. Although the intelligence officer of this area was exceptionally experienced and although the troops were most active it proved almost impossible to protect these brave men, many of whom were murdered.'[43] In short, the Protestant farmers were shot because they were informers: the official British source on the war, acknowledged by Hart to be 'the most trustworthy source' that we have, rather than supporting Hart's claim of sectarian killing by the IRA, effectively shows it to be false.[44]

If any possible doubt might remain on the issue, the views of Lionel Curtis, the shaper of events at the Paris Peace Conference, appear conclusive. Following a secret visit to Ireland in 1921, Curtis affirmed that 'Protestants in the south do not complain of persecution on sectarian grounds. If Protestant farmers are murdered, it is not by reason of their religion, but rather because they are under suspicion as Loyalists. The distinction is a fine, but a real one.'[45]

Hart's selective use of this official source did not end with this omission in regard to the Bandon area, the very area which was at the centre of his thesis. In his edited version of the *Record of the Rebellion* not only did he fail to acknowledge that he had made a selective use of the document in his book, but also he made, without any notification, another very significant omission. This omission concerned the attitude of the British army towards the IRA. In a section entitled, 'The People', the *Record of the Rebellion* stated: 'Judged by English standards the Irish are a difficult and unsatisfactory people. Their civilisation is different and in many ways lower than that of the English. They are entirely lacking in the Englishman's distinctive respect for the truth ... many were of a degenerate type and their methods of waging war were in most cases barbarous, influenced by hatred and devoid of courage.'[46]

Questions arise over these selective omissions. The title of Hart's book encompasses the IRA and its enemies: by the first omission the IRA are incorrectly presented as sectarian killers; by the second omission the enemies of the IRA (the British army) are protected from their manifest expression of racism. How does Hart explain these omissions? How does David Fitzpatrick, the series editor of *Irish Narratives* and the supervisor of Hart's original thesis, explain them? How does Foster reconcile them with the 'skill and empathy' that he has identified in Hart's work?

Moreover, many examples, both personal and institutional, might be chosen to show that the film correctly portrayed the religious character in the south of Ireland during the war years. The personal experience of Robert Barton, a Protestant landowner of county Wicklow, is extremely relevant to this theme. Barton had actually served in the ranks of the British army during the Rising; he was then elected to represent Sinn Féin for county Wicklow in the 1918 election; and, as a member of Dáil Éireann, he was appointed director of agriculture in August 1919. He was responsible for the plan for the re-afforestation of Ireland, which the British authorities at Dublin Castle did their best to frustrate, and the introduction of a national land bank.[47]

The National Land Bank provides an example of Protestants and Catholics working together to further the work of Dáil Éireann and of

Ireland. It was instituted by Robert Barton in December 1919 as part of his plans to help native Irish people acquire land and to improve their farms. Among the directors of the bank were to be found the names of other distinguished Protestants, such as Erskine Childers and Lionel Smith Gordon, a past pupil of Eton and Oxford. Draconian measures were taken by the government to prevent the success of this scheme: meetings were broken up; raids were made on banks holding National Land Bank accounts; and Barton himself was arrested and deported in January 1920. Significantly, the action was taken against him under the terms of DORA.[48]

Far from driving Protestants from the land, Irish republicans, as represented by Dáil Éireann, selected Protestants to be in charge of its land reform programme! Indeed, it was the actions of the British government, not those of Irish republicans, that provided the greatest threat to the harmonious working together of Protestants and Catholics in both the National Land Bank and the Co-operative Societies. Nothing could be further from the tenor and tone of Hart's and Foster's historical narrative on this matter. The work of two other organizations, the Irish White Cross Society and the Peace with Ireland Council, confirms this impression.

The Irish White Cross Society was founded in the early months of 1921 with the explicit aim of alleviating the distress and hardship caused by the actions of the crown forces. Leaders of the Catholic Church, the Church of Ireland, the Methodist Church, the Chief Rabbi of Dublin and many lay Protestants combined to take part in this work. As well as George Russell, Sir Horace Plunkett, Erskine Childers and Lionel Smith Gordon (chairman), whose names have featured in other organizations, among the other lay members were Professor Culverwell, James G. Douglas (honorary treasurer), Captain D. Robinson and a large number of women.

Among the Protestant women were Molly Childers, Dorothy Macardle, Dr Kathleen Lynn, Albinia Brodrick (the sister of the Earl of Midleton), Alice Stopford Green and Charlotte Despard (the sister of Lord French). Significantly, this large and influential group of Protestants supported the Irish White Cross Society even though the name of Michael Collins, then a wanted man and known to be in the IRA, was listed as a trustee of the society. Some Protestants did decline to join the society owing to the presence of Collins, but, it seems reasonable to ask, would so many leading non-Catholics have supported such relief work if the IRA had been engaged in a sectarian war?[49]

The Peace with Ireland Council, which was founded in October 1920 and based in London, concentrated on highlighting the atrocities committed by the crown forces. They did so through published pamphlets and public talks. Among its members were many Protestants, such as Lord

Henry Cavendish Bentinck, Basil Williams, John Annan Bryce, Oswald Mosley, Sir John Simon, Lord Buckmaster, George Bernard Shaw and the bishop of Winchester. D.G. Boyce, in his seminal, and still valuable, book on *Englishmen and Irish Troubles* (London, 1972) records in great detail the important work of the Peace with Ireland Council. Once again it seems reasonable to ask: would leading non-Catholics have contributed to the exposure of the actions of the British forces in Ireland if the IRA had been engaged in a sectarian war?[50]

Despite these evident signs of co-operation between Catholics and Protestants, Foster remains committed to the Hart version of a sectarian war: questions over Hart's use of sources have not qualified his judgement in any way. Perhaps this is not surprising as Foster himself, flying in the face of compelling contrary evidence, had earlier declared in his *Modern Ireland* that 'the emotions focussed by cultural revivalism around the turn of the century were fundamentally sectarian and even racist'.[51] Moreover, neither Foster in his *Modern Ireland* nor Hart in his *The IRA and its Enemies* have any reference in the index to the National Land Bank, the Irish White Cross Society or the Peace with Ireland Council. Moreover, the regular affirmations of distinguished Protestants throughout this period that there was no sectarian animosity among Irish people have not been able to influence the historical mindset of either Foster or Hart.

Douglas Hyde, the Protestant president of the Gaelic League, may have affirmed in 1913 that he had never known 'any member to be shaken or biased one iota by sectarian considerations' but his view cannot shake, or even shape, Foster's damning general conclusion that the cultural revival was 'fundamentally sectarian'.[52] In the same fashion, the words of George Russell (AE), published in letter form in June 1920, have not influenced the findings of Hart. Writing in the context of the pogroms against Catholics in the north of Ireland and at a time that is central to Hart's thesis, Russell declared that 'I, as an Irish Protestant and an Ulsterman by birth, have lived in Southern Ireland most of my life. I have worked in every county, and I have never found my religion to make any barrier between myself and my Catholic countrymen, nor was religion a bar to my work; and in that ill-fated Irish Convention (1917) one Southern Protestant Unionist after another rose up to say they did not fear persecution from their Nationalist and Catholic countrymen.'[53] For Roy Foster and Peter Hart to construct a narrative without taking cognisance of these Protestant voices raises important questions about the writing of Irish history.

The historical approach of both Foster and Hart, which ignores these evident signs of religious accord in the midst of much bitter conflict, has a distinct, if dubious, historical lineage. It finds an echo in the declaration of Dr John Pentland Mahaffy, Provost of Trinity College, to the Irish

Convention in 1917, where he stated that the differences between Catholics and Protestant marked 'the contrast not only of two creeds, but of two breeds, of two ways of thinking, of two ways of looking at all the most vital interests of men'. These words were not only cited by W. Alison Phillips, Lecky Professor of Modern History at Trinity College, but also endorsed by him in his 1923 history of *The Revolution in Ireland*. He asserted that 'creed marked the line of cleavage in everything that made for national sentiment. This is the fundamental fact which must be grasped, if the root cause of many of the subsequent troubles is to be understood.'[54]

One cannot but suggest that the historical narrative of Foster and Hart, strikingly reminiscent of that proposed by Mahaffy and Phillips, would have been far different, if it had embraced a wider range of sources and treated some selected sources more authentically. Apart from the specific lacunae relating to such issues as the Defence of the Realm Act, sectarianism and social/economic affairs, the major omission relates to their approach to the *Irish Bulletin* and the writings of those associated with it. The main contributors were Robert Brennan, Frank Gallagher and Erskine Childers. The *Bulletin*, the daily news sheet of the Dáil Éireann Publicity Department, began publication on 11 November 1919 and continued until the signing of the Treaty in December 1921. It presented a detailed account of the War of Independence from an Irish republican perspective and, although openly engaged in the work of propaganda, it attempted to achieve its purpose by being a journal of reliable record.

Hart ignores it; Foster ridicules it. Foster stated that the war of public opinion was conducted by British liberals and by 'Erskine Childers's tersely efficient propaganda machine, the *Irish Bulletin* (brilliant at scaling up any military activity into a "notorious" looting or sacking)'.[55] The accuracy of this disparaging assessment of the Bulletin may be measured by the accuracy of Foster's footnote on Erskine Childers, in which he is described as 'Minister for Publicity in the Dáil 1919–1921'. In fact Childers never enjoyed the title of 'Minister for Publicity' of Dáil Éireann. For some months in 1921, starting in February, Childers did act as substitute minister for Desmond Fitzgerald who, in turn, was acting as substitute minister for Lawrence Ginnell. He did not act as minister, even as substitute minister, for the years 1919 and 1920. This lack of accuracy in detail does not inspire confidence in the accuracy of Foster's general conclusions. Although some support for his strictures about the *Irish Bulletin* may be found in the contemporary writings of Major Street, association with Street is a very mixed blessing: he was officially engaged in the work of black propaganda during the Irish war.[56]

Street, based in the Irish Office in London, worked harmoniously with Basil Clarke, head of the propaganda office in Dublin Castle. In

March 1921 their views on propaganda were clearly expressed in a private exchange of letters. Clarke informed Street that 'I would say that the labelling of the news as some way as official ("Dublin Castle", "GHQ" etc.) is the essence of the whole thing: the whole system of news hangs on it.' Street fully concurred with these sentiments and expressed his approval in graphic terms: 'In order that propaganda may be disseminated … in order that it may be rendered capable of being swallowed, it must be dissolved in some fluid which the patient will readily assimilate. Regarding the press as the patient, I know of only two solvents, advertisement and news, of which the latter is by far the most convincing and most economical.'[57]

These men were concerned to win over the world at large to the British narrative of the war in Ireland. For our time the question remains as to how far the historical narrative of the Irish War of Independence has been influenced by the 'official' briefings of these propagandists. Herein lies the importance of the *Irish Bulletin*: it challenged, day in and day out, the 'official' version of the news. To ignore it and to reject it, as Hart and Foster have done, inevitably leads to a diminished historical narrative. Ultimately, it is in this context that Loach and Laverty, far from meriting criticism for their treatment of the Irish war, deserve commendation for discerning that Foster and Hart only tell part of the story, and that a partial one. A final brief observation, drawn from the experience of W.B. Yeats, provides further confirmation that the scenes presented by Loach and Laverty are not only dramatic but also authentic.

Foster's comprehensive study of W.B. Yeats contains clear evidence that Yeats was strongly opposed to reprisals and was critical of the conduct of the British crown forces in Ireland.[58] Speaking at the Oxford Union on 7 February 1921, Yeats proposed the motion 'that this House would welcome complete Self-Government in Ireland, and condemns reprisals'. The motion was adopted with a majority of ninety (219–129). Yeats, in his speech in favour of the motion, declared that he was sorry for the people of Ireland but 'his sorrow for England was greater: for Ireland was preserving her honour, and Freedom would triumph'. He maintained that in the county of Galway 'such even-handed justice as was administered by the Sinn Féin courts had been unknown in the days of the English ascendancy' and he added that 'nothing that the Prussians had done in Belgium was missing from the British tactics in Ireland'.[59]

The sentiments expressed in formal prose during Yeats' debating speech were also expressed by him in poetic imagery in a poem explicitly named 'Reprisals'. Foster mentions the poem but does not reproduce it. Written in late 1920, the poem laments that the life of a British airman, who died with honour in the Great War, is tarnished by the conduct of British soldiers in Ireland. The airman, although not named, was William

Robert Gregory, the son of Lady Augusta Gregory, who had been killed in January 1918. While Yeats was composing his poem, Lady Gregory was occupied in sending lists of Black and Tan atrocities to *The Nation* in order to make English people aware of the brutal actions taking place in their names. She was also annoyed that Yeats should use the death of her son to make political points and requested that he should not publish it.[60]

The setting of the poem was Kiltartan, county Galway, where Lady Gregory lived and where, in the early afternoon of 1 November 1920, Ellen Quinn had been shot dead by a police patrol passing by in lorries. Her death is referred to in the poem. Quinn, seven months pregnant and holding a baby of nine months in her arms, was standing in front of her farmhouse when she was hit in the stomach by a volley of gunfire. She died before midnight, in the arms of her husband, Malachy, with the blood still oozing from her wounds. The poem by Yeats reads:

> Half-drunk or whole mad soldiery
> Are murdering your tenants there.
> Men that revere your father yet
> Are shot at on the open plain.
> Where may new-married women sit
> And suckle little children now? Armed
> men
> May murder them in passing by
> Nor law nor parliament take heed.

These sentiments expressed by Yeats in regard to the killing of Ellen Quinn bear an uncanny resemblance to the ballad of Robert Joyce that provided the title for Loach's film. Malachy, the husband of Ellen Quinn, might well have lamented the death of his 'true love' in the same words as the subject of Joyce's ballad:

> And on my breast in blood she died
> While soft winds shook the barley.

One may only surmise why Roy Foster has chosen not to allow these events in the life of Yeats, the debate at Oxford and the poem 'Reprisals' to colour his review of the film. Whatever the reason for the omission, Foster's silence on the matter may offer some further explanation as to how Loach and Laverty could discern the historical reality of the Anglo-Irish war and Foster, himself, could not. They are to be congratulated not only for making this reality a feature of their film's broad historical canvas but also for painting that canvas in colours that convey deep personal experiences. The end result has been a truly golden achievement, which was rightly recognized as such at the Cannes film festival.

NOTES

1. *Daily Mail* (UK edition), 30 May 2006. See the Irish edition of the *Daily Mail*, 31 May 2006, for Tim Pat Coogan's response to the Dudley Edwards review. This did not appear in the UK edition
2. See *Irish Times*, 17 June 2006; *Irish Examiner*, 26 June 2006; Brian Hanley, History Ireland (September/October 2006); and the *Guardian*, 6 June 2006.
3. Roy Foster, 'The Red and the Green', *Dublin Review*, no. 24 (Autumn 2006), p. 51.
4. See Brian P. Murphy, 'The Easter Rising in the Context of Censorship and Propaganda with Special Reference to Major Ivon Price', in Gabriel Doherty and Dermot Keogh (eds), 1916: *The Long Revolution* (Cork, 2007), pp. 141–68.
5. Foster, *Dublin Review*, p. 46.
6. Charles Townshend, *The British Campaign in Ireland* (Oxford, 1975).
7. Roy Foster, *Modern Ireland 1600–1972* (London, 1988).
8. Foster, *Dublin Review*, pp. 47, 48.
9. *The Times*, 5 May 1919. See also Brian P. Murphy, 'Erskine Childers: the evolution of an enemy of empire – II', in Eoin Flannery and Angus Mitchell (eds), *Enemies of Empire. New perspectives on imperialism, literature and historiography* (Dublin, 2007), pp. 72–100.
10. *Report of Commission on the arrest and subsequent treatment of Mr Francis Sheehy Skeffington*, 1916, Cd. 8376, pp. 11–12.
11. J. Anthony Gaughan, *Memoirs of Constable Jeremiah Mee* (Dublin, 1975), p. 100.
12. *Irish Bulletin*, 5 August 1920; Frank Gallagher ('David Hogan'), *The Four Glorious Years* (Dublin, 1954) pp. 96–8; Colm Campbell, *Emergency Law in Ireland 1918–1925* (Oxford, 1994), pp. 27–9.
13. Thomas Jones and Keith Middlemas (eds), *Whitehall Diary*, vol. 111, Ireland 1918–1925 (London, 1971), p. 46.
14. Michael Hopkinson (ed.), *The Last Days of Dublin Castle: The Diaries of Mark Sturgis* (Dublin, 1992), p. 95.
15. Hanna Sheehy Skeffington, *British Militarism as I Have Known It* (Tralee, 1946), p. 14. General Tudor also settled in Canada and is buried in St Johns, Newfoundland.
16. Florence O'Donoghue, *Tomas MacCurtain, Soldier and Patriot* (Tralee, [1955] 1971), p. 166.
17. Foster, *Dublin Review*, p. 47.
18. Townshend, *British Campaign*, p. 149.
19. Foster, *Dublin Review*, p. 46.
20. Éamon de Valera, *Ireland's Claim for Recognitions as a Sovereign State* (Washington, 1920), pp. 20–1.
21. Ken Loach, 'Director's Note', *The Wind that Shakes the Barely* (Cork, 2006), pp. 7–9 and Foster, *Dublin Review*, p. 49.
22. Michael Collins Piper, 'The Rhodes Scholarships and the Drive for World Empire', in *The Barnes Review* (May/June 2004), p. 37.
23. Stephen Kinzer, *Overthrow: America's Century of Regime Change from Hawaii to Iraq* (New York, 2006), p. 81.
24. Seamus Ó Buachall (ed.), *The Letters of P.H. Pearse* (Gerrard's Cross, 1980), p. 373.
25. See David Onassi, *Air Power and Colonial Control* (Manchester, 1990) and Pat Walsh, *Irish Political Review* (June 2004).
26. *Daily News*, 2 July 1919.
27. Robert Lynd, *Who Began it? The Truth about the Murders in Ireland* (London, 1921).
28. The *Guardian*, 6 June 2006.
29. *The Times*, 27 September 1919.
30. Ibid., 18 December 1919.
31. *Daily News*, 19 April 1920.
32. See Mary Kotsonouris, *Retreat from Revolution: The Dáil Courts, 1920–1924* (Dublin, 1994).
33. See *Report of the Labour Commission to Ireland* (London, 1921), appendix 10, 'Report to November 1920 of Co-operative Creameries and other societies stated to have been destroyed or damaged by armed forces of the Crown', pp. 90–8.
34. Hugh Martin, *Insurrection in Ireland* (London, 1921), p. 69.
35. See evidence of Louie Bennett, secretary of Irish Women Worker's Union, *Evidence of Conditions in Ireland: The American Commission on Conditions in Ireland* (Washington, 1921), p. 994, citing Russell in the Irish Homestead.
36. Liam Cahill, *Forgotten Revolution: Limerick Soviet 1919 – A Threat to British Power in Ireland* (Dublin, 1990).

37. See Conor Kostick, *Revolution in Ireland: Popular Militancy, 1917–1923* (London, 1996), p. 180.
38. Peter Hart, *The IRA and its Enemies: Violence and Community in Cork, 1916–1923* (Oxford, 1998), p. 166.
39. Peter Hart, 'Youth Culture and the Cork IRA', in David Fitzpatrick (ed.), *Revolution? Ireland 1917–1923* (Dublin, 1990).
40. Foster, *Dublin Review*, p. 43.
41. *The Times*, 21 May 1998.
42. Hart, *IRA and its Enemies*, pp. 305–6.
43. Peter Hart (ed.), *Irish Narratives: British Intelligence in Ireland 1920–1921 – The Final Reports* (Cork, 2002), p. 49.
44. Hart (ed.), *Irish Narratives*, p. 6. For further discussion of Hart's use of sources see Brian P. Murphy, *The Origins and Organisation of British Propaganda in Ireland 1920* (Cork, 2006), pp 77–9.
45. See Meda Ryan, *Tom Barry: IRA Freedom Fighter* (Cork, 2003), p. 170. See also pp 156–70 for a critical assessment of Hart's views on the killing of some Protestants in west Cork at the end of April 1922. For a detailed study showing that most of the Protestants killed by the IRA were, in fact, informers, see John Borgonovo, *Spies, Informers and the 'Anti-Sinn Féin Society': The Intelligence War in Cork 1920–1921* (Dublin, 2006).
46. *Record of the Rebellion in Ireland, 1920–1921*, Imperial War Museum, London, pp. 31–2.
47. See Robert C. Barton, Witness Statement 979, Bureau of Military History, National Archives of Ireland.
48. Barton, WS 979, BMH and Peggy Quinn (ed.), *An Irish Banking Revolution: The Story of the National Land Bank Ltd.* (Dublin, 1995).
49. See *Report of the Irish White Cross to 31 August 1922* (Dublin, 1922).
50. D.G. Boyce, *Englishmen and Irish Troubles* (London, 1972).
51. Foster, *Modern Ireland*, p. 453. See also Brendan Clifford (ed.), *Envoi: Taking Leave of Roy Foster* (Aubane, 2006).
52. *Freeman's Journal*, 25 January 1913. See also Brian P. Murphy, 'The Canon of Irish Cultural History: Some Questions concerning Roy Foster's *Modern Ireland*', in Ciaran Brady (ed.), *Interpreting Irish History: The Debate on Historical Revisionism* (Dublin, 1994).
53. *Freeman's Journal*, 9 June 1920.
54. W. Alison Phillips, *The Revolution in Ireland 1906–1923* (London, 1923), pp. 52–3.
55. Foster, *Modern Ireland*, p. 499.
56. C.J. Street, (I.O.), *The Administration of Ireland 1920* (London, 1921) and Charles Townshend, *British Campaign*, pp. 118–19.
57. Murphy, *British Propaganda*, pp. 28–9, citing correspondence in the Colonial Office files.
58. Roy Foster, *W.B. Yeats: A Life, Volume II* (Oxford, 2003).
59. *Young Ireland*, 26 February 1921, reporting the speech of Yeats to the Oxford Union.
60. Judith Hill, *Lady Gregory: An Irish Life* (UK, 2005), pp. 318–19.

12

Rethinking the Republic: The Republican Movement and 1966

Matt Treacy

In 1966 the twenty-six county state seemed to be confidently facing into a future of prosperity and enhanced international standing. The economy was opening up to foreign investment and the Fianna Fáil government was talking about new houses and jobs and rising expectations. At Easter the state would commemorate the fiftieth anniversary of the 1916 Rising.

While official discourse was replete with the emotion and imagery of the revolution and full of the appropriate paeans to the goals of the 1916 leaders, the political elite was moving in a radically different direction. The previous year (1965) had seen the dramatic encounter between Taoiseach Sean Lemass and Northern Ireland Prime Minister Terence O'Neill. Despite the bluster and snowball throwing of Unionist extremists like Ian Paisley, the meeting represented as much a symbol of compromise on the part of the southern state as it did for Belfast.[1]

Alongside this, the Irish government was jettisoning all vestiges of its former protectionist economic policy. It had made a bid to join the European Economic Community in 1963, a bid which only failed when the British application had been vetoed. The Dáil also revised the legislation covering industrial investment in order to allow a hoped-for influx of foreign capital. The most dramatic manifestation of all, however, was the negotiation of a trade agreement with the British government in December 1965. This allowed for the phasing out of all tariffs by 1970.

The Dáil ratified the Anglo-Irish Free Trade Agreement on 7 January 1966 by sixty-six votes to nineteen. In proposing acceptance Lemass had painted a stark alternative of either moving towards free trade, with the agreement as an essential step and EEC membership as the ultimate goal, or of accepting economic stagnation and lower living standards.[1] In their critique, republicans were unapologetic about stating their preference for the latter rather than accepting what they saw as a retreat into the embrace of imperialism. For them national independence and sovereignty was a value to be placed above economic well being.

All Fianna Fáil TDs who were present in the Dáil voted in favour while the Labour Party opposed the measure. Fine Gael, sceptical of and loath to support any measure put forward by the government but equally reluctant to be seen to be in any sense 'anti-English', abstained. Party leader Liam Cosgrave claimed that 'the concessions obtained are small in the immediate future and limited and insecure thereafter'.[2] He warned that Irish businesses might suffer from being opened up to 'unfair competition'.[3]

The Labour Party, in opposing the Agreement, put many of the same arguments as republicans and claimed in their amendment to the government motion that the British would gain the balance of advantage from the deal. One of the Labour speakers, Denis Larkin, detected signs of a realignment in the politics of the Dáil that would open up the kind of opportunities for the left that were being envisaged by some republicans. He claimed that 'the debate revealed a union of souls between Fine Gael and Fianna Fáil, long awaited, long anticipated and we hope, in this year when we celebrate the 50th Anniversary of the Easter Rising, nearly realised'.[4]

The Wolfe Tone Society (WTS) organized a lobby of the Dáil on 4 January under the auspices of the Economic Independence Committee. This was established in 1964 and quickly became an influential ginger group dominated by supporters of those in the IRA leadership who were seeking to make the republican movement more relevant. The WTS congratulated the Labour Party which it said had 'returned to the position of its founder, James Connolly'.[5] Twenty-five of thirty-five Dublin TDs met the group. The Cork-based left-wing publication, *An Phoblacht*, which was critical of Cathal Goulding's wing of the movement, regarded the lobby as part of the process of conditioning republicans to accept participation in constitutional politics.[6]

The Wolfe Tone Society journal, *Tuairisc*, described the Free Trade Agreement as an act of national betrayal and claimed that the only force capable of defending national economic independence was a 'juncture of the forces of the labour and republican movements'. Another article contained a prescription for solving Ireland's problem that might have appeared strange to traditional republicans: 'Irish capital investment at home is the obvious answer to our lack of economic independence. This was the object of the rebels of 1916.'[7] The Agreement was regarded as the means by which the Republic would be brought back into the United Kingdom.[8] It was this objective that had led the British to encourage the Northern Ireland government to come to an accommodation with the Republic as internal reform. An end to partition could be accommodated in a situation in which the whole island was again part of the UK.[9]

Two days after the Free Trade Agreement was passed, Sinn Féin president Tomás MacGiolla addressed a meeting of the party's árd comhairle and other prominent republicans in Dublin. He claimed that the Dáil opposition could not respond to Lemass' taunt that they had no alternative because the only alternative to closer integration with Britain was 'to break the connection completely. This is the Sinn Féin alternative as the policy of Connolly and Pearse whom we are commemorating this year.' The *Irish Democrat*, published by the London-based Connolly Association, was fulsome in its praise of republican opposition to the Agreement, although it did give pride of place to the role of the Irish Workers Party, and depicted Sinn Féin and the IRA as 'fighting on many fronts'.[10]

The republican movement, in fact, was far from thinking about fighting in the sense of a renewed military campaign. In 1965 both the IRA army convention and a special Sinn Féin árd fheis had considered a detailed set of proposals, including one that would have allowed elected republicans to take seats in the Dáil and Stormont. This had been rejected. The internal debate had become public when the editor of the *United Irishman*, Denis Foley, wrote an editorial in March 1965 which strongly criticized the existing abstentionist policy, which he claimed was condemning the republican movement to irrelevancy.[11]

That caused outrage among defenders of the traditional policy and as a compromise the árd comhairle, which still had a majority opposed to change, adopted instead a reorganization plan based on the objective of building Sinn Féin to a position of strength whereby it would be capable of winning a majority of seats in Leinster House within five years. Ironically, this meant that the party was in effect committed to the same policy on which Fianna Fáil had been founded in 1926; that when it would win sufficient seats it would then be in a position to overturn the Treaty settlement. Given how badly Sinn Féin had done in the 1961 general elections such a policy was delusory. As a token of its seriousness Ruairí Ó Brádaigh and Tom Mitchell would stand in Fermanagh/South Tyrone and Mid-Ulster respectively in the forthcoming Westminster elections in the North.

The movement's education department, directed by Roy Johnston, published the *Republican Manual of Education* in 1966 as part of the effort to encourage IRA Volunteers and Sinn Féin members to buy into the new strategy of popular radicalization, rather than preparing for a new phase of armed struggle. Johnston wrote the material which attempted to link successive phases of struggle and republican organization to differing social classes and economic interests; the conclusion being that the failure to put the interests of the working class at the head of the national revolution after 1916 laid the basis for its defeat.[12] Nowhere did the *Manual* refer to the traditional republican belief in the *de jure* legitimacy of the Republic that was the basis of the abstentionist policy. Indeed there was the explicit statement that the alternative to Fianna Fáil in 1926, and presumably in 1966, would have been the formation by the movement of a 'disciplined, incorruptible political movement that would be prepared to work as a minority within the Dáil, until it gained enough support to make it a majority'.[13]

There was recognition of the fact that Fianna Fáil in power had attempted to create an independent economy but had failed to address basic problems.[14] Worse, these failures had in the 1950s induced them to jettison the old policies and open the economy up to foreign capital. The inevitable consequence of this would be a return to complete dependence on British imperialism. The Free Trade Agreement represented the final capitulation in this process and hence the leadership of the national struggle must pass to the republican and labour movements.[15] In recognizing the reasons for the failure of the 1956–62 border campaign, and in applying a 'ruthless realism' to prevailing conditions, republicans could provide the key to integrating the national and social struggles.[16]

It was in this context then that both the state and the republican movement prepared to celebrate the fiftieth anniversary of the Easter Rising as their foundation stone and legitimation. It was an event that both viewed in completely opposing ways. For the state it represented a revolutionary event that had laid the basis for the existing twenty-six county Republic. Although there were obvious differences between Fianna Fáil and Fine Gael, much of that conflict had been ameliorated by the declaration of the Republic in 1948. For the IRA and Sinn Féin, however, the aims of 1916 had not been realized. Therefore, the fiftieth anniversary was an occasion to re-dedicate themselves to their achievement, rather than one to celebrate the existing Irish state. Appropriate official references to bringing about an end to partition would be welcomed.

The fact that the IRA was still actively pursuing those aims came to public notice on 6 February 1966 when its chief of staff, Cathal Goulding, was arrested at Portlaoise. He was found to be in possession of a Luger pistol and 3,000 rounds of .303-rifle ammunition on bandoliers. No evidence was presented as to what Goulding was actually doing with the gun, although this was at a time when critics of the leadership were claiming that weapons were being collected from units to be placed under the control of Goulding's allies. He was remanded in custody but later released on bail. The heightened garda pressure on the republican movement prompted Sinn Féin to mount a picket on special branch headquarters at Dublin Castle on 15 May. They demanded that the Detective Unit be disbanded and accused the branch of using phone-taps, searches and intimidation against republicans.[17]

The jury in the Goulding case failed to agree on the charges and he was acquitted. Almost all of the violent incidents that took place in early 1966 had occurred immediately prior to the trial, and this was seen by some republicans as evidence of state manipulation of dissident provocateurs. His defence consisted of a complaint that he was the subject of intensive garda surveillance, stopping, searching and arrest. The jury may have inferred that Goulding would have been more cautious about carrying weapons. He didn't deny the charges but insisted: 'If you find me guilty of this charge, you are finding every Irishman of every generation from Tone to the men of 1916 guilty because they used the same methods I am seeking to use now for the same reasons.'[18] Goulding's detention was also significant in that he was replaced as chief of staff during his absence by Seamus Costello, who used the opportunity to push forward with more radical proposals for internal change than perhaps Goulding himself believed were acceptable at that time.

While Goulding remained in custody, the Connolly Association called on the Minister for Justice Brian Lenihan to release him, as a mark of the desire to commemorate 1916.[19] The Irish Workers' Group was more aggressive in its response, intimating that 'the names of the officers who arrested Mr. Goulding and of the prosecuting officer have been noted by the Irish revolutionary movement'.[20] This support from the Marxist left was grist to the mill of those who were alleging a communist takeover of the IRA. The *Sunday Independent* returned to that theme in January 1966 when a feature story alleged that persistent efforts by the Irish Communist Organization to gain influence in the IRA had come to fruition in 1965. It saw this as an exact replication of the situation in 1934 when elements of the IRA leadership had been 'seduced' by the Republican Congress which it described as a classic communist United Front organization. The article alleged that 'a leading member of the Communist organization was accepted into membership of the so-called IRA, was given effective charge of their propaganda machine and in that capacity has become a most sinister and influential figure in the physical force–Communist front combination'.[21] This was an obvious reference to Roy Johnston. It was claimed that the new alliance had been behind the Irish Telephonists' Association (ITA) strike, as well as ground rent agitations in Midleton and over-housing in Griffith barracks.

Significantly, when the newspaper solicited the views of Minister Lenihan on the allegations he replied that he 'would not wish to dissent in any way from the facts given in this article or indeed from the views expressed'.[22] The IRA's reply was an indication that it was no longer quite so frightened of the communist taint. It admitted that it had been involved in the agitations described, although its only contribution to the ITA was individual financial donations and advice that the workers settle their dispute within existing trade union structures. Republican opposition to foreign take-overs 'should not be interpreted as implying connections with any ideology or doctrine other than that of the 1916 Proclamation'. The IRA was opposed to the Free Trade Agreement and welcomed public scrutiny of republican ideas and policies.[23] MacGiolla issued a similar statement on behalf of Sinn Féin and called on Lenihan to investigate the infiltration of Fianna Fáil by pro-British and anti-national elements.

Another leading IRA figure, Sean Garland, who had been wounded in the Brookeborough raid in January 1957, was arrested by gardaí at Mountrath, county Laois on 7 May 1966. When searched Garland was found to be in possession of a document which had been drawn up following the 1965 IRA army convention. Parts of it were released to the press and extracts resurfaced in the appendix to the Cameron Report of 1969 as evidence of the long-term strategy being pursued by the IRA. On 9 May 1966 Garland was sentenced to two months' imprisonment for possession of illegal documents and membership of an illegal organization. The seizure of the documents was an embarrassment to the IRA, especially as they were being moved to avoid their loss in expected raids. This caused a minor panic among ordinary Volunteers who had heard rumours about what the material consisted of. An IRA statement of 15 May claimed that what the newspapers had christened the 'Garland Plan' did not represent IRA policy but rather was 'a suggested outline for a policy'. The organization also found it significant that the government had only released material that related to the twenty-six counties, whereas most of the proposals concerned the British presence in Northern Ireland.[24] The IRA also accused Lenihan of attempting to stir up an atmosphere that would be conducive to the introduction of internment.[25]

The press had only been given part of what had been captured, and it was the section that discussed the political reorientation of the IRA in the twenty-six counties. The military plan was not released; it was, not surprisingly, handed over to the RUC and later turned up as part of the state's evidence to the Scarman tribunal in 1971 in order to prove that the IRA had deliberately instigated the disturbances of 1969. It is significant too that the Irish government did not believe that the IRA was seriously planning any military offensive in the Republic. Had they done so, they would obviously have reacted in a somewhat different fashion. On foot of the Scarman disclosures, the Official IRA issued a statement on 23 May 1971 that again stressed that the 1965 plan was 'never in fact more than a draft for discussion purposes'.[26] The IRA was, however, being less than honest as it is clear from a garda special branch report that the army council had approved the 'Garland Plan' in August 1966. The Scarman tribunal was told that the document was passed to the RUC by an 'A.1 source' in mid-1968. The IRA claimed that the document must have been passed over in 1966 and that the source was the authorities in Dublin.[27] It is almost certain, however, given disclosures of the exchanges between the Northern Irish authorities and the British government in late 1965 and early 1966, that the RUC special branch had received reliable information on the IRA plan before Garland was arrested.

The reports of the sentencing of Garland mentioned that the captured documents referred to a Sinn Féin conference, a military plan, a report on the *Brave Borderer* incident, and a report concerning suspicions that an arms dump in the Kilkenny/Wexford area had been found by the Gardaí the previous October.[28] When Lenihan released some of the material to members of the Oireachtas he stated that it would not be in the public interest to release the retained sections. The *Irish Times* published extensive extracts from the political section and the 'Garland Plan' received wide coverage in all of the national newspapers.[29] The hope of the authorities obviously was that this would both embarrass the IRA and create public unease over the military plan that remained unseen.

It is ironic, therefore, that the political effect of publishing the 'Garland Plan' was not exactly what might have been intended. The presidential election campaign was in progress at the time and, speaking in support of the Fine Gael candidate Tom O'Higgins, Oliver J. Flanagan, TD for Laois/Offaly, accused Fianna Fáil of attempting to use the IRA document as an election gimmick. He appeared to imply that the whole thing might have been a fabrication designed to distract attention away from strikes, unemployment and high taxation.[30] Others chose to see the plan as evidence of the political progress being made by the republican movement. A meeting of the Universities branch of the Labour Party congratulated the IRA for the insight into the social and economic situation that was contained in the document.[31]

Irish Democrat, less surprisingly, regarded it as evidence that the movement was grappling with real problems, including the reorganization of the movement itself. 'If the attempt is successful it will undoubtedly be a development of major importance in modern Irish politics.'[32] Writing in *Hibernia*, Francis Grose said that the release of the 'Garland Plan' was another example of the use of the IRA 'bogeyman' by Fianna Fáil. He questioned the manner in which the special branch was allowed to operate and criticized the 'belligerently uncooperative attitude' taken by the Minister for Justice on all security issues.[33]

While the IRA leadership was intent upon furthering the reorganization of the movement, it was also forced to deal with situations in which some Volunteers or former members had become involved in violent incidents. The military plan agreed by the IRA convention in 1965 envisaged an almost immediate campaign of low-level operations as part of the strategy leading to another offensive against the British presence in the six counties. The first phase included the targeting of enemy agents and was explicitly designed to ensure that Volunteers were 'psychologically prepared for future killing'.[34] In reality, the IRA did not kill or attempt to kill anyone between the 1965 convention and the outbreak of the Northern conflict in 1969. In fact, what took place was a series of operations that belonged more properly to the second phase of 'stunt operations' but all appeared to have ceased by early 1966. Some of these, like the plan to attack the British naval vessel *Lofoten* in Cork, were authorized; others were carried out by IRA Volunteers apparently without official sanction. Some were the work of people who had been involved in the dissident groups of the 1956–62 period or who had subsequently left the movement.

Richard Behal was one of those prominently involved in many of the incidents which brought public focus on the IRA. Having already gained some notoriety from his role in clashes over the sale of Easter lilies and the protest over the visit of Princess Margaret Windsor, Behal was arrested and charged with involvement in the attack on the *Brave Borderer* at Waterford on 10 September 1965. That attack, in which shots were fired, had been approved by the army council. Scuffles attended the court hearings and in November 1965 Behal and Walter Dunphy were sentenced to nine months for assaulting a garda, while Edward Kelly received six months.[35] What caused the most concern for the IRA leadership were Behal's alleged subsequent unapproved activities, not least a prison escape and a series of bombings in county Kilkenny. It wasn't the actual illegality of Behal's actions that was a source of concern, but more the fact that Behal was drawing unwanted attention on the IRA. He escaped from Limerick prison on 20 February and while he was on the run his group was held responsible for blowing up the automatic telephone exchange at Kilmacow, county Kilkenny on 13 April. A poster proclaiming 'IRA Struggle for Freedom' was discovered at the scene.

What is striking about the Kilkenny incidents is that, apart from the blowing up of the telephone exchange, all were quite petty and must have been more of an aggravation to the locals than a major cause of concern to the gardaí. Between 12 and 22 April, eight incidents took place involving the blocking of roads and damage to telephone and telegraph wires.[36] At the end of April, Behal wrote to the newspapers to announce that the actions in south Kilkenny had ceased now that attention had been drawn to the brutality meted out to republican prisoners. He also stated that he was not responsible for any incidents that had taken place outside of Kilkenny. Two incidents that appear to have been connected to those in Kilkenny had taken place in Dublin. On 17 April an attempt was made to blow up the automatic telephone exchange in Merrion Street and posters demanding the release of republican prisoners were discovered at the scene. On 20 April a petrol bomb was thrown through the window of the gymnasium of Cathal Brugha barracks in Dublin. A youth was later arrested and charged.[37]

The IRA abducted Behal and the former Dublin brigade OC Phil O'Donoghue, who had been involved in the Brookeborough raid in 1957. According to the garda report, a court martial sentenced them to death for unofficial actions and seizing IRA weapons. The sentence was lifted on condition that they take no further actions, although Behal was later banished from the country by the army council and left Ireland on 27 May. This was intended to prevent Behal forming a splinter group.[38] Behal eventually made it to New York from where he described himself as a 'political refugee' in a letter he wrote in July 1967 to the *Irish Democrat* opposing EEC membership. The *Democrat* for its part believed that Behal was a 'fine patriot'.[39]

The run-up to the fiftieth anniversary of the 1916 Rising encouraged others to embark upon military escapades. On 24 February 1966 the Royal British Legion hall near the Dublin docks was set on fire. The *Evening Herald* suggested that a communist organization was responsible.[40] This may not have been totally off the mark as there was a rumour in Dublin republican circles that a group of individuals associated with the Irish Workers' Party were responsible for a number of these incidents. A prominent member of the anti-apartheid movement was also alleged to be involved in training a group of people to carry out similar operations. The IRA issued a statement denying responsibility for the attack on the British Legion: 'It must be pointed out that all such incidents are contrary to declared Republican policy.'[41]

On 1 March the home of the British military attaché, Brigadier R.N Thicknesse, at Eglinton Road, Donnybrook, Dublin, was petrol bombed.[42] The device was thrown through the kitchen window and caused extensive damage, although the family was out at the time.[43] No group claimed responsibility but the attackers left a note calling on the attaché, as a symbol of partition and British occupation, to leave Ireland by Easter Sunday. If he refused he would be shot.[44]

The most spectacular of the incidents took place on the morning of 8 March when Nelson's pillar in O'Connell Street, Dublin was blown up. At least eight people were arrested but all were released without charge.[45] The IRA again issued a statement denying it had anything to do with the event, even though it was popularly attributed to the organization. The garda special branch, however, was aware that it had not been an official action and blamed it on 'the IRA splinter group'. Some of its members and members of the IRA were arrested, but although incriminating documents were found in their possession no evidence was found to implicate any of them in the bombing.[46] That was the eventual conclusion of the garda investigation as conveyed by Peter Berry to the taoiseach, Jack Lynch, in

1968. The gardaí were 'reasonably satisfied as to the identity of some of them' but had insufficient evidence to bring charges.[47] In 2001, Liam Sutcliffe, a former member of the IRA in Dublin, admitted the bombing.

Special Branch believed that there were two groups of former IRA dissidents, one based in Dublin and the other in Cork. There were forty-one in the Dublin group based around a 'hard core' of former Volunteers. They were described as a 'vicious and undisciplined group and who are likely to engage in violent acts of disorder'.[48] They had arms and explosives and members who were fully trained in their use. Besides being suspected of various violent acts, the group had also become involved in social and economic agitation.[49]

While some of those who believed the IRA had blown up Nelson's pillar regarded it as an occasion for levity, or even a 'service to the nation', as the ballad written by Joe Dolan, later of the ballad group Sweeney's Men, and popularized that year by the Dubliners, put it, others took a dim view. A week after the event an article in the University College Dublin magazine *Campus* saw it as perhaps only a portent of things to come. The piece was entitled 'Extremism' and was written by Michael O'Dea: 'Although many of the trappings of the IRA and its preposterous newspaper seem laughable and even quaint, we shall ignore at our peril the threat that this body poses to law and order in Northern Ireland and in the Republic ... It looks as if many more bombs, north and south, will shatter the silence of the night before the year is out.'[50] An editorial in *Hibernia* in November 1965 had expressed similar fears that the anniversary would provide the occasion for an 'IRA renaissance'.[51]

Officially, Easter week began with Éamon de Valera reviewing a defence forces parade at the GPO on Easter Sunday 10 April. Six hundred veterans of the rising also took part. That night RTE television broadcast 'Cuimncheán', an hour-long film celebrating the events of the Rising. The Garden of Remembrance was formally opened on Easter Monday and on 12 April, Tomas MacAnna directed a pageant in Croke Park involving thousands of school children. There were also dozens of events organized in other parts of the state.

The largest republican movement commemoration took place in Dublin on Easter Sunday and was subject to sustained attack by the gardaí. In his address at Glasnevin, Sinn Féin President Tomás MacGiolla described Sean Lemass' meeting with Northern Ireland Premier Terence O'Neill in January as a 'total surrender' and as recognition of British rule in Ireland. Attempts were made by the gardaí, under the command of Chief Superintendent Michael Fitzpatrick, to seize the flag of the IRA's Dublin brigade. This was unsuccessful and the subsequent violence led the Labour Party to condemn the gardaí, who it claimed acted 'without any provocation from members of the procession'.[52]

Around 5,000 people took part in the commemoration that proceeded from Stephen's Green to Glasnevin cemetery. Seamus Costello, acting chief of staff while Cathal Goulding was being held on an arms charge, was chief marshal. Addressing the colour party, he said: 'Now here is the order – this flag is getting to Glasnevin cemetery, I don't care how it is getting there, but there it is getting.' The gardaí made several attempts to seize a flag that bore the inscription 'Oglaigh na hEireann – Cathlan Atha Cliath' but were thwarted. Eight men with addresses in Dublin were charged and sentenced to terms of two and three months for their part in the disturbances.

A publication issued by the movement to mark the anniversary, entitled *The Separatist*, was banned under the Offences against the State Act. It was clearly an IRA initiative but it spoke of the organization in the third person as though the authors were examining it from the outside. The introductory article noted Sinn Féin's commitment to abstaining from parliament but that the party was increasingly involved in social issues: 'At the moment the movement seeks to weld all labour and nationalist elements under the banner of freedom and equality.'[53]

The pamphlet included an interview with an IRA Volunteer who declared that before they could face the British in a military campaign they would have to 'unite the people in a mass freedom movement'.[54] Such a campaign would, however, assuredly come and the authors were confident that the IRA possessed the capability to ensure that the next time they would be successful: 'They are experts in guerrilla warfare and are confident that military action in the future, coupled with economic resistance now, will win them the support of the Irish people.'[55]

John O'Connell, Labour TD for Dublin South-West, raised the seizure of *The Separatist* in Leinster House on 5 May. He wanted to know why copies of the pamphlet had been taken from the Drogheda printers where it was produced.[56] Minister for Justice Brian Lenihan referred to the criminal proceedings that had been taken and, when asked by O'Connell whether he himself had read it, replied that he had and that he was satisfied that it contained 'much matter which was a direct incitement of subversive activity'.[57] O'Connell had earlier enquired on what grounds the gardaí had been ordered to seize the flag on Easter Sunday. Lenihan replied that the organizers of the demonstration had been warned in advance that its display would not be tolerated as it represented an illegal organization. When O'Connell pressed the minister, Lenihan retorted: 'If the Deputy wants to join some of these subversive organisations, let him do so openly.'[58]

As with the anti-partition campaign of the early 1950s, the official and unofficial commemorations of 1916 contributed to a heightening of interest in militant republicanism. Some of this no doubt led to young people deciding to join Sinn Féin and the IRA. Certainly, up to this point, the movement had made little impact on public consciousness. Maria McGuire, who later joined the provisional movement, described her awareness of the IRA while a student at Trinity College Dublin: 'No-one talked about the IRA, and I knew of them only as figures from the past who wore trench coats and carried Thompson sub-machine guns. I knew nothing of the IRA's campaign in the Six Counties of 1957 [sic]–62 and the single event that impinged on our consciousness was an explosion in March 1966 which wrecked Nelson's Pillar.'[59]

The Northern Ireland government was far more concerned over the threat posed by the IRA in the run-up to the fiftieth anniversary of the 1916 Rising than its Dublin counterpart. On 9 December1965 O'Neill wrote to the British secretary of state at the Home Office, Frank Soskice, to report that 'we have been advised by the RUC that preparations are on foot for an early resumption of IRA activities in Northern Ireland'.[60] Among the evidence O'Neill referred to were reports that Goulding and Garland had visited IRA units in the North and that arms had been brought in from the Republic. O'Neill felt that those who had been trained were 'impatient for action' and that in 'many aspects the present situation is on a par with that which prevailed immediately before the last IRA campaign was mounted in 1956'.[61]

There had been a number of incidents including the breaking up of a British army film show in Belfast in October 1965, and five men in semi-military uniform were arrested close to the home of the British army GOC, Northern Ireland command in November. The RUC also claimed that thirty-four training camps had been held in the Republic in 1965.[62] Lemass told the British that he was 'aware of IRA activities and was watching them carefully. On the whole he thought that reports of the IRA tended to be exaggerated but this did not mean that he was taking them lightly.'[63]

Unionist fears were heightened by a petrol bomb attack on an RUC Land Rover in Andersonstown, Belfast, on 10 February 1966, for which the IRA denied responsibility.[64] The *Belfast Telegraph* also claimed that the gardaí were preparing for an IRA campaign to begin at Easter, based on the intensive recruitment and training programme carried out by the IRA over the previous twelve months.[65] In the course of a series of interviews with the *Belfast Telegraph* in February, MacGiolla denied that the IRA had plans for a campaign. Indeed he claimed that the organization was badly equipped for such a venture.[66]

As Easter approached, Northern Ireland Home Affairs Minister Robert McConnell put it on notice that no infringements of the Public Order Act or the Flags and Emblems Act would be tolerated.[67] Wilson was informed of renewed concerns from Belfast but was assured by Home

Secretary Roy Jenkins that his office was in contact with their counterparts in Dublin 'who were being very co-operative'.[68] On 4 April Jenkins
sent the prime minster a lengthy report on the situation and the precautions that were being taken in the run-up to Easter: 'Information
received both from Scotland Yard and the Northern Ireland Government
shows that the threat is a real one. During the last year or so there has
been a steady build up of membership of the IRA, and it was estimated
at the end of last year that there were some 3,000 trained members or
supporters who could be called out in an emergency. Military training has
been carried out at camps held secretly in various parts of Ireland, and an
adequate supply of arms and ammunition is held.'[69] In response, the RUC
stepped up protection of personnel and installations and there were
plans to reinforce the police with the army if that was necessary.

Apart from minor incidents Easter 1966 passed off peacefully insofar
as the IRA was concerned. Despite the lack of evidence of any planned
actions by the IRA, the Northern authorities were still intent on taking
action against republicans apparently on the basis of new intelligence.
Unionist fears centred on plans for an Easter commemoration to be held
at the Casement Park GAA grounds in Belfast and the danger that this
would provoke a counter-demonstration by Paisleyites. In consequence,
the authorities had introduced a ban on cross-border rail traffic and mon-
itored road movements. They did not, however, believe that they would
require military assistance.[70]

Craig defended the actions of the Northern government as 'necessary
precautions to deal with the threatened IRA outbreak'.[71] While activity
had decreased, he claimed that republicans continued to pose a threat.
Stormont Republican Labour MP Harry Diamond ridiculed this as a
'mare's nest' and contrasted the hysteria over the IRA to the actual murders that had been carried out by the revived Ulster Volunteer Force.
Diamond was referring to the murder by the UVF of John Scullion in
Clonard on 27 May and of Peter Ward from Dublin on 26 June. Gusty
Spence and two others were arrested and charged with Ward's murder
and the UVF was proscribed.[72]

Whatever fears may have surrounded the fiftieth anniversary, there was
a suspicion that the Northern government had exaggerated the threat to
coincide with the Westminster election campaign in which polling took
place on 31 March. Republicans only stood in five of the twelve constituencies. Gerry Fitt, standing as a Republican Labour candidate, was
given a free run in West Belfast and won the seat with a majority of over
2,000. The republican candidates took 82,089 votes with Tom Mitchell
coming closest to being elected in Mid-Ulster with 47.75 per cent. The
overall vote in the five constituencies contested was slightly down from
1964 when they had secured 83,534.

The Wolfe Tone Society provided the most comprehensive outline of where it stood in the August 1966 issue of *Tuairisc* in a long article entitled 'Our Ideas'. It was written by Anthony Coughlan and outlined the strategy that republicans were to pursue through the civil rights movement. Coughlan's paper was read to the meeting at Kevin Agnew's home in Maghera that set the basis for the formal unveiling of the Northern Ireland Civil Rights Association in November 1966. According to 'Our Ideas', the purpose of the society was to provide the movement for a republic with 'the intellectual equipment' and ideology to defeat its enemies, to convince the Irish people that it was people thus equipped who deserved to be given the 'leadership of the nation'.[73] Republicanism was recognized as the 'conscience of the Irish people' despite its lack of intellectual vigour.[74]

Their project was one that might take many years. *Tuairisc* itself was 'small and select in its circulation' and aimed at 'opinion leaders'. The article was critical of the intellectual poverty of the republican movement. 'It is time that Irish republicans began to take ideas and theory seriously' and to counter the 'anti-national ideas and theories' that dominated discourse. 'We may ask where has the republican movement put forward an authoritative criticism of the Second Programme of Economic Expansion ... where is the ruthless analysis of the failure of either republicanism or Labour significantly to influence government policy in the twenty six counties since the southern state was founded?'[75]

The republican movement possessed people with the ability to do so but needed to overcome the 'stupid counterposing of the "practical" men and the "intellectuals"'.[76] There was a direct reference to the Cork-based *An Phoblacht* group who were using 'pseudo-revolutionary rhetoric and phraseology' to attack those in the republican movement who were seeking to organize a more vigorous struggle.[77] The appearance of such publications emphasized the need for the development of revolutionary republican theory. Defending the WTS against the attacks made on it, the writer claimed that those who were the object of attack were 'making an indispensable and powerful contribution to the movement for a free and independent republic'.[78]

The republican movement represented the working class, small farmers, small business people and progressive intellectuals and professionals. Co-operatives were the arena of struggle for small farmers and trade unions for workers but only a trade union movement with a national consciousness could work towards expanding employment and controlling the export of capital.[79]

Northern Ireland was undergoing rapid change. That placed the onus on republicans to develop the 'utmost flexibility and political astuteness and to strive to free their minds from outdated forms of thought'.[80] There was a possibility that British-imposed reform might lead to the coming together of Catholic and Protestant workers by destroying the mechanism of discrimination.[81] That echoed the argument made in C. Desmond Greaves' book, *The Irish Question*. The key to that was the broadest grass-roots organization and through the trade unions around the issues of the franchise, housing etc. It was also vital to secure broad unity and avoid antagonizing old feuds.[82] Such a strategy would help republicans to break out of their isolation and impotence.[83] It was argued: 'Republicans and nationally minded people should therefore be on their guard against provocateurs, people sent into their ranks mouthing pseudo-revolutionary phrases, pretending to act as firebrands, out to precipitate some incident which would give the Unionists an excuse for a pogrom. Let us be on our guard!'[84]

The writer predicted that the most likely outcome was a victory for the O'Neill faction in the Unionist Party and that this would destroy the illusions of Protestant workers in Orangeism. That would open up the 'long-term possibility' of reaching out to the Orange masses, and the people best placed to do so were republicans because of their democratic traditions and not being associated with Catholic sectarianism.[85] The August issue of *Tuairisc* also carried a piece by Jack Bennett, a Belfast Protestant and member of the Communist Party of Northern Ireland (CPNI), who wrote as 'Kanensas'. Bennett provided a somewhat different analysis of Paisleyism, not as an ultra-right-wing fringe but as 'the uninhibited expression of the fundamentals of Unionism'.[86] The logic of this was that the optimistic prognosis contained in 'Our Ideas' was unlikely to come about, but Bennett drew the opposite conclusion and claimed that most Protestants were repulsed by Paisley and that this would lead them to reject unionism 'as such'.[87] When MacGiolla was asked about the proposals in 'Our Ideas' he said that it did not necessarily reflect Sinn Féin policy but that much of their thinking was contained in it. Sinn Féin supported political action but if force was used against a political campaign then force might be justified.[88]

The main initiative taken by the WTS in 1966 was to organize the conference at Maghera that is generally regarded as the formal beginning of the civil rights movement. In June MacEoin began to make arrangements for the meeting and a sub-committee was established comprising himself, Coughlan, Johnston and Micheál Ó Loinsigh. MacEoin was also to contact republicans in Belfast regarding their attitude to the participation of Betty Sinclair of the CPNI who was a delegate to the Belfast Trades Council.[89] On 26 July it was agreed to hold the meeting at Kevin Agnew's house. The agenda was to focus on civil rights, discrimination and the trade unions.[90] Roy Johnston and Seamus MacGabhann gave a report from the meeting on 23 August where it had been agreed to establish a formal civil rights committee and to invite various organizations to participate. Former IRA Chief of Staff Sean Cronin wrote to Johnston from the United States on 5 September welcoming the imitative and urging that a campaign in support of something similar to the US Bill of Rights be established.[91]

There was evidence that the tenor of WTS proposals irked even some within the republican movement who were otherwise supportive of the new strategy of which it was an integral part. Although Prionnsias de Rossa wrote to Richard Roche requesting 'ideas' for the annual Dublin Sinn Féin Wolfe Tone week, he later complained over what he believed was a bias within the society towards the Labour Party.[92] He claimed: 'Labour has done very little to preserve or advance the national ideal and it is not likely to in the near future whereas Sinn Féin has a ready made national attitude and with encouragement and additional capable personnel could become a strong force within a short period. The negative attitude towards Sinn Féin will have to be changed. The sniping from the outside by otherwise sound republicans will have to stop if Sinn Féin is ever to gain ground.'[93] Despite his concerns, De Rossa was formally proposed as a member of the WTS on 13 September.[94]

The editorial in the July 1966 Cork *An Phoblacht* boasted that they were one of the groups described by the republican leadership as 'extremists' and 'splitters'. A later issue described the Wolfe Tone Society as 'a front for the clique which presently aspire to take over the IRA lock, stock and barrel'.[95] They also claimed to have information on the plan to disarm the IRA.[96] The group said that they based themselves, as a revolutionary socialist republican organization, on the IRA programme of 1933. There could be no compromise with a movement that had become reformist. Eoin MacDonaill attacked IRA General Army Order No. 8 which forbade military action in the twenty-six counties. He claimed that this obliged captured Volunteers to hand over weapons of better quality than any that had been available to the IRA of earlier periods. Much of the criticism was directed at the Sinn Féin social and economic policy.[97]

One of the issues that caused the most controversy within the movement in 1966 was a letter that Johnston wrote to the *United Irishman* in June in which he condemned the recitation of the Rosary at republican commemorations as sectarian.[98] Johnston also felt that commemorations were pointless unless those attending were given some written material that provided them with political direction. Johnston's letter on the Rosary led to a storm of protest with Seán MacStíofáin ordering that the paper not be distributed in his command area. MacStíofáin was suspended for six months, reduced on appeal to two, and re-elected at the IRA convention in October. In his autobiography MacStíofáin makes the point that his suspension had nothing to do with Goulding, who at the time was being held in prison.[99] Another consequence was that virtually the entire membership of Kerry Sinn Féin, one of the few parts of the country where it had genuine popular and electoral support, resigned in protest.

One of the themes of the new departure undertaken by the republican movement was unity between the republican and labour traditions. This was something that had long been advocated by Greaves in the columns of the *Irish Democrat*. It was taken up by Irish communists in 1961/62 and, by 1965, regularly referred to by the republican leadership. Addressing a conference of Labour students, MacGiolla spoke of how republicans were coming to understand the close relationship between republicanism and socialism.[100] Peadar O'Donnell, who had called for unity between the two movements, chaired the conference.[101] The April 1966 issue of the *Irish Democrat* carried a feature that asked a number of people how they thought Ireland had changed since 1916. Johnston saw the development of state industry in the twenty-six counties as the main achievement. On the question of republican/labour unity, Johnston didn't believe that was yet feasible but that it might come about as a consequence of republican involvement in social issues. An article by 'Enquirer' contained a somewhat convoluted definition of the republican movement as representative of 'classes intermediate between the capitalists and the working class; small businessmen, artisans, self-employed men, small professional men, teachers, lesser civil servants, white collar (but some manual) workers, and small farmers'.[102]

The Communist Party of Northern Ireland echoed the calls for unity: 'The Republican movement understands the relationship of economic problems to national independence. What is needed is an alliance between these two great movements such as we had in 1916 to defeat the plans of the people who would sell the whole country to monopoly capitalism.'[103] The Trotskyist Irish Workers' Group also called for the creation of a united front of labour, small farmers and republicans to resist government plans in the twenty-six counties.[104] Acting IRA chief of staff, Seamus Costello, when addressing the Belfast Easter commemoration, harked back to the brief display of solidarity between Protestant and Catholic workers during the 1932 Outdoor Relief dispute.[105] *The Irish Communist* welcomed what it saw as a return to a revolutionary nationalist position by the republican movement but claimed that an alliance between republicans and the labour movement was not yet possible.[106]

One of the areas to which the IRA paid particular attention during 1966 was the campaign by the National Farmers' Association (NFA). This involved withholding rates to support their demand for the state to provide more assistance to the sector. An army council meeting in October took the decision to become actively involved in the agitation and instructed command OCs to have local Volunteers infiltrate the NFA. On

25 October IRA general headquarters instructed Volunteers to take part but that only those who were actually farmers should do so. If the NFA organized another march in Dublin, each command area was to organize a group of republican farmers to participate. They would be co-ordinated by the IRA in Dublin to carry out whatever actions might take place during the course of the march. Ironically, the farmers' protests adopted as their theme an old IRA marching song, 'Off to Dublin in the Green', although few can have been aware of the close interest their republican contemporaries were taking in their activities.[107]

There was some evidence that the government was concerned about republicans and opposition from groups like the farmers and striking workers in 1966. In a speech to the Social Study Congress held in the National Stadium on 26 June 1966, Lemass referred to what he termed the ambivalent attitude of people towards illegal acts and organizations. While this could be taken as targeted at the IRA, the Taoiseach expanded his definition of what constituted unacceptable behaviour to include pickets placed on Leinster House and the conduct of industrial disputes. He may very well have been informed in such opinions by the content of the Garland document. As part of his preparations to meet the British prime minister, Harold Wilson, in December 1966, the new taoiseach, Jack Lynch (who succeeded Lemass on 10 November), requested that the Justice Department supply him with a 'brief note' on the current state of the IRA in case the British side should raise the issue. Lynch wanted to reassure the British that the IRA was not a current threat and that the gardaí were well informed of its intentions. While the republican movement did not seek to exploit the 1916 commemorations in the manner suspected by many of their adversaries, the IRA was certainly in the midst of an historic transformation.

NOTES

1. *Dáil debates*, Volume 219, 1140 ff.
2. Ibid., 1163.
3. Ibid., 1167.
4. Ibid., 1801.
5. *Tuairisc*, no. 5 (January/February 1966).
6. *An Phoblacht*, no. 4 (March 1966), p. 6.
7. *Tuairisc*, no. 5 (January/February 1966).
8. Ibid., no. 7 (31 August 1966), p. 6.
9. Ibid., p. 7.
10. *Irish Democrat*, January 1966.
11. *United Irishman*, March 1965.
12. *Republican Manual of Education*, Part I (1966), p. 19.
13. Ibid., p. 33.
14. Ibid., p. 37.
15. Ibid., p. 45.
16. Ibid., p. 46.
17. *Irish Times*, 16 May 1966.

18. Ibid., 20 April 1966.
19. *Irish Democrat*, April 1966.
20. *Irish Workers' News*, no. 72 (20 February 1966).
21. *Sunday Independent*, 2 January 1966, 'Communist's Quiet revolution in IRA Proves New Threat'.
22. Ibid.
23. Ibid.
24. *Irish Times*, 16 May 1966.
25. *United Irishman*, June 1966.
26. *Violence and Civil Disturbances in Northern Ireland in 1969: Report of the Tribunal of Inquiry*, Cmd.566, Vol. II (Belfast 1972), Appendix B, p. 52.
27. Ibid.
28. *Irish Times*, 10 May 1966.
29. Ibid., 14 May 1966.
30. Ibid., 19 May 1966.
31. Ibid., 23 May 1966.
32. *Irish Democrat*, June 1966.
33. *Hibernia*, July 1966.
34. Department of Taoiseach, National Archives of Ireland, 98/6/495, Garda report 3C/15/66, p. 25.
35. *Irish Times*, 25 November 1965.
36. Garda report, 3C/15/66, p. 51.
37. Garda report, 3C/15/66, p. 50.
38. Garda report, 3C/15/66, p. 52.
39. *Irish Democrat*, July 1967.
40. *Evening Herald*, 25 February 1966.
41. Irish Republican Publicity Bureau (IRPB) statement, 25 February 1966 in National Library of Ireland, MS, 22,938.
42. *Irish Press*, 2 March 1966.
43. *The People*, 6 March 1966.
44. Garda report 3C/15/66, p. 51.
45. *Irish Press*, 10 March 1966.
46. Garda report 3C/15/66.
47. DT, NAI, 99/1/22, Note from Peter Berry to Runaí, Department of Taoiseach, 17 January 1968.
48. Garda report, 3C/15/66, p. 56.
49. Garda report, 3C/15/66, p. 56.
50. *Campus*, I, 6 (15 March 1966).
51. *Hibernia*, November 1965.
52. *Irish Democrat*, May 1966.
53. *The Separatist*, Dublin (1966), p. 3.
54. Ibid., p.16.
55. Ibid.
56. *Dáil debates*, vol. 222, 1429.
57. Ibid., vol. 222, 1430.
58. Ibid., vol. 222, 1059.
59. Maria McGuire, *To Take Arms: A Year in the Provisional IRA* (London, 1973), p. 14.
60. Public Record Office, PREM 13/980, O'Neill to Soskice, 12 December 1965.
61. PREM 13/980, O'Neill to Soskice, 12 December 1965.
62. Ibid.
63. PREM 13/980, Wilson to RFD Shuffrey, Home Office, 13 December 1965.
64. *Belfast Telegraph*, 11 February 1966.
65. Ibid., 15 February 1966.
66. Ibid., 17 February 1966.
67. *Northern Ireland Commons debates*, vol. 62, 1529.
68. PREM 13/980, memo of 4 March 1966.
69. PREM 13/980, Jenkins to Wilson, 4 May 1966.
70. PREM 13/980, memo of 15 April 1966.
71. *Northern Ireland Commons debates*, vol. 64, 2280.
72. Ibid.

73. *Tuairisc*, no. 7 (31 August 1966), p. 1.
74. Ibid., p.2.
75. Ibid., p.3.
76. Ibid.
77. Ibid., p. 4.
78. Ibid.
79. Ibid., p. 5.
80. Ibid., p. 6.
81. Ibid., p. 7.
82. Ibid., p. 8.
83. Ibid., p. 9.
84. Ibid.
85. Ibid., p. 10.
86. Ibid., p. 11.
87. Ibid., p. 12.
88. *Irish Independent*, 16 August 1966.
89. Wolfe Tone Society minutes, 5 July 1966.
90. Ibid., 26 July 1966.
91. Wolfe Tone Society minutes, Letter of 5 September 1966 from Sean Cronin to Roy Johnston.
92. Wolfe Tone Society minutes, Letter of 16 May 1966 from Prionnsias de Rossa to Richard Roche.
93. Wolfe Tone Society minutes, Letter of 14 July 1966 from De Rossa to Roy Johnston.
94. Wolfe Tone Society minutes, 13 September 1966.
95. *An Phoblacht*, no. 8 (1966), p. 4.
96. Ibid., p. 5.
97. *An Phoblacht*, no. 6 (July 1966).
98. *United Irishman*, June 1966.
99. Seán MacStíofáin, *Memoirs of a Revolutionary* (London, 1976), p. 96.
100. *Irish Democrat*, March 1966.
101. Ibid.
102. Ibid., April 1966.
103. *Unity*, no. 5 (15 January 1966).
104. *Irish Workers' News*, 1 May 1966.
105. *United Irishman*, May 1966.
106. *The Irish Communist*, no. 6 (May 1966).
107. Garda report 3C/15/66, p. 25.

Appendix I:
The 1916 Proclamation

POBLACHT NA h-EIREANN
THE PROVISIONAL GOVERNMENT OF THE
IRISH REPUBLIC
TO THE PEOPLE OF IRELAND

IRISHMEN AND IRISHWOMEN: In the name of God and of the dead generations from which she receives her old tradition of nationhood, Ireland, through us, summons her children to her flag and strikes for her freedom.

Having organized and trained her manhood through her secret revolutionary organization, the Irish Republican Brotherhood, and through her open military organizations, the Irish Volunteers and the Irish Citizen Army, having patiently perfected her discipline, having resolutely waited for the right moment to reveal itself, she now seizes that moment, and, supported by her exiled children in America and by gallant allies in Europe, but relying in the first on her own strength, she strikes in full confidence of victory.

We declare the right of the people of Ireland to the ownership of Ireland, and to the unfettered control of Irish destinies, to be sovereign and indefeasible. The long usurpation of that right by a foreign people and government has not extinguished the right, nor can it ever be extinguished except by the destruction of the Irish people. In every generation the Irish people have asserted their right to national freedom and sovereignty; six times during the past three hundred years they have asserted it in arms. Standing on that fundamental right and again asserting it in arms in the face of the world, we hereby proclaim the Irish Republic as a Sovereign Independent State. And we pledge our lives and the lives of our comrades-in-arms to the cause of its freedom, of its welfare, and of its exaltation among the nations.

The Irish Republic is entitled to, and hereby claims, the allegiance of every Irishman and Irish woman. The Republic guarantees religious and civil liberty, equal rights and equal opportunities of all its citizens, and declares its resolve to pursue the happiness and prosperity of the whole nation and of all its parts, cherishing all the children of the nation equally, and oblivious of the differences carefully fostered by an alien government, which have divided a minority in the past.

Until our arms have brought the opportune moment for the establishment of a permanent National Government, representative of the whole people of Ireland and elected by the suffrages of all her men and women, the Provision Government, hereby constituted, will administer the civil and military affairs of the Republic in trust for the people.

We place the cause of the Irish Republic under the protection of the Most High God, Whose blessing we invoke upon our arms, and we pray that no one who serves that cause will dishonour it by cowardice, inhumanity, or rapine.   In this supreme hour the Irish nation must, by its valour and discipline and by the readiness of its children to sacrifice themselves for the common good, prove itself worthy of the august destiny to which it is called.

Signed on behalf of the Provisional Government,

THOMAS J. CLARKE
SEAN MaC DIARMADA
THOMAS MaCDONAGH
P.H. PEARSE
EAMONN CEANNT
JAMES CONNOLLY
JOSEPH PLUNKETT

Appendix II:
Introduction to
C. Desmond Greaves

1916 as History:
The Myth of the Blood Sacrifice

This essay was written in 1966 by the labour historian C. Desmond Greaves (1913–1988) on the 50th anniversary of the Easter Rising. That was before the 'Troubles' in Northern Ireland broke out in 1969 and before Ireland joined the European Economic Community in 1973. It was republished in pamphlet form on the occasion of the Rising's 75th anniversary in 1991, with references compiled by the present writer as Greaves' literary executor.

The pamphlet was written as a response to an article on the Rising in the magazine *History Today* by Mr. A.P. Ryan, assistant editor of the London *Times*. In his introduction, Greaves cautions that an essay written only fifty years after such a major event cannot offer 'the impossible, the mature assessment of 1916 in all its aspects'. Rather, his essay 'attempts to outline a basis for the criticism of the 'official' historical assessment of 1916 which has been presented in the press during the recent period'. He continued: 'I am of course not anxious to stand over every dot and comma of this account. But I offer for discussion as a more credible version of the history of 1916, and of 1916's significance for history, than that produced by the assistant editor of the Times'.

Why republish this essay? One reason is that in the course of his researches for his biographies *The Life and Times of James Connolly, Liam Mellows and the Irish Revolution* and *Sean O'Casey: Politics and Art*, Greaves got to know many participants in the Easter Rising, War of Independence and Civil War. This gave him a special insight into the causes, course and consequences of these events. A second reason is that Greaves was probably Ireland's leading Marxist historian and, as such, his analysis of the class interests involved in these events comprises an essential perspective.

A third reason is that the blood sacrifice myth is still influential. While claiming descent from 1916 is central to the myth of origin of Ireland's bourgeoisie and those running the contemporary Irish State, the initiators of the Rising clearly sought a different kind of Republic from that which we have now. For one thing, they sought an independent state in a country which was not partitioned. A century after the Rising nearly all shades of Irish nationalism and republicanism accept that, practically speaking, Ireland can only be reunited with the consent of a majority of the people of the North. That, in turn, entails Nationalists persuading contemporary Unionists, or a significant section of them, that a coming-together with their nationalist and Catholic fellow countrymen is in their best political and economic interests as Irish people. Greaves would have approved.

It was Greaves who pioneered in his political work in Britain from the mid-1950s onward the idea of a civil rights campaign as the way to break Unionist hegemony in Northern Ireland by removing the rational basis for unionism as an ideology of supremacy over Nationalists. This was an idea which was taken up by the 1960s Northern Civil Rights Movement, although Greaves would have held that the British Government has a duty to join the ranks of the persuaders as well.

The 1916 leaders sought a Republic in 'unfettered control of Irish destinies'. They saw such control as the prerequisite of a state that would 'cherish all the children of the nation equally'. The contemporary Irish state is clearly not in unfettered control of Irish destinies. The European Union makes the majority of Ireland's laws each year and has supremacy in any case of conflict. Ireland no longer possesses a currency of its own and, unlike all truly sovereign states, has no control over its rate of interest, credit conditions or exchange rates. It is barred from signing commercial treaties with other states yet legally obliged to seek to align its foreign policy with the rest of the European Union. Ireland is subject to periodic fines imposed from outside for failing to obey European laws.

The Irish Government and principal parties have approved a constitutional treaty which would give the EU the legal form of a European Federation, with its own legal personality, separate from and superior to its member states. This is similar to the manner in which the United States of America is separate from and superior to California and New York, and the relationship between Federal Germany and its constituent Lander.

Greaves' essay demolished the myth that 1916 was a semi-suicidal effort on the part of a group of idealists intent on a symbolical blood sacrifice. As matters transpired, the administrative blunder of General Maxwell's executions led to a national reaction which, in turn, stimulated an independence movement from which came the modern Irish state. Such a myth suits those who are reluctant to question the character of that state or to accept that it is far removed from that envisaged by those whose values and ideals were set forth in the Proclamation of the Republic of Easter 1916. That Republic is still worth striving for today.

Anthony Coughlan
2008

1916
AS HISTORY

The Myth of the Blood Sacrifice

C. Desmond Greaves

THE FULCRUM PRESS
DUBLIN 1991
The Desmond Greaves Estate

INTRODUCTION

A Jubilee coincides with the fifty year limit and is not therefore an ideal time for assessing an event historically. Official papers, for what they are worth, have yet to be fully opened. Eye-witnesses and participants are still alive, and protected by the law of libel. Old men and their families can have strong vested interests in past events. And of course in the general sense these past events are enshrined in surviving relationships which are part of the structure of living politics. This contribution does not therefore offer the impossible, the mature assessment of 1916 in all its aspects, but attempts to outline a basis for the criticism of the "official" historical assessment of 1916 which has been presented in the press during the recent period.

One thing is now clear. The Irish question is not dead. Britain still has, as she always had, an Irish policy. And it is well to bear in mind what that now is, and to note recent changes. Broadly speaking it can be defined as "integration within integration", the economic and political consolidation of these islands under the hegemony of British monopoly-capitalism as an aspect of the consolidation (through E.E.C. or other means) of neo-colonialist Europe. Obviously the propaganda necessary to popularising this line of development, given existing susceptibilities, calls for some reassessment of, not to say tinkering with, the facts of history.

Take for example the attitude of the British press to Mr Lemass's regime today, and contrast it with that taken towards Mr De Valera's. I well recall during the war a writer (in the Evening Standard, I think) describing De Valera's as "this rebel Government of doubtful authenticity". It had abolished the oath of allegiance to the British crown, taking advantage of the abdication of King Edward VIII – just as of old its predecessors of Grattan's Parliament availed of the insanity of George III. It had adopted a new constitution contrary to the provisions of the Free State Constitution Act of 1922. The implication was that it was not a genuine Government at all.

Before De Valera gave place to Lemass, a coalition had proclaimed a Republic and left the Commonwealth, and was pursuing an embarrassingly uncommitted policy in the United Nations. But on Mr Lemass's succession all was forgiven. "For the first time since 1922 there are men in Dublin with whom it is possible to do business" was one newspaper comment. And business was thereafter done. Big business shook hands across a border that was last week sealed to Republicans, even railway services being banned. (1)   There were plans to co-ordinate all Ireland economically for the benefit of British-controlled monopoly. Ireland followed Britain in applying for membership of the Common Market in 1961. And the independent line in foreign affairs faded away. Then came the 1965 Anglo–Irish Free Trade Agreement, which is seen by many in Ireland as an effort to re-establish the country's role as an agricultural hinterland to industrial Britain.

In the midst of this development came the jubilee of 1916. It was said by Professor Clarkson (2) when he was young and cynical that "in Ireland politics cannot be conducted without the aid of the glorious dead". How were the men who died for a Republic in 1916 to be harnessed to the task of re-establishing the Union? Clearly the Irish bourgeoisie must have a story. The story is roughly that into the quietly evolving affairs of a contented or indifferent people leapt a suicidal band of revolutionary idealists determined to save the soul of the nation through a blood sacrifice. They aroused not enthusiasm but hostility, and forfeited their lives. But then "a terrible beauty was born". All that was unchanged by the Rising was "changed utterly" by the executions. Thus from the British point of view General Maxwell's reign of terror was an unforgivable blunder. From the Irish it was the justification of the blood sacrifice. Inspired by the sacrifice the Irish people accomplised feats which otherwise would have been impossible, and thus finally was established the Ireland of today in which the national aspiration has been achieved and too enthusiastic Republicans can be put in jail.

MYTHS OF ORIGIN

Most ancient peoples have their myths of origin, which are often highly fanciful though usually revealing. We have before us simultaneously the Irish bourgeoisie's myth of how it achieved State power, and British Imperialism's myth of how it established neo-colonialism in Ireland. It is British policy we are mainly concerned with here, and I suggest that we examine it in the account given by the assistant-editor of the London *Times*, Mr A.P. Ryan, who published an article, "*The Easter Rising*", in the April issue of *History Today*. From internal evidence I am convinced that the article on the *Times* leader page shortly afterwards was from the same pen. As is known, Mr Ryan has published a *History of Ireland* and an account of the Curragh mutiny which most people have thought somewhat favourable to the Conservative Party. One of the points he made in it was that the

Unionist defiance of the Liberal Government, which as is known involved the establishment of a Provisional Government, the arming of Volunteers and extensive gun-running, was comprehensible in view of the fact that the Liberals in the 1910 election had asked for no mandate to introduce Home Rule into Ireland. That is worth bearing in mind.

I have quoted Yeats, that great myth-maker who assimilated every event to his own aristocratic romanticism. I must quote Ryan for the record. "A public opinion poll taken in Ireland . . . on the eve of the Dublin Easter Rising would have shown most men and women in favour of Home Rule, some content with the status quo, and only a small minority thinking in terms of armed insurrection." So much for the people. What of the authorities? "Poor Mr Birrell, the Irish Secretary, had allowed himself to say of the 'disaffected' men, 'I have them under the microscope.'"

Mr Ryan then continues, "What neither he nor other better judges of Irish form had reckoned with was a suicidal gesture in assertion of the rights of Ireland. But that is what happened." His evidence is Pearse's alleged admission at the Court-martial on 2 May that "he had been Commandant-General Commanding-in-Chief of the forces of the Irish Republic" (if the grammar seems curious I give it as 'twas given to me) and "had acted in fact in flat disobedience to superior orders."

Before quoting Ryan further here I must interpose that he omits the point that Pearse accompanied his acceptance of sole personal responsibility with the request that his life alone should be forfeit and his comrades should be spared. It is evidence of the position after the Rising, but is insufficient for founding an estimate of the Rising itself. Ryan records that "Volunteers taken prisoner were hooted by the Dublin crowds. For a day or two it seemed that Pearse's blood-bath had failed in its object. Then came the executions carried out by British military authority. They led to a complete revulsion of feeling.

The Rising drove Home Rule off the stage, created a climate of opinion in which the guerilla war against British troops and Black-and-Tans could be waged, and led through civil war and much bloodshed to the establishment of the Republic. Pearse won. How and why he did so makes a study in Irish psychology . . . ."

This quotation gives the curious impression that once Maxwell had carried out the executions, British Imperialism committed no more sins against Ireland. Ireland had done with it. Yet it contains a reference to the Black-and-Tans, who were certainly not in Ireland in 1916, and were only sent when the Royal Irish Constabulary, unreliable and weakened by resignations, was unable to control the country. That five years of class and national struggle could be motivated merely by a memory is to caricature Clarkson, and would certainly provide an interesting study in "psychology". That is, of course, if it were true.

Let us now compare the myth as it unfolds with the realities as far as we are able to ascertain them.

Bourgeois writers are always at their most naive in accounting for the mood of the masses. That the gas-worker, shop-keeper or taxi-driver is just as complex and individualized a product of history as the senator on the bench is incredible to him. That the mainstream of history runs through the lower orders seems preposterous. Hence the masses are either duped or inspired by agitators or idealists; or respond to some vague entity called the "spirit of unrest". Let us consider some of the actual experiences of the people just before 1916, when their mood will become more easily understood, and the absurd gallup-poll antithesis "are you for Home Rule or insurrection?" can be avoided.

IRELAND BEFORE 1916

In 1916 the majority of the Irish people still lived in the country. In the preceding thirty-five years revolutionary changes had taken place. As a result of the agitations led by the Land League, which at one time organized practically the whole agrarian population of Ireland, the tenantry had been progressively transformed into State mortgagees. The process began with the more prosperous tenants and being about half finished by the Birrell Act (3) left a countryside acutely divided along class lines but with its traditional leaders temporarily satisfied. Agrarian agitation nevertheless continued throughout the west, alongside agitation on behalf of town tenants. The larger farmers together with the bourgeoisie of the country towns (mostly merchants) were members of the United Irish League and supported its Parliamentary Party led by Redmond. It must be borne in mind, however, that there was great variety in the Irish countryside, the three main divisions, the cattle-breeding west, the cattle-fattening east and the dairy-farming south, forming an integrated system whose division of labour expressed itself in different proportions of family and wage labour. For the remaining tenantry and the landless men Home Rule meant that those who had already benefited from land division would hurry on with its completion; at the same time the fact that they seemed inclined to hurry slowly led to dissatisfaction. This expressed itself partly through the old secret agrarian societies, and partly through the physical force movement, the Irish Republican Brotherhood. It was thanks to the personal intervention of Sean MacDiarmada, one of the signatories of the Easter Proclamation, and himself a Connaught man, that the I.R.B. in Connaught were permitted to hold membership in the "moonlighting" societies. Home Rule was, of course, the demand of the bourgeoisie. Up to the eighteen-forties the demand had been "the repeal of the Union". In the eighteen-seventies this was scaled down to "federalism", a demand which had in O'Connell's day flourished mainly in Belfast. The effect of the Union had been both relative and absolute elimination of Irish industry by British competition, and a constant agrarian crisis thanks to cheap food from virgin lands. The essential demand was thus fiscal independence. Whether Gladstone's conversion to Home Rule was motivated by the high-minded considerations his biographers attribute to him, or whether he was also weighing the advantages of transferring the cost of land-purchase to an Irish Exchequer, control of tariffs neither he nor his successors would grant. Home Rule was thus born in chains. Worse than that, the Irish bourgeoisie were split on its method of application. The last time the industrialists of the North joined forces with the merchants and small manufacturers of the South was in 1896. That was in a common front against the over-taxation of Ireland. Thereafter, with tariff control withheld, every instalment of land-purchase seemed to detract from the value of Home Rule to the northerners who held the main taxable capacity. Throughout this period the southern bourgeoisie preferred to give concessions in hope of bourgeois unity rather than vigorously fight Britain for a better Bill. For to do so would have set the masses in action. The smaller bourgeoisie were of course not so inhibited. Now let us turn to the working class. These were concentrated in Belfast and Dublin, together with the large coastal towns. This population distribution shows the predominantly mercantile character of Irish capitalism apart from Belfast. While they were capable of considerable industrial militancy, the political tradition of the workers had been to support the capitalists. Why? Because they gave work. Their continued existence in competition with English manufacturers was the Irish worker's passport to live in his own country. The farmer was a different matter. He was blamed for the fact that butter and bacon were dearer in Dublin than in London. Home Rule to create more work was one thing. Home Rule to subsidize the farmer was another. Nowhere was this suspicion of the agrarian south stronger than among the Protestant workers of Belfast who enjoyed a privileged position as against their Catholic fellow workers. To them the papist was typically a countryman.

Thus the split in the ranks of the bourgeoisie communicated itself to the working class quite readily as the history of Carson's agitation shows only too well. The Ulster Volunteers were formed and armed ostensibly to defend the Protestant workers from "popery". (4) The Redmondites' intention to play off country against town was revealed clearly in the electoral clauses of the Home Rule Bill, which favoured the countryside with disproportionate representation in the proposed local Parliament.

The fundamental cause of all this disunity was the refusal of British Imperialism to concede the one right, control of tariffs, without which Home Rule was little more than a sham. The I.R.B. who were strong among the artisans and tradesmen of the towns, as well as having a following among the intellectuals of the Gaelic language movement, prepared first for a "patriot opposition" which would fight within the local Parliament for the enlargement of its rights. After the final concession to the Unionists, when Redmond accepted the principle of the partition of Ireland (that is to say the split in the bourgeoisie was to be made the basis of a division of the national territory) (5) the need for a revolution which would precede the establishment of Home Rule and thus avoid partition became a matter of discussion. When successive postponements aroused the suspicion that Home Rule was not coming at all, a revolution to free Ireland once and for all became the obvious alternative.

WORLD WAR ONE

It is clear therefore that the issue of Home Rule was entangled in a most complex set of class antagonisms. If the average patriotic Irishman thought that he should support it because that was all he could get, still those who offered it him were not unfaulted idols. The brutal measures taken by 404 Dublin employers in hopes of destroying militant Trade Unionism before Home Rule came into force were well known and understood. (6) Connolly had no difficulty in winning support for his policy of defeating the Liberals at the three 1913 by-elections. And it was the Home Rulers who squealed. Again let it be said, the people were by no means satisfied that the Redmondites were capable of bringing home the bacon. Hence the Irish Volunteers, founded in November 1913 as a broad military organization controlled by the I.R.B. From the formation of the Volunteers until June 1914 the Parliamentarians sought first to weaken, then to control the Volunteers. There is no doubt whatsoever that their titular head, Eoin MacNeill, used his position on the organization committee with undue freedom. He opened negotiations with the Parliamentarians and allowed their appetite to be whetted by encouragement until they demanded that to the provisional committee of twenty-five should be added a further twenty-five. Since the provisional committee contained some of their adherents the result was to give them control. This was conceded so that when the war broke out it was possible for Redmond to offer Asquith the defence of Ireland for the Empire through the Volunteers. Then followed negotiations for putting the Volunteers under the British War Office by means of the Territorial Army Act. Finally in September Redmond made his notorious speech at Woodenbridge urging the Volunteers to join up for service in Flanders.

The result was a split. The original committee resumed its freedom of action. The Volunteers had become a mass organization numbering over 100,000. Every town and village had its company. The officers were drawn from the merchants and larger farmers with a sprinkling of artisans and tradesmen. The split followed class lines. In both country and town there was a new gathering centre for small men. The Trade Union movement declared against the war and Connolly described the tactics to be adopted by the united movement of workers and small-bourgeoisie in terms very different from the supposed blood sacrifice:

> *The Germans are in Boulogne where Napoleon projected an invasion of Britain. To Ireland is only a twelve hour run. If you are itching for a rifle, itching to fight, have a country of your own; better to fight for our own country than for the robber empire.*

And he wrote further:

> *Starting thus Ireland may light a fire which will not burn out until the last capitalist bond and debenture will burn to ashes on the grave of the last warlord.*

In those early months of war the Irish Neutrality League was founded. Organizers were despatched throughout Ireland to rebuild the Irish Volunteers. There was general understanding that England's difficulty was to be Ireland's opportunity, and to Connolly at least (and his newspaper had wide circulation, reaching up to 80,000 for some issues) Irish tactics were to be based on the resolutions of the Basle and Stuttgart conferences of the Socialist International. (7) The imperialist war was to be turned into a war of national liberation.

There are no records of Connolly's meetings at this time being broken up by hostile mobs. There are no records of opposition to the marching Volunteers or Citizen Army in Dublin, though this is recorded of cities such as Limerick and towns like Tullamore in less than a year's time. But there are records of 500 prosecutions under the Defence of the Realm Act between the outbreak of war and the Rising, and the suppression of every single paper of the national opposition.

That the promising anti-war movement languished there is little reason to doubt. In part the suppression of newspapers contributed to this result. But more important were the economic results of the war. The farmers could sell all they produced and could employ their sons and hired men. Recruitment took off the surplus labour force, providing some homes with regular earnings for the first time in years, and separation allowances brought "affluence" even into the ranks of the lumpen-proletariat. The Home Rule Act was on the statute book (together with an amending Act suspending its operation until after the war) and while for the time being the people were enjoying as a result of war the economic benefits which they hoped to get from Home Rule, after the war was over they expected to continue to enjoy them under Home Rule.

The first effect of the war was to sharpen class contradictions; its second effect was to place them in suspense. And it was this suspense, while all the issues remained unresolved, which appeared on the surface to be acquiescence. The mood of the masses was to make economic hay while the sun shone. This was not the time for rocking the boat. Imperialism, as Connolly put it, was "buying the souls of men". But this was a temporary phenomenon resulting from a particular stage in the war. The many recent writers who have extended it backwards over the years miss its distinctive character. Lenin accurately summarized the situation when he said that the struggle had not yet matured. But all the factors were present.

Now for the thoughts of Dublin Castle. That Mr Ryan is right about "poor Birrell" is confirmed elsewhere. Thus on 10 April Major Price, Chief of the Military Intelligence in Ireland, wrote:

> *The general state of Ireland, apart from recruiting and apart from the activities of the pro-German Sinn Féin minority, is thoroughly satisfactory. The mass of the people are sound and loyal as regards the war, and the country is in a very prosperous state and very free from ordinary crime.*

This confirms what has been said. Ireland had been restored to the position she held before the repeal of the Corn Laws, and held a highly favoured position in the British market. The two provisos are however noteworthy. The people were sound and loyal but did not want to join up. And they seem to have managed to tolerate the "pro-German Sinn

Féin" (meaning the Volunteers) for nearly two years. This might be held to imply that they still regarded the Volunteers as a rod in pickle in the event of Home Rule not coming up to expectations.

GOVERNMENT TAKEN BY SURPRISE

Accepting Birrell's complacent statement at its face value Mr Ryan can only suggest that no Government can be expected to anticipate suicide. But more is known than that about the situation within Dublin Castle. Professor Leon O'Broin has recently published an analysis of the documents so far available. (8) These show that what can be conveniently termed the "Home Rule crisis" was affecting the ruling class as deeply as those classes contending for power. From the introduction of the Home Rule Act onward no official knew for certain who was going to be his boss next year. This uncertainty led to a weakening of the vigilance of the R.I.C., and a loosening of the traditional loyalties of the entire civil service. More than that, it led the authorities at the Castle to give far more weight than would have been otherwise possible to the opinions of the Parliamentary leaders. They regarded themselves in a sense as a caretaker administration paving the way for Redmond and Dillon who would in due course take over. Repeatedly from his arrival at the end of 1914, landlords and others with eyes to the ground were urging on Birrell strong action against the Volunteers. The under-secretary, Nathan, was not averse from obliging. At the end of 1914 he listed the "seditious press" and considered suppressing it. He sent copies of the Irish Volunteer and Ireland to Birrell in London. Birrell consulted Dillon and Devlin who advised against suppression on the grounds that far from harming them it would rally support. In any case the "Sinn Feiners" (note this is the title given them by their enemies, not that which they themselves chose) (9) were an insignificant minority. Nathan replied that he was tired of hearing the Sinn Feiners called an insignificant minority; they were not an insignificant minority and it was not true to say they had no influence. And Nathan had his way and the papers were suppressed. There is preserved a letter in which he suggested that in order to help the good work Mr Dillon, the Nationalist leader, should include in one of his speeches the suggestion that if Ireland were invaded by the Germans, the "Sinn Feiners" would help the Germans.

The funeral of O'Donovan Rossa at the beginning of August 1915 was a tremendous demonstration of the depth and extent of national feeling. The military suggested action to prevent the collection of money for arms. Birrell forbade it. In November, after the Citizen Army had carried out a mock attack on Dublin Castle, Lord Midleton demanded that the Volunteers be forcibly disarmed. Nathan reported that "the Nationalist party had lost control of the country and with the avowed purpose of preparing to resist conscription, the extremists were everywhere organizing and gaining strength."

In early December he warned that "Sinn Féin was edging out Mr Redmond, their Volunteers were doing much mischief, and the young priests who supported them were very extreme." He described the difficult role Redmond had to play. "He had been honestly imperial in the war, but by going as far as he had had lost his position in the country." But still Dillon advised him to "keep his hands off the organizers."

On 20 January 1916, Lord Midleton saw Birrell himself and drew attention to the speeches being made by Fr Michael Flanagan to the alleged effect that Ireland should be an independent country in alliance with Germany, and he mentioned a circular from the Cork Volunteers declaring that opposition to conscription should be backed by armed force if necessary. Inevitably the failure of recruiting was bringing the issue of conscription to the fore. And it had been agreed by the Irish Neutrality League, or a broad committee under its aegis, that in the event of conscription, an attempt to disarm the Volunteers, or a German landing, the Volunteers should make an insurrection. As the war proceeded, despite the economic prosperity, these issues increasingly darkened the horizon. On the question of the German arms ship it appears that though British intelligence knew of its journey (though not the correct date) Nathan was kept in ignorance out of concern lest the source of the information (required for even more momentous matters) should leak out.

The explanation for the unpreparedness of the authorities thus lies in the general situation vis-à-vis the transfer of power. It was essential for the bourgeoisie to maintain its influence against a coalition which though organizationally far weaker at the time, could expand very rapidly if certain issues were raised. And of course it was not a question of suicide. If Redmond and Dillon were anxious not to take the offensive against what was in essence Republicanism, it did not follow that Republicanism would not take the offensive against the war forces. And this is indeed what happened.

MILITARILY SOUND, POLITICALLY PREMATURE ?

Since it is not now a question of explaining a suicidal blood sacrifice, perhaps we should now consider why the Volunteers and Citizen Army undertook an insurrection which while (as I hope to show) militarily sound was politically premature.

The reason was basically the fear that the war might end before the opportunity was taken. There had been many reverses for the Entente arms. These, for example the disaster of Suvla bay, had helped to discourage recruitment and to encourage the movement against conscription. In January 1916 Countess Markievicz with characteristic ingenuousness expressed from a public platform the hope that the rumours of peace were unfounded. She drew sharp rebukes from the pacifist Sheehy-Skeffington, who subsequently was murdered in cold blood by a British officer when trying to effect mediation between the parties during the fighting. And it is generally accepted that in the early part of 1916 the British cabinet were giving serious consideration to a negotiated peace. (10) The seizure of power was thought of as a stimulus to this negotiated peace, in which Germany would prove relatively stronger than she had been at the outbreak of war, and if power could be held long enough for the establishment of any kind of administration, then that administration could claim belligerent rights and expect international recognition in the peace settlement. The problem was thus how to seize enough territory for the establishment of an administration and how to hold it long enough. In his analysis of the military objectives of the Rising that actually took place, Col Eoghan O'Neill of the Military College at the Curragh expressed his conviction that the mission decided upon was the occupation of Dublin. (11) This opinion was based on an analysis of the military disposition actually made. It may be added that he considered the careful planning shown as completely at variance with the theory of a suicidal blood sacrifice, although he held the view that a number of mistakes were made.

What were the problems? The first problem arose from the immaturity of the mass movement. This expressed itself within the liberation front. Griffith and his Sinn Féin (the only group at that time entitled to the name Sinn Féin) were not in favour of an offensive insurrection. Had Britain attempted conscription or the disarming of the Volunteers they would probably have offered resistance. But this might not necessarily have involved an armed rebellion. Even prominent members of the I.R.B., for example Bulmer Hobson, had been converted to a preference for guerilla tactics. He wrote a pamphlet entitled "Defensive warfare". Those in favour of armed insurrection were confined to the Citizen Army under Connolly and Mallin, and the Supreme Council of the I.R.B. In mid-January the Supreme Council met and elected a full "military council" which was authorised to prepare secretly an armed insurrection at a date within their discretion, and in doing so to come to an accommodation with Connolly.

The proposal made to Connolly was to organize a Rising on Easter Sunday under cover of manoeuvres, relying on Pearse's position as director of organization and the cadre of I.R.B. men within the Volunteers, to effect the transformation without MacNeill's knowledge. He would find himself the leader of an insurrection and could go on or drop out as he pleased. It must be recalled at this point that MacNeill had only two years previously taken it upon himself to negotiate a new constitution for the Volunteers with the Redmondites. Under this constitution the men who were now proposing to deceive him would have been excluded from their positions. Connolly thought this course dangerous. It is not known what precisely he urged. But from what he said on other occasions it seem he was generally in favour of changing the leadership. His colleagues thought that this might act as a warning to the authorities and bring about an attempt to disarm the forces before they were prepared. And Connolly, says Desmond Ryan, conceded with much misgiving. (12)

The next problem was arms. Arrangements were made that these should be landed at Fenit in Co. Kerry. Railwaymen were to run a special train up the west coast dropping arms at Limerick, which was to be by-passed by the Ballysimon loop, Ennis, Crusheen, Gort and Tuam but above all at Athenry. These arms were to be used on the line of the Shannon, thus drawing off forces from the west of Dublin and making it difficult for the British to invest the city. As for the Volunteers elsewhere they must make do with what they had or could capture. It should be noted that it was in the west that the Volunteers had their largest reserves of unarmed manpower.

A further problem was created when at the end of March a number of Volunteer organizers were arrested and deported to Britain. These included Mellows who was to take command on the Shannon. He was traced to his place of exile by his brother who impersonated him for sufficient time to let him out of the country in disguise. He reached his headquarters at Killeeneenmore, near Athenry, the day the Rising began.

The final problems were the failure of the arms landing and the discovery by MacNeill that the manoeuvres were indeed to be an insurrection. The failure of the arms landing was basically due to the arms ship not being equipped with radio, and thus not receiving last-minute orders to delay the landing. Strangely enough this last-minute message was intercepted by the British who thus did not discover the ship on the day she actually arrived. The ship was scuttled when discovered and Casement who landed from a submarine was arrested.

Almost simultaneously MacNeill and Hobson discovered the truth, and for several days orders, confirmations and countermands were flying between headquarters and the outlying companies. The confusion was indescribable. MacNeill made certain that all would know of the cancellation of the manoeuvres by inserting an advertisement in the Sunday Independent. This may have allayed the fears of the authorities who were now (possibly subject to the results of the emergency cabinet then meeting) preparing plans for mass arrests and disarming the Volunteers. But it could not bring into action the many Volunteers who had retired in disgust. After a long and serious meeting in Liberty Hall the military committee decided to put into action as much of the original plan as was possible on the Monday. Code messages were sent out in all directions. The Volunteers who took part in the Rising were substantially the members of the I.R.B., plus the Citizen Army.

Colonel O'Neill considers that to hold Dublin for a week with the forces available would be regarded as a very remarkable achievement even for a professional army. This opinion by a professional military man is of great importance where the "blood sacrifice" theory is in question. It should be noticed too that the political aim was still intact. It is interesting to speculate what would have happened if at the Cabinet meeting it had been decided to seek a negotiated peace. In the west something approaching a thousand square miles of Irish territory was held for several days. The insurgents in Wexford held out even after Dublin had surrendered.

HOW THE PEOPLE REACTED

We can now turn to the question of the attitude of the Irish people. Here it would seem there was a significant gulf between town and country. Too much should not be made of it of course, as policemen are spread thinner in the country and the walls do not have ears. Nobody who reads Mellows's story of the rising in Galway or speaks to his surviving comrades can doubt that the popular nature of the insurrection was well understood. The Athenry area had benefited from the land division, but this was by no means complete. The town tenants' agitation had been exceptionally intense as recently as 1907. The I.R.B. was strong and had assisted the small farmers and landless men in their agitation. After the Rising was over the R.I.C. reported to the commission of enquiry. Anybody familiar with East Galway will immediately be struck by the confusions and contradictions. Sometimes the distances between well-known towns are ludicrously wrong. It should be remembered of course that these officers were reporting to people who probably did not know the district. There are detailed descriptions of events which were both topographically unlikely and chronologically suspect. The explanation of this is that from Ballinasloe to Galway city, some forty miles, and from Tuam to Gort, some thirty odd, the R.I.C. evacuated all outlying posts and shut themselves up in their barracks in the few large towns, sometimes providing accommodation in addition for the larger merchants or prominent members of Redmond's party. That the landlord classes screamed for help is undoubted. And there are fanciful stories only explicable, in my opinion, as elaborate explanations of why it was not forthcoming.

When the Volunteers camped at Moyode they were almost embarrassed by the swarms of young children who came pressing on them their (unnecessary) services as scouts. The farmers' wives baked bread for them, and offered onions, potatoes and vegetables. In the field kitchen which supplied several hundred men these combined with the rumps of bullocks commandeered from the local landlords to make appetising Irish stew. Police were taken prisoner and when the cease-fire was being negotiated one of the objections was that the police prisoners would identify the insurgents. They gave their word of honour not to do so. And it is still said locally that some of them kept it. Why? Because otherwise it would not be very healthy living in the district. The Rising in Galway was a kind of peasant war accompanying the national revolution in Dublin.

Recently the Liverpool Echo published an account of the Rising which seems to have indicated that the people were bitterly opposed to it. A correspondent who claimed to have lived on Dublin's Navan Road as a little girl told in reply how she had seen a fleet of cars carrying wounded men and was extremely upset asking the local people what was wrong." Don't worry. They are great heroes and are fighting for Irish freedom", she was told. They had been involved in the battle of Ashbourne. Again to return to Dublin, there is ample evidence in the extensive literature for sympathy with the rebels among the people. There was a widespread fear that they would give in too soon and thus become an object of ridicule. But there is also evidence that the lumpen-proletariat which had indulged in looting before the fire got too hot, did assemble near the quays and do a bit of booing. But even in 1916 this was not a dense residential area, and certainly not typical of the working class. In Grafton Street, the Bond Street of Dublin, well-dressed ladies and gentlemen showed their breeding by spitting at the prisoners. But just after an insurrection, when a city is still smoking, when there is martial law and thousands of men, women and boys have been arrested, is not the time when even the most optimistic sympathiser could be expected to come out and cheer. Those who were in sympathy would naturally keep their opinions to themselves. Certainly they would not express it to the numerous British press men who thronged the city. (13)

PEARSE'S BLOODBATH?

Mr Ryan calls the Rising "Pearse's bloodbath" oblivious of that other bloodbath which was simultaneously claiming millions of the youth of Europe. "It is better to die 'neath an Irish sky Than at Suvla or Sud-el-bar" runs the famous song.

But Pearse, the only one among the revolutionaries who had ever given voice to sentiments of "blood sacrifice", was by no means the lonely central figure he is alleged to be. The notion of establishing a secret society to prepare an insurrection to free Ireland had occurred to James Stephens while an exile in Paris following the abortive Risings of 1848 and 1849. In 1855 he founded the Irish Revolutionary Brotherhood with this object. A Rising was attempted in 1867. The organization, now called the Irish Republican Brotherhood, played an enormous part in the Land League struggles and formed a backcloth to the militant parliamentarianism of Parnell. It fell on lean times after his fall, being so to speak entangled in the debris. But it continued uninterruptedly, was revivified soon after the turn of the century by Hobson and McCullough, and in 1907 by the return of Tom Clarke. These, with Sean MacDiarmada, built up the organization throughout Ireland, and over the whole period there was training in the use of arms which took its first organized form some months before the foundation of the Irish Volunteers. Pearse did not become a member of the I.R.B. until the end of 1913.

Of the seven signatories Connolly will be known to many. "How do you know so much about revolution Mr Connolly?" an interrupter once shouted up at him. "My business is revolution, madam" he replied. Tom Clarke had spent many years in jail in Britain on dynamite charges; he had survived thanks to an iron will and strong constitution under conditions where some of his fellow-prisoners went mad. While in the U.S.A. he was a member of the Engineers' Trade Union. There was nothing suicidal about either of these men.

Sean MacDiarmada was born in Co. Leitrim but as a youth emigrated to Glasgow where he became a tram driver and bartender. Later he worked a while in Belfast where he met Hobson and McCullough. For several years after 1905 he toured Ireland on a bicycle forming circles of the I.R.B. wherever he went. Eamonn Ceannt was a clerical worker who strongly supported the workers in the lock-out of 1913. His character is shown in his last message sent out before his execution:

> *leave for the guidance of other Irish revolutionaries who may tread the path which I have trod, this advice: never to treat with the enemy, never to surrender to his mercy, but to fight to a finish. I see nothing gained but grave disaster caused by the surrender which has marked the end of the Irish insurrection of 1916 – so far as Dublin is concerned. The enemy has not cherished one generous thought for those who with little hope, with poor equipment and weak in numbers, withstood his forces for one glorious week. Ireland has shown that she is a nation. This generation can claim to have raised sons as brave as any that went before; and in years to come Ireland will honour those who risked their all for her honour at Easter in 1916.*

There is no trace of a death-wish here, except perhaps for a few more of his enemies. The remaining two signatories, Plunkett and MacDonagh, were intellectuals. Plunkett was the youngest but was seriously ill. Nevertheless he managed to get married in prison before he was executed. As for MacDonagh his every word and line breathes irrepressible gaiety and love of life.

As for the rank and file, one can imagine the 200 odd sturdy Trade Unionists of the Citizen Army engaging in a blood sacrifice. One might just as well call an unsuccessful strike a "work sacrifice"!

A quotation from the official enquiry will throw some light on the temper in the west:

> *"My lord", said Inspector Clayton, R.I.C., "It all started in Craughwell in 1907. Secret societies followed and branches were organized in Loughrea, At Henry and Kilrea. And then that fellow Mellows came from Dublin. He was a paid organizer and he enrolled every youth in every parish. Lord Hardinge: The Sinn Feiners were pretty well known to" you I suppose?*

Inspector: Yes, my lord, they were.
Lord Hardinge: Were there any people of superior class or
  education among them?
Inspector: No, my lord, none.
Lord Hardinge: What class did they come from?
Inspector: Small shop-keepers, blacksmiths, publicans and
  farmers' sons.
Lord Hardinge: There were no literary types among them?
Inspector: No, my lord."

It is only necessary to appreciate this class composition of the insurgents to see how impossible it would be, after MacNeill had already given everybody who wished to withdraw a perfect excuse for doing so, for Pearse to lead these men into a "blood sacrifice" even if he had wished to do so. His gallant offer to take full responsibility, coupled with a romantic streak in some of his writings, are not (as was stated earlier) adequate for the assessment of an insurrection of this magnitude and complexity. (14)

That the executed men took their place alongside Tone and Emmet as a result of the executions is of course plain. But to say as Mr Ryan does in the concluding paragraph of his article, that Kitchener and Maxwell "performed their involuntary roles as founding fathers" (of the Irish Republic that exists today) is to miss the essence of the situation in 1916. Tone was executed in 1798 and became a hero at once. Did any revolution follow? Emmet was executed after an unsuccessful insurrection in1803. He has remained a hero sung in verse from that day. Did any revolution follow? The Manchester martyrs were hanged and every year from then on throngs assembled to commemorate them. Was there a revolution? What then distinguished the insurrection of 1916? It was that the Rising took place as the first breach in the world imperialist war front, that the crisis in Ireland was a real crisis, affecting both rulers and ruled, and merely hastened, did not create, the inevitable reassertions by history of the actual relationships of Irish life, which had been partially (and only partially) obscured for the short space of just over a year.

NATIONAL RESURGENCE

What had been implicit in the situation all along now shone out with blinding certainty. The British were not in the war to establish the independence of small nations. The Redmondites who were supporting them had thrown away, not utilized, Ireland's advantage. The merchants, large farmersand industrialists were left without a policy. Simultaneously the results of the decision taken in London to prosecute the warmore vigorously began to take effect. Prices rose. Small farmers began to agitate for land. Where they secured the land the threat of conscription hung over their labour force, their children. The expected expansion of war-production in Ireland did not take place. The new party established by the small-bourgeoisie was given Griffith's name of Sinn Féin, but had De Valera as president and Griffith as vice-president. It grew from strength to strength. In the 1918 election it won 73 of Ireland's 100 territorial constituencies.

It was when British imperialism refused to accept the verdict of the people in 1918 that the most intense phase of the national struggle began. Dail Eireann, established in defiance of the British power, reaffirmed Irish independence and began the de facto administration of the country, with its own finance department, local government department, courts, police and even jails. Against it Imperialism sent soldiers and Black-and-Tans. That the inspiration of the men of 1916 still encouraged there is no doubt. But the struggle was against actual evils being perpetrated by imperialism, the murders, incendiarisms, shooting-up of whole towns, to say nothing of the herding of the men of Ireland into jails and concentration camps. It was now that Imperialism was fought to something approaching a standstill and Lloyd George adopted the alternative policy of seeking an accommodation with more compromising elements (notably Griffith and Collins) who had become the guardians of bourgeois interests after the old bourgeois party had disintegrated. It was this accommodation, not the Rising of 1916, nor the Anglo-Irish war, that gave rise to the present partitioned Ireland, one of whose States is the Republic that Mr Ryan fathers on General Maxwell.

Finally it is worth dealing with the frequently made speculation that had Maxwell not introduced the white terror the revolution which followed 1916 would never have taken place.

What would the alternative have been? Obviously no government so defied in the midst of a war could afford to let everybody go scot free. What then was the minimum reprisal possible consistent with remaining the Government? Or consistent with continuing the war? The imprisonment of the sixteen men who were executed and all others let off? This line of thought leads to a fantasy. Once the act of defiance had been committed, provided that imperialism remained imperialism, that Ireland remained a subject nation, that the crisis of the world war was there and bound to develop further – granted these concretely existing conditions, there was no course of action British imperialism could adopt which would not serve to strengthen the national liberation movement.

It is interesting to compare Mr Ryan's description of the Rising as a "suicidal gesture" with that of Karl Radek (15) who stigmatized it as a "putsch". His article appeared in the Berner Tagwacht under the title "a dead letter". In his criticism of Radek's thesis Lenin commented that it was an odd coincidence that the "representative of the imperialist bourgeoisie" Kulisher (a Russian "Cadet") dubbed the Rising "the Dublin putsch".

According to Radek it was a "putsch" that could come to nothing. He wrote his article for the issue of 9 May, possibly before he had heard of any executions. His disdainful approach to the Irish National movement arose from his belief that the "Irish problem was an agrarian problem" and that the peasants having been appeased with reforms the national movement was now a "purely urban, petty-bourgcois movement which not withstanding the sensation it caused, had not much social backing",

As we have seen, land purchase was far from complete despite the Birrell Act, and there was required another Act (the Free State Land Act of 1924) before the way could be cleared for completing the agrarian revolution. Second the whole course of the Home Rule crisis had shown how widely the masses were involved in the national movement. The imperialist Mr Ryan sees in the Rising something that should never have happened. At the end of his article he expresses the view that the Irish should remember "not without shame" the British soldiers who were killed while suppressing the insurrection, and he suggests that candles should be lit in the Dublin churches to them as well. This expression of chauvinism fits exactly his opinion that the unnatural event could never have happened but for the sublime madness of Pearse and the administrative folly of Maxwell. How many times have we heard such analysis applied in India, Egypt or Vietnam?

To the leftist Radek on the other hand the Rising could not possibly be justified because it did not coincide with his preconceived opinion of what was worth revolting about.

Lenin described his opinion as "monstrously doctrinaire and pedantic" and his reply (16) is worth rereading in full:

> The term 'putsch' in the scientific sense of the word may be employed only when the attempt at insurrection has revealed nothing but a circle of conspirators or stupid maniacs, and has aroused no sympathy among the masses. The

centuries old Irish national movement, having passed through various stages and combinations of class interests . . . expressed itself in street fighting conducted by a section of the urban petty-bourgeoisie and a section of the workers after a long period of mass agitation, demonstrations, suppression of the press etc. Whoever calls such a Rising a 'putsch' is either a hardened reactionary or a doctrinaire hopelessly incapable of picturing a social revolution as a living thing.

"For to imagine that social revolution is conceivable without revolts by small nations in the colonies and in Europe, without the revolutionary outbursts of a section of the petty bourgeoisie with all its prejudices, without the movement of politically non-conscious proletarians and semi-proletarian masses against landlord, church, monarchical, national and other oppression – to imagine that means repudiating social revolution. Very likely one army will line up in one place and say 'We are for socialism' while another will line up in another place and say 'We are for imperialism' – only from such a ridiculously pedantic angle could one label the Irish rebellion a 'putsch'.

"Whoever expects a 'pure' social revolution will never live to see it. Such a person pays lip-service to revolution without understanding what revolution really is."

Further on in the same article Lenin returns to the subject and adds:

"If on the one hand we were to declare and to repeat in a thousand keys that we are 'opposed' to all national oppression and on the other hand we were to describe as a 'putsch' the heroic revolt of the most mobile and enlightened section of certain classes in an oppressed nation against its oppressors, we would be sinking to the same stupid level as the Kautskyites. The misfortune of the Irish is that they have risen prematurely, when the European revolt of the proletariat has not yet matured. Capitalism is not so harmoniously built that the various springs of rebellion can of themselves merge at one effort, without reverses and defeats. On the other hand, the very fact that revolts break out at different times, in different places, and are of different kinds, guarantees wide scope and depth to the general movement; only in premature, partial, scattered and therefore unsuccessful revolutionary movements do the masses gain experience, get to know their real leaders, the socialist proletarians, and in this way prepare for a general onslaught, in the same way as separate strikes, demonstrations, local and national, outbreaks in the army, outbursts among the peasantry, etc. prepared the way for the general onslaught in 1905".

A STRUGGLE NOT YET ENDED

How then are we to look at 1916? Not surely in isolation from the events which followed. One way of viewing its history is to regard the entire period from 1912 to 1923 as the Irish revolution, and the Home Rule crisis, the distortion of its development through the war, the Rising and aftermath, the national resurgence, declaration of independence, Anglo-Irish war, truce and civil war, as the concrete forms the struggle took in its successive phases. Historically it took the forms we have enumerated. But the process as a whole, with all its accidents and contradictory developments, was a product of the opening stages of the general crisis of capitalism. That in the end the victory was only partial, that the bourgeoisie recovered the initiative and appropriated to itself some (though not all) of the gains won by the people, and seems now prepared to retreat still further, indicates that the struggle has not yet ended.

Now what is the effect of the myth, which we referred to at the opening of the discussion? First the pretence that 1916 was the struggle for the existing Republic in the Twenty-Six Counties embellishes the present regime. It obscures partition and the facts of neo-colonialism. It fits in well with the current affectation that "imperialism is dead" in general and the Irish question in particular. By resting the Irish revolution on the accident of "suicide" and the accident of Maxwell's undue harshness, the irreconcilability of British imperialism and the Irish people's movement for national democracy is concealed.

The last thing I would wish to suggest is that Mr Ryan worked up his theories for that deliberate purpose. That these theories are very widespread anybody who has read the British (or Irish) papers in recent times will testify. What is being concealed is the responsibility of British imperialism for forcing the Irish to accept something less than they fought for in 1916. And under these circumstances the integration which is equally enforced, but under economic pressure, can be represented as the voluntary action of a free people.

I am of course not anxious to stand over every dot and comma of this account. But I offer it for discussion as a more credible version of the history of 1916, and of 1916's significance for history, than that produced by the assistant editor of *The Times*.

NOTES

1. An action of the Northern Ireland Unionist regime in Stormont.
2. J.D. Clarkson, author of *Labour and Nationalism in Ireland*, New York 1925.
3. The 1909 Land Act which provided more money for land purchase.
4. Elsewhere C.D. Greaves writes of these forces of Unionist counter-revolution as follows: *"The Unionists' first necessity was to silence all contrary voices among the bourgeoisie ...Liberals who protested found their Orange associates reluctant to do business with them. The storm-troopers of Unionist reaction were recruited from the brazen hoodlums of the Belfast slums. The leaders who directed them were mostly the brainless pups of aristocratic families. They appeared anachronistically from their parks and demesnes to join with their most abject victims in putting the clock back. Orange elements hitherto too respectable for ruffianism learned the example from their betters, and a pressure of intimidation was started which increased from day to day."* Life and Times of James Connolly, London 1961, p.285; And again, *"The first fascist movement of the century stalked unrecognised on to the stage of history."* Liam Mellows and the Irish Revolution, London, 1971, p. 47.
5. In March 1914, when the Parliamentary Party leaders Redmond and Devlin accepted Asquith's proposal for "two Irelands", with individual counties to be permitted to opt out of the Home Rule Act.
6. The great Dublin lock-out, which commenced in August 1913 and continued until the following spring.
7. Congresses of the Socialist International at which the member parties committed themselves to opposing their own national governments in the event of war. Only the Irish, Russians and Serbs fulfilled their commitment.
8. O Broin, *Dublin Castle and the 1916 Rising: the Story of Sir Mathew Nathan*, Dublin 1966, and *The Chief Secretary: Augustine Birrell in Ireland*, London 1969.
9. *Sinn Féin*, meaning "we ourselves", not "ourselves alone" as it is often rendered. The notion is one of self-reliance, not exclusivity.
10. See for example, CJ. Lowe and M.L. Dockrill, *British Foreign Policy 1914–1922*, Vol. 2: *The Mirage of Power*, London 1972, p. 238 et seq.: *"Serious consideration of peace terms in Britain started in 1916 with the growing US pressure on the belligerents to end the war. It was a reflection, partly, of the necessity of not offending Wilson, partly of a growing consciousness that it might not be possible to gain a sufficient ascendancy over the Central Powers to impose the peace the British Government wanted."* Peace proposals were discussed in the War Committee in March.
11. Col Eoghan O'Neill, *"The Battle of Dublin 1916: A Military Evaluation of Easter Week"*, An Cosant óir, Vol. 26, 211–222, 1966. In 1991 Col J.P. Duggan discovered important new material on the military plans for the uprising in the German archives in Berlin. It related to proposals made by Joseph Plunkett to the German High Command during a visit he made in 1915. These envisaged a complex nationwide revolt by the

Volunteers, interacting with the landing of German arms and an expeditionary force at Limerick. Professor F.X. Martin described the new data as "of utmostimportance" to historians. *"Now at last we have evidence of the existence of a plan for an All-Ireland rising that was not hare-brained."* Dr Donal McCartney, Professor of Modern Irish History at UCD, said *"one cannot help wondering what might have happened had the Germans shown a real interest."* (*Sunday Press* 31 March 1991) This material confirms the validity of the earlier military assessment of Col. O'Neill and the judgement of C.D. Greaves in the present work.

12. D. Ryan, *James Connolly*, London 1924.

13. In an article in the *Irish Democrat*, Feb. 1991, P. Berresford Ellis draws attention to a hither to ignored contemporary reference in F.A. McKenzie, The Irish Rebellion, London 1916. McKenzie was a Canadian journalist eye-witness of the surrender of the insurgents, although he was unsympathetic to their cause. He writes *"I have read many accounts of public feeling in Dublin in these days. They are all agreed that the open and strong sympathy of the mass of the population was with the British troops. That this was so in the better parts of the city, I have no doubt, but certainly what I myself saw in the poorer districts did not confirm this. It rather indicated that there was a vast amount of sympathy with the rebels, particularly after the rebels were defeated. The sentences of the Courts Martial deepened this sympathy."* Among other details he describes people cheering a column of arrested insurgents, some of them women, marching singing a rebel song between lines of British soldiers near Dublin Castle on the Sunday evening following surrender. See p. 92 et seq.

14. In this connection revisionist publicists have poured reams of cant over a few rhetorical sentences of Pearse's. They seem unaware that part of the Zeitgeist of 1914–15 and the years leading up to then was a romanticising of the heroism and self-sacrifice of war by way of contrast to the "bourgeois" complacency of the long peace since 1870. This was a common theme of European writers at the time. See D.H. Lawrence and Rupert Brooke amongst others. The rational kernel to Pearse's rhetoric of blood-sacrifice is the idea that political and social salvation must come from within. America's Thomas Jefferson will scarcely be accounted bloodthirsty because he wrote *"The tree of liberty must continually be watered with the blood of martyrs and of tyrants!"*

15. Leader of the International Left Wing Conference at Zimmerwald, Switzerland, 1915, where the call was made for the organizations of the working class *"to stand for the emancipation of the oppressed nations as well as of the enslaved classes."*

16. In VX Lenin on Britain, Vol. 22, pp. 338–42, London 1960; reprinted in O.D. Edwards and F. Pyle, *The Easter Rising 1916*, London, 1968.

Appendix III:
Nominal Roll of the
Irish Citizen Army

NOMINAL ROLL OF THE IRISH CITIZEN ARMY

Army No.	Army Section Name/No.	Name	First Name	Address	R M Fox
1	Capel St no 4 (Commandant General, Dublin Division, Irish Republican Forces)	Connolly	James	Liberty Hall	GPO
2	Inchicore Crumlin no 3 (Commandant)	Mallin	Michael	Emmet Hall, Inchicore	St Stephen's Green/ College of Surgeons
3	Church St no 9	Kain	Thomas	11 Arran Quay	St Stephen's Green/ College of Surgeons
4	High St no 1 (Lieutenant)	Jackson	P.	40 Augustine St Lr	St Stephen's Green/ College of Surgeons
5	High St	Kelly	Michael	Back Lane	St Stephen's Green/ College of Surgeons
6	Aungier St no 2	Donnelly	Michael	113 St Stephen's Green	St Stephen's Green/ College of Surgeons
7	North Strand no 6	Robbins	Frank	39 Nth William St	GPO/City Hall
8	Gloucester St no 5	Poole	John	50 Marlboro St	St Stephen's Green/ College of Surgeons
9	Church St no 9	Hyland	Jas	11 Lr Bridge St	GPO/ Henry and James
10	Gloucester St no 5	Connolly	Edward	58 Lr C Gloucester St	St Stephen's Green/ College of Surgeons
11	Sth C Rd	Little	Jas	31 Upper Clanbrassil St Rear	St Stephen's Green/ College of Surgeons
12	North Strand no 6	Byrne	John	56 Summerhill	
13	North Strand no 6	Elmes	Elliot	32 Leinster Ave, Nth Strand	
14	Sth C Rd	Henry	Fred	25 Charlmont St	St Stephen's Green/ College of Surgeons
15	Dorset St no 8 (Sergeant and Assistant QMG)	McGowan	Seamus	3 Blessington St	GPO
16	High St	Oman	William	48 High St	St Nicholas Graveyard
17	High St (Commander)	Oman	George	48 High St	GPO/Imperial Hotel
18	North Strand no 6	Halpin	William	6 Valentine Tce	City Hall
19	Gloucester St no 5	Nelson	Thomas	40 Gardiner St Middle	City Hall
20	Gloucester St no 5	Dwyer	James	20 Rutland Sq	City Hall
21	High St	Clarke	Philip	65 Cork St	St Stephen's Green/ College of Surgeons
22	High St	Keogh	James	11 Brabazon St	St Stephen's Green/ College of Surgeons
23	High St	Walsh	James	11 Brabazon St	
24	Inchicore Crumlin no 3	Bradley	Patrick	1 St Mary's Tce, Inchicore	St Stephen's Green/ College of Surgeons
25	High St	O'Shea	Jas	28 The Coombe	St Stephen's Green/ College of Surgeons
26		De Coeur [crossed out]	R.	77 Aungier St	St Stephen's Green/ College of Surgeons
27	Inchicore Crumlin no 3 (Commander)	Kinsella	Peter	2 St James Place, Inchicore	
28	Inchicore Crumlin no 3	Keogh	Edward	24 Park St, Inchicore	St Stephen's Green/ College of Surgeons
29	North Strand no 6 (Commander)	Norgrove	George	15 Strandville Ave	St Stephen's Green/ College of Surgeons
30	Gloucester St no 5 (Commander)	Reilly	John	12 Lr Gardiner St	GPO/City Hall
31	Sth C Rd	Cooper [crossed out]	John	30 Lennox St	

Army No.	Army Section Name/No.	Name	First Name	Address	R M Fox
32	Capel St no 4 (Sergeant)	Doyle	Joseph	117 Capel St	St Stephen's Green/ College of Surgeons
33	Aungier St	[crossed out]			
34	Capel St no 4	O'Keeffe	John	8 Mary's Abbey	Synod Hall
35		[crossed out]			
36	Dorset St no 8	Lawlor	Patrick	17 Russell Place, N C RdSt	St Stephen's Green/ College of Surgeons
37	Capel St no 4 (Commander)	Kelly	John	5 Swifts Row	St Stephen's Green/ College of Surgeons
38	Gloucester St no 5	Findley	John	39 Nth Parade	
39		[crossed out]			
40	Aungier St	Tuohy	Patrick	43 Bride St	GPO/Imperial Hotel
41		Tuohy	Michael	43 Bride St	
42	Gloucester St no 5	Connolly	Michael	58 Lr Gloucester St	GPO/ Henry and James
43	Capel St no 4	Halpin	William	53 Dominick St	
44		McDonnell	Patrick	19 Lr Gardiner St	St Stephen's Green/ College of Surgeons
45	Capel St no 4	Williams	Patrick	25 Stafford St	
46		[crossed out]			
47	Townsend St no 12 (Commander)	McGuire	Terence	10 Tara St	
48	North Strand no 6	Egan	Andy	15 Summerhill	
49	Gloucester St no 5	Darcy	Charlie	4 Murphy's Cottages off Gloucester St	GPO/ Henry and James
50	Gloucester St no 5	Connolly	Matthew	61 Ballybough St	City Hall
51	Gloucester St no 5	Dwyer	Michael	20 Rutland Cottages	St Stephen's Green/ College of Surgeons
52		O'Neill	John	61 Ballybough Rd	GPO
53	Gloucester St no 5 (O/C Boys' Corps)	Carpenter	Walter	110 Lr Abbey St	GPO
54		Connolly	Sean	108 Phillipsburg Ave	City Hall
55		de Markievicz		Leinster Rd	
56	Dorset St no 8	O'Neill	John.	14 Grenville St, Mountjoy Square	St Stephen's Green/ College of Surgeons
57	(Captain) Inchicore Crumlin no 3	Bradley	Luke	1 St Mary's Tce, Sarsfield Rd, Inchicore	Guardroom, Upper Castle Yard
58		Conroy	John	40 Railway St	St Stephen's Green/ College of Surgeons
59	Dorset St no 8	Charleton	Michael	27 Portland Place	St Stephen's Green/ College of Surgeons
60	Aungier St	Fitzpatrick	Frank	35 Aungier St	City Hall/Evening Mail office
61	Dorset St no 8	Coyle	Thomas	5 Eglinton Ave, Phibsborough	City Hall
62	Aungier St	Fox	Patrick	8 Peter St	St Stephen's Green/ College of Surgeons
63	Sth C Rd	Frank	Henry	5 Fennells Cottages	
64	Aungier St	Thomas	Scully	7 Pitt St	
65	Gloucester St no 5	Brady	Christy	32 Foley St	Guardroom, Upper Castle Yard

Army No.	Army Section Name/No.	Name	First Name	Address	R M Fox
66	Church St no 9	O'Reilly	Felix	18 Benburb St	
67	North Wall no 10	O'Reilly	Joseph	38 Commons St	GPO
68	Gloucester St no 5	Daly	Thomas	13 Lr Gloucester St	Guardroom, Upper Castle Yard
69	Gloucester St no 5	Farrell	Denis	6 Millett Place	GPO/City Hall
70	Capel St no 4	Blair	Thomas	3 Little Strand St	
71	High St		Patrick	40 East Essex St	
72	Gloucester St no 5	Poole	John	93 Foley St	
73	Church St no 9	Burton	James	37 Ashford St	
74	Sth C Rd (Commander)	Kelly	Jas	4 Clanbrassil St Upper	St Stephen's Green/ College of Surgeons
75	Sth C Rd	Joyce	James	4 Union Place, Grove Rd	St Stephen's Green/ College of Surgeons
76	Dorset St no 8	Kelly	Jas ?	93 Dorset St Lr	St Stephen's Green/ College of Surgeons
77	Dorset St no 8	Kelly	Joseph	93 Lr Dorset St	
78	Dorset St no 8 (Commander)	Carton	Owen	21 Temple St Nth	St Stephen's Green/ College of Surgeons
79		Tuke	James	83 Green St	St Stephen's Green/ College of Surgeons
80	High St	Ryan	Fred	3 High St	St Stephen's Green/ College of Surgeons
81	Gloucester St no 5	McManus ?	William	50 Marlboro St	
82	Capel St no 4	Joyce	Edward	29 Charles St, West Ormond Quay	St Stephen's Green/ College of Surgeons
83	Church St no 9	Lawerence	Richard	39 King St ?	GPO
84	Dorset St no 8	Dwyer	James	7 Inns Quay, formally 49 Rutland SQ	St Stephen's Green/ College of Surgeons
85	Capel St no 4	Doyle	Thomas	45 Dominick St Lr	
86	Capel St no 4	Turner	Michael	18 Nth Anne St	
87	Church St no 9	[crossed out]			
88	Baldoyle no 7	McDonagh	Joseph	18 Cottage Sutton Rd, Baldoyle	GPO
89	Baldoyle no 7	McCormack	James	13 Sutton Cottages	GPO
90	Baldoyle no 7	Nolan	Michael	Borough Field Cottages, Baldoyle	GPO
91	Baldoyle no 7	Roche	Joseph	Moynetown, Baldoyle	
92	Baldoyle no 7	Roche	Patrick	Moynetown, Baldoyle	
93	Baldoyle no 7	Kennedy	William	13 Sutton Cottages	
94	Baldoyle no 7	Roche	Philip	New Road, Baldoyle	
95	(Commander)	O'Donoghue	Thomas	1 Mountjoy St Mid	St Stephen's Green/ College of Surgeons
96	High St (Commander)	Burke	Edward	63 Meath St	St Stephen's Green/ College of Surgeons
97		Adams	John	109 Cork St	St Stephen's Green/ College of Surgeons
98	Inchicore Crumlin no 3	Conroy	Andrew	131 Inchicore Rd	GPO (Also served at Hopkins & Hopkins. Wounded.)
99	Inchicore Crumlin no 3	King	William	4 [address faded]	

Army No.	Army Section Name/No.	Name	First Name	Address	R M Fox
100	Inchicore Crumlin no 3	Daly	James	3 Labourers Cottages, Crumlin	
101	Gloucester St no 5	King	Daniel	18 Nth Cumberland St	
102	Inchicore Crumlin no 3	Quinn	John	7 Windmill Lane, Crumlin	
103	Townsend St no 12	White	Jack	21 Luke St	
104	Baldoyle no 7	Doherty	Patrick	5 Sutton Tce, Sutton	
105	Gloucester St no 5	O'Leary	Phillip	4 Gardiner St Mid	
106	High St	Maguire	James	32 St Michaels Tce, Blackpitts Buildings	St Stephen's Green/ College of Surgeons
107		Gough	James	1 Nth Richmond St	St Stephen's Green/ College of Surgeons
108	High St	Craven	Barney	21 Poole St, Pimlico	St Stephen's Green/ College of Surgeons
109	Dorset St no 8	[crossed out]			
110	Sth C Rd	[crossed out]			
111	Baldoyle no 7	Fox	Patrick	9 Sutton Rd, New Cottages, Baldoyle	
112	Baldoyle no 7	Gough	Joseph	Kilbarrack/ Sutton	
113	Baldoyle no 7	Rooney		Borough Sutton	
114	Baldoyle no 7	Blake	Charles	Moynetown, Baldoyle	
115	Baldoyle no 7	Rooney	James	Borough Sutton	
116	Baldoyle no 7	Blake	John	Moynetown, Baldoyle	
117		King	Arthur	25 St Ignatius Rd	
118		King	Martin	n/s	
119		Duffy ?	Hugh	48 Elizabeth St, Clonliffe Rd	
120		[crossed out]			
121		Wade	Michael	24 Nth Great Charles St	
122	Dorset St no 8	Hanratty	John	23 Upr Blessington St	
123	Capel St no 4	Byrne	Patrick	28 Bolton St	Synod Hall
124		Doyle [crossed out]	Joseph	19 Emerald St	
125	North Strand no 6	Hughes	John	23 St Mary's Rd off Church Rd East Wall	
126	North Wall no 10	Murphy	Fred	9 North Wall	St Stephen's Green/ College of Surgeons
127	Townsend St no 12	Johnson	William	12 Denzille St	
128		Scott	W.	7 New Row, Inchicore	
129	High St	Lacey	Phil	8 Brabazon St	St Stephen's Green/ College of Surgeons
130	High St	Redmond	Andrew	79 The Coombe	St Stephen's Green/ College of Surgeons
131	North Wall no 10	McHugh	Patrick	16 Commons St	GPO/Imperial Hotel
132	Sth C Rd	Redmond	Timothy J.	9 Curzon St /2 Verdon Cottages, Terenure	
133	Sth C Rd	Lambert	Thomas	Rear Old Bridge House, Milltown	
134	North Wall no 10	Nolan	Henry	37 Newfoundland St	

Army No.	Army Section Name/No.	Name	First Name	Address	R M Fox
135		King	George	25 St Ignatius Rd	GPO
136	Dorset St no 8	[blank]			St Stephen's Green/ College of Surgeons
137	High St	Cassidy	Henry	36 The Coombe	St Stephen's Green/ College of Surgeons
138	High St	Burke	Matthew	Brabazon St	St Stephen's Green/ College of Surgeons
139	High St	Byrne	Joseph	10 Braithwaite St	St Stephen's Green/ College of Surgeons
140		Fullerton	George	22 Bow Lane, Jan House?	GPO/ Henry and James
141	Gloucester St no 5	Donnelly	James	66 Railway St	
142	Dorset St no 8	McCullough	James	3 Clonturk Ave	
143	North Wall no 10	Duff	Thomas	29 Seville Place Cottages	
144	High St	O'Connor	John	18 Francis St	St Stephen's Green/ College of Surgeons
145	North Wall no 10 (Commander)	Mahon	John	4 Nixon St	St Stephen's Green/ College of Surgeons
146	North Wall no 10	Bryan	Thomas	31 Guild St	St Stephen's Green/ College of Surgeons
147	Church St no 9	Finnigan	Michael	4 Ushers Lane, Ushers Quay	GPO/Imperial Hotel
148	Aungier St	Delaney	Michael	31 Peter St	St Nicholas Graveyard
149	Dorset St no 8	O'Shea	Robert	37 Upr Gardiner St	St Stephen's Green/ College of Surgeons
150		Bannon	John	68 Foley St	St Stephen's Green/ College of Surgeons
151	Dorset St no 8	Campbell	George	18 Hardwick St	St Stephen's Green/ College of Surgeons
152	North Wall no 10	Conway	Peter	11 Leland Place/Common St	
153	North Wall no 10	Corbally	Richard	7 Moore Row	GPO
154	High St	Smith	Thomas	7 Rainsford Ave, Thomas Court	
155	North Wall no 10	[blank]		3 Piles Buildings, off Wood St	St Stephen's Green/ College of Surgeons
156	Aungier St	Murphy	Joseph	3 Back Lane	City Hall/Evening Mail office
157	High St (Commander)	Kelly	Martin	33 Newfoundland St	St Stephen's Green/ College of Surgeons
158	North Wall no 10	Quigley	James	115 Townsend St	St Stephen's Green/ College of Surgeons
159	North Strand no 6	Byrne	James	10 Gloucester St Upr	
160	Gloucester St no 5	McCarthy	Mick	40 Gardiner St	St Stephen's Green/ College of Surgeons
161		Nelson	Jas	129 Summerhill	
162	North Strand no 6	Dillon	Patrick	9 Bishop St	
163	Aungier St	Kelly	William	21 Little Denmark St	St Stephen's Green/ College of Surgeons
164	Capel St no 4	Foy	M.	40 Waterford St	
165		Murphy	William	29 Arran Quay	
166	Church St no 9	Walsh	Joseph	18 Richmond St Sth	St Stephen's Green/ College of Surgeons
167	Sth C Rd	McNamara	Patrick	15 Dominick St Lr	
168	Capel St no 4	Pettigrue	H.	4 Gardiner St Mid	
169		O'Leary	William		St Stephen's Green/ College of Surgeons

Army No.	Army Section Name/No.	Name	First Name	Address	R M Fox
170	Aungier St	Fitzpatrick	Matthew	8 Digges Lane	
171		Hannon [crossed out]	John	63b Corporation Buildings, Foley St	
172	North Strand no 6	Byrne	James	30 Summerhill	
173	North Wall no 10	Moore	John	9 Newfoundland St	GPO/Imperial Hotel
174	North Wall no 10	[blank]			
175		[blank]			
176	North Strand no 6	Murray	Henry	2 Sherriff Place	
176	North Strand no 6	Murray	Con	21a Summer Place	
177		Whelan	Thomas	43 Church St, East Wall	
178	North Wall no 10	Grogan	Patrick	2 Emily Place, Sherriff Place	
179	North Strand no 6	Sheehan	Thomas	2/3 Loyalty Rd, West Road	
180	North Wall no 10	Hughes	Peter	13 Church Rd, Nth Wall	
181		Kelly	Charles	38 Lr Gloucester St Lr	
182	North Wall no 10	Hosey	Murtagh	10 Nixon St	
183	High St	Bermingham	P.	1 Raleigh Place, Dolphins Barn	St Stephen's Green/ College of Surgeons
184	North Wall no 10	Brown	Robert	10/12 Nixon St	
185	High St	Connell	Christy	21 Allingham St or 20 Maxwell St	
186	North Strand no 6	Barker	Denis	4 Empress Place, Portland Row	
187	Gloucester St no 5	Carpenter	Peter	110 Foley St	GPO/Metrople hotel
188	North Wall no 10	Seery	James	10 Beresford Place	Guardroom Upr Castle Yard
189	Dorset St no 8	Sexton (see also 276)	Michael	28 Broadstone Ave	GPO/City Hall
190	Dorset St no 8	Murtagh	Patrick	11 St Ignatius Rd	
191	North Wall no 10	Nolan	John	13 Mayor St Upr	GPO/City Hall
192	Church St no 9	[crossed out]			
193	Capel St no 4	Fitzgerald	Edward	20 Little Denmark St	
193	Inchicore Crumlin no 3	Kelly	James	13 Barns Place, Old Kilmainham	St Stephen's Green/ College of Surgeons
194	Capel St no 4	[blank]			
195	(Captain)	Poole	Christy	5 Rutland St Lr	
196	Gloucester St no 5	Mills	David	43 Gloucester St	St Stephen's Green/ College of Surgeons
197		Brogan	Christy	7 Frankfort Cottages, Killarney St	
198		Kelly	William	23 Waterford St	
199	North Strand no 6	Courtney	Daniel (Also served at Annesley Bridge.)	43 Bessboro Ave, Nth Strand	GPO

Army No.	Army Section Name/No.	Name	First Name	Address	R M Fox
200	Gloucester St no 5	Lacey	Michael	43 Gloucester St Lr	GPO/Imperial Hotel
201	Gloucester St no 5	Smith	Charlie	43 Foley St	St Stephen's Green/ College of Surgeons
202	North Wall no 10	Coates	Peter	12 Oriel St Upr	
203	Aungier St	Donnelly	James	8 Digges Lane	
204	Aungier St	Ryan	John	2 Little Digges Lane	
205	Capel St no 4	Carroll	John	78 Dominick St Upr	
206	Capel St no 4	Darling	Jack	22 Dominick St Lr	
207	North Wall no 10	Boyd	Larry	45 Mayor St Lr	
208	Capel St no 4	Kearns	Joe	5 Aston Quay	
209		O'Rourke	Shaun	30 Lr Gardiner St or 24 Gloucester St	
210	Dorset St no 8	Coyle	Thomas	7 Henry St Grocers, 2 Myrtle St, Mountjoy SQ	
211	Capel St no 4	Gleeson	Thomas	50 Dominick St Lr	St Stephen's Green/ College of Surgeons
212	Aungier St	Hand	Matt	12 Lr Longford St	St Stephen's Green/ College of Surgeons
213	Capel St no 4	Quirke	Thomas	4 Dominick St	
214	Dorset St no 8	Hawthorne	Percy	2 Fitzgibbon St	
215	High St	Boylan	John	23 St Michael's Tce	
216	Aungier St	Byrne	James	28 Stephen's St Lr	
217	Gloucester St no 5	John	Louis	67b Corporation Buildings	
218	Capel St no 4	Doyle	Ed J	7/8 Bachelors Walk	
219		Leddy?	Peter	14 Buckingham St Upr	
220	Capel St no 4	Ellis	James	47 East Arran St	
221		Chaney	William	5 Northcote Ave, Church Rd	St Stephen's Green/ College of Surgeons
222		Laird [crossed out]		3 Foley St	
223	Townsend St no 12	Murphy	Robert	6 Repeal Place, Powerscourt Lr	
224	Townsend St no 12	Martin	Chris	62 Shelbourne Rd	
225	North Wall no 10	Cullen	James	14 Jane Place Upr	
226	Townsend St no 12	Henry	Robert	92 Mount Lr	
227	High St	Kelly	Thomas	3 Watkins Cottages, Ardee St	
228	North Wall no 10	Kearney	Christopher (Pickfords)		
229	Townsend St no 12	Johnson	Jack	2 Sherriff St Upr	
230	North Wall no 10	Cullen	Francis	67 Sir John's Quay	
231	Inchicore Crumlin no 3	Woods	Patrick	14 Mayor St Upr	
232	Church St no 9	Walsh	William	15 Inchicore Rd	
				27 Arran Quay	

Army No.	Army Section Name/No.	Name	First Name	Address	R M Fox
233	Church St no 9	Keegan	John	76 Benburb St	
234	Church St no 9	Keegan	Laurence	72 Benburb St	
235	Aungier St	Hinch	William	53 Aungier St	
236	High St	Hinch	Patrick	23 Blackpitts Buildings	
237	Gloucester St no 5	Maher	Edward	8 Gloucester St Upr	
238	Dorset St no 8	Brennan	John	5 Grenville Place	
239	Dorset St no 8	O'Reilly	Patrick	43 Geraldine St	St Stephen's Green/ College of Surgeons
240	Dorset St no 8	O'Reilly	Thomas	43 Geraldine St	
241		McDonnell	James	n/s	City Hall/Evening Mail office
242	High St no 4	Shannon	Martin	12 The Coombe	St Stephen's Green/ College of Surgeons
243	Dorset St no 8	O'Reilly	John	43 Geraldine St	City Hall
244	Townsend St no 12	Smith	Jas	8 Queens St	St Stephen's Green/ College of Surgeons
245	Gloucester St no 5	McNamara	Mick	22 Gloucester St Upr	
246	Capel St no 4	Gahan	John	33 Lr Dominick St	
247		Daniel	Henry	6 Gardiner St Lr	
248		Donnelly	Mick	66 Railway St	
249	North Strand no 6	Hitchcock	William	16 Northbrook Ave, Lr Nth Strand	
250	North Strand no 6	Clarke	John	22 Queens Cottages, N Strand	
251	North Strand no 6	Tierney	John	1 Synott Place, Nth Strand	
252	Aungier St no 6	Mahony	Joe	2 Little Digges St	
253	North Wall no 10	Murphy	Patrick	5 Julian Place, Nth Wall	
254	Capel St no 4	Curley	John	12 Coleraine St	
255		Curly	James	41 Marlboro St	
256	North Wall no 10	Seery	John	10 Beresford Place	
257	Townsend St no 12	O'Sullivan	James	John's Quay ?	St Stephen's Green/ College of Surgeons
258	Gloucester St no 5	Mooney	Patrick	10 Gardiner St Middle	
259		Jordan	John	9 Gardiner St Middle	
261		Conroy [crossed out]		40 Railway St	
262	Townsend St no 12	Carroll	Mick	24 George's Quay	St Stephen's Green/ College of Surgeons
263	Townsend St no 12	Freeman	John	2 Mark's Court, Townsend St	
264	North Strand no 6	Dunne	Mick	25 Upr Noctor Ave	
265	North Wall no 10	Boyle	Peter	32 Sherriff St Upr	
266	North Strand no 6	Farrelly	John	4 Empress Villas	
267	North Wall no 10	Conroy	Mick	15 Nixon St, Nth Wall	
268	Townsend St no 12	McDonnell	Patrick	9 Shaw's Cottages	
269	North Strand no 6	Cleary	Christy	29 Summerhill	

Army No.	Army Section Name/No.	Name	First Name	Address	R M Fox
270	Dorset St no 8	Fleming	William	44 Upr Wellington St	
271	Capel St no 4	Osborne	J.	87 Capel St	
272	Townsend St no 12	Ryan	Denis	2 Erne Cottages, Lr Erne St	
273	Townsend St no 12	Carroll	Simon	186 Townsend St	
274	Church St no 9	Roche	Christy	21 Merchants Quay	
275	Townsend St no 12	Le Strange	Patrick	5 Eden Gardens Townsend St	
276		Sexton	Mick	28 Broadstone Ave	
277	Aungier St	McLoughlin	M.	77 Bride St	
278		Whelan	A.	2 Moore's Cottages	
279	Dorset St no 8	Holden	J.	4 Mountjoy Place	
280	Church St no 9	Hicks	C.	27 Winetavern St	
281	Capel St no 4	Cullen	P.	12 Parnell St	
282	Capel St no 4	Kelly	F.	152 Parnell St	
283		Darcy	James	4 Murphy's Cottages	
284	Townsend St no 12	Lawlor	D.	51 Queen's St	
285	Gloucester St no 5	Tully	W.	15 Gloucester St Upr	
286	North Wall no 10	Masterson	J.	16 Guild St	
287	Gloucester St no 5	Flynn	J.	6 Lr Gloucester St	
288	North Wall no 10	Kirwan	P.	10 Beresford Place	
289	Capel St no 4	Connolly	Michael	20 Swifts Row	
290	Capel St no 4	White	M.	1 Swifts Row	
291		O'Flynn	J.	24 Gardiner St Lr	
292	North Strand no 6	Feeney	J.	2 Shamrock Cottages	
293		Clements	W.	157 Parnell St	
294	Gloucester St no 5	O'Leary	J.	33 Railway St	
295	Aungier St	Walsh	Tom	52 Cuffe St	GPO/City Hall
296	North Wall no 10	Clarke	William	3 Church St, Nth Wall	
297		Nathan	George	19 Waterford St	
298	High St	Hudson	Patrick	130 Cork St	
299		Byrne	James	3 Emerald Place	
300	North Strand no 6	Madderly	Tom	21 Summerhill	
301		Cox	Tom	4 Rutland Cottages, Rutland Square	
302		John	Breen	53 Marlboro St	
303	High St	John	Craven	3 Ardee St	
304	North Strand no 6	Keogh	Will	7 Nth Clarence St	
305		Venerables		7 Chamber St	

Army No.	Army Section Name/No.	Name	First Name	Address	R M Fox
306	Aungier St	Walsh	Patrick	17 Great Ship St	
307	Gloucester St no 5	Carroll	Peter	15 Gloucester St	
308	Gloucester St no 5	Hughes	Henry	41 Upr Gloucester St	
309	North Strand no 6	Nolan	Will	41 Upr Rutland St	
310	Aungier St	Kavanagh	Will	53 York St	
311		Beresford	Will	8 Gloucester St	
312	Sth C Rd	Cantwell	George	1 Upr Leeson St	
313		Coleman	James	2 Waterford St	
314		Purfield	John	19 Townsend St	
315		Comerford	Joe	184 Iveagh Trust Buildings, Block P	
316	Capel St no 4	Cahill	Henry	71 Abbey St Middle	
317	Sth C Rd	Murphy	Chris	19 Westmoreland Park	
318		Malone	Will	29 Parnell St / 1 High St	
319	Capel St no 4	Byrne	Mick	29 Parnell St	
320	Capel St no 4	Cumberton	W.M.	15 Temple Bar	
321		McBride	Bernard	8 Killarney St	
322		Devanny	Ben	n/s	
323	Capel St no 4	Geoghegan	Matt	7 Baldoyle	
324		Lynch	William	8 Dorset St	
325		Giltrap		Finglas	
326	Townsend St no 12	Colgan	John	20 City Quay	
327	Sth C Rd	Maire	Louis	17 Grantham St	
328	Sth C Rd	Connolly	Roderick	Surrey House, Rathmines	
329	Capel St no 4	Egan	William	98 Capel St	
330	Aungier St	Bryan	Denis	8 Vances Buildings, Bishop St	
331	Dorset St no 8	Killeen	Robert	14 Vances Buildings, Bishop St	
332	High St	Murray	Edward	14 Ormond Quay	
333		Healy	Tom	23 Oriel St Lr	
334		O'Neill	James	St Catherine's, Lucan	
335		Poole	Patrick	50 Marlboro St	
336		Maher	John	1a Montague St	
337	Gloucester St no 5	Walsh	Thomas	23 Upr Gloucester St	
338		Purcell	John	3 Bella St	
339		Dunne	Andy	179 Brunswick St Sth	

Index